Encyclopedia of
Cyber Warfare

Encyclopedia of Cyber Warfare

PAUL J. SPRINGER, EDITOR

An Imprint of ABC-CLIO, LLC

Santa Barbara, California • Denver, Colorado

Library of Congress Cataloging-in-Publication Data

Names: Springer, Paul J., editor.
Title: Encyclopedia of cyber warfare / Paul J. Springer, editor.
Description: ABC-CLIO, LLC : Santa Barbara, CA, [2017] | Includes bibliographical
    references and index.
Identifiers: LCCN 2016058373 (print) | LCCN 2017002115 (ebook) |
    ISBN 9781440844249 (hardcopy : alk. paper) | ISBN 9781440844256 (eBook)
Subjects: LCSH: Cyberspace operations (Military science)—United States—
    Encyclopedias. | Cyberterrorism—Encyclopedias.
Classification: LCC U163 .E45 2017 (print) | LCC U163 (ebook) |
    DDC 355.4/1—dc23
LC record available at https://lccn.loc.gov/2016058373

ISBN: 978-1-4408-4424-9
EISBN: 978-1-4408-4425-6

21 20 19 18   2 3 4 5

This book is also available as an eBook.

ABC-CLIO
An Imprint of ABC-CLIO, LLC

ABC-CLIO, LLC
130 Cremona Drive, P.O. Box 1911
Santa Barbara, California 93116-1911
www.abc-clio.com

This book is printed on acid-free paper ∞

Manufactured in the United States of America

Contents

List of Entries

Guide to Related Topics

INDIVIDUALS

Alexander, Keith B.
Alperovitch, Dmitri
Arquilla, John
Assange, Julian
Brenner, Joel F.
Bush, George W.
Carpenter, Shawn
Cebrowski, Arthur K.
Clarke, Richard A.
Cray, Seymour
Evron, Gadi
Gates, Bill
Gates, Robert M.

Hayden, Michael V.
Kaspersky, Yevgeniy "Eugene" Valentinovich
Libicki, Martin C.
Mandia, Kevin
Manning, Bradley
Mitnick, Kevin
Obama, Barack
Panetta, Leon E.
Putin, Vladimir
Rogers, Michael S.
Rumsfeld, Donald H.
Snowden, Edward J.
Tenenbaum, Ehud "Udi"

U.S. GOVERNMENT ORGANIZATIONS

Central Intelligence Agency (CIA)
Defense Advanced Research Projects Agency (DARPA)
Defense Information Systems Agency (DISA)
Department of Defense (DoD)
Department of Energy (DOE)
Department of Homeland Security (DHS)
Department of Justice (DOJ)
Federal Bureau of Investigation (FBI)
National Infrastructure Advisory Council (NIAC)

National Institute of Standards and Technology (NIST)
National Security Agency (NSA)
President's Commission on Critical Infrastructure Protection (PCCIP)
Second Army/Army Cyber Command
24th Air Force
U.S. Coast Guard Cyber Command (CGCYBER)
U.S. Cyber Command (USCYBERCOM)
U.S. Tenth Fleet

PRIVATE CORPORATIONS

Apple Inc.
Baidu
FireEye
Google
Intel Corporation
Internet Corporation for Assigned Names and Numbers (ICANN)

Kaspersky Lab
Mandiant Corporation
McAfee
Microsoft Corporation
RAND Corporation
Russian Business Network (RBN)
Second Life

NIPRNet
Patriotic Hacking
Phishing
Programmable Logic Controller (PLC)
Red Team
Remote Administration Tool (RAT)
Server
SIPRNet
Social Engineering
Software
Solid-State Drive (SSD)
Spear Phishing
Spoofing
Spyware
SQL Injection

Supervisory Control and Data Acquisition
    (SCADA)
The Onion Router (TOR)
Tier 1 Internet Service Provider
Torrent
Transmission Control Protocol/Internet Pro-
    tocol (TCP/IP)
Trojan Horse
Weapons of Mass Disruption
White Hat
Whitelist
Wi-Fi
Worm
Zero-Day Vulnerability

CYBER WARFARE ATTACKS AND PROGRAMS

Aramco Attack
Code Red Worm
Conficker Worm
EINSTEIN (Cyber System)
Estonian Cyber Attack (2007)
Flame Worm
Gauss Worm
Georbot
Georgian Cyber Attack (2008)
GhostNet
ILOVEYOU Virus
JPMorgan Hack
Low Orbit Ion Cannon (LOIC)
Minimum Essential Emergency Communi-
    cations Network (MEECN)
Moonlight Maze
MS Blaster Worm
MyDoom Virus
Nimda Worm
Office of Personnel Management Data
    Breach

Operation Ababil
Operation Aurora
Operation Babylon
Operation Buckshot Yankee
Operation Cartel
Operation Cast Lead
Operation Night Dragon
Operation Orchard
Operation Payback
Operation Shady RAT
Operation Titan Rain
PRISM Program
Rustock Botnet
Shamoon Virus
Solar Sunrise
Sony Hack
SQL Slammer Worm
Stuxnet
Target Corporation Hack
TJX Corporation Hack

CYBER GUIDELINES

Comprehensive National Cybersecurity
    Initiative (CNCI)
Cyber-Defense Exercise
Cyber-Equivalence Doctrine
Cyberspace Policy Review (2009)
Foreign Intelligence Surveillance Act (FISA)
Information Warfare Weapons Treaty

Just War
Laws of Armed Conflict
National Cyber Security Strategy
National Infrastructure Protection Plan
    (NIPP)
Net-centric Warfare (NCW)
Presidential Decision Directive 63 (1998)

Quadrennial Defense Review
Tallinn Manual

Unrestricted Warfare
USA PATRIOT Act

NONSTATE CYBER ACTORS

Al Qaeda
Anonymous
Islamic State in Iraq and Syria (ISIS)

LulzSec
Silk Road
Syrian Electronic Army (SEA)

INTERNATIONAL ORGANIZATIONS

Cyber Defence Management Authority
  (CDMA)
Interpol
NATO Cooperative Cyber Defence Centre
  of Excellence (CCDCOE)

North Atlantic Treaty Organization (NATO)
People's Liberation Army Unit 61398
Riga Summit

List of Documents

Preface

In the 21st century, nations, nonstate actors, and individuals have a new avenue to engage in conflict. The development of the Internet has had many unforeseen effects on human society, enabling massive changes in communications, commerce, and conflict. So far, the Internet has not fundamentally changed human nature; it has only allowed for a new means of engaging in normal human behavior, including some of the worst human activities. Thus, it is unsurprising that humans have chosen to continue their criminal, espionage, sabotage, and warfare activities in the new cyber domain.

Cyber space is definitely not the same as the physical realm, and using it as a means of conflict does not always follow the same approaches used in the physical world. In some ways, warfare in the cyber domain is less terrifying than conflict on land, at sea, or in the air, in part because, to date, no humans have been killed by a cyber attack. Currently, cyber activities tend to be an enabling mechanism supporting conflict in other domains, rather than being an entirely separate vector for violence. However, as more devices are connected and societies become more dependent upon cyber networks, the possibilities for causing harm grow in proportion. Further, because the Internet is by definition an international network that does not halt at national borders, it blurs the line between domestic and global activities, pushing past the assumed limitations of domestic and international law. Because a nation may choose to respond to a cyber attack by retaliating in the physical domain, cyber warfare offers a certain potential for crossover effects. Ultimately, whether an attack is perceived as an irritant or an act of war will largely depend on the preferences, motivations, and capabilities of the victim more than the intentions of the actor.

The cyber domain has special characteristics that make it a unique arena for human conflict. Unlike the physical domains (land, sea, air, and space), the cyber domain is entirely artificial—and it remains an evolving platform. Although certain behaviors in cyber space are governed by the limits of what can be performed within a computer network, it is unclear whether other forms of government truly apply to the Internet. Certainly, the establishment of computer networks has challenged many assumptions regarding the limits of legal and ethical behavior. Because the Internet has outgrown all projections for both its utility and its dangers, it is impossible to predict how it will develop in even the near future, much less over the remainder of the 21st century.

This volume seeks to provide some clarity about the history and current capabilities of the cyber domain. Its authors have largely, though not exclusively, focused on the Western experience, particularly that of the United States. In part, this is due to the availability of open-source, unclassified data. Not only are the sources readily available, but they tend to be more applicable to the target audience for this work. The authors come from a wide variety of backgrounds, with a substantial number of them serving in the military or other governmental institutions. As such, it needs to be stated that the ideas and arguments presented in this volume are the opinions of the individual authors, based on their expertise, and do not represent the position of any government, military entity, or institution.

There have been an almost limitless number of key contributors to the production of this work, beginning with Padraic (Pat) Carlin and Steve Catalano, the editors at ABC-CLIO, who conceived of it and pushed it through to fruition. In the production process, Subaramya Durairaj and Magendra Varma of Lumina Datamatics provided enormous assistance. Thanks also to Pete Feely, production manager at Amnet Systems, and copyeditor Lisa Crowder. Of course, a work of this magnitude is only as strong as the contributions of its creators, without whom it would still be a collection of blank pages. Thus, it is gratefully dedicated to the 59 authors who contributed their time, their expertise, and their efforts to produce first-rate entries that will help the reader grapple with the unique challenges of cyber warfare.

Introduction

The use of information as a means to conduct warfare is a concept that has existed for centuries. However, the rise of massive cyber networks and increasingly powerful computers has led many military strategists to conclude that the cyber realm should be considered a new domain of warfare, akin to the land, sea, air, and space domains previously developed and utilized in warfare. Over the past two decades, humans have become increasingly reliant on information networks, which in turn have become a part of the very fabric of society, influencing virtually every person on the planet. Even those who have never used a computer are affected by these networks, both in positive and negative ways. Just as conflict has touched every nation on earth and has had at least some effect on almost every life, so too has human conflict spread into the machine realm. As such, the cyber domain is being used in new and creative fashions to shape the conflicts of the physical world and, at times, to carry out attacks with effects every bit as tangible as those using conventional weaponry.

Because the cyber domain is entirely manmade, it is not governed by the same properties as the physical world. In fact, there are no rules within the cyber domain that cannot be changed, either by altering the hardware that creates the environment or changing the programming that controls it. Given this changing nature of the cyber environment, developing a national cyber strategy to secure a country from cyber attacks is a continual problem. The only sure way to become immune to cyber attack is to sever all connections to the cyber domain—but such a drastic decision would also essentially remove a nation from the modern world. Thus, nations are forced to engage in the cyber domain, regardless of preferences, priorities, or national capabilities.

Cyber assets are typically associated with communications, economic activities, and maintaining vast amounts of information, and cyber attacks are thus most commonly assumed to be new forms of espionage or crime. However, cyber networks are increasingly able to influence the physical world through the control of infrastructure assets such as electrical grids, meaning that a cyber attack can potentially inflict harm on not only computer hardware but also the people living in the cyber-enhanced environment. Whereas earlier cyber attacks might be considered a problem best addressed by intelligence agencies or law enforcement, these more advanced cyber attacks might cross the threshold into warfare, particularly if they directly or indirectly cause the loss of human life. Already, cyber attacks are being used as an enhancement mechanism to enable or improve kinetic attacks in the physical world, but soon, they may be utilized in place of conventional violence, achieving the same ends without incurring the same risks to the attacker.

Although the cyber domain is largely a positive innovation, for most of its users, the Internet is a vast, poorly understood environment. Most computer owners do not realize the inherent dangers that it represents or how their interaction with sites on the Internet might enhance the ability of malevolent actors to carry out acts of crime, espionage, sabotage, terrorism, and warfare. While this should not scare citizens into departing the cyber domain entirely, in some ways, the subjects discussed in this work should remind users that there are often far greater consequences to seemingly innocent activities in the cyber domain. They should be aware of the types of organizations using the Internet for their own purposes, ranging from hostile nation-states seeking avenues of attack and new means of information theft to terrorist organizations attempting to recruit new members and spread their propaganda. Cyber criminals, too, have found the Internet to be a vast new trove of potential targets, many of whom unknowingly volunteer their information without regard for the dangers involved.

This encyclopedia serves as a reference guide to the reader seeking to gain a better understanding of the nature of the cyber domain and the threats that it presents to the citizens of the world. It seeks to offer an overview of the key individuals, organizations, and actions that have shaped the modern cyber networks and how state and nonstate actors have come to rely on the Internet as a means of interaction with other states. After examining the entries in this work, readers are encouraged to consult the further readings offered with each entry and those listed in the bibliography to enhance their knowledge of subjects of interest.

ADVANCED PERSISTENT THREAT (APT)

The term *advanced persistent threat* (APT) refers to highly sophisticated actors conducting stealthy offensive operations in computer networks, usually through the Internet. The goal of such operations includes any combination of espionage, financial gain, sabotage, or reconnaissance. Such actors are often shown to work on behalf of nation-states, typically under the control of the military or intelligence services. They may also be private entities contracted by nation-states or, more rarely, operating purely for personal profit (i.e., sophisticated criminals). In some cases, the distinction between criminal and agent of a nation-state may be hard to draw, with the same individuals or groups exhibiting both characteristics at different times.

The term APT appears to have been in use since 2006, first appearing in documents authored by U.S. Air Force personnel, and became mainstream with the 2013 *APT1* report by Mandiant. APTs share a number of attributes that differentiate them from other malicious actors:

- Mission Focus: APTs often have narrowly defined missions and goals, which may require that they gain access to specific networks or organizations. Such targets may be more difficult to successfully compromise than the average network or individual computer. This is in contrast to criminal actors, who generally exhibit a more opportunistic behavior, which may, for example, manifest as massive (and therefore noisy) spear-phishing campaigns. However, the strategic goals for an APT may be defined quite broadly (e.g., obtaining information pertaining to a technical area or technology from any available source), and the tactics used when targeting a large organization may come to resemble those of a less sophisticated actor; sometimes this is a deliberate choice by the APT to avoid drawing attention to the attack itself or to sow confusion as to the identity of the attacker.
- Sophistication: APTs often have custom tools that have been developed over a long period of time, the expertise and resources to develop new capabilities as needed, and the training and discipline to use such tools to conduct large-scale operations while minimizing cross-contamination across operations. The majority of publicly disclosed APT campaigns point to the extensive use of spear-phishing attacks as the preferred method of initial compromise, but APTs have been known to use a variety of other attack tactics, including watering hole, malicious advertising, credential theft, social engineering, SQL injection, and software exploitation.

- Resources: APTs generally have access to sufficient resources to pursue a number of different attack strategies over a long period of time against a chosen target, including potentially developing or procuring previously unknown vulnerabilities for which no known fix exists and no forewarning is possible. In addition, APTs may devote significant resources and time in developing the necessary attack infrastructure and tools needed to conduct operations. However, APTs will not always use sophisticated tools and tactics; rather, the mission characteristics, including risk profile, urgency, and the sophistication (or "hardness") of the target, will dictate the conduct of operations.
- Persistence: Criminal actors on the Internet are typically interested in activities that result in short-term financial payoff, which may also be inherently very noisy, such as stealing financial information or installing ransomware (e.g., CryptoLocker). In contrast, APT missions generally require prolonged presence on a target network, such as for continuous collection of sensitive information. As a result, APTs need to operate in a stealthy manner so as to minimize the time to detection and to establish backdoors for regaining access should they be discovered.

While the primary concern of an APT is completion of the mission, secondary objectives include remaining undetected so as to avoid exposure of tools, techniques, and infrastructure; evading the association of a detected operation with the specific APT; and avoiding associating the APT with the correct country. The relative priority of these concerns depends on the specific APT and may change over time and across missions.

Proactive defenses such as firewalls, deep packet inspection, and attachment detonation chambers can play a role in hardening an organization's security posture, therefore requiring more effort to gain an initial foothold. However, the scale and complexity of modern enterprises and the individual systems within them suggest that resourceful and patient adversaries will generally manage to gain a foothold. The problem becomes even more complex when considering dependencies on external partners, resources, and services that may in turn be targeted by an APT to assist in gaining access to its target. As enterprise security has traditionally focused on perimeter defense, APTs have generally found it easy to expand their initial access and achieve their goals through a combination of lateral movement, privilege escalation, and the introduction of backdoors.

Much effort has been expended in developing tools and techniques for detection of such threats beyond the initial stages of compromise and for the forensic analysis of their activities. Such techniques have primarily focused on the analysis of massive volumes of logging information to identify potentially anomalous events; on identifying anomalous or "known bad" communication patterns, both within an enterprise network and at its external boundaries (e.g., at the firewall); and on the generation, sharing, and action upon indicators of compromise (IOC), which represent externally observable and, at least in theory, invariant elements of the APT tools or infrastructure. Such IOCs include, but are not limited to, file hashes, Internet Protocol (IP) addresses, network protocol signatures, and Windows Registry values. To the extent that an APT reuses tools and infrastructure (and therefore IOCs) across different operations, threat information sharing has the potential to significantly reduce the mean time to next detection (MTTND) and to increase the ability of defenders to attribute an attack.

Angelos D. Keromytis

See also: Cyber Attack; Cyber Crime; Cyber Defense; Cyber Espionage; Mandiant Corporation; People's Liberation Army Unit 61398; People's Republic of China Cyber Capabilities; Social Engineering; Spear Phishing

Further Reading

Brenner, Joel. *America the Vulnerable: Inside the New Threat Matrix of Digital Espionage, Crime, and Warfare.* New York: Penguin Press, 2011.
Lindsay, Jon R., Tai Ming Cheung, and Derek S. Reveron, eds. *China and Cybersecurity: Espionage, Strategy, and Politics in the Digital Domain.* New York: Oxford University Press, 2015.
Mandiant Corporation. *APT1: Exposing One of China's Cyber Espionage Units.* Alexandria, VA: Mandiant Corporation, 2013.

AIR GAPPING

The term *air gapping* is commonly used to describe a security measure taken to protect a computer system from intrusion. To air gap a computer system, it must be isolated from any local area network or public wireless network. The military, intelligence agencies, financial entities, and even some advocacy groups air gap certain systems because of the sensitive information contained within. Though primarily a security measure, air gapping can also refer to a procedure that transfers data from one classified system to another. It is commonly used to take material from the *low side* (unclassified machines) to the *high side* (classified machines). Data is cut to a CD-ROM on the low side and inserted on the high side. Even isolating the system from a network may not totally protect it.

Recent exploits have shown why air gapping is essential for critical systems. A hacker recently claimed he infiltrated a flight control system through the plane's media network. More famously, the Stuxnet virus that attacked centrifuges in Iran was introduced through a USB drive connected to the machine. Even if the system's external connections prevent the system from being subject to electromagnetic or other electrical exploits, they still cannot prevent the system from insider mistakes or threats. Under the National Security Administration's (NSA) TEMPEST program (Telecommunications Electronics Material Protected from Emanating Spurious Transmissions), the U.S. government developed standards to help air gap computer systems. The standards recommend minimum safe distances for the system as well as enclosing the system in a Faraday cage to prevent intrusion.

Melvin G. Deaile

See also: Cyber Security; Hardware; Internet

Further Reading

Clarke, Richard A., and Robert K. Knake. *Cyber War: The Next Threat to National Security and What to Do about It.* New York: HarperCollins, 2010.

Libicki, Martin. *Cyberspace in Peace and War.* Annapolis, MD: U.S. Naval Institute Press, 2016.

ALEXANDER, KEITH B.

General Keith B. Alexander (1951–) served as director of the National Security Agency (NSA) and chief of the Central Security Service (CSS) starting in August 2005 and concurrently as commander of U.S. Cyber Command (USCYBERCOM) from 2010 until his retirement in 2014. Alexander was born December 2, 1951, in Syracuse, New York, and was commissioned as an army second lieutenant at the U.S. Military Academy at West Point in 1974. During his military career, he earned several master of science degrees from Boston University (business administration), the Naval Postgraduate School (systems technology and physics), and the National Defense University (security strategy). Alexander also graduated from the U.S. Army Command and General Staff College and the National War College.

Through USCYBERCOM, Alexander was responsible for planning, coordinating, and conducting operations in defense of Department of Defense (DoD) computer networks under the authority of U.S. Strategic Command (USSTRATCOM). He also held overlapping responsibilities, in his capacity at the NSA and CSS, for select DoD national foreign intelligence and combat support missions and the protection of U.S. national security information systems. As a career military intelligence officer, Alexander served in several significant intelligence posts prior to assuming the directorship at the NSA, including U.S. Army deputy chief of staff, G-2; commanding general of U.S. Army Intelligence and Security Command; director of intelligence at U.S. Central Command (CENTCOM); and as deputy director for requirements, capabilities, assessments, and doctrine (J-2) for the Joint Chiefs of Staff (JCS).

Alexander succeeded General Michael Hayden to the NSA directorship when the latter was promoted to his fourth star and appointed to serve as deputy to Ambassador John Negroponte, President George W. Bush's appointee to the newly created position of director of national intelligence (DNI). Alexander's tenure at the NSA was marred by controversies over the legality and efficacy of the NSA's data collection activities. The first of them erupted in December 2005 when the *New York Times* reported that the NSA had been conducting warrantless surveillance of U.S. citizens' phone conversations and e-mail since 2001. The second and most personally damaging of these scandals came when Edward Snowden, then a contracted employee of the NSA, leaked thousands of classified documents to journalists in June 2013. The trove of stolen files revealed the extent of the NSA's access to private communication through penetration of the information infrastructure and secret agreements with telecommunications and Internet service providers.

The Snowden revelations unleashed a storm of criticism against the NSA. Alexander offered to resign from the NSA after the extent of the leaks became known, but President Barack Obama declined his offer, defending both the NSA's programs and the agency's embattled director. Alexander retired from military service the following year.

Robert Y. Mihara

See also: Hayden, Michael V.; National Security Agency (NSA); Obama, Barack; Snowden, Edward J.; U.S. Cyber Command (USCYBERCOM)

Further Reading

Harris, Shane. *The Watchers: The Rise of America's Surveillance State.* New York: Penguin Press, 2010.

Hayden, Michael V. *Playing to the Edge: American Intelligence in the Age of Terror.* New York: Penguin Press, 2016.

ALPEROVITCH, DMITRI

In 2011, Dmitri Alperovitch cofounded and became the chief technology officer of CrowdStrike, a security technology company focused on helping enterprises and governments protect their intellectual property and secrets against cyber espionage and cyber crime. Alperovitch holds an MS in information security and a BS in computer science from the Georgia Institute of Technology. Alperovitch worked at a number of computer security start-ups in the late 1990s and early 2000s, including the e-mail security start-up CipherTrust, which invented the TrustedSource reputation system. When CipherTrust was acquired by Secure Computing in 2006, he led the research team that launched the software as a service business. Alperovitch became vice president of threat research at McAfee when it acquired Secure Computing in 2008. In January 2010, he led the investigation, named Operation Aurora, into the Chinese intrusions of Google and two dozen other companies. He also led the investigation of the Night Dragon espionage operation of Western multinational oil and gas companies and traced them to a Chinese national living in Heze City, Shandong Province, People's Republic of China. Also in 2011, Alperovitch was awarded the prestigious Federal 100 Award for his contributions to U.S. federal information security. In 2013 and 2015, Alperovitch was recognized as one of *Washingtonian*'s "Tech Titans" for his accomplishments in the field of cyber security. He was also selected as one of *MIT Technology Review*'s "Top 35 Innovators under 35" in 2013. In addition to his position at CrowdStrike, Alperovitch is currently a nonresident senior fellow of the Cyber Statecraft Initiative at the Atlantic Council. Alperovitch has conducted extensive research on reputation systems, spam detection, Web security, public-key and identity-based cryptography, and malware and intrusion detection and prevention.

Lisa Beckenbaugh

See also: Cryptography; Encryption; McAfee

Further Reading

"Atlantic Council Programs Report: July 2015." Atlantic Council, August 3, 2015. http://www
.atlanticcouncil.org/for-members/atlantic-council-programs-report-may2015-3.

"Dmitri Alperovitch." CrowdStrike. http://www.crowdstrike.com/dmitri-alperovitch.

"Innovators under 35: Dmitri Alperovitch, CTO, CrowdStrike." MIT Technology Review,
October 10, 2013. https://www.technologyreview.com/s/521371/innovators-under-35
-dmitri-alperovitch-cto-crowdstrike.

AL QAEDA

Al Qaeda is a Sunni jihadist group that was founded by Osama bin Laden and others around 1988. Al Qaeda translates to "the base," which aptly characterizes how the organization has provided a base of training and knowledge to subsidiaries around the world. The group is considered a terrorist organization by many states, including the United States, which launched its War on Terror against Al Qaeda after the attacks of September 11, 2001. Despite U.S. efforts to target much of its central leadership, many analysts argue that Al Qaeda remains a strong and diversified organization through its many "franchises," which exist in more than 30 countries.

Al Qaeda emerged from Afghan resistance to Soviet occupation, but it found its primary motivation in opposing all things Western, particularly those representing the United States. This includes Western ideas such as democracy. Strategically, Al Qaeda sought to lure the United States into attacking and invading a Muslim country, which would subsequently provoke insurgents to resist occupation forces. It then planned to expand the conflict throughout the region, further drawing the United States into a long and costly war. At the same time, it would launch terrorist attacks against U.S. allies. Finally, by 2020, it hoped the U.S. economy would collapse, and with it the world economy. Al Qaeda would then initiate a global jihad and institute a global caliphate.

Since 9/11, Al Qaeda has increasingly sought to use cyber terrorism against the United States in the belief that cyber targets are just as open as airports were prior to 9/11. Al Qaeda draws its recruits from disaffected but often well-educated circles, thus it has access to those conversant in technology.

Still, it has spent far more time threatening to carry out cyber attacks than successfully making them. In 2007, for example, members of Al Qaeda attempted to attack numerous Western Web sites with distributed denial-of-service (DDoS) attacks but failed. In January 2015, Al Qaeda Electronic (AQE) emerged, the first cyber franchise connected to the organization, although its exact relationship to Al Qaeda is unknown. So far, AQE has mostly engaged in Web site defacement, which is one of the easier forms of hacking. It has yet to target a high-profile Web site. Its Twitter site currently only has a few hundred followers and lists its physical location as Kandahar, Afghanistan.

Unlike the Islamic State in Iraq and Syria (ISIS), which has adroitly managed its online presence, Al Qaeda has been more hesitant to embrace technology because leaders have been fearful that technology will reveal their locations and thus subject them to U.S. airstrikes. Technology has been focused within to maintain communication rather than on the external world in seeking to recruit or connect to followers.

With the death of Osama bin Laden and other leaders, there is debate over whether Al Qaeda is more of a working philosophy or an organization. Some believe that Al Qaeda actively directs its many national variants, serving as the strategic vision and guiding the parameters of its attacks. Others argue that Al Qaeda serves as an umbrella, with its loosely affiliated spin-offs waging their own independent campaigns that consist of both a local focus on corrupt Muslim regimes as well as a broader goal of attacking anything with Western ties.

In its system of beliefs, Al Qaeda is similar to ISIS in that it follows Salafi ways of thought, which seek to purify Islam from Shiites and others seen as failing to adhere to Islam as it existed in the days of Muhammad. In opposition to ISIS, however, bin Laden had warned against establishing a state too quickly because of the speed at which the United States overthrew previous attempts. Although ISIS has seemed to eclipse Al Qaeda as of 2016, if Osama bin Laden is correct, that is a temporary aberration because Al Qaeda's approach is more enduring.

Heather Pace Venable

See also: Cyber Terrorism; Distributed Denial-of-Service (DDoS) Attack; Islamic State in Iraq and Syria (ISIS)

Further Reading

Chen, M. Thomas. *Cyberterrorism after Stuxnet.* Strategic Studies Institute and United States Army War College Press, June 2014. http://www.strategicstudiesinstitute.army.mil/pdf files/PUB1211.pdf.

Ibrahim, Raymond, ed. *The Al Qaeda Reader: The Essential Texts of Osama Bin Laden's Terrorist Organization.* New York: Broadway Books, 2007.

Liu, Eric. "Al Qaeda Electronic: A Sleeping Dog?" A report by the Critical Threats Project of the American Enterprise Institute, December 2015. http://www.criticalthreats.org /al-qaeda/liu-al-qaeda-electronic-december-2-2015.

Mendelsohn, Barack. *The Al-Qaeda Franchise: The Expansion of Al-Qaeda and Its Consequences.* New York: Oxford University Press, 2016.

Wright, Lawrence. *The Looming Tower.* New York: Vintage, 2007.

ANONYMOUS

Anonymous is the name used by a collective of hackers, hacktivists, human rights advocates, and online pranksters scattered across the globe. The organization itself is amorphous and hard to define by goals, members, or activities. The group claims to be leaderless, and members are often even unknown to each other as the only concept that bands this collective together is respect for anonymity. Digitally, Anonymous is known by their logo of a suited man whose head has been replaced by a question mark surrounded by branches symbolizing peace. It is supposedly based on a surrealist painting by artist Rene Magritte. Additionally, individuals claiming to be members of Anonymous often upload videos in which they disguise their voices and wear Guy Fawkes masks made famous by the movie *V for Vendetta*. Their tagline is

> We are Anonymous.
> We are Legion.
> We do not forgive.
> We do not forget.
> Expect us.

The group can trace its roots to an Internet message board known as 4chan. On this message board, users can post on various topics without having to create a username. Rather, they can create posts under the user identification of "Anonymous." From this forum, the group Anonymous adopted its name. The group first began coordinating Internet trolling activities in 2003, the most famous being an online raid of the chatting site and virtual teenage hangout Habo Hotel. The group infiltrated the Web site by joining with the same character, a black man in a gray suit with an Afro. They flooded the Web site and then organized to form various figures, such as a swastika.

Originally intending to troll purely for the entertainment value, or "lulz," the group slowly began to coordinate efforts against groups that they believed stifled freedom of speech. One of the first politically charged coordinated attacks occurred in 2008 against the Church of Scientology. The church attempted to censor a leaked video of Tom Cruise speaking about Scientology. In the first wide-scale coordinated effort, the "hive," as they were called at the time, called on hackers to join together against Scientology through a 4chan message board under the name "Project Chanology." Followers launched a series of distributed denial-of-service (DDoS) attacks on the Church of Scientology's Web site in an attempt to crash it, prank called the Scientology hotline, and sent faxes that printed nothing but large black blocks to waste ink. This was followed by the uploading of a video in which an unknown speaker in a robotic voice warned that they would expel and systematically dismantle the Church of Scientology. Ten days later, this was followed by a mass protest in which Anons, or members of Anonymous, gathered together in real life throughout various cities to protest Scientology. The largest protest occurred in Los Angeles, where a thousand protestors, many wearing Guy Fawkes masks, marched outside the Church of Scientology building. Later that same year, the Federal Bureau of Investigation (FBI) began to take the threat of Anonymous seriously.

Soon after the success of the Scientology protests, the group suffered infighting over whether it should continue to engage in such politically motivated activities. Participation in the group soon waned, but by late 2010, Anons had reemerged to launch Operation Payback against the Recording Industry Association of America and the Motion Picture Association of America. These organizations had attempted to bring down file-sharing sites such as The Pirate Bay. Their attacks expanded to include organizations that they felt had attempted to silence Julian Assange or WikiLeaks, such as Amazon.com, PayPal, and Visa. This attack led to the subsequent arrest of 14 hackers by the FBI. Anons also participated in support of the Arab Spring movements, releasing software to protect Web browsers from government surveillance and organizing DDoS on various government sites. Anonymous or its offshoot LulzSec is also said to have been responsible for attacks on the computer security firm HBGary Federal, the government of Uganda, the Westboro Baptist Church, and Sony. Anons participated in support of the Occupy Wall Street movement and have targeted various child pornography and revenge pornography sites.

Currently, the hacker collective Anonymous continues to claim responsibility for a variety of actions in real life and cyber space. The group organized a protest known as the Million Mask march and has become involved in protests in Ferguson, Missouri. Anonymous has also targeted the Web sites of Islamic extremist groups and the Ku Klux Klan. The group hosts a YouTube channel that allows individuals to keep up-to-date with its current operations.

Barbara Salera

See also: Assange, Julian; 4chan; Hacktivist; LulzSec

Further Reading

Coleman, Gabriella. *Hacker, Hoaxer, Whistleblower, Spy: The Many Faces of Anonymous.* London: Verso, 2014.

Olson, Parmy. *We Are Anonymous: Inside the Hacker World of LulzSec, Anonymous and the Global Cyber Insurgency.* New York: Back Bay Books, 2012.

ANTIVIRUS SOFTWARE

Antivirus software is a program or collection of programs designed to protect computers from malware. This is done by scanning a computer's memory and any programs that are running in search of indications that malware is present. A computer virus is a program that attaches itself to a file and then seeks to replicate itself inside of the system, infecting other files. The term *virus* came into use in relation to computer viruses because they are similar to biological viruses: a digital virus cannot live on its own and survives by multiplying until it takes over a host. Viruses can carry payloads with them when they infect a computer. Therefore, a virus programmer can add various attacks on behalf of the one seeking to infiltrate a computer or network. Viruses seek to hide themselves from detection by users and antivirus software. Such malware can be dangerous because it can be programmed for anything, from general advertising spam, to stealing personal and business information, to destroying hardware.

Computer viruses take on three main forms: file infectors, boot-sector viruses, and macro viruses. The first viruses discovered were file infectors that need to be attached to a program that is installed on a computer. Boot-sector infections run in the computer memory upon start-up and then infiltrate the hard disk or any removable disks that are used with the computer. Macro viruses can be hidden in the scripts of programs that are embedded in data files rather than programs. This makes them more common and enables such infections to spread rapidly, as users are more likely to share smaller files. The rise of Internet usage has enhanced the devastation of macro viruses because of the increased ease with which people can transfer data files.

The technologically driven modern world has increased the importance of needing to ensure that computer systems and networks are protected. Antivirus software provides protection against the harmful effects of an infected computer. A virus tries to hide from detection by concealing itself in a file or program. Then, it attempts to run unobserved in the background and to carry out its designed task. Initially, contamination was largely seen by inclusion of viruses on disks with programs intended to be installed on a computer. Once the program was introduced, so too was the virus. With the increased usage and reliance on the Internet in the 21st century, threats to cyber security have grown exponentially.

Programs designed to detect and remove viruses operate by searching for patterns that give away the presence of an infection. Because malware is designed to not leave a trace, it is not easy for an individual user to detect it. Software is engineered to look for signs of concealment, which prove to be clues that something is hidden from plain view. Makers record code of known viruses and install these markers into their software so that the engine can recognize and remove the virus code if it detects the presence. However, it is more difficult to uncover viruses that companies are not aware of. This is why antivirus software is programed to look for suspicious activity from files and other programs that appear to be attempting to conceal something more sinister under the surface.

Antivirus software was expanded to detect and capture other forms of malware, including worms, spyware, adware, and phishing scams. This change caused an increased importance on ensuring that antivirus programs are up-to-date and operating properly. These threats not only include the potential of personal attacks, but businesses and even governments can also be vulnerable if proper steps are not taken. Some of the main concerns for an individual or corporation include the loss of such sensitive data as financial information and personal documents. Also, in some cases, national security has been threatened when nations have experienced cyber attacks seeking to uncover hidden information or shut down operations.

The list of companies producing antivirus software is vast, but a few of the more well-known corporations are Kaspersky Lab, McAfee, Bitdefender, Symantec Corporation (Norton), and Webroot. Various providers offer unique services, but they all strive to succeed in uncovering, blocking, and removing any malware that may attempt to infect a computer system. Some of the providers offer free software for use in fighting viruses, while others are paid protective services.

Ultimately, it is important for users to make sure that they have up-to-date antivirus software installed. Such programs are critical in the attempt to prevent leaking of sensitive information and the shutdown of computer systems.

Jason R. Kluk

See also: Cyber Crime; Hacker; Kaspersky Lab; Malware; McAfee; Phishing; Software; Spear Phishing; Symantec Corporation

Further Reading

Barile, Ian. *Protecting Your PC*. Boston: Charles River Media, 2006.

Schneier, Bruce. *Secrets and Lies: Digital Security in a Digital World*. New York: John Wiley & Sons, Inc., 2000.

Solomon, Alan. *PC Viruses: Detection, Analysis, and Crime*. London: Springer-Verlag, 1991.

APPLE INC.

Apple Inc. is a technology giant that makes hardware and software for mobile devices and desktop computers. Apple is known for driving innovation by popularizing the graphic user interface (GUI), the mouse, apps, and the "post–PC world" as well as customer loyalty, innovation in design and marketing, and the mystique of secrecy the company maintains. Apple is headquartered in Cupertino, California; employs over 115,000 workers worldwide; and operates over 300 Apple Stores.

Apple was founded in 1976 by Steve Jobs (1955–2011) and Steve Wozniak (1950–). The company created workstations throughout the next two decades, including the immensely popular Macintosh, the first mass-market workstation with such intuitive elements as a GUI and a mouse. After declining in the 1990s, the company was revitalized by Jobs and Jonathan Ive, who took it into the post–PC world with the release of the iPod, iPhone, and iPad alongside traditional desktops and laptops running Apple's OS X operating system and digital offerings such as iOS and iTunes. At the time of Jobs's death in 2011, Apple was one of the largest and most important tech companies in the world.

Apple's unique approach, the "magic of Apple," sets it apart from its competition in several ways. Apple products are largely purpose-built, allowing little customization or differentiation from the base model. Its customers tend to be extremely brand loyal, especially to its desktop and laptop products and software. As a result, Apple customers often consider themselves to be a part of the Apple "family" and remain fiercely loyal to its products.

Apple has largely played a peripheral role in cyber crime and cyber warfare. During the heyday of the Apple workstation in the 1980s, many early cyber attacks were directed at Apple products, including Elk Cloner and the first large-scale virus, Festering Hate/CyberAIDS, in 1987. As the popularity and market share of Apple products declined, so did interest in attacking them. This caused many Apple users to believe that Apple computers and devices were "unhackable," a belief encouraged by the company that remains to the present. However, the shift to mobile products has prompted an upsurge in attacks on Apple products. The 2010s saw a major increase in viruses and other attacks directed at Apple users, including malware such as WireLurker, XcodeGhost, and MacDefender. In 2016, the first ransomware attack on Apple computers, called KeRanger, occurred. Apple is often slow to respond to vulnerabilities: 2008's FinFisher/FinSpy exploit in iTunes took months to close, as opposed to shorter times for competing companies. Many security companies now rate Apple as the most vulnerable large tech company because of these two factors.

Apple has an increasing role in cyber warfare. The San Bernardino terror attacks of December 2015 involved an iPhone 5C owned by one of the attackers; the FBI requested that Apple unlock its encryption, but Apple refused on principle and was backed by its fellow tech companies. However, tech companies have a longstanding policy of cooperating with the U.S. government, including Apple. The company signed on to the NSA PRISM program in 2012, the last-known major tech company to do so. Much of this cooperation fed into the NSA metadata program, as revealed by the Edward Snowden leaks. The San Bernardino case was resolved by a third party, but it indicates the increased role of Apple in cyber-security issues.

Jonathan Abel

See also: Cloud Computing; Cyber Security; Encryption; Federal Bureau of Investigation (FBI); Google; Malware; Microsoft Corporation; National Security Agency (NSA); PRISM Program; Snowden, Edward J.

Further Reading

Dormehl, Luke. *The Apple Revolution: The Real Story of How Steve Jobs and the Crazy Ones Took Over the World.* New York: Virgin Books, 2013.
Harris, Shane. *@War: The Rise of the Military-Internet Complex.* New York: Houghton Mifflin Harcourt, 2014.
Lashinsky, Adam. *Inside Apple: How America's Most Admired—and Secretive—Company Works.* New York: Business Plus, 2012.

ARAMCO ATTACK

A cyber attack on Saudi Aramco (Saudi Arabian Oil Company) occurred on August 15, 2012, using the Shamoon virus. Aramco is Saudi Arabia's state-owned oil company, the world's largest producer, which supplies more than 10 percent of the global oil demand. Aramco's headquarters is located in Dhahran, Saudi Arabia. At its peak production, Aramco produced approximately 12 million barrels per day of crude oil, but it averaged 10.2 million barrels per day in 2015.

The attack on Aramco was one of the most destructive virus attacks since Stuxnet, according to U.S. Secretary of Defense Leon E. Panetta. The attack was started by an insider, a disgruntled Saudi Aramco employee, who infected a computer system within Aramco's internal network. The employee was alleged to be working for the Iranian government. Sometime after the attack occurred, the Cutting Sword of Justice, a previously unknown hacker group, claimed responsibility for Shamoon. As proof of their involvement, the hacker group posted thousands of Aramco computer IP addresses. The Shamoon virus infected nearly 30,000 Aramco computers, which were rendered completely unusable after the attack. It took Saudi Aramco over a week to restore services after isolating their system. Armaco's main internal network service was restored by August 26, 2012. The Shamoon virus did not reach the drilling or refining operations control system computers, but much of the drilling and production data were lost because of data corruption by the virus. This critical data had not been backed up that day, allegedly due to Ramadan.

Normally, data was supposed to be manually backed up twice per day. The attack also affected the company's public-facing Web site, which still experienced significant downtime, even after the announced recovery. The Shamoon attack appears to have been a form of cyber sabotage.

The Shamoon virus is a self-replicating modular computer virus that affects Microsoft Windows–based machines. The virus was primarily targeted for oil and energy companies. The virus is spread from one infected computer to other computers within the network. According to Symantec, the virus contains three components: a dropper, a wiper, and a reporter. The dropper is the primary component that initiates the copying and execution of itself as well as embedding the other components into the system. The wiper is the destructive component that deletes files and overwrites files with corrupted JPEG images. The reporter transmits the virus information back to the attacker. The virus basically renders the computer systems unusable. The Aramco cyber attack demonstrates the dangers of neglecting network security and directly connecting critical systems to the Internet.

Steven A. Quillman

See also: Cyber Attack; Cyber Espionage; Shamoon Virus

Further Reading

Libicki, Martin. *Cyberspace in Peace and War.* Annapolis, MD: U.S. Naval Institute Press, 2016.

Mackenzie, H. "Shamoon Malware and SCADA Security—What Are the Impacts?" *Tofino Security*, October 25, 2012.

Sandle, T. "Shamoon Virus Attacks Saudi Oil Company." *Digital Journal*, August 18, 2012.

Springer, Paul J. *Cyber Warfare: A Reference Handbook.* Santa Barbara, CA: ABC-CLIO, 2015.

ARPANET

The Advanced Research Projects Agency Network, or ARPANET, was a computer network that preceded the Internet and served as its original central network. It was established and initially operated by the Advanced Research Projects Agency (ARPA), a Department of Defense organization later renamed the Defense Advanced Research Projects Agency (DARPA). In the 1960s, ARPA contracted with universities to conduct computer science research and sought a way to consolidate data and share resources among the various geographically separated laboratories. The solution was to establish a network to forward data from a computer host by breaking messages into small, manageable "packets" and routing them via redundant links ("switching") to the recipient host. The problem of incompatibility between the hosts was overcome by the establishment of a "subnet" of smaller computers, known as Interface Message Processors (IMPs), which would communicate with each other through a standardized set of commands, known as a Network Control Protocol (NCP). Host computers sent data to their local IMP, which then broke up the message and routed it through the other IMPs to its destination, where the IMP at that location reassembled the message and forwarded it to its host computer.

The original four nodes of ARPANET—at the Stanford Research Institute (SRI), University of California–Los Angeles (UCLA), University of California (UC) Santa Barbara, and the University of Utah—were operational by December 1969.

ARPANET's development benefited from the fact that many of its users were also its designers. An informal Network Working Group (NWG) formed to discuss improvements and standards for usage, documenting their findings in modestly titled Requests for Comments (RFCs). The advent of electronic mail (e-mail) in 1972 as part of ARPANET's File Transfer Protocol (FTP) soon supplanted resource sharing as the network's key feature. As early as 1973, e-mail messages comprised three-fourths of all network traffic. Online communities arose as a result of this new form of interaction.

As other computer networks developed throughout the United States and the world, designers began to consider ways to connect them together into a single "Internet." A team led by ARPA developed a concept that would allow messages to pass from one network to another through a "gateway" computer. This concept required new protocols, the first being the Transmission Control Protocol (TCP) as a common language for network messaging and the second being the Internet Protocol (IP) for sending messages through gateways. In 1983, ARPANET officially transitioned from NCP to TCP/IP and became the main hub of the Internet.

Network demand soon began to outpace ARPANET's capacity. The development of personal computers (PCs) and local area networks (LANs) caused usage to climb exponentially in this period. Another government agency, the National Science Foundation, had established its own network (NSFNET) for any university willing to pay for a subscription. It had a "backbone" of five supercomputers and thus a much higher capacity than ARPANET. By the end of the 1980s, DARPA had decided to terminate ARPANET operations, transferring the host connections to NSFNET. ARPANET was officially decommissioned on February 28, 1990.

Christopher G. Marquis

See also: Defense Advanced Research Projects Agency (DARPA); Domain Name System (DNS); E-commerce; Ethernet; Internet; Sun Microsystems; Transmission Control Protocol/Internet Protocol (TCP/IP)

Further Reading

Abbate, Janet. *Inventing the Internet.* Cambridge, MA: The MIT Press, 2000.

Hafner, Katie, and Matthew Lyon. *Where Wizards Stay Up Late: The Origins of the Internet.* New York: Simon & Schuster, 1996.

Moschovitis, Christos J. P., Hilary Poole, Tami Schuyler, and Theresa M. Senft. *History of the Internet: A Chronology, 1843 to the Present.* Santa Barbara, CA: ABC-CLIO, 1999.

ARQUILLA, JOHN

John Arquilla, an American academic specializing in international relations and cyber warfare, was born in 1954. Arquilla completed his BA at Rosary College in 1975. After working from 1975 to 1987 as a surety bond executive, he received his

MA and PhD in international relations from Stanford in 1989 and 1991, respectively. During that time, he worked as an analyst for RAND Corporation before becoming an assistant professor of national security affairs at the Naval Postgraduate School (NPS) in Monterey, California, in 1993. Since 2005, he has held the title of professor of defense analysis at NPS. He continues to work at RAND as a senior consultant. Notable publications include *Afghan Endgames: Strategy and Policy Choices for America's Longest War* (2012); *Insurgents, Raiders, and Bandits* (2011); *Worst Enemy: The Reluctant Transformation of the American Military* (2008); *Information Strategy and Warfare* (2007); *The Reagan Imprint: Ideas in American Foreign Policy from the Collapse of Communism to the War on Terror* (2006); *Networks and Netwars: The Future of Terror, Crime, and Militancy* (2001); and *In Athena's Camp: Preparing for Conflict in the Information Age* (1997).

Arquilla played a prominent role in shaping U.S. military policy in the age of emerging cyber technology. He worked as a consultant to General H. Norman Schwarzkopf Jr. during Operation Desert Storm and advised American secretaries of defense John Hamre and Donald Rumsfeld. Netwar, or cyber "swarm-tactics," ranks as his most notable contribution to military affairs. Rejecting the hierarchical structure of modern militaries, Arquilla has advised the adoption of network structures by modern states to defeat dispersed and decentralized terrorist groups such as Al Qaeda. He has also argued that cyber warfare represents a new means of conducting information warfare but that the concept of information dominance has been a part of warfare for centuries.

Jordan R. Hayworth

See also: Cyber War; Net-centric Warfare (NCW); Rumsfeld, Donald H.

Further Reading

Arquilla, John. *Networks and Netwars: The Future of Terror, Crime, and Militancy.* Santa Monica, CA: RAND, 2001.

Arquilla, John, and Douglas A. Borer, eds. *Information Strategy and Warfare: A Guide to Theory and Practice.* New York: Routledge, 2007.

ASSANGE, JULIAN

Julian Assange is the Australian-born founder and editor-in-chief of WikiLeaks. He is currently wanted for rape charges in Sweden, but he has been granted asylum and is currently living in the Ecuadorian embassy in London to avoid extradition to Sweden and eventually the United States.

Assange first started hacking as a teenager in Australia. Under the hacker name Mendax, Assange, along with a few others, formed the group International Subversives. The group successfully hacked into many U.S. military and corporate networks, such as the Pentagon, U.S. Air Force, U.S. Naval Intelligence, NASA, and Lockheed Martin, just to name a few. Eventually, he was arrested and convicted of 25 counts of hacking and related crimes charges. He was ordered to pay restitution and released on good behavior

In 2005, Assange first developed the idea for WikiLeaks. He wanted to create a Web site where anyone could post information anonymously about anything. In 2006, with the help of John Young, WikiLeaks secured a Web address, and Assange worked tirelessly, traveling around the world, to get the Web site off the ground. The Web site's first impact came in the release of documents that outlined a plan to assassinate members of the Somali government.

In 2010, Assange and WikiLeaks became a household name when the WikiLeaks founder released a video titled "Collateral Murder" that showed the American military opening fire on what appeared to be unarmed civilians and children. Soon after, through his contact Private First Class Bradley Manning, WikiLeaks published thousands of U.S. government documents online. A year later, the Swedish government issued a warrant for Assange's arrest on sexual assault charges. He fought extradition, fearing the Swedish government would hand him over to the United States. The United States has not filed charges against Assange, though he is currently still in hiding.

Barbara Salera

See also: Anonymous; Hacktivist; Manning, Bradley; Snowden, Edward J.; WikiLeaks

Further Reading

Fowler, Andrew. *The Most Dangerous Man in the World: The Explosive True Story of Julian Assange and the Lies, Cover-ups and Conspiracies He Exposed.* New York: Skyhorse, 2011.
Greenberg, Andy. *This Machine Kills Secrets: Julian Assange, the Cypherpunks, and Their Fight to Empower Whistleblowers.* New York: Plume, 2013.

ATTRIBUTION

Attribution is the ability to determine those responsible for disruption, intrusion, or a cyber attack; convincing a would-be attacker that you have the ability to identify them and determine their culpability is one premise of deterrence in cyber space. Four levels of attribution have been proposed by researchers Don Cohen and K. Narayanaswamy:

1. Identification of the specific hosts (machines) involved in the attack
2. Identification of the controlling host (machine)
3. Identification of the actual human actor(s)
4. Identification of the higher organization with a specific purpose to the attack

The level of attribution required depends on the type and severity of the cyber attacks; however, these attacks are intrinsically difficult to deter because of the network architecture, variable levels of security, and the ability for attacks to be launched via unknowing third parties or over international borders.

Once attacked, attribution in cyber space can be difficult because, unlike traditional circuit switching networks such as analog telephones, the Internet is a packet-switching network that does not establish a path prior to transferring information between addresses. While it is the case that both the telephone network and the Internet are a patchwork of privately owned, independent networks with architecture supporting different technology platforms across jurisdictions that have evolved their own laws, attribution on the Internet is more difficult because it does not require dedicated paths for message transfer. Instead, Internet messages are broken up and transmitted along many different paths, information is subdivided into packets, and each packet is routed through a different path to its intended destination. Packets can be combined or fragmented, as required, and at the final address, the process is reversed and the data reassembled into its original form.

One analogy is that a packet-switched network resembles the postal system. Packets are sent without the nework knowing the entire route beforehand. As a packet arrives at a post office (router), the next post office is then determined by the system's protocols; this is repeated many times until the packet reaches its final address. There is a further complication: as dedicated paths are not required, a packet-switched network allows multiple users simultaneous use of a shared network to a far greater degree than is the case for a circuit-switched network; the Internet, therefore, can be more dense in terms of traffic and information.

Attribution is possible. Identification of the IP address of a machine (level 1 attribution) can be accomplished by each router maintaining a record of all packets that move through it; this record can be queried to identify the next router an attack passed through and, ultimately, the point of origin. To mitigate the resulting data-storage issue and maintain privacy, only the header information—the source and destination of the packet, known as *metadata*—needs to be stored. A further technique is referred to as a *hack back*. Rather than just following the attack chain through the routers, it is possible for a victim of an attack to penetrate a series of host machines by inserting a host-monitoring capability, thereby exploiting the same vulnerabilities to identify infected machines until the attack origin is determined (level 2 attribution); should personal data be held on this machine, level 3 attribution might be achievable.

Unfortunately, there are problems with implementing these approaches. To be effective, every country and ISP would have to agree to record and store data on packet traffic, and this would generate an inordinate amount of mixed-format data that would be expensive to analyze; moreover, even if the origin of the attacks could be identified, they may be from public-access areas such as cyber cafés or public libraries. As far as a hack back, infecting and monitoring intermediate machines in an attack chain may constitute a potential violation of privacy laws for individuals who are already unwitting victims. Notwithstanding the legal impediments, more sophisticated attackers can eliminate the vulnerabilities that might otherwise have facilitated a defender hack back, or due to the nature of the attack, hack backs may have to be accomplished while the attack is underway. Overall, attackers enjoy an asymmetric advantage over defenders because of architectural and technical limitations such as static network configurations and fixed IP addresses as well as regulatory hurdles.

Recently, research has led to experimentation that has successfully used surplus IP address capacity in networks. Elements of the network (the subnet gateways and network controllers) can be used to create short-lived random IP addresses at variable rates. Whereas the defending network administrators are still able to monitor their own unchanged hosts and gateways, potential attackers are confronted by constantly changing pseudo IP addresses that shroud the actual network behind a fog of moving data; they cannot fix their target. By creating an ever-changing attack surface, the target appears more unpredictable to attackers and is thus harder to exploit and more resilient to attacks; attackers will potentially perceive their advantages to have been reduced, along with their likelihood of success.

Graem Corfield

See also: Cyber Attack; Cyber Deterrence; Hacker; Internet; Internet Protocol (IP) Address

Further Reading

Cohen, Don, and K. Narayanaswamy. *Survey/Analysis of Levels I, II, and III Attack Attribution Techniques.* Research Project Sponsored by Advanced Research and Development Activity (ARDA), Los Angeles: CS3 Inc., 2004.
Libicki, Martin C. *Cyber Deterrence and Cyber War.* Monograph, Arlington: RAND Corporation, 2009.

AUTHENTICATION

Authentication is the process of verifying the identity of a user, process, or device, or verifying the source and integrity of data. Authentication is necessary because creating an online identity leads to the registration of credentials that can be used to access systems, applications, or data; authentication is a transaction to test those credentials.

Credentials are typically classified in three categories:

- Something you know (username, password, PIN)
- Something you have (device, cryptographic key)
- Something you are (biometric feature)

Depending on the consequences arising from a compromise, authentication may be single-factor, two-factor, or multifactor, with credentials being constructed from any combination of the three categories. Additionally, authentications can consist of a single step or several steps, with the user presenting an alphanumeric string of characters that is validated against a stored record or generated as part of the authentication transaction. In practice, this will be a username or password or, alternatively, a one-time pass code or biometric measurement. Authentication processes can be driven by rules that reflect evaluation of risk, such as a user providing single-factor authentication when attempting to log in from a known computer and address but otherwise being required to provide two-factor authentication. Alternatively, authentication requirements can be driven by the nature or value of a transaction; a retailer may ask for a photographic ID or utility bill with proof of address in addition to a means of payment that includes entering a PIN.

Static authentication methods are essentially a binary decision process consisting of three subprocesses: enrollment, presentation, and evaluation. During enrollment, information is collected about the individual and stored to be used as a template for authentication. During presentation, an individual requests to use the system, and when prompted, the individual presents his or her identity and an authentication factor. The evaluation is then triggered, which consists of comparing the presented credentials against the stored profile, resulting in either a match or nonmatch. While it is common to validate a user with a one-time authentication process at the beginning of an online session, this does leave the system vulnerable thereafter, as static authentication does not continuously verify the identity of the user once he or she has logged in.

Continuous authentication consists of reauthenticating the user repeatedly throughout the lifetime of the session by repeatedly checking the authentication credentials of the user while the session is still in progress. One of the key measures of the strength of the authentication mechanism is how often the credential changes; referred to as *entropy*, this increases the uncertainty that an attacker faces if credentials are falsely presented. Continuous authentication works by continuously monitoring user behavior and uses this as basis to reauthenticate periodically throughout a log-in session. As an alternative to password-based user authentication, continuous authentication can use biometrics: the identification of humans by their physical characteristics, such as the user's face, fingerprint, iris, or behavioral traits, such as gait, keystroke pattern, or typing rate.

Graem Corfield

See also: Cyber Defense; Cyber Security; Encryption

Further Reading

Bryen, Stephen D. *Technology Security and National Power: Winners and Losers.* New Brunswick, NJ: Transaction Publishers, 2016.

Rosenzweig, Paul. *Cyber Warfare: How Conflicts in Cyberspace are Challenging America and Changing the World.* Santa Barbara, CA: Praeger, 2012.

B

BAIDU

Baidu is the most prominent and frequently used search engine in the People's Republic of China (PRC). Baidu was founded on January 18, 2000, by Robin Yanhong Li and Eric Xu Yong with the purpose of providing Internet users with an efficient method for finding information and services online. As of 2016, the current chief executive officer of Baidu is Robin Yanhong Li, and the company headquarters is located in Beijing, China.

Baidu services are offered in Mandarin Chinese and allow users to search for Web sites, audio recordings, and images. Additionally, Baidu provides other services, such as searching news, Web directories, social networks, dictionaries, government information, maps, an encyclopedia, online shopping, finance, statistics, entertainment, music, travel booking, e-readers, cloud storage, international postal codes, international legal cases, translations, missing persons, games, and international patents.

Baidu has generated a lot of controversy for its extensive online censoring of topics and Web sites deemed provocative or inappropriate by the PRC government. These actions have raised concerns about the objectivity of search results provided to users. In the case *Zhang et al. v. Baidu.com Inc.*, activists in the United States alleged Baidu violated the U.S. Constitution by suppressing and censoring political and prodemocracy speech. Judge Jesse Furman dismissed the lawsuit and stated Baidu could use its own editorial judgment and has the legal right to censor and block search results for their product.

Roger J. Chin

See also: Google; Peoples' Republic of China Cyber Capabilities

Further Reading

Fuchs, Christian. "Baidu, Weibo and Renren: The Global Political Economy of Social Media in China." *Asian Journal of Communication* 26 (2016): 14–41.

Jiang, Min. "The Business and Politics of Search Engines: A Comparative Study of Baidu and Google's Search Results of Internet Events in China." *New Media & Society* 16 (2014): 212–233.

BITCOIN

Bitcoin is the first decentralized digital currency. It is a peer-to-peer digital currency with no centralized banking distribution authority. It is also sometimes called a *cryptocurrency* because it uses cryptographic principles, such as hashing and encryption algorithms, as the basis of its function. Bitcoin was invented by a person using the alias Satoshi Nakamoto in 2008 and began circulating as open-source software in 2009. Bitcoins come into circulation through miners. Miners are individuals or groups of individuals who compete to earn payment in bitcoins as a reward for using their computing power to provide the record keeping for all Bitcoin transactions on the Bitcoin network.

Transactions are recorded in blocks, and blocks are sequenced together in chronological order into a blockchain, which serves as the public ledger for accounting. The blockchain is considered the main technological innovation of Bitcoin. Bitcoin came into public consciousness most famously by its use in the online black market site Silk Road, which was shut down by the FBI in 2013. It is reported that over 9 million bitcoins were used to make purchases on the site. Digital currencies are also appealing for international financial transactions, as they are independently issued and not backed against any other currency or controlled by any government.

Deonna D. Neal

See also: Cyber Crime; Dark Web; Silk Road

Further Reading

Tapscott, Don, and Alex Tapscott. *Blockchain Revolution: How the Technology behind Bitcoin Is Changing Money, Business, and the World.* New York: Penguin, 2016.

Vigna, Paul, and Michael J. Casey. *The Age of Cryptocurrency: How Bitcoin and the Blockchain Are Challenging the Global Economic Order.* New York: St. Martin's Press, 2015.

BLACK HAT

A black hat is a hacker who gains unauthorized access to a computer or network out of malice or for personal gain. The term refers to villains in early Western films who often wore black hats to signify their evil to viewers.

For many years, black hat hackers only operated individually or in small groups to attack individual Web sites. In 2004, black hat hacker Jeremy Hammond argued that black hats should collectivize and use their power and skills to enact political change. The spread of such ideas helped give rise to hacker collectives such as Anonymous and its offshoot, LulzSec, which can initiate global cyber insurgencies against large corporations and government entities. Attacks by these black hat collectives can possibly jeopardize national security or cost companies millions of dollars.

The term has two other related uses. In 1997, cyber-security expert Jeff Moss held the first Black Hat Briefings, a conference that brought together professionals in the burgeoning field of information security. Initially held annually in Las Vegas, Black Hat Briefings have since expanded to multiple continents. Also, director Michael Mann adapted the term for his 2015 cyber-espionage film *Blackhat* about a hacker released from prison to identify the culprit of a series of devastating cyber attacks.

Ryan Wadle

See also: Anonymous; Hacker; Hacktivist; LulzSec; White Hat

Further Reading

Reitman, Janet. "The Rise and Fall of Jeremy Hammond: Enemy of the State." *Rolling Stone*, December 7, 2012. http://www.rollingstone.com/culture/news/the-rise-and-fall-of-jeremy-hammond-enemy-of-the-state-20121207.

Rosenzweig, Paul. *Cyber Warfare: How Conflicts in Cyberspace Are Challenging America and Changing the World.* Santa Barbara, CA: Praeger, 2013.

BLACKLIST

A blacklist is a grouping of identifiers that represent malicious entities or content. It is typically used to block communication with such entities, to prevent blacklisted content from entering a system or network, or to detect the presence of such communications or content. A variety of blacklists have been introduced over the years, and some are widely used. There are blacklists that contain file hashes (e.g., of known malware); Uniform Resource Locators (URLs); Internet Protocol (IP) addresses (of hosts that have exhibited behavior such as denial of service, scanning, or sending spam); domain names (hosting malicious services); and e-mail addresses (typically identifying spam senders). Some blacklists are maintained by individual private or commercial entities, while individuals or organizations maintain others in a collaborative fashion and make them accessible on the Internet.

New identifiers are inserted in the list once the maliciousness of the corresponding entity is established. The technical means for establishing maliciousness depends on the type of identifiers and the purpose of the blacklist. For example, a blacklist of spamming mail servers may require a certain number of e-mail messages from that server to be flagged as spam over a given period of time. The criteria for such insertion are the most important characteristics of a blacklist. For collaboratively maintained blacklists, one additional concern is the presence of possibly malicious participants, who may be trying to either prevent their insertion to the list or degrade its effectiveness. Blacklists also often have defined criteria for the removal of entities that may have been misclassified, especially when the insertion criteria are subject to misinterpretation or false positives.

Angelos D. Keromytis

See also: Cyber Defense; Distributed Denial-of-Service (DDoS) Attack; Firewall; Internet; Whitelist

Further Reading

Brenner, Joel. *America the Vulnerable: Inside the New Threat Matrix of Digital Espionage, Crime, and Warfare.* New York: Penguin Press, 2011.

BOTNET

A botnet is a group of compromised Internet-connected computers that have been forced to operate on the commands of an unauthorized remote user, usually without the knowledge of the computer's owner. This term, which combines bot from robot and net from network, usually has a negative or malicious connotation. The core components of a botnet are the infected computers and command and control. Home-based computers connected to the Internet that have not been effectively protected with a firewall and other safeguards are most susceptible to being compromised by a hacker, computer virus, or Trojan horse and turned into a bot or zombie (under remote direction). Although computer owners may be unaware that their system has been compromised, there are a number of possible signs. A computer that is infected could slow down, display mysterious messages, and may even crash.

The number of computers comprising a botnet can range in size from a dozen to hundreds of thousands. The network of infected computers is usually limited to a few hundred or a couple thousand, however, to prevent detection. There are a number of countermeasures to protect a computer from becoming a bot. Installing top-rated security software, configuring software settings to update automatically, increasing browser security settings, limiting user rights when online, and ensuring a system is patched with the most recent updates are good ways to help protect an Internet-connected computer. It is also advisable to never click on attachments unless the source can be verified.

Botnet controllers go by a variety of names, including bot-herders or botmasters. The controller can send a single command to activate a zombie army attack. Two of the major forms of command and control used by botmasters are client-server and peer-to-peer (P2P). In the client-server model, a single host or a small collection of hosts are used to manage the bots comprising the botnet. The major disadvantage of this model is that if the central control entity is removed, the network is destroyed, as the bots cannot connect to a nonexistent server. In the P2P type, the command and control aspect is decentralized, making shutting them down more difficult. Member bots participate equally in passing on traffic. This helps to provide anonymity to the controller because their system appears to be just another bot. Among the first P2P botnets was Sinit, released in September 2003. Since that time, millions of computers have been co-opted into botnets.

The typical bot life cycle starts with infection through various methods, including a hacker exploiting software vulnerabilities or an owner unintentionally installing a Trojan camouflaged as a helpful software application that was initiated by a spam e-mail, social media, or a game application. Once infected, the computer attempts to contact command and control in a process called *rallying*. When this process is successful, the computer goes into a waiting state until given a command by the botmaster.

Botmasters can program bots to perform a number of tasks or attacks. One basic attack is distributed denial-of-service (DDoS). A DDoS is a targeted attack against one Web site or network. In a coordinated effort, bots target a specific victim at a certain date and time and are instructed to request information from the targeted site, overloading its ability to answer or process the requests and causing the site to become overloaded and crash. Botnets can also spread viruses, generate e-mail spam, and commit other types of crime and fraud, including click fraud and Bitcoin mining. Click fraud is when bots are used to boost Web advertising billings by automatically clicking on Internet ads. Spyware can also be loaded onto the computers to steal personal and private information, including credit card numbers, bank credentials, and other sensitive personal information. The goal for many of these attacks is financial, but other motivations include a thrill for the bot-herder, crippling competitors, or as part of a larger military operation.

An example of a botnet used as part of a military operation is the Patriot botnet. A group of Israeli hackers created the botnet to initiate distributed denial-of-service attacks against anti-Israel Web sites. Unlike the normal procedure of gathering computers into the botnet surreptitiously, the creators invited people to voluntarily infect their computers to join the botnet. It was created, in part, to combat the cyber attacks launched by anti-Israeli groups following Israel's attack and invasion of the Gaza Strip, from December 27, 2008 to January 18, 2009.

An ongoing concern is that botnets can be used as cyber weapons to attack governmental entities and infrastructure. They can be used to collect information and to disable computers and Web sites. There are already some examples of this type of attack against the Republic of Georgia (Georbot). Botnets are not limited to individuals or nonstate actors. They can also be used by nation-states for DDoS attacks and other cyber-warfare operations.

Lori Ann Henning

See also: Cyber Attack; Cyber Weapon; Distributed Denial-of-Service (DDoS) Attack; Georbot; Hacker; Operation Cast Lead

Further Reading

Dunham, Ken, and Jim Melnick. *Malicious Bots: An Inside Look into the Cyber-criminal Underground of the Internet*. Boca Raton, FL: CRC Press, 2009.

Johnson, Thomas A., ed. *Cybersecurity: Protecting Critical Infrastructures from Cyber Attack and Cyber Warfare*. Boca Raton, FL: CRC Press, 2015.

Lee, Wenke, Cliff Wang, and David Dagon. *Botnet Detection: Countering the Largest Security Threat*. New York: Springer, 2008.

BRENNER, JOEL F.

Joel F. Brenner is a cyber-security expert. He also has a law practice at Joel Brenner LLC in Washington D.C., is a senior adviser for the Chertoff Group, and is a Robert Wilhelm Fellow at the MIT Center for International Studies. His expertise includes cyber and physical security, classified information and facilities, sensitive foreign transactions, intelligence law, privacy, and internal investigations. Brenner received his BA from University of Wisconsin–Madison in history (1969); his PhD at the London School of Economics and Political Science (1972); and his JD at Harvard Law School (1975).

Brenner has had a long and distinguished career in cyber and physical security, information privacy and securities, and intelligence law. With his standing on the Committee on Foreign Investment in the United States (CFIUS), he regulated sensitive transactions concerning foreign acquisitions and overseas operations, export controls, and liabilities of foreign governments. He also has many years of experience both inside and outside the government in homeland security.

Brenner began as a trial lawyer for the Department of Justice and moved on to private practice. In April 2002, he became the National Security Agency's inspector general, overseeing internal audits and investigations with functions of intelligence oversight. By 2006, he was chair of the National Counterintelligence Policy Board, which is responsible for integrating counterintelligence activities for 17 departments, including the FBI, CIA, DoD, Homeland Security, and others. He implemented strategy, policy, and compliance of the various departments. Brenner then became the senior counsel of the National Security Agency (NSA) in 2009, advising on public and private Internet security and industrial espionage. In March of 2013, he opened his private practice. He has published several books and dozens of articles about cyber threats to the United States.

Raymond D. Limbach

See also: Cyber Defense; Cyber Security; National Security Agency (NSA)

Further Reading

Brenner, Joel F. *America the Vulnerable: Inside the New Threat Matrix of Digital Espionage, Crime, and Warfare.* New York: Penguin, 2011.

Brenner, Joel F. *Glass Houses: Privacy, Secrecy, and Cyber Insecurity in a Transparent World.* New York: Penguin, 2013.

BUSH, GEORGE W.

George W. Bush served as the 43rd president of the United States from 2001 to 2009. Building upon the policies of his predecessors, President George W. Bush identified cyber security as a top priority. He signed the National Strategy to Secure Cyberspace in February 2003. The strategy identified the protection of critical infrastructure as the primary national security goal for the United States in cyber space. During this time period, it was identified that many critical industries relied on cyber space for either commerce or command and control of devices in the physical world. The use of Supervisory Control and Data Acquisition (SCADA) systems raised a serious concern that the U.S. and world economies could be significantly affected from widespread cyber disruptions. SCADA systems replaced manual control systems and allowed greater efficiency through remote access, but many of these systems were developed without a robust plan for protecting the controllers from cyber threats.

Widespread cyber espionage also arose during Bush's presidency. His administration considered private-public partnerships the foundation of the strategy, but there was also considerable effort spent reforming U.S. government organizations to protect against cyber threats. Cyber security in the Bush presidency focused almost entirely on securing American networks inundated with intrusions. It established the National Cyber Investigative Joint Task Force (NCIJTF) to coordinate operations against significant cyber threats.

Although nation-state cyber threats certainly preceded the Bush presidency, collective understanding about these threats had reached an unprecedented level. During Operation Buckshot Yankee, the penetration of classified networks by a foreign intelligence service led to the creation of U.S. Cyber Command. President Bush believed that U.S. dependence on cyber space required a coordinated effort by the federal government to encourage better security practices, and his strategy for cyber space reflected this belief.

Zachary M. Smith

See also: Cyber Defense; Operation Buckshot Yankee; Supervisory Control and Data Acquisition (SCADA); United States Cyber Capabilities

Further Reading

Bush, George W. *Decision Points.* New York: Crown Publishers, 2010.
The White House. *The National Strategy to Secure Cyberspace.* Washington, D.C.: Government Printing Office, February 2003.

C

CARPENTER, SHAWN

Cyber-security expert Shawn Carpenter is best known as the whistle-blower who exposed a Chinese cyber-espionage program code-named Titan Rain by the FBI. Carpenter graduated in computer science from the University of Nebraska–Lincoln in 1990 and joined the U.S. Navy. After completing the Naval Nuclear Power School in 1993, he worked as a nuclear propulsion plant operator and chemist until 1997. Upon leaving the U.S. Navy, Carpenter joined Sandia National Laboratories, a nuclear lab and a subsidiary of the Lockheed Martin Corporation, as a senior network intrusion detection analyst.

In 2003, Carpenter investigated a series of security breaches at Sandia, which also affected Lockheed Martin, Redstone Arsenal, NASA, and U.S. military instillations. He traced the attacks back to Chinese IP addresses. Carpenter requested permission from Sandia to hack back the cyber attacks but was denied. He was told his only concern should be Sandia and not to share information of the attacks with other affected organizations or the FBI. Carpenter then launched an independent investigation and shared the results with the Army Counterintelligence Group and the FBI. In 2005, Sandia fired Carpenter after discovering his work with the FBI. Carpenter then sued Sandia for wrongful termination and defamation. In February 2007, a New Mexico jury ruled in Carpenter's favor and awarded him almost $4.7 million in damages. After Sandia appealed the verdict, the two parties reached a private settlement in October 2007.

Since 2005, Carpenter has worked for a number of organizations, including the U.S. Department of State and NetWitness Corporation, and he is currently the senior vice president of cyber at Cybraics.

Mary Elizabeth Walters

See also: Cyber Security; Federal Bureau of Investigation (FBI); Operation Titan Rain; Peoples' Republic of China Cyber Capabilities

Further Reading

Libicki, Martin. *Cyberspace in Peace and War.* Annapolis, MD: U.S. Naval Institute Press, 2016.
Steinnon, Richard. *Surviving Cyberwar.* Lanham, MD: Government Institutes, 2010.

CEBROWSKI, ARTHUR K.

Arthur K. Cebrowski (1942–2005) was a U.S. Navy vice admiral who pioneered the concept of *network-centric warfare* and helped spearhead the transformation of the U.S. military in the 1990s and 2000s. While serving at the Naval War College from 1998 until 2001 and as the civilian head of the Office of Force Transformation from 2001 to 2005, Cebrowski developed the concept of net-centric warfare (NCW), which postulated that information and speed would trump mass and firepower in future wars. To accommodate this vision, Cebrowski argued for a fundamental restructuring of the Department of Defense to place it on par with innovative civilian technology companies. He also advocated weapons systems that fulfilled his vision, including smaller aircraft carriers and—in concert with analyst Wayne Hughes—a cheap, stripped-down "streetfighter" warship that later served as the basis for the navy's Littoral Combat Ship program.

Born August 13, 1942, in Passaic, New Jersey, Cebrowski received a BA in mathematics from Villanova in 1964. He served two tours as a naval aviator in the Vietnam War. In 1973, he received an MA in computer systems management from the Naval Postgraduate School. He later commanded the USS *Guam*, the USS *Midway* during Operation Desert Storm, and the USS *America* battle group. He died on November 12, 2005, after a battle with cancer.

Ryan Wadle

See also: Net-centric Warfare (NCW)

Further Reading

Blaker, James K. *Transforming Military Force: The Legacy of Arthur Cebrowski and Network Centric Warfare.* Westport, CT: Praeger Security International, 2007.

CENTRAL INTELLIGENCE AGENCY (CIA)

With the fall of the Cold War and the rise in a focus on terrorism after September 11, 2001, the Central Intelligence Agency (CIA) dramatically changed from an organization focused on collecting intelligence about foreign threats to one charged with undertaking secret paramilitary wars against terrorist groups. These secret wars have entailed problematic tactics. Many have criticized the CIA's questionable moral standards, particularly in regard to the use of brutal interrogation techniques, such as one suspect who was waterboarded 83 times. They have also challenged whether torture produced the kind of intelligence the CIA claimed it did. It also operated a series of secret prisons in a number of foreign countries. The drone attacks particularly favored by the Obama administration have also been heavily criticized. Some argue these attacks create more terrorists than they eliminate. The Obama administration announced in early 2016 that it would release records regarding these attacks with the hope that transparency would bring more support for its operations.

Director John Brennan was appointed in 2013. He recently reorganized the CIA by creating 10 centers based on regions of the world or specific missions, such as counterterrorism. These centers integrate analysts and operatives, who had long been divided. Brennan hopes the centers will lead to a greater sharing of information and a sense of community. This change seeks to repeat the successes of the CIA's Counterterrorism Center by integrating two subcommunities to identify, locate, and, ultimately kill terrorists. Brennan, who had served as an analyst within the agency, is mistrusted by many operatives because they believe he is undermining key espionage operations. They also charge that the CIA's reorganization is adding more bureaucracy, which will only make it more lethargic.

Now, the CIA is seeking to reinvent itself again as it transforms into an agency concerned with cyber espionage, putting the digital domain at the forefront of its operational focus. Although it is unclear exactly what role it played, the CIA worked with the National Security Agency (NSA) and the Israeli government to create the malware used in the Stuxnet cyber attacks launched against an Iranian nuclear reactor. This 2010 operation represented the first time an industrial-type hacking account had been carried out successfully.

In 2015, the CIA launched its Directorate for Digital Innovation (DDI), the first new directorate created in 50 years. The CIA has four other directorates: the Directorate for Science and Technology's responsibilities include the invention of gadgets, the Directorate of Support oversees logistics and administration, the Directorate of Intelligence has been renamed the Directorate of Analysis, and the National Clandestine Service returned to its traditional name of the Directorate of Operations.

DDI's creation was a response to a series of embarrassing cyber attacks against the United States, including North Korea's attacks on Sony Pictures in 2014, which included the theft and destruction of data, and an Iranian cyber attack against a Las Vegas casino. Whereas cyber previously had been compartmentalized within the agency, it is now organized to infuse it.

The CIA will maintain its focus on human intelligence gathering as opposed to the NSA's signal intelligence. Or, in other words, the NSA watches espionage from afar, while the CIA concentrates on acting against it on the ground in numerous ways. For example, a spy could infiltrate a group or a foreign military facility to implant malware. It could also seek to identify the "digital dust" of persons of interest. For example, it will track a potential target's cell phone as he or she travels. The CIA also plans to use cyber data to better identify potential foreign recruits.

Still, the CIA is challenged by its legacy IT equipment, which badly needs updating. The CIA has not kept pace with technological change to the extent that the NSA has. Although not directly related to its cyber equipment, the CIA's director was embarrassed when a teenager hacked into his personal AOL e-mail account in the fall of 2015.

Heather Pace Venable

See also: Cyber Espionage; Israel Cyber Capabilities; National Security Agency (NSA); Stuxnet; United States Cyber Capabilities

Further Reading

Greenberg, Andy. "Cyberespionage Is a Top Priority for CIA's New Directorate." *Wired*, March 9, 2015. http://www.wired.com/2015/03/cias-new-directorate-makes-cyberespionage-top-priority.

Hosenball, Mark. "CIA to Make Sweeping Changes, Focus More on Cyber Ops: Agency Chief." *Reuters*, March 6, 2015. http://www.reuters.com/article/us-usa-cia-idUSKBN0M223920150306.

Morrell, Michael. *The Great War of Our Time: The CIA's Fight against Terrorism—From al Qa'ida to ISIS*. New York: Twelve, 2015.

CERTIFICATES

Certificates are signed digital identity documents. The signatures usually originate with a third party. Certificates contain an identity and the public portion of an asymmetric key pair. They provide evidence that the entity named in a document is the sole holder of the private portion of the key pair. The mathematical relationship between the two halves of the key pair allows the owner of the certificate to prove he or she holds the private half of the key pair without revealing it. The signatures likewise involve asymmetric cryptography, which makes the certificate easy to verify but difficult to forge.

Anyone can sign certificates. Certificates rely on trust as well as verification. If the person verifying the certificate does not trust the signatory, he or she will not trust the certificate. As a result, there are lists of trusted certificate authorities. The listed authorities have widespread acceptance as trustworthy signatories. Most Internet browsers employ one of these lists. These lists are subject to change. If new certificate authorities form, they may be added to the list. If certificate authorities suffer a breach, they may no longer be considered trustworthy and therefore be removed. This fragility of trust is a weakness of the system. There are a number of external mechanisms, such as certificate cross-signing and certificate pinning, that partially mitigate this problem.

Certificate authorities can delegate the authority to sign certificates to other entities. In such cases, the delegating authority issues a certificate to that effect. These delegating certificates may be limited in scope, allowing the subsidiary to only issue certificates for subdomains of a single Web site, or they can be broader, allowing the subsidiary authority to further delegate. A certificate signed by a subsidiary authority is only valid in conjunction with all the delegating certificates. These certificates construct a chain of trust that leads back to the original trusted certificate authority. The construction of the chains means that if any signatory in the chain realizes it has been compromised, it can invalidate the signatures of all the certificates down the chain.

Certificates have limited durations. This limits the period during which damage can occur if the signatory's key is compromised. In all cases, the signatures on certificates rely on the signatory's private key remaining secure to prevent forgeries. If a signatory's private key is compromised, they can add the public portion of the key to a revocation list that alerts the public to not trust that particular key in future. This also invalidates all previously issued certificates, meaning that the compromised signatory must reissue all prior certificates under a new key.

Jonathan Hoyland

See also: Authentication; Cyber Security; Encryption

Further Reading

Brenner, Joel F. *America the Vulnerable: Inside the New Threat Matrix of Digital Espionage, Crime, and Warfare.* New York: Penguin, 2011.
Libicki, Martin. *Cyberspace in Peace and War.* Annapolis, MD: U.S. Naval Institute Press, 2016.

CLARKE, RICHARD A.

Richard A. Clarke is a former U.S. government advisor on cyber security and was the counterterrorism czar during the 9/11 attacks. He was born on October 27, 1950, in Dorchester, Massachusetts. He earned his bachelor's degree from the University of Pennsylvania in 1972, and in 1973, he began working as an analyst of European security issues in the U.S. Department of Defense. In 1978, he earned a master's degree in management from the Massachusetts Institute of Technology.

In 1985, Clarke became the deputy assistant secretary of state for intelligence, and he later became the assistant secretary of state for political-military affairs under the George H. W. Bush administration. During Bill Clinton's presidency, Clarke became the counterterrorism coordinator for the National Security Council (NSC), until George W. Bush made him the special advisor to the president on cyber security. Before the 9/11 attacks, Clarke advised that the U.S. should arm groups in Afghanistan and increase drone surveillance of Al Qaeda, the Taliban, and Osama bin Laden.

After 9/11, Clarke focused on issues of cyberterrorism in the public and private sectors. Since resigning in 2003, he has been outspoken against the Bush administration's counterterrorism efforts and the invasion of Iraq. Clarke has written several books and has been an advocate of increasing cyber security nationwide.

Michael Hankins

See also: Cyber Terrorism; National Cyber Security Strategy

Further Reading

Clarke, Richard A., and Robert K. Knake. *Cyber War: The Next Threat to National Security and What to Do about It.* New York: HarperCollins, 2010.
Summers, Anthony, and Robbyn Swan. *The Eleventh Day: The Full Story of 9/11 and Osama Bin Laden.* New York: Ballantine Books, 2011.

CLOSED NETWORK

A closed network is any electronic system that tries to limit usage to anything but full public access. Militaries and businesses can close their networks by using cryptography or sophisticated frequency-hopping schemes. One of the most widespread commercial closed networks is cable television, which requires a subscription to access signals over a coaxial cable or fiber optic cable, while broadcast networks allow any viewer with an appropriate tuner to access RF television signals.

Wi-Fi networks can be closed, allowing only a predetermined list of users, or users who know network-specific access credentials, to access a network. Some Wi-Fi networks limit access by not broadcasting network-specific Service Set Identifier (SSID) data (which is one way that users can locate and join a network). This may seem to increase network security, as the closed network is difficult to find and more difficult to join, but it usually only serves to limit casual usage. Sophisticated intruders can still use specialized passive electronic means to identify the closed-network SSID and intrude on the network. In addition to providing little extra security, closed Wi-Fi networks that require verbatim SSID entries and associated credentials incur higher user error rates during access.

Jeffrey R. Cares

See also: Hardware; JWICS Network; NIPRNet; SIPRNet; Wi-Fi

Further Reading
Bayuk, Jennifer L. *Cyber Security Policy Guidebook.* Hoboken, NJ: Wiley, 2012.

CLOUD COMPUTING

Conventional computers require software programs to be installed directly on the computer's hard drive for the software to operate. As more programs are required, the hard drive requires more capacity. As corporate networks become larger and software increases in sophistication, software installation and maintenance costs and hard drive memory costs increase as well.

Very rarely will any user in a network run every software program on their computer at once, so at the corporate level, there is significant excess software and memory capacity at any instant. With the advent of high bandwidth networking, it became possible to run software from across a corporate network rather than resident at each workstation, requiring less software maintenance and less local memory (and therefore cheaper computers). The software can now be centrally installed, run, and maintained, and the data are produced by running the centrally stored software. Such a network is said to run its services "in the cloud" because, to users, the software and data do not appear in a physical location (for example, resident in the computer on their desks).

Although the original impetus was to decrease overall costs, cloud service business models can be more expensive than conventional computing because more programs may be accessed (on a pay-as-you-go model, for example) by more users than might have been the case when software installation and maintenance limited a user base.

Jeffrey R. Cares

See also: Hardware; Software

Further Reading

Mahmood, Zaigham, ed. *Continued Rise of the Cloud: Advances and Trends in Cloud Computing*. London: Springer, 2014.

CODE RED WORM

The Code Red worm is a computer virus released on July 12, 2001, by unknown parties at Foshan University in China. One of the fastest-spreading computer viruses ever recorded, it infected 350,000 computers within a week. The worm was discovered by Marc Maiffret and Ryan Permeh of eEye Digital Security. They named it "Code Red" after the type of Mountain Dew they were drinking when they found it.

The worm used a buffer overflow loophole in Microsoft's Internet Information Services (IIS) software to allow the virus to run on the target machine. If the infection occurred before the 19th of the month, the worm used the machine to infect other systems running IIS by generating a random Internet Protocol (IP) address and attempting to send the worm to that machine. After the 19th of the month, the worm began a distributed denial-of-service (DDoS) attack on the White House Web site, crashing the page by overloading it with information. It also defaced Web pages hosted on the infected IIS software so that the page informed visitors it had been hacked by the Chinese.

Although Microsoft promptly issued a patch to close the loophole exploited by the Code Red worm, numerous computers were infected before users fully adopted the patch. It is estimated that of the 6 million computers running vulnerable IIS software, one in eight were infected by the worm before the vulnerability in the software was finally fixed on August 10, 2001.

Benjamin M. Schneider

See also: Distributed Denial-of-Service (DDoS) Attack; Malware; People's Republic of China Cyber Capabilities; Worm

Further Reading

Kizza, Joseph Migga. *Guide to Computer Network Security.* London: Springer, 2015.
Wang, Jie, and Zachary A. Kissel. *Introduction to Network Security: Theory and Practice.* Hoboken, NJ: Wiley, 2015.

COMPREHENSIVE NATIONAL CYBERSECURITY INITIATIVE (CNCI)

The Comprehensive National Cybersecurity Initiative (CNCI) was enacted by President George W. Bush in National Security Presidential Directive 54/Homeland Security Presidential Directive 23 (NSPD-54/HSPD-23) in January 2008. This CNCI consisted of 12 initiatives that would secure the United States in cyber space and multiple government agencies. It is still largely classified.

Since the 1990s, the U.S. government has balanced cyber-defense efforts into two priorities: securing government systems and protecting the American people and the economy. CNCI was to tackle the protection of government systems. It focused entirely on cyber security to help stop the loss of terabytes of sensitive information on military networks. It received a budget of $40 billion over a five-year period, funneled into the military and intelligence community.

In February 2009, President Barack Obama directed a 60-day interagency cyber-security review, which led to the declassification of limited material regarding CNCI. He implemented recommendations to the Cyberspace Policy Review that the CNCI activities should evolve and become key elements of an updated cyber-security strategy. Major goals were to establish a front line of defense against today's immediate threats, defend against the full spectrum of threats, and strengthen the future cyber-security environment. President Obama ordered the summary of the CNCI released to support transparency efforts.

The CNCI has 12 initiatives:

1. Manage the federal enterprise network as a single network enterprise with Trusted Internet Connections;
2. Deploy an intrusion detection system of sensors across the federal enterprise;
3. Pursue deployment of intrusion prevention systems across the federal enterprise;
4. Coordinate and redirect research and development (R&D) efforts;
5. Connect current cyber operations centers to enhance situational awareness;
6. Develop and implement a government-wide cyber counterintelligence (CI) plan;
7. Increase the security of classified networks;
8. Expand cyber education;
9. Define and develop enduring "leap-ahead" technology, strategies, and programs;
10. Define and develop enduring deterrence strategies and programs;
11. Develop a multipronged approach for global supply chain risk management;
12. Define the federal role for extending cyber security into critical infrastructure domains.

Obama claimed that the developers of the CNCI consulted with privacy experts to protect citizens' privacy and civil liberties. While securing cyber space is important to the nation's defense, it cannot come through trampling on constitutional rights. On January 6, 2011, the National Security Agency (NSA) built the first of a series of data centers, the Community Comprehensive National Cybersecurity Initiative Data Center at Camp Williams, Utah, also called the Utah Data Center, which some critics have claimed is being used to build extensive electronic profiles of U.S. citizens. One of the major criticisms of the CNCI has been the charge of a lack of transparency. Certain detailed aspects must remain classified; claims have been made that they hinder accountability to Congress and the public. Also, current classifications make it difficult for certain agencies and the private sector to interact and contribute to successful CNCI projects.

Raymond D. Limbach

See also: Cyber Defense; National Cyber Security Strategy; National Security Agency (NSA); PRISM Program

Further Reading

Clarke, Richard A., and Robert K. Knake. *Cyber War: The Next Threat to National Security and What to Do about It.* New York: HarperCollins, 2010.

Obama, Barack. *The Comprehensive National Cybersecurity Initiative.* Washington, D.C.: White House, 2009. https://www.whitehouse.gov/issues/foreign-policy/cybersecurity /national-initiative.

COMPUTER EMERGENCY RESPONSE TEAM (CERT)

Computer emergency response teams (CERT) are groups of cyber-security teams located around the world that provide expertise on cyber-related security issues. Formed to combat the increasingly complex threats of the cyber age, CERTs provide fast and reliable feedback on cyber- and information-security issues for governments, whose bureaucratic structures typically lack adequate expertise in cyber security. In common usage, CERTs are often misidentified as computer emergency readiness teams and are also often called computer security incident response teams (CSIRTs).

Researchers at Carnegie Mellon University first utilized the term CERT in the late 20th century. Specifically, CMU operationalized the first CERT after the Morris worm, an early version of a computer worm, attacked the Internet on November 3, 1988, and led to much panic. The U.S. government supported CMU's efforts to develop professional systems to counter the new threats to the country's cyber infrastructure. After 2000, the term was adopted by other agencies and institutions. In addition to their emergency response functions, CERTs assist in the dissemination of security information to governments and corporations. CERTs often collaborate between public and private entities to promote cyber security. As the threats from cyber space have increased in the form of malware, so too have the number and types of CERTs. Emerging as local or national entities, such as US-CERT, CERTs have now been created for some transnational organizations. To protect vulnerable and high-target systems such as water treatment plants and the power grid, some CERTs have been developed for the industrial sector.

As of 2016, there were approximately 250 organizations worldwide that utilized the name CERT. One such organization, US-CERT, was created by the U.S. Department of Homeland Security's (DHS) cyber-security division in 2003. It was charged with coordinating America's cyber-defense operations as part of the National Cybersecurity and Communications Integration Center (NCCIC). In 2014, DHS defined cyber security as its fourth priority mission. US-CERT is the 24-hour operational arm of DHS and NCCIC and is the leading organization involved in maintaining the country's cyber-security posture. It coordinates the sharing of cyber information and assesses and responds to potential cyber-security risks. US-CERT is also charged with protecting the constitutional rights of American citizens.

From 2012 to 2016, DHS spent $706 million annually on cyber-security programs, a large portion of which went to CERT. Despite US-CERT's efforts, malware has continued to achieve some success against America's cyber-security apparatus. In 2013, hackers broke into the network of the U.S. Army Corps of Engineers to access information on 85,000 dams. That same year, the Federal Communications Commission's Emergency Broadcast System broadcasted an alert of an ongoing zombie attack to residents in Michigan, Montana, and North Dakota after a hacking incident. Most seriously, in 2015, Chinese and Russian hackers breached the U.S. Office of Personnel Management and the White House's unclassified network, gaining access to information on federal employees with security clearances. These are just a few of the examples of threats dealt with by CERTS on a regular basis.

Jordan R. Hayworth

See also: Department of Homeland Security (DHS); Office of Personnel Management Data Breach

Further Reading

Andress, Jason. *Cyber Warfare: Techniques, Tactics and Tools for Security Practitioners.* Waltham, MA: Syngress, 2014.

Coburn, Tom. *A Review of the Department of Homeland Security's Missions and Performance.* Washington, D.C.: U.S. Senate Report, January 2015.

Singer, Paul W., and Allan Friedman. *Cybersecurity and Cyberwar: What Everyone Should Know.* New York: Oxford University Press, 2014.

CONFICKER WORM

Conficker is a highly sophisticated, stealthy, self-propagating computer worm, first detected in November 2008, that targets Microsoft Windows operating systems. Conficker's other known aliases are Downup, Downadup, and Kido. Conficker exploits an October 2008 Microsoft Windows Server Service Remote Procedure Call. This vulnerability allows the attacker to run arbitrary code on Windows operating systems without authentication. The main impact of Conficker was its ability to disable, reconfigure, or terminate an infected computer's operating system and other security services. Conficker disables the Windows security measures as well as third-party firewalls and antivirus products, which leaves the system vulnerable. The virus also blocks access to the third-party security sites for infection removal tools. Conficker uses several advanced malware techniques to make it hard to contain and control the virus.

Once installed on a machine, Conficker copies itself into the system directory with a random name, registers itself as a service, and adds itself to the registry. The worm then uses specific sites to find the infected machine's IP address, check the speed of the current Internet location, and obtain the current date and time. Once the IP address is known, Conficker downloads a small HTTP server that scans other machines for vulnerabilities. When a target is found, Conficker packages itself as a payload for infection, continuing the cycle. At Conficker's peak, it was one of the fastest and largest botnet worm infections. There were an estimated 6.5 million machines infected with Conficker in 2010.

In 2009, a task force was created to combat the Conficker pandemic. The group was called the Conficker Working Group or Conficker Cabal. The group included representatives from AOL, F-Secure, Facebook, Georgia Tech, ICANN, McAfee, Kaspersky Lab, IBM-ISS, Cisco, Sophos, Symantec Corporation, Microsoft Corporation, SRI International, Trend Micro, SecureWorks and others. Microsoft has offered a $250,000 reward leading to the capture and conviction of the worm's creators. The authors of this virus are unknown, but Conficker allegedly originated from the Ukraine, based on digital cues within the code.

Steven A. Quillman

See also: Botnet; Malware, Microsoft Corporation; Microsoft Windows; Worm

Further Reading

Andress, Jason, and Steve Winterfield. *Cyber Warfare: Techniques, Tactics and Tools for Security Practitioners.* Waltham, MA: Syngress, 2011.

Bowden, Mark. *Worm: The First Digital World War.* New York: Grove Press, 2011.

Kirk, J. "Cleaning Up Botnets Takes Years to Complete." *Computerworld*, August 3, 2015.

Springer, Paul J. *Cyber Warfare: A Reference Handbook.* Santa Barbara, CA: ABC-CLIO, 2015.

CRAY, SEYMOUR

Seymour Cray (1925–1996), an American electrical engineer, helped found a number of computer corporations dedicated to producing the world's fastest computers during his long and distinguished career. Cray was born in Chippewa Falls, Wisconsin, on September 28, 1925, and he died in Colorado Springs, Colorado, on October 5, 1996, as a result of injuries from a car accident.

Cray joined Engineering Research Associates (ERA), a firm known for developing early drum memory systems and codebreaking machines for the U.S. Navy, in 1951. After ERA was acquired by a succession of other computer firms, Cray, like many members of the firm, eventually joined the new Control Data Corporation (CDC) and specialized in developing fast high-end scientific computers that were termed *supercomputers*. In succession, Cray designed the ERA 1103 (1953), CDC 1604 (1958), and CDC 6600 (1965), the first commercial supercomputer. Cray's designs did not rely on the brute force speed of the processors to achieve their computational power. Instead, he emphasized other elements, including cooling systems and input-output bandwidth management, to ensure instructions and data arrived on time to optimize processing.

Cray ultimately left CDC in 1972 to found Cray Research in his hometown. He developed a series of Cray computers that advanced the state of the art in supercomputing until he founded another company, Cray Computer Corporation (CCC), in 1989 in Colorado Springs. CCC went bankrupt in 1995, and he founded his final company, SRC Computers, to leverage massive parallel processing to advance supercomputing until his untimely death.

John G. Terino

See also: Hardware

Further Reading

Ceruzzi, Paul E. *Computing: A Concise History.* Cambridge, MA: The MIT Press, 2012.
Murray, Charles J. *The Supermen: The Story of Seymour Cray and the Technical Wizards behind the Supercomputer.* New York: John Wiley & Sons, 1997.

CRYPTOGRAPHY

Cryptography is the practice of concealing the true meaning of language within a code that is unreadable to all except the intended recipient. Encryption is achieved by replacing the plaintext, or the original language, with a cipher. Cipher is the name given to code used to convert the original text. Initially, codes were simple for people to remember and the process easy enough to allow for quick retrieval of messages. However, with the advent of computers, ciphers became increasingly complex, and security grew exponentially.

Cryptography may appear to be a young science, but it is a practice that dates back thousands of years. The first documented use of concealment can be traced back to the ancient Egyptians and Greeks. They disguised messages by using non-traditional written languages or physically concealing information so it could not be found without knowledge of how to retrieve it. This was considered a necessity due to the long period of time it took to deliver messages over great distances. In U.S. history, George Washington (1731–1799) was noted to have used various methods of encryption to protect the vulnerability of messages during the American Revolution.

Cryptography slowly gained the attention of a larger portion of the world population. This was aided by the increased reference to secret codes in literary works and other publications. Edgar Allan Poe is a chief example of a 19th-century writer who employed the usage of ciphers and hidden meaning inside of his stories to great effect. History is full of narratives about the usage of cryptography as well.

Cryptanalysis is the theory of devising methods of uncovering ciphers in the hope of intercepting secret information. Some of the most notable uses of cryptanalysis occurred during times of war. Military operations were undertaken with high levels of secrecy involving the movements of troops, the intention of battle plans, and other sensitive data that would prove problematic if opposing forces were to intercept such missives. World War I proved to be successful for the United States by implementing a code that was able to withstand attempts to break it while succeeding in cracking the German naval code. Subsequent naval battles were influenced by the information gleaned from the intercepted transmissions.

Another example in the 20th century of successful decryption occurred during World War II, when the Allied Forces were able to crack a code that the Germans were using to communicate. With this information, the Allies gained an advantage in knowing enemy plans and how best to react. The intelligence learned from the unmasked German correspondence was referred to as "Ultra." This was the name associated with intelligence the Allies learned from infiltrating the German channels. This triumph was in addition to the work done in London at Bletchley Park. Together, the British and Americans were able to defeat the Enigma Code, the encryption system employed by the Germans.

Within the modern business world, there are concerns about cyber security that force businesses to allocate part of their budgets to ensure they do not suffer from any information leaks or attacks seeking to steal materials. Antivirus software and other computer-security programs run various forms of cryptography to weave a protective layer around a personal computer or server. On the other side, there are individuals employing cryptanalysis in an effort to circumvent the security measures. There is a constant struggle between both factions. The biggest struggle for individuals to study this field is that they are tasked with attempting to predict ongoing methods of cryptography in the present in addition to any advancements. The secretive nature of cryptography means that outsiders are unsure of what progress has been made in the field until time has passed and secrets are revealed and can be studied.

Cryptography evolved to become a part of everyday life, as evidenced by the development of the public-key method of cryptography. This system of encryption works by assigning individuals both public and private codes. Therefore, if a person needed to send a message by a secure method to another, he or she would not need to worry about prearranging a set cipher system beforehand, such as in the past. Instead, one simply needs to encrypt with the other person's readily available public code, thereby ensuring that only the intended recipient will be able to read the message with his or her unique private code.

There is constant debate surrounding the idea of privacy. The public and private sector argue over the balance between liberty and security. For a state or agency to provide adequate protection to the people it serves, there must be an understanding from the citizens that some of their freedoms may be infringed on in pursuit of providing such defense. Opposite this point of view, there are individuals who feel that they have the right to privacy and who deplore the idea of giving others access to important personal information.

A current example of this in the United States was the contest between the electronics company Apple and the Federal Bureau of Investigation (FBI) in 2016. During this dispute, the government agency felt that Apple had a duty to give the FBI access to a suspect's personal information contained on his cell phone. However, the company refused, citing that they felt it was wrong to help the government infringe on the public's interest of self-security. Ultimately, the FBI was able to break the phone's encryption without the company's assistance. However, this debate will continue with no clear resolution, as the best option is to find a balance between safety and private security.

Overall, cryptology has advanced a long way since its inception. What began as a literal system of hiding information from view has transformed into an extremely complex system designed to disguise language in plain sight. In the 21st century, cryptography is not only employed by governments but is also valuable for business and personal use. The constant struggle between code makers and those trying to break codes will continue to push the discipline further. Such developments no doubt will also enhance the reliance on ciphers and the element of privacy that they provide.

Jason R. Kluk

See also: Encryption; Federal Bureau of Investigation (FBI); National Security Agency (NSA)

Further Reading

Kippenhan, Rudolf. *Code Breaking: A History and Exploration.* New York: The Overlook Press, 1999.
Konheim, Alan G. *Cryptography: A Primer.* New York: John Wiley & Sons, 1981.
Rosenheim, Shawn James. *The Cryptographic Imagination: Secret Writings from Edgar Poe to the Internet.* Baltimore: The Johns Hopkins University Press, 1997.
Singh, Simon. *The Code Book: The Evolution of Secrecy from Mary Queen of Scots to Quantum Cryptography.* New York: Doubleday, 1999.
Weber, Ralph, E. *United States Diplomatic Codes and Ciphers, 1775–1983.* Chicago: Precedent Publishing, 1979.
Winterbotham, F. W. *The Ultra Secret.* New York: Harper & Row, 1974.

CYBER ATTACK

The term *cyber attack* has not always been applied discriminately, and as a consequence, it is often taken to refer to a much broader set of circumstances than are prescribed by laws, treaties, and conventions. One common definition of a cyber attack is an attack initiated from a computer against a Web site, network, or individual computer that compromises the confidentiality, integrity, or availability of that system or stored information.

There are an increasing number of methods applied to carry out a cyber attack, including distributed denial-of-service (DDoS), malware, phishing, and social engineering leading to data theft. DDoS attacks are intended to isolate targets from the network by flooding them with packets of very large amounts of data, thus saturating all the capacity of the network. As a consequence, legitimate requests are lost or the service becomes too slow to function. Although DDoS is not technically challenging when compared to other methods, its effectiveness can be considerable and protracted, and for this reason, the systems targeted by this kind of attack tend to be symbols of important infrastructure or organizations, rather than the infrastructure or organizations themselves.

The adoption of a variety of operating systems by an increasingly broad consumer base has incentivized the development of cross-platform malware that is effective against more than just PC-based Windows systems. Additionally, metamorphic and polymorphic malware is designed to change its coding such that each successive version differs from its predecessor; in this way, it evades detection by conventional antivirus programs, even those that are routinely updated. More so than methods such as DDoS, creating polymorphic code presents a technical challenge to the belligerent as well as the intended target because of the need to employ multiple transforming techniques such as registry renaming, code permutation, expansion, and shrinking. Some culpability may lie with the intended victims because cross-platform malware is facilitated by the attacks being able to migrate seamlessly across different devices and operating systems that have been chosen exactly because they are common, free downloads with software that is open source; and yet, despite the inherent vulnerabilities, many of these Web applications manage key business assets, such as company social media feeds.

The concept of *phishing* centers on the ability to use e-mail to allow anyone to contact any other person, regardless of whether they are a stranger, an existing contact, or in one's group of social or business contacts. In particular, the e-mail system is an open door, and when reaching out to groups of individuals directly or as cc's (carbon copies) and bcc's (blind carbon copies), it is not unusual for a filter to not be applied to such communications. This facet of nonexclusivity is further exacerbated by Simple Mail Transfer Protocols (SMTP) being readily exploited because SMTP requires no authentication of the address associated with incoming e-mails.

Beyond phishing, social engineering entails more direct targeting interaction. Contrasting with malware, social engineering is nontechnical intrusion that relies on social interaction whereby targets are tricked into disclosing information that will directly or indirectly facilitate access to a network and its data. The human vulnerability being exploited is the reasonable predisposition of most individuals toward courtesy and helpfulness, rendering them vulnerable to giving away valuable information out of a desire to be courteous.

More sophisticated and systematic efforts by coordinated adversaries can attempt to infiltrate a sensitive system, remain undetected for as long as possible, and leave unnoticed. Referred to as advanced persistent threats (APTs), a significant fraction of cyber, corporate, and intelligence espionage is attributed to nation-states and their actors, who actively pursue classified and sensitive information from Western nations. Bolstering conventional cyber defenses does not offer sufficient protection against APT, and multiple layers of physical, organizational, and cyber defenses; knowledge of the threat; and advanced skills to detect and react to ongoing and successful attacks are required; this is referred to as *continuous persistent monitoring* (CPM). Examples of CPM techniques include secure browsing applications, hardware, and transaction-signing devices to monitor users. CPM techniques also include analyses of the relationships between internal and external users to detect misuse or collusive behaviors; as such, forensics systems and tools are installed onto networks to continuously monitor and record all traffic and activity. In the event that a network has been infiltrated and the intruder subsequently attempts to eradicate evidence of his or her presence, separate network traffic recorders can provide information on how, when, and where the infiltration occurred and what information may have been compromised.

As distinct from all other activities on networks, in conflict and warfare, the use of the term *attack* has to be applied with discrimination, as various bodies of international rules and standards regulate conduct where the law of armed conflict (*jus in bello*) applies. The Geneva Conventions of 1949 define an attack as an act of violence; whether undertaken as part of an offensive or defensive action, its strict application or interpretation is important in predicating or prohibiting the behaviors of all the actors in a conflict. In conflicts, attacks (cyber or physical) must be predicated on four cumulative conditions for them to be lawful. The target of any attack has to be a military objective, and the means or method used by the attacker must be lawful. The attacker must take specified precautions, and, finally, the attacker must ensure that the attack does not cause damage to civilian objects, or civilians, disproportionate to the gains being sought.

Any attack that does not meet these cumulative criteria is considered unlawful; therefore, the question of what constitutes that threshold of attack in cyber space is critical to ensuring that acts of espionage are not mistaken for a prelude to a wider attack. This allows nations to control whether, and how, the emerging situation escalates with a lawful proportionate response. Unfortunately, uncertainty in applying international law arises because few of the technical or operational methods employed in cyber space existed at the time the Geneva Conventions were agreed on when the measure of what is termed "consequential harm" was determined by damage, destruction, injury, and death as a result of conventional violent kinetic force.

Following a DDoS attack that caused widespread disruption to electronic commerce in Estonia in 2007, the North Atlantic Treaty Organization (NATO) instituted the Tallinn process to ascertain the applicability of international humanitarian law and the doctrines of *jus ad bellum* (criteria that are met before engaging in war that is lawfully permissible and considered just) to cyber conflicts. The resulting guidance (set out in the *Tallinn Manual*) considered cyber operations conducted against cyber infrastructure and cyber activities conducted against physical objects that rely on computer systems and data and concluded that a cyber attack was a cyber operation, whether offensive or defensive, that is reasonably expected to cause injury or death to persons or damage or destruction to objects.

The Tallinn process confirmed that earlier references to "acts of violence" in the 1949 amendments to the Geneva Conventions were not limited in scope to activities that release kinetic force, such as conventional munitions. Additionally, it ruled that as cyber operations have cyber consequences, it followed that there could be consequential harm. Should that consequential harm exceed *de minimis* damage, leading to destruction, injury, or death that could be reasonably foreseeable, it would exceed the threshold of consequential harm and constitute an attack. As a consequence of the rulings set out in the Tallinn process, it is unlikely that cyber operations against online infrastructure, such as Web sites as opposed to network infrastructure, would constitute an attack; therefore, the cyber operations targeting Estonia could not be considered an attack. As with subsequent cyber operations in Georgia, where Web sites were rendered unusable by defacement or DDoS, the purpose of the operations was to confuse, stymie, and control news and a narrative. Media, financial institutions, and government departments have also been disrupted by cyber operations attributed to the Russian Federation and had the effect of capping public support for target governments and led to local loss of market confidence—all as part of a hybrid warfare campaign.

Contentions remain about whether using cyber operations to interfere with the normal operation of a physical device or system can be termed an attack. It has been argued that if the functionality of a system or device requires subsequent replacement of physical components, this damage exceeds the threshold of consequential harm, but this does not apply in the cases where operating system software is the required remedy. As opinions given in the Tallinn process were divided, no definitive ruling has yet been offered in this specific case

Means also exist to affect cyber operations that are intended to deliver only partial or temporary interference against physical devices and systems; damage is partial and not permanent. In 2007, the Israeli Defense Force launched Operation Orchard to strike against a suspected strategic target inside Syrian borders. The air attack was successful and was achieved without losses, despite the target being protected by advanced integrated air defense systems (IADS). There has been speculation that the attack incorporated a variation of a cyber tool developed by the United Kingdom's BAE Systems that facilitates penetration of communications links to IADS. Known as the Suter airborne network attack system, rather than jamming radar signals, it instead hacks into the IADS to control the functionality of time-critical operations by locating emitters precisely and then directing data streams into them that can include false targets and message algorithms. In examining whether the use of a Suter-type weapon constitutes an attack, or disruption with damage, it would be necessary to consider whether any consequential damage, destruction, injury, or death at either the target or within the IADS could have been reasonably foreseeable and whether mitigating actions were taken by the belligerent.

Graem Corfield

See also: Cyber Espionage; Cyber War; Cyber Weapon; Distributed Denial-of-Service (DDoS) Attack; Estonian Cyber Attack (2007); Georgian Cyber Attack (2008); Just War; Malware; Operation Orchard; Phishing; Social Engineering; Spear Phishing; *Tallinn Manual*

Further Reading

Graham, David. "Cyber Threats and the Law of War." *Journal of National Security Law & Policy.* Vol. 4:87, 2010.

Libicki, Martin. *Crisis and Escalation in Cyberspace.* Santa Monica, CA: RAND, 2012.

Libicki, Martin. *Cyberdeterrence and Cyberwar.* Santa Monica, CA: RAND, 2009.

Rosenzweig, Paul. *Cyber Warfare: How Conflicts in Cyberspace Are Challenging America and Changing the World.* Santa Barbara, CA: Praeger, 2012.

Schmitt, Michael. "Classification of Cyber Conflict." *Journal or Conflict & Security Law.* Vol 12(2), 2012.

Schmitt, Michael N., ed. *Tallinn Manual on the International Law Applicable to Cyber Warfare.* New York: Cambridge University Press, 2013.

CYBER CRIME

Criminals have more possibilities in the new age of cyber space. Cyber crime offers the criminal more security in contrast to classical forms of crime, such as a bank robbery. For cyber crime, a computer is the only essential requirement. In fact, the computer can be both the tool of the crime and its object. Cyber criminals can use computers to commit crimes such as fraud or theft. What started as the activities of a small group of hackers in the early years of the Internet has become an enormous security issue in recent years; groups of organized cyber criminals have begun using malware to carry out a new form of criminal opportunity created by an ever-growing Internet. There are four factors that enable cyber crime: there are no borders for cyber criminals; the equipment is rather inexpensive compared to traditional criminal tool sets; the criminal is not forced to meet the victim; and the Internet grants anonymity. For those reasons, the future will face an increasing number of cyber crimes. This form of crime could consequently become a more dangerous threat than terrorism, although cyber terrorists might also use cyber crime as a method to secure resources.

Cyber crime is immense and cost the global economy almost $400 billion in 2012. The national-security strategy of numerous Western nation-states already considers cyber crime as a major threat, comparable to terrorism or military crises between nation-states. This is not an overemphasis of the problem. The 2012 Norton Cybercrime Report named a yearly number of 556 million victims of cyber crime worldwide. Most of these crimes seem to be solely the consequence of ignorance or laziness by the human Internet user, but the methods of the criminals also get more and more sophisticated. For only $150, one can purchase a hack for a Gmail account, and for $350, a Trojan horse can be bought that would allow one to screen someone else's computer activity.

Especially in regions where countries are preoccupied with basic health issues or political instability, such as Africa, the increase of cyber crimes is tremendous. While governments deal with traditional crimes in these regions, inexpensive equipment allows groups of organized cyber criminals to establish their operational bases in these regions. The lack of legal measures and insufficient IT knowledge on the official side of the law make it hard to counter the establishment of such organized groups that can act from a relatively safe harbor to commit crimes all around the globe. South African leadership has started measures to introduce more cyber space–oriented legislation, but many other African countries will need years to be ready to deal with such issues. But the increase of cyber crime is not solely a problem of the developing world; it is also stimulated by the Western world and its lack of interest and shortsightedness.

In the United States, it is the government more than the private user that seems to be interested in issues of cyber security. While a virus is seen as an interruption of the workday for many desktop users, it is seen as a possible major threat by public officials and cyber specialists. Vulnerabilities were already obvious in 2000, when commercial Internet sites such as Yahoo and eBay were victims of cyber attacks. Consequently, computer crime entered a more official debate. The U.S. Congress elicited several bills that should particularly focus on computer crime. However, when such laws are discussed in public, there is always the general argument for Internet users' privacy as well. How much control is wanted by those who are using the Internet anonymously but might also be victims of a cyber attack? Is the privacy of the Internet worth the possible cost? New technology allows hackers to invade Internet users' privacy, such as by stealing credit card information related to online billing accounts. Unfortunately, the criminal is granted the same privacy when committing a crime, as it is easy to work with fake IP addresses or over several foreign servers.

Robert Mueller, the former director of the Federal Bureau of Investigation (FBI), warned that cyber threats might be the most dangerous ones in the future. In 2001, EUROPOL police chief Jürgen Storbeck warned Internet users to be aware of the threat. He referred to previous hacks, during which cyber criminals were easily able to hack the credit card information of more than 1,000 guests of the World Economic Summit. For Storbeck, cyber crimes represented the first step toward cyber terrorism, something that could be referred to by observing the conflict in the Near East. Organized crime already used the anonymity of the Internet to transfer millions of U.S. dollars every year, so terrorists might be willing to use the same tactics for their financial transfers in the future.

Another danger was identified by the use of cyber-crime tactics by states or actors working on behalf of a state's interests. In the struggle between China and the United States, cyber crimes play an active and aggressive role, meaning that the cyber crimes could easily be transformed into measures of a full-scale cyber war. However, cyber crimes in China also seem to be a genuine problem, as 70 percent of all maliciously registered domains were used by Chinese cyber criminals to attack Chinese targets, in large part because the majority of Chinese computer users have pirated copies of Microsoft Windows, which are blocked from receiving security updates.

Official agencies that want to defend themselves and their citizens against such cyber crimes, no matter whether they are committed by individuals, organized crime groups, or foreign governments, are in an ambivalent position. On the one hand, there is a need to be prepared for the possibilities the Internet and the cyber space provide to the criminals, but on the other hand, the public is resistant to a government that is too involved in cyber security. There will be a further discussion about a possible loss of privacy to gain more security, but whatever the outcome might be, it is sure that further measures are needed to secure the Internet for the common user against cyber criminals, organized crime groups, and foreign state intervention.

Frank Jacob

See also: Cyber Attack; Cyber Security; JPMorgan Hack; Office of Personnel Management Data Breach; Russian Business Network (RBN); Sony Hack; Target Corporation Hack; TJX Corporation Hack; Trojan Horse

Further Reading

Bucci, Steven. "Joining Cybercrime and Cyberterrorism: A Likely Scenario." In *Cyberspace and National Security: Threats, Opportunities, and Power in a Virtual World.* Edited by Derek S. Reveron. Washington, D.C.: Georgetown University Press, 2012.

Carr, Jeffrey. *Inside Cyber Warfare: Mapping the Cyber Underworld.* Sebastopol, CA: O'Reilly Media, 2009.

Hardy, Marianna, ed. *The Target Store Data Breaches: Examination and Insight.* New York: Nova Science Publishers, 2014.

Singer, P. W., and Allan Friedman. *Cybersecurity and Cyberwar: What Everyone Needs to Know.* New York: Oxford University Press, 2014.

Springer, Paul J. *Cyber Warfare: A Reference Handbook.* Santa Barbara, CA: ABC-CLIO, 2015.

Stiennon, Richard. *Surviving Cyber War.* Lanham, MD: Government Institutes, 2010.

CYBER DEFENCE MANAGEMENT AUTHORITY (CDMA)

The Cyber Defence Management Authority (CDMA) is the focal point for the North Atlantic Treaty Organization's (NATO) political and technical application of cyber defense in protection of Alliance Communications and Information Systems (CIS) and provides support to NATO member defense capabilities when requested. The cyber-coordination body went operational in April 2008 in direct response to unprecedented cyber attacks against Estonia in 2007.

The CDMA establishment marks a significant shift in policy from infrastructure protection of NATO systems by adding member state defense capabilities and Alliance augmentation as a core function. This effort provides operational defense with real-time monitoring focused on threat mitigation under the umbrella of the North Atlantic Council (NAC) and was formally ratified by NATO heads of state during the 2008 NATO summit in Bucharest, Romania.

Cyber attacks have become a political concern for Alliance members. During the 2002 NATO Prague Summit, cyber defense emerged for the first time as a key political agenda issue. This issue was reiterated by Alliance leadership in 2006 through a stated need to protect information systems. The Estonian attacks in 2007 solidified NATO's position and served as the catalyst for the CDMA. Additionally, it resulted in an increased level of commitment formally approved in NATO's Policy on Cyber Defense and the NATO Defense Planning Process.

Furthermore, since 2007, there has been a shift in NATO members' commitment to prevent cyber attacks and the use of Article 5, Collective Defense, versus Article 4, Consultation and Coordination. In 2009, the NATO Parliamentary Assembly officially decreed, "Cyber defense poses a special problem for NATO policymakers, who are seeking to maximize the deterrent effect of the Alliance. . . .The decision to announce an expansion of Article 5 to encompass cyber attacks may cause potential aggressors to think twice." As a result, the CDMA will play an increasing role in NATO's security capability for the foreseeable future.

Fundamentally, the strength of the CDMA rests in the integration of capabilities and collaboration with broader NATO and European organizations such as the NATO Smart Defense Initiative, national computer emergency response teams

(CERTs), and strategic initiatives of the Cooperative Cyber Defense Centre of Excellence (CCDCOE). Through this cooperative effort, capabilities and expertise will continue to grow in support of NATO Alliance members.

Jose Alberto Rivas Jr.

See also: Computer Emergency Response Team (CERT); Estonian Cyber Attack (2007); NATO Cooperative Cyber Defence Centre of Excellence (CCDCOE); North Atlantic Treaty Organization (NATO); Patriotic Hacking

Further Reading

Duyvesteyn, Isabelle. "Between Doomsday and Dismissal: Cyber War, the Parameters of War, and Collective Defense." *Atlantisch Perspectief* 38(7), 2014.

Hughes, Rex B. "NATO and Cyber Defence, Mission Accomplished?" *Atlantisch Perspectief* 33(1), 2009.

McGee, Joshua. "NATO and Cyber Defense: A Brief Overview and Recent Events." Center for Strategic & International Studies, July 8, 2011.

NATO Parliamentary Assembly. "NATO and Cyber Defence." 2009 Annual Session. Brussels, 2009.

Schmitt, Michael N., ed. *Tallinn Manual on the International Law Applicable to Cyber Warfare.* New York: Cambridge University Press, 2013.

CYBER DEFENSE

Cyber defense is necessary but not a sufficient part of cyber resilience—a holistic approach to countering cyber threats. For the U.S. government, a holistic approach to countering threats of all types consists of five steps:

1. *Prevent* attacks
2. *Protect* from attacks when they do occur
3. *Mitigate* the impact of attacks
4. *Respond* to the attacks
5. *Recover* from attacks

These five different preparedness mission areas are addressed in the National Planning Frameworks, which in turn are part of the National Preparedness System. Specific cyber actions are discussed in the Cyber Incident Annex to the National Response Plan. The Federal Emergency Management Agency (FEMA) is responsible for this planning and preparedness system under the aegis of the Department of Homeland Security (DHS).

Cyber operations happen in the information environment, which consists of the physical, informational, and cognitive dimensions. The physical dimension is the hardware, and the informational dimension is the software. The cognitive dimension is sometimes called *wetware* and consists of the thoughts of human beings.

Everyone needs to perform cyber defense. At the individual level, this typically consists of following proper cyber hygiene. This includes purchasing, installing, and updating a competent antivirus program; using a firewall; running periodic security scans; selecting and maintaining passwords that are difficult to break; backing up data; and securing personal data. It also includes commonsense actions, such as not opening suspicious communications, not clicking on unknown links, and managing connections on social media as well as controlling access to a home Wi-Fi router.

Organizations have to be more careful. They have entire information technology systems to protect, a large workforce, and information or assets that other organizations, criminals, or even states would like to access. The most important issue for organizations is that their leadership understands the importance of cyber security, stresses organizational cyber-security performance, and budgets enough for cyber security. Additionally, organizations need to train their personnel on security awareness, safeguard large amounts of data, and hire skilled personnel to manage their cyber-security systems.

States are responsible for all the activities of these organizations. They must develop and maintain cyber-security legislation, policies, and organizations. They must coordinate with the education system to ensure that it is producing enough cyber-security professionals. They also must integrate cyber security into national security, safeguarding national secrets as well as maintaining national command and control.

Cyber defense is built into the first three steps of the National Planning Framework. The last two steps are manifestations of resilience, or the ability to bounce back from an attack, which is part of preparedness but not of defense. Cyber defense is designed to defend a system or systems against cyber attack. There are two types of cyber attacks: semantic and syntactic. Semantic attacks use language to shape cognition. Syntactic attacks use the computer codes themselves. As an example, the first phase of a phishing attack is a semantic attack, where the attacker convinces the target to click on the link. As soon as the link is clicked, the phishing attack goes into the second, or syntactic, phase of the attack, unleashing the malware into the target system.

There are two types of effects that a cyber attack can achieve: manipulation and denial. Manipulation describes any change. It can mean shaping cognition, where the thoughts of the target are manipulated, or the manipulation of coding via a syntactic attack. There are three forms of denial: degradation, disruption, and destruction. Degradation means denying access to, or operation of, a target to a level represented as a percentage of capacity. Disruption mean completely but temporarily denying access to, or operation of, a target for a period of time. Destruction of a target means to permanently, completely, and irreparably deny access to, or operation of, a target.

Cyber defense is designed to be part of the system to prevent attackers from conducting semantic or syntactic attacks to manipulate data and thought or to deny access to a system. There is no such thing as a perfect cyber defense. If a person can write a code or design a system, another person can find a vulnerability in the code or in the system. As such, a holistic approach to defense accepts the inevitability of successful attacks. The holistic system combines defense with resilience, or the ability to bounce back from a successful attack.

Cyber defense takes cyber attacks into account and seeks to prevent them from succeeding. A cyber attack follows a pattern called the *cyber kill chain*. The steps to the cyber kill chain are the following:

- *Reconnaissance* of the target system identifies targets.
- *Weaponization* is the preparation and staging phase of an attack.
- *Delivery* of the malware to the target launches the operation.
- *Exploitation* of a software, hardware, or human vulnerability occurs.
- *Installation* of a persistent backdoor maintains access.
- *Command and control* of the malware opens a command channel to enable the adversary to remotely manipulate the victim.
- *Actions on the objective* accomplishes the goal of the mission.

The Department of Defense (DoD) refers to Defensive Cyberspace Operations (DCO), which are passive and active cyber-space operations intended to preserve the ability to utilize friendly cyber-space capabilities and protect data, networks, net-centric capabilities, and other designated systems. Another part of DoD's defense repertoire is defensive cyber-space operation response action (DCO-RA). These are deliberate, authorized defensive measures or activities taken outside of the defended network to protect and defend Department of Defense cyber-space capabilities or other designated systems. This could be seen as a type of counterattack. Although many organizations and some individuals would like to perform cyber counterattacks as part of deterrence after intrusions, private-sector response actions would in most cases violate the Computer Fraud and Abuse Act (CFAA), especially Title 18 United States Code (USC) 1030 (a) (3) and (5).

A truly holistic large-scale defense system is appropriate for larger organizations and states. It has six major goals:

1. *Redirect* directs adversaries' activities away from defender-chosen targets so that attackers' efforts cease or become mistargeted or misinformed.
2. *Obviate* renders attackers' efforts ineffective by making sure that their efforts or resources cannot be applied or are wasted.
3. *Impede* makes attackers work harder or longer to achieve intended effects. This recognizes that sometimes you cannot prevent attackers from achieving their intended effects, but it causes them to invest more resources or undertake additional activities.
4. *Detect* identifies attackers' activities or their effects, which makes their activities susceptible to defensive responses
5. *Limit* attackers' effectiveness by restricting the consequences of adversarial efforts.
6. *Expose* attackers by developing and sharing threat intelligence, which takes away attackers' advantages and allows defenders to get better prepared.

Redirecting includes deterring, diverting, and deceiving the attacker. Deterring discourages the adversary from undertaking further activities by instilling fear or doubt that those activities will achieve the intended effects, with a goal that the attacker stops activities. Diverting leads the attacker away from defender-chosen targets so that the attacker refocuses activities on different targets and wastes his or her efforts. Deceiving leads the attacker to believe false information about defended systems, missions, or organizations or about defender capabilities so that his or her efforts are wasted.

Obviating includes preventing and preempting. Preventing makes the attacker's activity ineffective, while preempting ensures that the attacker cannot apply resources or perform activities because resources are destroyed or made inaccessible.

Impeding includes degrading and delay. Degrading decreases the effectiveness of the attacker's activities so that the attacker achieves some but not all of the intended effects or achieves all intended effects but only after taking additional actions. Delaying increases the amount of time needed for an attacker's activity to achieve its intended effects, which may expose the attacker to greater risk of detection and analysis.

Limiting is a type of mitigation that includes containing, curtailing, recovery, and expunging. The defender seeks to contain by restricting the effects of an attacker's activity to a limited set of resources, reducing the value of the activity to the attacker. Curtailing limits the duration of an attacker's activity, limiting the attacker's ability to perform all of his or her missions. Recovery is part of resilience and rolls back the attacker's gains, causing the attacker to fail to retain mission impairment due to recovery of the capability to perform key mission operations. It minimizes the denial effect of a cyber attack. Expunging removes attacker-directed malware and repairs corrupted data, which seeks to prevent further advantages from the latter stages of the cyber kill chain: exploitation, installation of a persistent backdoor to maintain access, command and control, and actions on the objective.

Exposing includes analyzing and publicizing. Analysis allows the target to understand the attacker better, based on analysis of adversarial activities, types of malware used in attacks, and their effects, so that the attacker loses the advantages of uncertainty, confusion, and doubt and the defender can recognize the attacker's tactics, techniques, and procedures (TTPs).

Publicize means to increase awareness of an attacker's characteristics and behavior across the stakeholder community through organizations such as Information Sharing and Analysis Organizations (ISAOs) or Information Sharing and Analysis Organizations (ISACs). The attacker loses the advantage of surprise and deniability and the ability to compromise one organization's systems to attack another organization.

In 2016, the most popular types of cyber defense included the following:

- Network-based antivirus software
- Advanced malware analysis and sandboxing
- Secure e-mail gateway (SEG)
- Secure Web gateway (SWG)
- Web application firewall (WAF)
- Data loss and leak prevention (DLP)

- Denial-of-service (DoS) and distributed denial-of-service (DDoS) prevention
- Intrusion detection and prevention systems (IDS/IPS)
- Security information and event management (SIEM)
- Security analytics and full-packet capture and analysis
- Network behavior analysis (NBA) and NetFlow analysis
- User behavior analytics and activity monitoring
- Next-generation firewall (NGFW)
- Threat intelligence service

It is not critical that individuals understand the details of cyber defense—they simply need to understand that cyber defense is important. Attackers are constantly attempting to exploit any vulnerability in personal or organizational systems to manipulate or deny access. Human error allows for the inevitability of attackers achieving one or both of these goals, even if individuals and organizations subscribe to best practices.

Humans are the most vulnerable component of any cyber system. The best approach to defending against both semantic and syntactic attacks is the holistic one. It is especially important to subscribe to the best practices, use software known to be safe and stable, and cooperate within one's company and sector to mitigate the risk of cyber attacks. Above all else, individuals must maintain constant vigilance for effective cyber defense.

G. Alexander Crowther

See also: Antivirus Software; Cyber Attack; Cyber Security; Cyber Weapon; Department of Homeland Security (DHS); Malware

Further Reading

Brenner, Joel. *America the Vulnerable: Inside the New Threat Matrix of Digital Espionage, Crime, and Warfare.* New York: Penguin, 2011.

Carr, Jeffrey. *Inside Cyber Warfare: Mapping the Cyber Underworld.* Sebastopol, CA: O'Reilly Media, 2009.

Clarke, Richard A., and Robert K. Knake. *Cyber War: The Next Threat to National Security and What to Do about It.* New York: HarperCollins, 2010.

Libicki, Martin. *Cyberspace in Peace and War.* Annapolis, MD: U.S. Naval Institute Press, 2016.

Singer, P. W., and Allan Friedman. *Cybersecurity and Cyber War: What Everyone Should Know.* New York: Oxford University Press, 2014.

Springer, Paul J. *Cyber Warfare: A Reference Handbook.* Santa Barbara, CA: ABC-CLIO, 2015.

Stiennon, Richard. *Surviving Cyber War.* Lanham, MD: Government Institutes, 2010.

CYBER-DEFENSE EXERCISE

Cyber-defense exercises are live simulations of cyber-attack and cyber-defense scenarios. Typically, two or more teams of cyber specialists are pitted against each other to compete for control over individual computers or networks of computers.

The exercises are held to train and evaluate the cyber unit's readiness, technical aptitude, and effectiveness at offensive and defensive strategy in the cyber domain. Participants in defense exercises are logically divided into red teams and blue teams, whose responsibility is to attempt attacks in real time and to defend against ongoing attacks, respectively.

Red teams assume the role of cyber intruders seeking to gain a foothold on the target network. A red team performs computer network exploitation activity and furthers its access by systematically searching for and progressively compromising assets on the target network. Achieving access typically involves the construction or sourcing of exploits for security vulnerabilities present in the target infrastructure. Red teams then seek to exfiltrate sensitive information and attempt to maintain a covert but persistent presence on compromised systems by planting backdoors.

Blue teams are tasked with defending the computer network and individual nodes against malicious influence exerted by the attacker, such as denial-of-service or arbitrary code execution. The team must typically defend unpatched, out-of-date, or misconfigured network services against any and all exploitation attempts. In the event of a security compromise, the blue team aims to swiftly counteract and recover from the attack by monitoring the network traffic for signs of malicious command and control communications, discovering the attacker's presence on systems, disabling implanted malware, and reconfiguring default settings to deny future attack vectors.

The spectrum of skills and the expertise level required from participants vary according to a number of factors, including the realism and complexity of deployed network- and system-level security measures, the scale and diversity of equipment that forms part of the target infrastructure, and the extent of knowledge given to attackers a priori about the topology of the target network. A fine balance between cyber offense and defense ideally results in a competitive but constructive coevolution of attack methodology and security technology.

Military organizations, penetration testing companies, and computer security conferences, and many others, run annual cyber-defense exercises and competitions. A popular instantiation of cyber-defense exercises is the attack and defense model employed by capture-the-flag competitions. These competitions, hosted worldwide in both online and face-to-face form, aim to distill the present-day wide-spectrum computer-security work, involving cryptanalysis, exploit synthesis, and vulnerability discovery, into short and objectively measurable exercises.

Dusan Repel

See also: Cyber Security; National Security Agency (NSA); Red Team; White Hat

Further Reading

Clarke, Richard A., and Robert K. Knake. *Cyber War: The Next Threat to National Security and What to Do about It.* New York: HarperCollins, 2010.
Libicki, Martin. *Cyberspace in Peace and War.* Annapolis, MD: U.S. Naval Institute Press, 2016.
Reveron, Derek S., ed. *Cyberspace and National Security: Threats, Opportunities, and Power in a Virtual World.* Washington, D.C.: Georgetown University Press, 2012.

CYBER DETERRENCE

Cyber deterrence refers to a state of affairs where a potential adversary does not launch a cyber attack because of the risks inherent in or responses elicited by such an action. Potential responses include cyber "counterattack," which may involve hack back confined to the specific attack and related infrastructure; more generalized cyber attacks against the attacker, whether proportionate or not; or the capture, neutralization, or exposure of the infrastructure, tools, and techniques used by the attacker. However, responses may not be confined to the cyber domain and may involve the use of military (also referred to as *kinetic*), diplomatic, economic, legal, or any other means that would have an undesirable impact to the attacker.

Cyber deterrence is a matter of both perception and fact, as it relies on an assessment by the putative attacker of the defender's technical capabilities (both defensive and offensive) and likelihood of response. From a game-theoretic perspective, deterrence assumes a multiround game with rational players, who may, however, have incompatible worldviews or risk profiles. In general, it is very difficult for a defender to estimate the degree of deterrence that is projected, except perhaps at a very abstract level, as that would require intimate and continuous knowledge of the potential attacker's planning and strategy.

The primary technical elements in cyber deterrence relate to the relative quality of the defense and offense, the ability of the defender to attribute the attack to the right entity, and the ability of the defender to effectively counterattack, as modulated by the ability of the attacker to defend against it.

The Effect of Defense Quality

One of the risk-related considerations for attackers is the impact of being detected. In addition to loss of access to the target network, alerting the defender about the attacker's interests and objectives, and potentially not achieving the mission, a key concern is the exposure of techniques, tools, and infrastructure (TTI). As these may take significant time and resources to develop, their exposure can significantly hamper the ability to conduct future operations. Furthermore, to the extent that the same or similar TTIs are used across multiple operations, their exposure may imperil any such concurrent activities. This has become a significant risk, as various systems for the rapid sharing of indicators of compromise (IOCs) have been widely adopted across both the private and public sectors. As an illustration of the trade-off space, one may consider the two extreme ends of relative power between offense and defense: in the probably unattainable (and thus largely theoretical) case of "perfect" defenses, an attacker would be deterred from any offensive action due to the certainty of failure or detection; in the equally unlikely case of perfect offense (i.e., guaranteed to succeed and remain undetected), an attacker would have no risk-related reasons to refrain from undertaking any operation (i.e., attacking any target of interest).

Attribution

As a follow-on to detection and as a prerequisite to most responses to a cyber attack, whether such responses are conducted through the cyber domain or otherwise, the defender must be able to attribute the attack to an entity. Such entities may be individuals, organizations or units thereof, or nation-states. The granularity of attribution may be dictated by the technical capabilities or limitations of the defender; the needs of the possible response options (e.g., economics sanctions on individuals vs. nation-states); the necessary proof detail that must be obtained and provided to third parties (e.g., in a "name and shame" vs. a legal indictment); and other nontechnical considerations (e.g., diplomatic sensitivities). Note that attribution may be based on both intrinsic and extrinsic evidence to the specific cyber attack (e.g., captured malware sample and foreign intelligence collection, respectively). The primary challenges with attribution relate to acquiring sufficient and convincing evidence linking an attack to a specific entity and being able to reveal such evidence to the public (e.g., in a court of law) without revealing information about defensive capabilities. A significant complicating factor is deception or "false flag" operations conducted by the attacker to misdirect the defender's attribution efforts.

Retribution Capability and Attacker Sensitivity

For deterrence to be effective, there must exist a set of outcomes driven by defender action that would result in the attacker being worse off overall than if the cyber action had not been undertaken. These outcomes may be drawn from any number of domains, including economic and financial (e.g., the gain from stealing financial or intellectual property information is offset by the impact of economic sanctions or loss of personal liberty due to imprisonment), public perception, diplomatic, political, and even existential (e.g., kinetic operations against terrorist-supporting hackers). As stated earlier, most such outcomes require good attribution, which in turn usually requires good cyber defenses. The sensitivity of different attackers to the same response options will vary, as will their susceptibility to any given response. For example, "name and shame" (i.e., bad publicity) has negligible effect on terrorist actors (and in fact may be beneficial to their goals), whereas it is generally acceptable to respond with military action against such actors but not (so far) against nation-states. The calculus for what constitutes an appropriate and proportional response is complex; some of the relevant parameters to be taken into consideration include the quality of the proof, the severity of the initial attack, and the collateral damage from any response.

It should be obvious from the above that cyber deterrence is significantly more complex than deterrence in other domains. The often-invoked analogy to nuclear détente (also known as the mutually assured destruction, or MAD, doctrine) may be an oversimplification of the problem space. The main complexities arise from the clandestine nature of cyber operations, the difficulty of attribution, the mutability of digital artifacts, and the relationship of cyber activities to intelligence gathering.

Angelos D. Keromytis

See also: Attribution; Cyber Attack; Cyber Defense; Cyber Escalation; Escalation Dominance

Further Reading

Libicki, Martin. *Cyberdeterrence and Cyberwar.* Santa Monica, CA: RAND, 2009.

Libicki, Martin. *Cyberspace in Peace and War.* Annapolis, MD: U.S. Naval Institute Press, 2016.

Springer, Paul J. *Cyber Warfare: A Reference Handbook.* Santa Barbara, CA: ABC-CLIO, 2015.

CYBER-EQUIVALENCE DOCTRINE

The cyber-equivalence doctrine is the notion, first propagated in 2011, that the United States will regard cyber attacks as one among a spectrum of potential attacks and will respond using any available means that it deems appropriate. As such, this concept essentially moved future cyber attacks into the category of acts of war, should the U.S. government wish to treat them as such. It also points out that the United States does not feel bound to limit its responses to cyber attacks to the cyber domain, effectively stating that the American response to a cyber attack might come in the physical domain. This decision parallels earlier U.S. declarations that any attack upon American military forces using a biological or chemical weapon would be encompassed by the broader term *weapon of mass destruction*, a category of attacks that includes nuclear weapons. Because the United States chooses not to maintain significant stockpiles of biological and chemical weapons, it is incapable of responding in kind to such an attack, and hence claims it will use nuclear weapons in their place.

This type of declaration serves many different functions. The first is that it potentially creates a major deterrent effect—nations cannot probe U.S. cyber defenses, or launch cyber attacks upon American infrastructure, without potentially triggering a retaliatory attack. Even if an enemy has a greater cyber capability than that possessed by the United States, it cannot guarantee that a cyber conflict will remain confined to the cyber realm; hence, cyber attacks carry a greater risk to the nation that initiates them.

The cyber-equivalence doctrine opens the door to significant escalation in response to a cyber attack. Most theorists consider a kinetic attack to be an act of war, while a cyber attack might not reach that threshold. A cyber attack on the United States, if it is not met with an equal response in the same domain, might trigger a cycle of escalation that leads to catastrophic damage. Of course, cyber attacks tend to be accompanied by an attribution problem. It is difficult to launch a major physical attack without revealing the identity of the attackers. Most cyber attackers deliberately hide their identities and might even try to shift blame to an uninvolved actor. If successful, this might also shift the U.S. retaliation onto an innocent nation, and if the American response is overt and physical, it could create a chain of cascading attacks that leave the initiator unharmed.

Paul J. Springer

See also: Attribution; Cyber Attack; Cyber War; National Security Agency (NSA); Obama, Barack; Panetta, Leon E.; United States Cyber Capabilities

Further Reading

Libicki, Martin. *Crisis and Escalation in Cyberspace.* Santa Monica, CA: RAND, 2013.

Obama, Barack. *International Strategy for Cyberspace: Prosperity, Security, and Openness in a Networked World.* May 2011. https://www.whitehouse.gov/sites/default/files/rss_viewer /international_strategy_for_cyberspace.pdf.

CYBER ESCALATION

Cyber escalation refers to the potential for a cyber attack to increase negative effects or damage to the cyber capability of an enemy or result in actual, violent kinetic activity separate from or in consonance with an actual cyber war. This increased volatility initiated in the cyber realm parallels Herman Kahn's concept of the "escalation ladder" created in conjunction with deterrence and escalation theories regarding nuclear weapons. Specifically, cyber escalation is driven by a belligerent's cyber operations or capacity for them and the resulting perception of intent and effect held by affected parties; perceptions are often hazy in cyber space.

Cyber escalation becomes likely when confronted with a cyber crisis. Such a crisis may result from increased tension due to an actual cyber attack, concern that an attack has occurred, or simply the fear that one is imminent. Potential third-party activity in cyber space exacerbates the possibility of misperceptions and erroneous responses. Given that cyber crises are often ambiguous, cyber escalation is largely speculative, and the ability to calculate its potential unintended consequences is difficult at best.

Regarding cyber deterrence, consideration must be given to the potential for an attacker to escalate into kinetic violence, including the use of nuclear weapons when such capability exists. With this in mind, a state may choose to warn off a potential aggressor by declaring its intent to respond to any cyber attack with any weapon available, including special weapons. However, attacks may continue to escalate if the attackers believe retaliation in the cyber realm is unwarranted; if they are facing political pressure to respond in an aggressive, costly manner; or if they believe they will lose any cyber conflict but can dominate a foe in another operating domain, such as conventional military conflict.

Explanations of escalation are fraught, and use of the term when discussing cyber war is all the more perplexing given the complexity and vagueness of the cyber domain. Arguably, concerns about cyber escalation may be mitigated if a nation's war goals are limited in nature and military activities toward those ends follow suit. Managing or limiting cyber escalation in a wartime environment is especially difficult when trying to link intentions, effects, and perceptions.

Ronald N. Dains

See also: Cyber Attack; Cyber War; Escalation Dominance

Further Reading

Clarke, Richard A., and Robert K. Knake. *Cyber War: The Next Threat to National Security and What to Do about It.* New York: HarperCollins, 2010.

Kramer, Franklin D., Stuart H. Starr, and Larry K. Wentz. *Cyberpower and National Security*. Dulles, VA: NDU Press and Potomac Books, Inc., 2009.

Libicki, Martin C. *Crisis and Escalation in Cyberspace*. Santa Monica, CA: RAND Corporation, 2012.

Libicki, Martin C. *Cyberdeterrence and Cyber War*. Santa Monica, CA: RAND Corporation, 2009.

CYBER ESPIONAGE

The term *cyber espionage* encompasses invasions by state and nonstate actors onto government and private computer systems and networks that are designed to steal delicate information that may be used for military, political, or economic gain. Cyber espionage is similar to traditional clandestine intelligence-gathering operations that seek to gain protected information; they only differ in platform. As part of a state's cyber strategy, cyber espionage can include the theft of intellectual property and is a key component of major state actors, including but not limited to China, Iran, North Korea, Russia, and the United States.

One of the earliest cases of cyber espionage occurred during the Cold War, before cyber security had grown into an item of national security. In 1986, Cliff Stoll, a systems administrator at Lawrence Berkeley National Laboratory, noticed accounting discrepancies within the computer systems. Later, after working with the Federal Bureau of Investigation (FBI) to set a trap known as a *honeypot*, they discovered a German hacker named Markus Hess had been recruited by the KGB, the Soviet intelligence service, to infiltrate and steal military information for the Soviet Union. It was discovered that army and air force bases were additional targets. Cyber espionage has transformed much since the 1980s, and the era of the lone wolf–style hacker has ceased to exist, as hacking has changed from mere hobby to an element of warfare.

Modern hackers now face an advanced and well-trained adversary in security specialists that have a plethora of defensive mechanisms at their disposal. As a result of the changing environment of cyber warfare, hackers' methods of attack typically fall into three categories. The opportunistic approach targets millions of potentially vulnerable systems, seeking the handful that are unprotected for the purpose of either monetary gain or to use the computing power of the compromised systems. In some cases, malicious software like the Code Red worm scans millions of systems in search of specific vulnerabilities. This phishing method is also associated with the semitargeted attacks that are aimed at specific organizations and public institutions. These two methods of approach of cyber espionage are typically focused on the private sector, as they cast a wider net. The most threatening of approaches focuses on government and military systems and is known as the advanced persistent threat (APT).

APTs have numerous motivations but are commonly placed into four main categories: activism, cyber crime, corporate espionage, and those with a political or military agenda. APTs use advanced technologies and remain focused on specific targets for months and even years. APTs have this ability because they have almost unlimited resources at their disposal. They are most commonly military units, government-funded entities, or groups funded by an outside corporation conducting corporate espionage—in an attempt to steal trade secrets and intellectual property. APTs that have military or political agendas are usually state-sponsored and use cyber espionage as one element of a cyber strategy against a nation's adversaries. Many governments are known or suspected of supporting APTs.

It is a widely supported belief that the Chinese government supports a group of APTs known as "APT1," and they are suspected of being connected with a group called "Unit 61398" of the Chinese People's Liberation Army. In 2014, one of the more well-known cyber-espionage acts occurred when the National Security Agency (NSA) reported that the Chinese military had stolen terabytes of information that included data from the United States' top-secret F-35 fighter program. These losses affect the long-term balance of airpower superiority, as it has been suggested that certain elements of the F-35 have appeared in the Chinese next-generation fighter, the J-31. The data taken from the program also has had both a national and economic impact. Billions of dollars spent on the research and development phase of the program to ensure the cutting edge on the battlefield have been lost via cyber espionage. The Chinese are not alone in their cyber-espionage activities, as discovered by WikiLeaks in 2010 and Edward J. Snowden in 2013. Both released military and diplomatic secret documents to the press.

Combating such cyber espionage in the Unites States is the U.S. Cyber Command (USCYBERCOM) created in 2010. Located at Fort Meade, Maryland, USCYBERCOM was commanded by General Keith B. Alexander, who also headed the NSA until his retirement in 2014, when he was replaced by Admiral Michael Rogers. USCYBERCOM's goal is to plan, coordinate, and conduct operations and the defense of the Department of Defense's (DoD) information networks. USCYBERCOM is a unified organization that is composed of each military service branch, representing the 24th Air Force (Air Forces Cyber), Second Army (Army Cyber Command), U.S. Tenth Fleet (Fleet Cyber Command), and the Marine Corps Cyberspace Command. Each of these commands is responsible for operations within their own branch of service. USCYBERCOM has five core objectives: to view cyber space as an "operational domain," to implement new security measures, to build international partnerships for improved and collective security, to develop cyber warriors, and to innovate new methods concerning how the military can fight in cyber space.

John J. Mortimer

See also: Advanced Persistent Threat (APT); Alexander, Keith B.; Code Red Worm; Cyber Warriors; Department of Defense (DoD); Federal Bureau of Investigation (FBI); Moonlight Maze; National Security Agency (NSA); Operation Night Dragon; Operation Shady RAT; Operation Titan Rain; Phishing; Rogers, Michael S.; Second Army/Army Cyber Command; Snowden, Edward J.; Solar Sunrise; U.S. Cyber Command (USCYBERCOM); WikiLeaks

Further Reading

Chapple, Mike, and David Seidl. *Cyberwarfare: Information Operations in a Connected World.* Burlington, MA: Jones and Bartlett Learning, 2015.

Heickerö, Roland. *The Dark Sides of the Internet: On Cyber Threats and Informational Warfare.* Translated by Martin Peterson. New York: Peter Lang Publishing Group, 2013.

Schmidt, Michael N., ed. *Tallinn Manual on the International Law Applicable to Cyber Warfare.* New York: Cambridge University Press, 2013.

Shakarian, Paulo, Jana Shakarian, and Andrew Ruef. *Introduction to Cyber-warfare: A Multidisciplinary Approach.* Waltham, MA: Syngress, 2013.

Singer, P. W., and Allan Friedman. *Cybersecurity and Cyberwar: What Everyone Needs to Know.* New York: Oxford University Press, 2014.

CYBER ETHICS

Ethics is one of five branches of philosophy that deals with the study of moral principles that govern a person's or group's behavior. Metaethics is concerned about the nature of ethics and moral reasoning. Normative ethics is interested in determining the content of moral behavior, exemplified by the question, what *ought* I to do? Applied ethics deals with specific domains of human action, such as medicine, law, or war, and seeks to craft criteria for how to act in those domains. Cyber ethics falls within the domain of applied ethics. The word *cyber* is most commonly used as an adjective that characterizes the culture of computers, information technology, computer networks, and virtual reality. Thus, cyber ethics is the study of moral principles appropriate to the use of computers, information technology, and virtual reality.

Computer ethics, now considered part of cyber ethics, was founded by MIT professor Norbert Weiner during World War II, while helping to develop an anti-aircraft cannon capable of shooting down fast warplanes. This technology required an understanding of feedback systems, which Weiner coined "cybernetics." In 1950, Weiner wrote what is now considered the seminal text in computer ethics, *The Human Use of Human Beings: Cybernetics and Society.*

Cyber ethics, which includes information ethics and computer ethics, often groups into the following categories: (1) privacy, to include data collection and protection; (2) property, to include intellectual property rights and digital rights management; (3) accessibility, to include freedom of information and the digital divide; (4) censorship, to include net neutrality, sexuality, pornography, and gambling; and (5) ethical codes of conduct for information technology professionals.

The usage of computers and other information technologies does not occur in its own hermetically sealed domain; computers permeate multiple domains of human activity. As such, it is difficult to discuss cyber ethics abstracted from other normative principles that govern other human activities. For example, the ethical use of information technology in medicine needs to take place within the wider discussion of the normative principles that govern medical practice. Consequently, the use of information technology in medicine may yield different ethical requirements than might be appropriate for the use of information technology by the Department of Defense. It is the particular challenge of cyber ethics to identify, delineate, and delimit how the vast array of applications of computers and information technology, which interpenetrate other domains of human activity and have their own normative values, can and should be used justly.

There is also considerable debate in cyber ethics about whether computers and information technologies introduce a whole new class, *sui generis*, of ethical concerns, or whether they just bring existing ethical principles into sharper relief. For example, are online communities *moral* communities, that is, communities in which there are certain duties and obligations among individuals that should be expected and enforced, or are online communities nonmoral communities? If they are moral communities, should these communities abide by the same moral principles followed by off-online communities, or are there new moral principles that need to be *invented* to adequately capture the moral dimensions of online communities? If online communities are *not* moral communities, then what moral principles, if any, should govern human interactions online? Should members of online communities expect privacy, autonomy, and freedom of speech to the same degree individuals possess these rights off-line? Why or why not? In short, does the online world require a whole new set of rules that cannot (or should not) be analogously applied from the off-line world? It is the task of cyber ethicists to ask, investigate, and provide answers to these questions.

With respect to cyber warfare, cyber ethics deserves special mention. The term *cyber* is now deployed as a noun and labeled and treated as the fifth operational military domain, in addition to the four "air, land, sea, and space" domains. As such, the use of computers and information technology by the Department of Defense to wage war or operations other than war (OOTW) has become an important area of study. With respect to its use by the military, cyber ethics is most often discussed with respect to cyber warfare and the ethics of war. Similar to the discussion above, there is considerable debate about whether the just war tradition, that is, the normative framework for moral deliberation about when it is justified to go to war (*jus ad bellum*) and proper conduct in war (*jus in bello*), is robust enough to contemplate the new kinds of uses and effects computers and information technology introduce as tools for warfighting and espionage. For example, is targeting programmable logic controllers, which allow the automation of electromechanical processes used to control machinery, and in turn disabling those machines (the method used by Stuxnet) the ethical equivalent of destroying those machines by a conventional weapon? Questions about what may be classified as a cyber weapon and how it should be regulated are still unclear. The seminal debate that took place on whether the just war tradition is sufficient to the task of classifying and regulating the uses of cyber technologies in war can be found in the *Journal of Military Ethics*, Volume 9.4 (2010), between Randall Dipert and James Cook.

Deonna D. Neal

See also: Cyber Attack; Cyber Crime; Cyber War; Cyber Weapon; Intellectual Property; Just War; Net Neutrality; Stuxnet

Further Reading

Alfreda, Dudley, and James Braman. *Investigating Cyber Law and Cyber Ethics: Issues Impacts and Practices.* Hershey, PA: IGI Global, 2011.

Lucas, George. *Ethics and Cyber Warfare: The Quest for Responsible Security in the Age of Digital Warfare*. Oxford: Oxford University Press, 2016.

Spinello, Richard A. *Cyberethics: Morality and Law in Cyberspace*. Sudbury, MA: Jones & Bartlett, 2011.

Taddeo, Mariarosaria. *The Ethics of Cyber Conflicts: An Introduction*. London: Taylor and Francis Group, 2016.

CYBER SABOTAGE

Attacks against the critical infrastructure have long been a key aspect of warfare. In particular, intelligence organizations have sought to conduct acts of sabotage behind the lines of modern wars, undermining critical war production, an enemy's ability to move forces and resources, or the communications of an opponent. Modern electrical grids, transportation networks, and communication systems rely on computers to function. Computers are used to track inventory and determine shipments that need to be made from regional distribution centers to point-of-sale terminals. They are also used to regulate traffic on the nation's rail and road networks and to shift electrical power drains from one station to another to prevent regional blackouts. These innovations make for more efficient systems, so long as they function, but they can also trigger serious cascade effects when they fail. Thus, while they are extremely useful, they can also make a small problem into a catastrophe under the right circumstances.

There has been a disturbing trend of evidence pointing to the emplacement of backdoors and logic bombs in the U.S. infrastructure controlling the electrical grid, suggesting that one or more potential enemies have taken steps to facilitate cyber sabotage should a war erupt. Such attacks, planned in advance, could theoretically be executed without warning as part of a first-strike approach to warfare, or they might be triggered to disrupt efforts by the United States to project power around the globe. The failure of U.S. government agencies and infrastructure companies to properly secure their communications networks has all but guaranteed that hostile nations will attempt some form of infrastructure sabotage via the cyber domain in the event of a conflict with the United States, and doing so will have significant indirect effects upon the civilian population.

Paul J. Springer

See also: Cyber Attack; Cyber Security; Cyber War; Infrastructure; Logic Bomb; National Infrastructure Advisory Council (NIAC); National Infrastructure Protection Plan (NIPP); Stuxnet; Trojan Horse

Further Reading

Brenner, Joel. *America the Vulnerable: Inside the New Threat Matrix of Digital Espionage, Crime, and Warfare*. New York: Penguin, 2011.

Singer, P. W., and Allan Friedman. *Cybersecurity and Cyber War: What Everyone Should Know*. New York: Oxford University Press, 2014.

Siroli, Gian Pietro. "Strategic Information Warfare: An Introduction." In *Cyberwar, Netwar, and the Revolution in Military Affairs*. Edited by Edward Halpin, Philippa Trevorrow, David Webb, and Steve Wright. New York: Palgrave Macmillan, 2006.

CYBER SECURITY

Cyber security is a concept that evolved in government strategy and organization, private industry systems design, and as a subject of study. Cyber security exists as a government and private reaction to a complex world full of threats in cyber space. Therefore, cyber security is more effectively considered a strategy. Cyber security, which is threat-based, is distinctly different from cyber-space communications, which is connectivity-based. Where *communications* describes the purpose for which cyber space was built, *cyber security* describes the necessary addition of security to protect networks from threats that seek to exploit flaws in the system. Cyber security evolved in policy as threat activity increased and nations grew dependent on cyber space for governance and commerce. Soon, nation-states began to operate through computer networks to accomplish state tasks such as espionage and warfare. Cyber-security strategy evolved through numerous administrations and is often used to describe an end state that the United States is trying to achieve through policy actions, though cyber security as an end state is problematic due to the complexity of the cyber-space environment and the threat landscape. Nevertheless, the U.S. government has made a substantial investment in building cyber security as a strategy under the umbrella of national security.

The creation of computer networking and cyber space did not include the creation of cyber security. In late 1969, only months after Apollo 11 landed on the moon, scientists created the Advanced Research Projects Agency Network (ARPA-NET). As scientists tested ways to create reliable communications, there was little concern about the security of the creation. The scientists involved inherently trusted each other; it was possible to easily verify the identity of all users and endpoints on an almost entirely closed system. The true power of the Turing machines, or computers, used in the construct was the versatility of the system. New ways to move data, such as e-mail, were created to add functionality to the system, which was built to maximize flexibility. As this system grew and more users were added, it became increasingly apparent that there were ways to exploit the lack of security. At the point the scientific community came to that realization, the foundation was already laid and could not be dug up and restarted. The world of cyber space moved on without security built in, but the experiment of computer networking started to provide functionality that was never conceived by the original scientists. As more commerce and governance became networked, it became clear that there was risk in the system that was never planned for.

When Ronald Reagan assumed the presidency, the world was at the height of its concern over the growth of communism; at the same time, there was a rapidly growing culture, as a subset of the computer science community, that focused on finding flaws in the system. The community called themselves *hackers*. Hackers that exploited flaws in the telephone system were called *phreakers*. Some within this community used their talents to further criminal activity and were hunted by the federal government. Kevin Mitnick is a notable example of this type of hacker. Although hacking rose in notoriety as a crime, the movie *WarGames* may have provided the catalyst to the federal government to treat cyber security more seriously.

In the film, Matthew Broderick's character hacks the U.S. Air Force computer at the North American Aerospace Defense Command responsible for nuclear weapons launch. President Reagan reportedly watched the film and was so bothered by the implications that he tasked the National Security Council to investigate the feasibility of the movie's premise. These government studies led to National Security Decision Directive 145. Although the term *cyber security* was not yet prevalent, this document was the first White House policy on the subject of security for computers and information systems.

The White House gave the National Security Agency (NSA) authority to assess the vulnerability of government networks, but it also made the NSA responsible for approval of standards and equipment used in telecommunications and automated systems security. In 1987, Congress passed the Computer Security Act that appointed the National Institute for Standards and Technology (NIST) to maintain telecommunication and cyber-security standards instead of the NSA. Under Reagan, the hacking community had definitively intersected with national security, and hacking was now a threat that was going to be taken seriously by the government.

During the 1990s, the threat from hacking continued to grow, with significant incidents directly linked to national security. As tensions grew between the United States and Iraq, the Department of Defense detected a series of computer intrusions at such locations as Andrews Air Force Base that were based on a vulnerability in the Sun Solaris operating system. A computer task force was assembled to track these incidents; it was called Solar Sunrise. The Federal Bureau of Investigation (FBI) and the Air Force Office of Special Investigations were able to determine the incident was actually not linked to the Iraqi government but was the work of a small group of young Israelis. A cyber wargame called Eligible Receiver, combined with Solar Sunrise, demonstrated to the government how serious a threat hacking posed in the hands of a sophisticated government adversary instead of bored Israeli teenagers.

Moonlight Maze was one of the earliest publicly known cyber incidents believed to be linked to such an adversary. This breach was actually a series of incidents lasting at least two years and believed to be attributed to Russia. Compromised victims included the National Aeronautics and Space Administration (NASA) and the Department of Energy. Although attribution was never positively linked, the implications were that the state of security in cyber space was not adequate to defend networks critical to national security.

As the United States entered the 21st century, national security faced numerous challenges, and the state of cyber security in the United States continued to appear inadequate. President George W. Bush began his administration with the most significant terrorist attacks in U.S. history, and it was feared cyber space could provide a new avenue for terrorist attacks on critical infrastructure. Building on the incidents of the previous decade, the United States assessed how vulnerable these critical systems were to terrorist attack. At the same time, a chain of cyber intrusions called Titan Rain spread across the Department of Defense. Titan Rain was the first publicly known incident of organized Chinese cyber-espionage activity against the Department of Defense. At that point, in the Bush White House, the national-security staff faced significant terrorist threats throughout the world, national cyber infrastructure with security added as an afterthought, and several nations building robust cyber capabilities in their militaries and espionage services. It appeared that the nation was unprepared to defend against the range of threats it would face in this new domain. The result was President Bush's plan to secure cyber space.

President Bush's new strategy was built around the concept he referred to as *cyber-space security*. The two documents authored by the White House included National Security Presidential Directive 38 and a released version called the 2003 National Strategy to Secure Cyberspace. The Bush White House dissected the concept of cyber security and set priorities for the federal government and industry to meet. The term *cyber security* became widely used in both the public and private sector, and significant government spending was associated with modernizing the U.S. cyber infrastructure. According to the White House, the linkage between the public and private sector was key to cyber security. As a government strategy, cyber security in the Bush administration was critically dependent on the private sector increasing its level of security, as the private sector managed the bulk of cyber space and critical infrastructure. Market pressures and government action led software developers, antivirus vendors, hardware manufacturers, and network engineers to focus more resources on security during design phases or attempts to update aging systems. Furthermore, industries that had grown dependent were encouraged to focus on ensuring their networks met a baseline standard for security.

During the Bush presidency, cyber-security focus and funding grew substantially. In National Security Presidential Directive 54, the White House implemented the Comprehensive National Cybersecurity Initiative (CNCI) to manage the growing funding streams for cyber security–focused organizations and improving the defensive posture of government networks. Despite the government focus, it is questionable whether the United States moved any closer to achieving cyber security as an end state. Although national strategy may have provided a framework and plan, cyber space continued to grow at an unprecedented rate, and security needs struggled to keep pace with the expansion of the Internet.

There was now a rapidly growing culture of cyber security within the U.S. government and the private sector, but significant cyber incidents were still on the rise. In a rare declassification of cyber intrusions, the Department of Defense acknowledged that one of its most significant cyber incidents occurred in 2008. Called *Buckshot Yankee*, official statements claimed a thumb drive plugged into computers in the Middle East contained a virus that was able to infect classified networks. Based on multiple sources, the Russian government was believed to be responsible for the penetration. This incident shocked the military and put into question whether U.S. military cyber security was prepared for conflict in the 21st century. With the cumulative weight of previous major cyber incidents, Buckshot Yankee served as a catalyst to form the U.S. Cyber Command (USCYBERCOM) to centralize the defense of military cyber space, with the director of the National Security Agency as its commander.

During the Obama administration, the cyber-security industry continued to grow significantly, as nearly every major corporation and government agency grew cyber-security departments, but this boom in cyber security failed to keep pace with the rate of growth of cyber space. During the time between 2005 and 2015, social media exploded into the homes and mobile devices of nearly every American family. Commerce also moved significantly into cyber space as more companies grew considerably more dependent on online capabilities. During this time, the Internet integrated into every major corporation, and enough cyber-security professionals simply did not exist to meet the needs of government and the private sector. Instead of building better cyber security and growing networks out from that foundation, many corporations assimilated older networks and continued expansion into cyber space at even faster rates because of competition. Cyber security was often considered a constraint on the expansion and integration of networks into commerce and collaboration. As more valuable data moved online, the cyber-security industry struggled to keep up.

The Obama administration heavily focused on cyber-security policy as a wide range of threats focused on exploiting flaws in cyber-security practices. As the Global War on Terror came to a close and terrorism funding lines were reorganized, cyber-security funding continued to increase to approximately $13 billion per year. During the Obama administration, nations focused heavily on developing cyber-weapons programs, and the growth of commerce online provided potent targets for criminal threats to exploit. There was a wide range of notable incidents that demonstrated how vulnerable world networks were to increasingly advanced cyber attacks. Unattributed malware called *Stuxnet* penetrated control systems for nuclear centrifuges in Iran, effectively destroying them. The North Korean government stole data and destroyed the functionality of computers belonging to Sony Entertainment. In addition, there was a wave of high-profile cyber-espionage incidents that occurred during the same time period. The cyber-security section of the National Security Council became the driving force behind a series of cyber-security policies. The most noteworthy policies include Executive Order 13636: Improving Critical Infrastructure Cybersecurity, Presidential Policy Directive 20 (PPD-20), and the President's Cybersecurity National Action Plan. The U.S. government now treats cyber security as a critical department of national security, a position unlikely to change with a new administration.

Despite significant amounts of attention from multiple administrations, most experts still consider U.S. cyber security far from adequate to meet the threat landscape. Cyber security is now intertwined with global communications, but it was not originally part of the design of computers or networks. Unlike the early stages of cyber-space development, cyber security is now implemented at various stages of software, hardware, and network development. Cyber insurance is also a growing industry to provide some financial protection from network compromises. Today, cyber security is a multibillion-dollar industry and a significant policy area for the U.S. government. Cyber security served as a reaction to threats and has grown in importance since the Reagan administration. Each president since has added additional policies and focus to cyber-security efforts as globalized communications continued to invade every part of governance, commerce, and even daily life. Cyber security is now a critical part of the global communications industry and the government and will remain so for the foreseeable future.

Zachary M. Smith

See also: Cyber Deterrence; Cyber War; Moonlight Maze; National Cyber Security Strategy; Operation Buckshot Yankee; Operation Titan Rain; Solar Sunrise; Sony Hack

Further Reading

Brenner, Joel. *America the Vulnerable: Inside the New Threat Matrix of Digital Espionage, Crime, and Warfare.* New York: Penguin, 2011.

Carr, Jeffrey. *Inside Cyber Warfare: Mapping the Cyber Underworld.* Sebastopol, CA: O'Reilly Media, 2009.

Clarke, Richard A., and Robert K. Knake. *Cyber War: The Next Threat to National Security and What to Do about It.* New York: HarperCollins, 2010.

Libicki, Martin. *Cyberspace in Peace and War.* Annapolis, MD: U.S. Naval Institute Press, 2016.

Singer, P. W., and Allan Friedman. *Cybersecurity and Cyber War: What Everyone Should Know.* New York: Oxford University Press, 2014.

Springer, Paul J. *Cyber Warfare: A Reference Handbook.* Santa Barbara, CA: ABC-CLIO, 2015.

Stiennon, Richard. *Surviving Cyber War.* Lanham, MD: Government Institutes, 2010.

CYBERSPACE POLICY REVIEW (2009)

The 2009 Cyberspace Policy Review (CPR) is a document initiated by President Barack Obama to review U.S. policies and bureaucratic structures for cyber security. The document revealed significant gaps in the nation's security infrastructure pertaining to cyber space and called for increased government attention. In early 2009, President Obama called for a 60-day comprehensive review of U.S. cyber security. A team of cyber-security experts conducted the review, engaging with leaders in industry, academia, privacy advocacy groups, state governments, international organizations, and the federal government. Completed in May 2009, the Cyberspace Policy Review summarized the team's conclusions while providing a road map for increasing America's cyber security.

The review concluded that the United States faced a crossroads between continuing to expand access to cyber space to promote efficiency and innovation while simultaneously ensuring security and privacy rights. According to the review, the United State could no longer accept the status quo and a national dialogue on cyber security was needed. The review determined that the United States should embrace internationalism as a cyber-security strategy, arguing that cyber isolationism will no longer work. In addition, it called for greater private and public sector engagement. As the federal government must protect and defend the country, the review supposed that its powers and responsibilities in cyber security were clear and essential. While calling for an overall government approach to create a new cyber-security infrastructure, the review recommended that the White House assume the primary leadership role.

A near-term action plan called for a variety of steps to implement specific recommendations. These included appointing a cyber-security official to coordinate American cyber-security policies and activities alongside a strong National Security Council (NSC) directorate; preparing an updated national cyber-security strategy; designating cyber security as a key management priority of the POTUS; appointing a privacy and civil liberties official to the NSC directorate; formulating and clarifying legal roles for various cyber-security agencies across the federal government; increasing public awareness of cyber security through expanded educational initiatives; increasing the number of government positions devoted to cyber security; preparing a response plan in the event of a cyber-security incident; supporting research for the development of new technologies to gain an edge in cyber-security strategy; and protecting privacy and civil liberties while securing the nation's cyber infrastructure. While continued cyberattacks against America's information systems demonstrate the persistent ability of enemy states and organizations to damage the United States, the Cyberspace Policy Review initiated a major government effort and raised public attention to this emerging threat and reality.

Jordan R. Hayworth

See also: Cyber Security; National Cyber Security Strategy; Obama, Barack

Further Reading

Cyberspace Policy Review: Assuring a Trusted and Resilient Information and Communications Infrastructure. Washington, D.C.: Office of the President of the United States, May, 2009.

CYBER TERRORISM

The Internet is something that changed the world, and not solely in a good way. Today, almost all terrorist organizations use the Internet as a recruiting tool. However, the Internet provides a more dangerous field of action, namely, cyber terrorism. The Internet is used to spread propaganda videos on social media Web sites, to exchange money using bitcoins or other Internet currencies, to train or recruit new members of a terror organization, and even to launch attacks by using a dangerous new Internet virus. As a consequence of the low-intensity conflicts, methods of asymmetric warfare, including those that incorporate the Internet, are intensively spreading.

Terrorism itself is not a modern phenomenon, but an old weapon to threaten the existent order by the unexpected use of violence, mostly in a shocking way (e.g., against innocent civilians). Today, terrorism in its classical and new cyber forms is posing a dangerous threat for international peace as well as the transnational standards that are based on law and order. Yonah Alexander called the aim of terrorism a "pervasive fear for the purpose of achieving political goals." To achieve it, the Internet and the use of the cyber space as a new battleground seem to have flourished in the last decade.

There are terrorist groups in more than 60 countries that are using information and communication technology (ICT) to achieve their aims. Especially after the strengthening of counterterrorist activities in the aftermath of 9/11, terrorists have tried to gain a stronger grip on the possibilities the World Wide Web provides. The globalization that has been a by-product of this development allows single groups to coordinate a worldwide agenda and keep their own national or regional focus at the same time. With regard to communication and the connection of terrorist individuals or smaller groups, the Internet and its new communication technologies provide a large pool for possible actions.

In contrast to cyber crimes, cyber terrorism always utilizes fear to achieve a political aim. It wants to weaken or put pressure on a particular political system that is considered to be the ideological or religious enemy of the terrorist group and its members. There are two types of cyber terrorism, state or nonstate, which generally are performed by an individual or a group. The goal is usually to put political pressure on an enemy or to create as much chaos as possible. As there has been a general growth of terrorist acts since the 1990s and the collapse of the Soviet Union, more and more cases draw attention to the newer communication and information technologies that are involved to commit such terrorist acts. The easier availability of communication systems, technology, and international travel stimulated the growth of global terrorism in the last two and a half decades. Initially, mainly states or rich individuals, such as Osama bin Laden, sponsored terrorist activities, but today, the cheap cost of cyber terrorism makes it even more dangerous.

Despite these dangers, people are seldom aware of what cyber terrorism really implies, often confusing it with cyber crime or other forms of cyber attack. It is the motivation and the attacker that defines it as a terrorist act. Michael Vatis specifically defined it as "computer-to-computer attacks intended to cause significant damage in order to coerce or intimidate a government or civilian population." The Internet therefore becomes the connecting part in the terrorist network that brings target and terrorist into contact. A cyber terrorist consequently acts like a hacker, but not with the same intention. In addition, cyber terrorists might be used by foreign governments as a form of cyber-guerrilla tactic in a low-intensity conflict.

Financially, cyber terrorism is also much cheaper than conventional attacks. A person with Internet access is usually not a threat, but a participant in a global and fast communication exchange network. However, almost everyone has access to this network, and a person that has rather dangerous aims can easily pose a threat against stock markets and government Web sites. Only an individual's technological skill limits the possibilities for the individual or a terrorist group. For sure, the sophistication of the government to protect probable targets from a cyber terrorist and an attack is important. That is why some state agencies are recruiting hackers for their security systems, as these people already know the tools that could be used in terrorist scenarios. Also, not only hackers but also states such as Iran and China, jihadi terrorist groups, and other malevolent organizations are already screening cyber space for possible leaks or weak spots to attack. For all of them, the cheap costs are attractive, as one only needs a computer, Internet access and sufficient skills to launch an attack. In addition, these attacks of cyber terrorism could be launched from everywhere around the globe. That also makes it almost impossible to predict an attack before it begins. The only way to counter it is to be prepared for the possibility that it could happen. In particular, the difficulties in tracking an attack are what make it so attractive for terrorists. After the attack, they can send their messages to the world without being located and punished for their actions.

Once malicious code is planted, it does not have to cause an immediate action, meaning that cyber terrorists could plan their action beforehand and wait for it to be untraceable before the launch of their attack. Potential targets are numerous, ranging from power plants, to airports, to hospitals. Considering horror scenarios about how electricity or communication might be interrupted by hackers already causes fear, and not only in the Pentagon. Every agency that is concerned about national security has to train specialists to counter such scenarios in a fast and adequate way. Steady preparation of defense systems, the analysis of changes, and sufficient communication capabilities on the side of the defending agencies are needed to be prepared for possible attacks in the future. Swift countermeasures and transnational cooperation by global security networks are also needed to limit the utility of cyber space for terrorist activities in the future.

That cyber attacks could have been used already is known. Since the U.S. invasion of Afghanistan, terrorist organizations have explored the possibilities provided by the Internet. It might be true that online training is not really useful, when one compares it to personal education; however, the methods for terrorist attacks could be easily deployed after having been trained in person. The Council of Europe Cybercrime Convention has failed to gather sufficient support for transnational cyber-crime regulations that would grant easier access to and measures against terrorists; however, the discussion is not over yet. Cooperation, especially in the legal sector, is needed to be able to follow leads on international terrorist groups who use the advantage of anonymity in the World Wide Web to cover their traces.

In addition, national security has to be equally protected against hackers who might solely act as individuals or small groups in the interests of their government. Intrusions into U.S. government systems and the available evidence strengthen the idea that such attacks might have been directed by foreign governments, such as China or Russia, to politically weaken the United States, and the acts might be classified as cyber terrorism rather than cyber war. Furthermore, the acceptance of such hacker networks stimulates black-market sales of malware and technology that could cause much greater damage in the future, especially in cases in which the malware causes a process of destruction that cannot be stopped by the attackers themselves.

Frank Jacob

See also: Al Qaeda; Anonymous; Cyber Attack; Cyber Crime; Hacker; Iran Cyber Capabilities; Islamic State in Iraq and Syria (ISIS); Malware; Syrian Electronic Army (SEA)

Further Reading

Alexander, Yonah. *International Terrorism: National, Regional and Global Perspectives.* New York: Praeger, 1976.

Awan, Imran, and Brian Blakemore. *Policing Cyber Hate, Cyber Threats, and Cyber Terrorism.* Burlington, VT: Ashgate, 2011.

Demchak, Chris C. *Wars of Disruption and Resilience: Cybered Conflict, Power, and National Security.* Athens, GA: University of Georgia Press, 2011.

Vatis, Michael: "The Next Battlefield: The Reality of Virtual Threats." *Harvard International Review* 28(3) (2006): 56–61.

Weiman, Gabriel. *Terror on the Internet: The New Arena, the New Challenges.* Washington, D.C.: USIP, 2006.

Westby, Jody R. "Countering Terrorism with Cyber Security." *Jurimetrics* 47(3) (2007): 297–313.

CYBER WAR

A war is usually a form of collective violence between two or more states that is ordered and performed by professionals to achieve an economic, political, or religious aim that could or would be prevented by the antagonist group. A war in cyber space does not follow such a definition, as a single person with a laptop and an Internet connection could start a war in this environment by attacking a foreign government using methods well-known from diverse cyber crimes. While superpowers such as the United States seem to be well prepared to fight a war in the material world (land, sea, air, space), actions that are performed in cyber space are something that could threaten national security. Cyber war was not even a possibility some decades before, when the first computers were built, but today, it seems to offer a cheap alternative to classical battlefields, not only to terrorists but to state actors as well. Former CIA director Leon E. Panetta claimed in 2012 that the United States' next Pearl Harbor could be a cyber attack, suggesting that this form of assault might presage the next major conflict.

In contrast to acts of war, most cyber attacks, regardless of whether they are state-sponsored, try to gain something by espionage, sabotage, or subversion. That these activities might lead to a more powerful use of the cyber space as a battleground seems to be clear. Those who deal with such possibilities claim that the war is inevitable, and there would not be something surprising, such as an attack out of nowhere. Not only private companies but whole governments prepare themselves to counter the initial attacks of a future cyber war. In addition, laboratories try to develop new technologies that will not only help with such a defense strategy but also support an initial attack. That cyber space is already a sphere of warfare is obvious. In 2007 and 2008, Estonian and Georgian Web sites were attacked, presumably by Russian hackers, and these attacks showed that cyber attacks can damage foreign governments.

The possible scenarios are broad and include attacks against airports, hospitals, and banks. In 2010, the Stuxnet virus was used to significantly damage the Iranian nuclear program and was probably developed by Israel or the United States explicitly for this reason. Those who studied the Stuxnet worm described it as the first "cyber super weapon" that could be used in more destructive cases. It is still debated whether the use of this virus was an act of war, as it was not violent and no humans suffered physical harm from it. However, it destroyed or at least sabotaged the Iranian atomic program and therefore must be seen as a violent act of someone to destroy the progress of the Iranian government. Such an act is hostile, but one cannot claim it to be an act of war because we do not know exactly how far governments were involved in its creation, use, and target selection or even which governments ordered its use.

Information warfare (IW) is not limited by borders and allows militaries to act in multiple ways, such as attacking facilities, creating disorder in the enemy's territory, or using cyber space as a platform for propaganda that is intended to weaken the morale of the enemy's supporters. As modern societies have based their lives on the use of technology, attacks against or though this technology seems to be more likely in a future war in the age of information. Numerous scenarios especially deal with such a war in East Asia, where tactics of cyber warfare seem to have become a key component of war preparations, especially in the People's Republic of China (PRC). Analysts agree that the war of the future will not follow classical terms of warfare; at the very least, it will incorporate the possibilities cyber space is offering.

More driving are the questions of national security related to the issues of cyber attacks, cyber terrorism, and cyber war. The fact that cyber attacks are so inexpensive make them extremely dangerous, especially because such states as the PRC, which would not be able to compete with the United States on a military level, assume that a war based on such cyber attacks might not only be winnable but affordable for its military. State and nonstate actors can use this affordability to recruit skilled hackers into the ranks of terrorist organizations or war parties alike. Paramilitary cyber groups, often called *patriotic hackers*, are already being incorporated into cyber armies It is likely that future cyber wars will be asymmetric conflicts from the start, and these low-intensity conflicts might be more dependent on the skills of the cyber warriors than the supply of war material.

Next to destroying infrastructure in enemy territory, accompanying cyber attacks could be launched during an act of war to gather information, steal state secrets, or to sabotage the foreign government in several ways, including attacks on communication facilities. Conventional attacks could simply be combined with cyber attacks, something the United States already did during the Iraq War. Systems that were used to command or control Iraqi troops were blocked, creating an advantage for the U.S. troops that were invading on the ground.

However, the United States is not the only nation-state that has already adopted the new technology for its military doctrine. Cyber warfare, at least on the doctrinal level, has already been developed by several national armies whose aim is to limit costs while achieving a high potential to threaten such superpowers as the United States. The most well-known examples for this trend are China and Russia, where hackers seem to be actively recruited into the ranks of the military. However, Beijing and Moscow are not the only state actors that show an increased interest in the use of modern technology in war. France, India, Iran, Israel, North Korea, and

Pakistan are also interested and well aware of the damage that could be produced by cyber attacks in a future war. Most experts assume that more than 100 states are currently in possession of technology that could be specifically used for measures and acts in a possible cyber war.

The idea of a total war in the future is occupying the minds of Chinese military leaders. They believe in a future war that will decide the Chinese fate. Due to related fears, the military planners in Beijing are strongly focusing on cyber warfare, which would be an essential part of a war without limits. PRC colonels Qiao Liang and Wang Xiangsui made this clear in their seminal work *Unrestricted Warfare*. Like a guerrilla war, a cyber conflict would be unlikely to follow the conventional laws of war, which is why China needs to be prepared to fight on all fronts. Data networks need to be secured while the soldiers for such a new war are trained. Consequently, military education in China involves more and more technology- and information-based components. Beijing's military leaders seem to be well aware of the fact that they would be unable to defeat the United States in a direct confrontation, which is why all means are mobilized to change this inferiority. Cyber warfare, therefore, becomes a modern equivalent to Mao's teaching of guerrilla warfare. The new guerrilla is the hacker, who is able to attack the imperialist enemy without a physical or timely limitation.

In the cyber realm, there is the possibility to attack without being identified as an aggressor. Cyber attacks are usually launched with an attempt to conceal the attacker's identity. The use of such attacks might consequently happen without a clear identification of which nation-state launched it. Cyber war could consequently lead to a conflict without a conventional engagement, such as a campaign of cyber terrorism by state-backed hackers. Such attacks might also have different meanings. It could fulfill the sole purpose of letting the enemy know that a so-far unknown technology is available. Causing a threat to force the enemy to change its position from aggressive to defensive is therefore an option for such an attack. It can, however, also be the aim of the attacker to weaken the enemy without letting anyone accuse the originating nation of aggression. A third party could always be made to look responsible. As long as there is no definitive proof, attacks might be easy, untraceable, and therefore extremely attractive.

In cyber conflicts, data networks are usually the targets of cyber attacks, with viruses or physical mechanisms of transmission, such as flash drives, used as the means to initially place the hacker malware into the target system. With some degree of success, the attack will cause the data networks to be paralyzed and create as much trouble as possible. This is achieved when electrical networks or other key elements of infrastructure are attacked. An attack against the enemy's mass media would also lead to turmoil and panic. The options are endless, something that has to be taken into consideration when discussing the dangers of a possible cyber war in the future. The PRC military, in particular, is focusing its activities on such networks and their possible weaknesses for a cyber attack. Furthermore, attacks against the communication systems of the enemy are trained for as well. However, the most likely scenario is not a war solely confined to cyber space, but the combination of cyber attacks and physical attacks that take place in the real world. That the first strikes have to be well prepared for, on the attacking as well as the defending sides, is important to be understood.

Everyone can get access to cyber space as long as a computer or laptop and a connection to the Internet is available. Everyone can therefore act like a hacker with sufficient technical know-how. In contrast to the military, the possible pool of willing "combatants" might be larger, as this kind of war is not related to the danger of getting physically wounded or killed by the enemy. Military planners understand this potential, and they created a simulation center for information warfare in the 1990s. The idea of a psychological war, which would rely on the use of computer-based attacks to influence the mind-set of enemies, became increasingly attractive. Wei Jincheng, a leading PRC strategist, declared that information warfare needs to be seen as a "new form of People's War." Human intelligence would be combined with technological capabilities to secure Chinese interests against an enemy that could not easily be defeated without the mobilization of competing cyber capabilities to augment conventional forces. Information warfare has consequently been actively chosen as a weapon that could change the asymmetric situation between the United States and China in a possible war. A relative inferiority with regard to military hardware is made even by the use of "military software" and hacking skills.

The Twelfth Five-Year Plan (2011–2015) expresses these ideas as cyber combat or espionage and are named as major military tools. Software engineers and hackers have been recruited to prepare the Chinese military for the possible event of a major war in the future. This policy directly counters the concept of a free Internet. This might be dangerous for the regime, but it is also a major tool of self-defense. Therefore, only those who agree on China's policy seem to gain all access to the dangerous options the Internet could create in cyber space. To put it simply, nationalist hackers are promoted, and liberal ones are punished. Computer warfare units have been established in Guangzhou, Jinan, and Nanjing, with hundreds of cyber troops at each location.

The Japanese Ministry of Defense has already mentioned the danger of possible attacks, probably fearing such from China or North Korea, in a White Paper on Defense in 2011. While cyber terrorists or hackers are a phenomenon that is well-known, the real dangers of cyber attacks in a war scenario are rather unknown to the wider public. However, the danger is still increasing, especially as more and more technology is used in our daily lives. As more Internet connections are established, the scenario of a cyber war becomes more dangerous. Thus, the most Internet-dependent nations trade the convenience of advanced networks for the danger that they might be exploited.

While the public is not yet aware, the U.S. military has reacted to counter the increasing menace. The Pentagon initiated its "Strategy for Operating in Cyberspace" in 2011. This strategy, however, was solely defensive and not an aggressive one. The idea was not to militarize the Internet, but to be prepared for future cyber attacks that would decrease the American ability to counter foreign war efforts. Regardless of this statement, the idea of offensive operations is gaining traction, and the industries for cyber security and cyber weapons are booming. Computer scientists are also animated to specialize in cyber vulnerabilities to develop methods for attack that could be used in information warfare. While the industry is scouting skilled personnel for their valuable computing skills, the government is competing for the same pool of people to enhance national security. One potential successful application of cyber warfare was reported by David Sanger, who covered the Stuxnet virus and stated that Israel and the Pentagon had developed the cyber worm. Sanger named the attack "America's first sustained use of cyber weapons" and thereby claimed that the American strategy might be more than solely defensive.

Following the Stuxnet attack, the discussion about cyber warfare left the theoretical sphere to become a more real discourse that also involved public opinion. As a cyber attack had realistically shown what was possible, more vivid scenarios were envisioned. Physical destruction by a cyber attack was demonstrably possible, so a new dimension of threat was visible for everyone, whether the attack had been launched by the United States or not. Those who wanted to believe that there had been U.S. involvement claimed that the American military was in possession of offensive technology already; those who doubted it demanded the development of such a technology. In addition to the classical four domains of warfare (air, ground, space, water), cyber space was declared to be the fifth domain. The budget for the cyber arsenal was increased, and the air force, moving to assume primacy in the domain, requested a budget of $4 billion to pursue cyber superiority.

The 21st century is likely to see another arms race, but this time it may not be airpower or space programs that are important so much as cyber space and its possibilities for the use of the computer networks in war. Those nation-states that are able to defend their own communication and data networks while being able to attack the enemy's might become the superpowers of the digital age. This fact will cause trends and changes in military training, civil education, and the business world. The hard work by governments, companies, and skilled operators will be needed to keep a superior position in this struggle that is not only waged by nation-states but hacker networks and terrorists alike.

Frank Jacob

See also: Cyber Attack; Cyber Weapon; Iran Cyber Capabilities; Israel Cyber Capabilities; National Security Agency (NSA); North Korea Cyber Capabilities; People's Republic of China Cyber Capabilities; Russia Cyber Capabilities; United States Cyber Capabilities; U.S. Cyber Command (USCYBERCOM)

Further Reading

Brenner, Joel. *America the Vulnerable: Inside the New Threat Matrix of Digital Espionage, Crime, and Warfare.* New York: Penguin, 2011.

Carr, Jeffrey. *Inside Cyber Warfare: Mapping the Cyber Underworld.* Sebastopol, CA: O'Reilly Media, 2009.

Clarke, Richard A., and Robert K. Knake. *Cyber War: The Next Threat to National Security and What to Do about It.* New York: HarperCollins, 2010.

Liang, Qiao and Wang Xiangsui. *Unrestricted Warfare.* Beijing: PLA Literature and Arts Publishing House, 1999.

Libicki, Martin. *Cyberspace in Peace and War.* Annapolis, MD: U.S. Naval Institute Press, 2016.

Rid, Thomas. *Cyber War Will Not Take Place.* New York: Oxford University Press, 2013.

Singer, P. W., and Allan Friedman, *Cybersecurity and Cyber War: What Everyone Should Know.* New York: Oxford University Press, 2014.

Springer, Paul J. *Cyber War: A Reference Handbook.* Santa Barbara, CA: ABC-CLIO, 2015.

Stiennon, Richard. *Surviving Cyber War.* Lanham, MD: Government Institutes, 2010.

CYBER WARRIORS

Cyber warriors are individuals engaged in offensive and defensive cyber operations. The goal of cyber warriors is to ensure a stable cyber domain, including the security of weapon systems, command and control systems, and national industrial assets. Although technology is important in the cyber-space domain, the U.S. Army concluded that cyber warriors will determine the success of operations. These men and women typically require extensive training beyond what is normally expected of civilian and military workers in the same field to defend networks and use complex computer systems. As of 2013, there was great demand for cyber warriors by the U.S. government and military. One of the biggest issues with the cyber-warrior workforce is a lack of common definitions for the various roles across all departments and offices.

The defensive aspect of cyber warriors was defined by the Department of Defense (DoD) as countermeasures designed to detect, identify, intercept, and destroy or negate cyber activity that is deemed a threat or that is attempting to penetrate or attack government or military networks. The U.S. Marine Corps (USMC) has embraced the offensive aspect of cyber warfare by training their cyber warriors for offensive as well as defensive operations. The USMC Combat Development Command has even considered training cyber warriors to go into the field with marine expeditionary forces. In 2011, 78 percent of the cyber workforce engaged in defensive operations were civilians; however, in following years, the military took a slightly larger role in cyber warfare. U.S. Cyber Command (USCYBERCOM) was focused on recruiting several thousand cyber warriors by 2015.

By 2012, all of the military branches had created professional roles for both offices and enlisted personnel in the field of cyber warfare. The unique aspect that the military provides for the cyber workforce is that of being cyber warriors. The military embraced their role as warriors in the new cyber age and focused on this aspect to separate their role from that of the civilian cyber workers. Furthermore, the army outlined four values that define cyber warriors: professionalism, elite teams trained in cyber warfare; trust; discipline, to trust a person in cyber space as you would on the battlefield; and precision, because collateral damage can be as harmful in cyber space as on any other battlefield.

Some cyber warriors are recruited with the necessary skills needed to join the cyber workforce, but many more positions offer increased training opportunities. Training, such as the Joint Cyber Analysis Course, which is a six-month course provided at the Center for Information Dominance at the navy's Corey Station base in Pensacola, Florida. This course teaches students to handle a wide range of cyber missions. The navy, marine corps, and army offer service-specific training courses in cyber operations at their respective technical schools and centers. On-the-job training through developmental assignments gives soldiers additional experience in the workplace. In addition to training as cyber warriors, most of these military men and women receive all of the traditional training that their branch requires.

Christopher Menking

See also: Cyber War; United States Cyber Capabilities; U.S. Cyber Command (USCYBERCOM)

Further Reading

Li, Jennifer J., and Lindsay Daugherty. *Training Cyber Warriors: What Can Be Learned from Defense Language Training?* Santa Monica, CA: RAND, 2015.
Libicki, Martin. *Conquest in Cyberspace.* New York: Cambridge University Press, 2007.

CYBER WEAPON

Cyber weapon is a term used to describe programs, equipment, tactics, techniques, and procedures used for offensive cyber operations. Cyber power is the ability to use cyber space to create advantages and influence events in the other operational environments and across the instruments of power. As a domain, cyber is an operating environment. This does not do justice to all that cyber is, however. Cyber is also a platform that enables leaders to achieve effects in the electromagnetic spectrum and the information environment. It is even possible to achieve physical effects via cyber power. Because of this, cyber power facilitates all other operations that use the elements of national power (diplomacy, information, military, and economic) as well as more purely military activities such as command, control, communications, computers, intelligence, surveillance, and reconnaissance (C4ISR).

There are two types of cyber attacks: semantic and syntactic. Semantic attacks use language to shape cognition. Syntactic attacks use the computer codes themselves. As an example, the first phase of a phishing attack is a semantic attack, where the attacker convinces the target to click on the link. As soon as the link is clicked, the phishing attack goes into the second, or syntactic, phase of the attack, unleashing the malware into the target system.

There are two types of effects that a cyber attack can achieve: manipulation and denial. Manipulation describes any change. It can mean shaping cognition, where the thoughts of the target are manipulated, or the manipulation of coding via a syntactic attack. There are three forms of denial: degradation, disruption, and destruction. Degradation means to deny access to, or operation of, a target to a level represented as a percentage of capacity. Disruption is to completely but temporarily deny access to, or operation of, a target for a period of time. Destruction of a target means to permanently, completely, and irreparably deny access to, or operation of, a target.

A cyber attack follows a pattern called the *cyber kill chain*. The steps to the cyber kill chain are the following:

- *Reconnaissance* of the target system identifies targets.
- *Weaponization* is the preparation and staging phase of an attack.
- *Delivery* of the malware to the target launches the operation.
- *Exploitation* of a software, hardware, or human vulnerability occurs.
- *Installation* of a persistent backdoor maintains access.
- *Command and control* of the malware opens a command channel to enable the adversary to remotely manipulate the victim.
- *Actions on the objective* accomplishes the goal of the mission.

The most popular types of attacks in 2016 included the following:

- Watering hole attacks
- Zero-day attacks
- Web application attacks
- Advanced persistent threats (APTs)/targeted attacks
- Distributed denial-of-service (DDoS) attacks
- SSL-encrypted threats
- Phishing attacks
- Drive-by downloads

A watering hole attack can happen if an attacker figures out what Web pages people from the target organization visit and then infects one or more of those Web pages with malware, which then infects the visitors who take it back to their system.

Zero-day attacks exploit vulnerabilities in software that are not publicly known (and therefore not defended against). Prominent examples include Stuxtnet and Shamoon.

Web application attacks use characteristics of coding to manipulate the code to achieve a certain effect. They include remote code execution, SQL injections, format string vulnerabilities, cross-site scripting (XSS), username enumeration, and buffer overflows. They all allow attackers to take advantage of vulnerabilities or underlying characteristics of software. Remote code execution allows an attacker to run arbitrary, system-level code on the vulnerable server and retrieve any desired information contained therein. Format string vulnerability and SQL injection allow an attacker to access crucial information from a Web server's database. XSS requires the victim to execute a malicious URL, which may be crafted in such a manner to appear to be legitimate at first look, a popular approach in phishing attacks. Username enumeration is where the backend validation script tells the attacker whether the supplied username is correct or not, allowing the attacker to determine usernames by experimenting. A username is often sufficient to supply access to a system. A buffer overflow is when data written to a buffer is bigger than the buffer can handle, possibly causing errors and crashes and sometimes allowing attackers to write data into areas near the buffer.

An APT is group, such as a government, with both the capability and the intent to target, persistently and effectively, a specific entity. This phrase gained popularity with the Mandiant Report, which identified Unit 61398 from the Chinese People's Liberation Army (PLA) as APT1, which had systematically conducted cyber espionage over years, penetrating 141 companies spanning 20 major industries and maintaining access to victim networks for an average of 356 days, with the longest exploitation being 1,764 days.

Distributed denial-of-service (DDoS) attacks actually deny service, usually by overwhelming the target network. A DDoS attack comes from a number of computers that are all attacking the same target. This technique was used by Russia against Estonia in 2007 and Georgia in 2008.

SSL-encrypted threats refers to threats that use cryptographic Internet Protocols to move malware past security controls because many traditional network-security products are not designed to inspect SSL traffic.

Phishing attacks involve a semantic attack to get the target to click on a link, at which point malware takes over and makes a syntactic attack on the target's system. Spear-phishing is a phishing attack designed for a certain person in an organization, and a whaling attack is a phishing attack against a high-value target, such as an executive. Clone-phishing is a type of phishing attack where the attacker takes the content and recipient addresses from a legitimate e-mail that contains an attachment or link and uses it to create an almost identical, or cloned, e-mail.

Drive-by downloads happen when visiting a legitimate Web page. The user clicks on a link provided by a pop-up, which then downloads the malware onto the victim's computer.

Each of these types of attacks uses a syntactic weapon, while many include a semantic weapon as well.

G. Alexander Crowther

See also: Advanced Persistent Threat (APT); Cyber Attack; Cyber Warriors; Distributed Denial-of-Service (DDoS) Attack; Estonian Cyber Attack (2007); Georgian Cyber Attack (2008); Malware; People's Liberation Army Unit 61398; Phishing; Shamoon Virus; SQL Injection; Stuxnet; Zero-Day Vulnerability

Further Reading

Brenner, Joel. *America the Vulnerable: Inside the New Threat Matrix of Digital Espionage, Crime, and Warfare.* New York: Penguin, 2011.

Carr, Jeffrey. *Inside Cyber Warfare: Mapping the Cyber Underworld.* Sebastopol, CA: O'Reilly Media, 2009.

Clarke, Richard A., and Robert K. Knake. *Cyber War: The Next Threat to National Security and What to Do about It.* New York: HarperCollins, 2010.

Libicki, Martin. *Cyberspace in Peace and War.* Annapolis, MD: U.S. Naval Institute Press, 2016.

Singer, P. W., and Allan Friedman. *Cybersecurity and Cyber War: What Everyone Should Know.* New York: Oxford University Press, 2014.

Springer, Paul J. *Cyber Warfare: A Reference Handbook.* Santa Barbara, CA: ABC-CLIO, 2015.

Stiennon, Richard. *Surviving Cyber War.* Lanham, MD: Government Institutes, 2010.

D

DARK WEB

The dark web, a tiny grouping of Web sites with hidden Internet Protocol (IP) addresses, is a small portion of the deep web that enables users to anonymously access hidden Web sites using specialized tools and technical knowledge. For example, whistle-blowers pass data to the press, legal authorities, or government agencies about corruption in an organization via the dark web. Drug dealers, hackers, hit men for hire, and others also use the dark web to offer services. Available data says dark web content is "balanced," but its users are mostly and preferably unknown.

The dark web's original design and current use provide some detail about this portion of the Internet. In 2002, the Naval Research Lab fielded a concept of anonymous Web activity that enabled U.S. government intelligence activities via downloadable software called The Onion Router (TOR). TOR's expanding global network includes at least 6,000 nodes designed to ensure their users surf the Web or host data without revealing anything. This hidden activity champions privacy, freedom of speech, security, and human rights but also hosts child pornography, illegal drug marketplaces, terrorist chat rooms, and other illegal or illicit data, interestingly, at about the same rate according to a TOR content study from 2013. Increasing illicit activity masks "legitimate" dark web activity. Therefore, some anonymous surfing or data hosting is harmless, while other illegal or illicit activities lead to radicalization, jail, or self-destruction.

The dark web uses anonymizing software (AS) and encryption to protect all who use it. TOR is the most common AS, but other options include virtual private networks (VPNs), peer-to-peer (P2P), or the Invisible Internet Project (I2P). TOR protects Web traffic by encrypting it in layers and bouncing those layers randomly across its global nodes three times, stripping off a layer at each hop. Hopping is a common AS practice because it hides user and data host IP addresses. It also protects identity and makes identification of origin very difficult.

Why users connect is hard to say. Privacy zealots, dissidents, journalists, law enforcement, spies, hackers, drug dealers, terrorists, and pedophiles are common. Of the 3.3 billion Internet users globally, most estimates claim dark web users only account for 0.03 percent of Web activity.

Jeremy Cole

See also: Cyber Crime; Cyber Terrorism; Deep Web; Encryption; Internet; Silk Road; The Onion Router (TOR)

Further Reading

Bartlett, Jamie. *The Dark Net: Inside the Digital Underworld.* New York: Melville House, 2015.

Libicki, Martin. *Cyberspace in Peace and War.* Annapolis, MD: U.S. Naval Institute Press, 2016.

Rosenzweig, Paul. *Cyber Warfare: How Conflicts in Cyberspace Are Challenging America and Changing the World.* Santa Barbara, CA: Praeger, 2012.

DEEP WEB

The deep web is a portion of the Internet that requires users to input specific data to gain access to a specific resource. For example, if a six-year-old wants to watch a Disney movie on Netflix, his or her parents must have set up a Netflix account and paid the monthly fee. With just a username and password, deep web access is granted and the movie starts. This is not the evil child porn or terrorist chat room commonly and incorrectly associated with the deep web. The deep web is where most data on the Internet resides. Sundry users input data to get into its vast stores. While less than 1 percent hosts illicit Web content, most is legitimate.

Size, data, and security elements define this commonly known iceberg-like entity. The seminal estimate of 2001 said the unindexed deep web contains 7,500 terabytes of information, equal to a 4-minute MP3 that could play continuously for 14,000 years. Today's deep web data is what most Internet users look for; it encompasses e-mail, Amazon, Netflix, or a database that one works with daily. For example, the 2015 hack of the Office of Personnel Management (OPM) databases that compromised the personal information of 22 million U.S. government personnel penetrated a deep web resource. Such a sizeable and valuable database illustrates the need to secure deep web databases. The deep web is incomprehensibly enormous and contains the data users want or work with daily; it must be protected.

Access controls are the primary means to connect users to deep web data. For example, users normally establish accounts and passwords to access specific resources, such as e-mail, Facebook, Twitter, online banking sites, and paid subscription sites. Because these sit behind a unique username and password and are not accessible to indexing search engines, they are part of the deep web. Organizational intranets and research and development databases also require specific access that is often controlled by username and password or digital chip technology. To get into the deep web, authorized users must present authorized credentials.

There are many deep web user types. Standard users check e-mail, transfer funds, pay bills, scour indexes for deceased relatives, or rely on a plethora of other deep web resources. Entrepreneurs like Amazon and Facebook advertise or sell products. The mysterious dark web, whose users account for only 0.0625 percent of deep web activity and content, comprises only a tiny portion of normal Web activity. These users require specialized software and technical knowledge. Despite user diversity, the overwhelming majority use the deep web for innocuous, mundane activity.

Jeremy Cole

See also: Dark Web; Internet; Office of Personnel Management Data Breach

Further Reading

Libicki, Martin. *Cyberspace in Peace and War.* Annapolis, MD: U.S. Naval Institute Press, 2016.

Rosenzweig, Paul. *Cyber Warfare: How Conflicts in Cyberspace Are Challenging America and Changing the World.* Santa Barbara, CA: Praeger, 2012.

DEFENSE ADVANCED RESEARCH PROJECTS AGENCY (DARPA)

The Defense Advanced Research Projects Agency (DARPA) is a Department of Defense (DoD) research and development organization established by President Dwight D. Eisenhower in February 1958. It was created in response to the October 1957 launch of the first man-made satellite by the Soviet Union, *Sputnik*. This launch demonstrated that the Soviets had a viable intercontinental ballistic missile (ICBM) capability with their R-7 rocket. Although the United States had advanced rocket designs ready for production, such as the Atlas, the public perception was that the United States had lost its technological edge; the Eisenhower administration had to show firm action to assuage the public.

The creation of the Advanced Research Projects Agency (ARPA) in February 1958 was one component of their response. ARPA was originally chartered to boost capabilities in rocketry and space, solve issues related to reentry vehicles, develop methods of nuclear test detection (Project Vela), and advance missile defense technology (Project Defender). It also sponsored work on Transit, a predecessor of GPS championed by the navy. With the creation of the National Aeronautics and Space Administration (NASA), by 1960 most of the space-related research efforts were removed from ARPA's portfolio. ARPA initiated Project Agile, a study of methods to improve counterinsurgency techniques, technologies, and communications to assist in the conflict in Southeast Asia, shortly after President Kennedy took office in 1961. Research in these areas also advanced technical developments in sensors, surveillance, and directed energy in the 1960s and later in the 1980s.

Beginning with the Kennedy administration, ARPA was revectored to a role that it has largely maintained to the present. It serves as a technology booster for projects and areas that are too risky, too new, too urgent, are of uncertain feasibility, or obviously not within the purview of any single military service to support and pursue. ARPA could fund basic research that, in many ways, could be equated with military security. ARPA had the advantage of minimizing bureaucratic red tape and developed a methodology that often focused on creating a few centers of excellence to ensure long-term potential in key areas while also supporting technology demonstrators that might result in revolutionary technological change. At the same time, ARPA attempted to lessen the chance of technological surprise in an effort to help maintain America's technological edge as a nimble organization devoted to excellence.

From the 1960s onward, ARPA supported significant research in materials science and computer science that had tremendous implications for the direction of research, the development of academic organizations, the future of military technology, and the creation and growth of industries associated with the high-technology sectors related to computers and communications in the late 20th century. Project Pontus was an ARPA-sponsored initiative to boost the research base, number of PhDs, and overall capabilities in material science and engineering by establishing a handful of interdisciplinary laboratories (IDLs) on select college campuses throughout the United States. Improvements in this area had significant ramifications in improving structural and power-conversion materials essential for advancing technologies associated with advanced propulsion, solid-state electronics, and high-strength materials associated with space and other military applications. By the early 1970s, when the program was turned over to the National Science Foundation (NSF) for administration on a permanent basis, the IDLs had provided a home for material science and engineering that firmly established the field as an interdisciplinary growth center, and the number of PhDs produced had skyrocketed at least fourfold in many instances along with a concatenate increase in applicable research by universities and industry.

In the emerging field of computer science, ARPA played a major role in developing time-sharing techniques, networking protocols, human factors engineering, and the advancement of the concept of artificial intelligence (AI) that made computers both more useful and provided a goal for future research in the field. Starting in 1963, the agency also established the foundations of the Internet by initiating the first time-shared computer systems. ARPANET (the first wide-area packet-switching network) became a four-node network in 1970 and grew to 23 hosts in a year as the major issues associated with physically connecting the computer nodes, economically using the expensive communication lines that connected the sites, and dealing with differences in hardware and software among the time-sharing systems were solved. Expanded use of the system and burgeoning capabilities, such as electronic mail (e-mail), helped grow the network and laid the foundation for its development beyond scientific and academic uses and for the commercial success that propels the World Wide Web, or the Internet, today.

After 1972, the organization was renamed the Defense Advanced Research Projects Agency (DARPA) and narrowed in scope to sponsoring only defense-related projects. This led to a mass migration of computer science expertise to the private sector and a flowering of private industry in that economic sector as the agency reduced its sponsorship. Advances in semiconductors, very-large-scale integration (VLSI), and other promising areas of computer science led to speculation that major leaps in computing power could lead to improved machine intelligence. By the early 1980s, DARPA had seized on this speculation and attempted to boost AI with its Strategic Computing Initiative. The effort largely failed to achieve anything close to what was promised regarding AI, which might be fitting for an organization dedicated to high risk, high reward efforts. In the end, DARPA achieved more modest advances in AI, such as expert systems, speech recognition, high-performance computing, and logistics loading, that have shown up in commercial and military applications. Advances in automatic target recognition, space-based sensors, propulsion, and materials sponsored by DARPA were employed to enhance missile defense and the National Aerospace Plane (NASP) research efforts in the 1980s as well.

Recently, DARPA has sponsored projects in robotics, remotely piloted aircraft (RPA), powered exoskeletons, and cancer research.

John G. Terino

See also: ARPANET; Department of Defense (DoD); Internet

Further Reading

Abbate, Janet. *Inventing the Internet.* Cambridge, MA: The MIT Press, 1999.

Campbell-Kelly, Martin, William Aspray, Nathan Ensmenger, and Jeffrey R. Yost. *Computer: A History of the Information Machine.* Boulder, CO: Westview Press, 2013.

Edwards, Paul N. *The Closed World: Computers and the Politics of Discourse in Cold War America.* Cambridge, MA: The MIT Press, 1996.

Hafner, Katie. *Where Wizards Stay Up Late: The Origins of the Internet.* New York: Simon and Schuster, 1998.

Hughes, Thomas P. *Rescuing Prometheus.* New York: Pantheon Books, 1998.

Roland, Alex, and Philip Shiman. *Strategic Computing: DARPA and the Quest for Machine Intelligence, 1983–1993.* Cambridge, MA: The MIT Press, 2002.

DEFENSE INFORMATION SYSTEMS AGENCY (DISA)

The Defense Information Systems Agency (DISA) is part of the U.S. Department of Defense (DoD). It was founded in 1960 and was known as the Defense Communications Agency (DCA) until 1991, when it was given its current responsibilities and new title. The agency conducts the day-to-day management of the DoD's communication networks, computer-based information systems, and the Global Information Grid (GIG). DISA is under the portfolio of the assistant secretary of defense, network information, and integration. DISA also assists and advises the secretary of defense on computer network policies, such as security and procurement, information technology (IT), network operations, and information assurance. They are also responsible for providing strategic-level guidance and oversight for computer network operations (CNO) of the DoD. This includes network operation and information assurance for the various branches of the DoD, including the Joint Chiefs of Staff (JCS). Providing high-level advice to the DoD is an important function of DISA. Constantly changing conditions involving IT require up-to-date research into new technologies and trends, and they possess the education and resources to be able to do this for the DoD. DISA offers an important service to the DoD, as they offer advice and support to military leaders who may not have any background in IT or Internet-security issues.

Response to the various threats from both state and nonstate actors to the DoD's CNO at bases and installations all over the world, including the GIG, falls to DISA. Tracking these threats has become more difficult, as both state and nonstate actors have attempted to hack DoD network systems, including the CNO. It is simply no longer enough for the DoD to worry about other nations when it comes to cyber threats. Nonstate actors now have the ability to hack DoD network systems and have caused major disruptions to military communications and technology. The motivations of these nonstate actors can range from social concerns, terrorism, and patriotic intentions in times of conflict. Covert support from other groups or governments may be the motivation for these cyber attacks. Stopping these attacks is very difficult, especially if they come from another nation. The DoD can rarely track hackers outside the United States. DISA must support efforts to put in place measures to stop attacks before they happen and advise the entire DoD of the need for security for its CNO.

The U.S. military has increasingly become dependent on information technology (IT) to run its communications and military hardware; therefore, cyber security has become a very important element of military defense. This technology must be protected from hacking attempts. Hackers can use software to gain control of the IT in military weapons and shut them down or destroy them. This challenge is very difficult for DISA, as new cyber threats appear every day. Prevention is the only effective method of stopping attacks. As DISA provides support for the entire DoD, all manner of threats must be investigated. Defensive measures against them need to set up to protect the large number of weapons and communications systems relying on IT and related hardware. The DoD, with advice from DISA, has purchased commercial off-the-shelf technology. This leaves them vulnerable to attacks from hackers, who can learn the technology more easily than proprietary equipment made especially for the DoD. The need to keep expenditures down is the reason for these purchases, but they open up American military forces to more cyber-based threats.

The DoD has many intelligence subdepartments, and IT is an important part of each. Today's intelligence agencies rely on IT to gather information on threats to the United States and its troops and bases aboard. DISA provides advice and technology for these intelligence activities and is therefore crucial to protecting the DoD and its activities.

Brad St. Croix

See also: Attribution; Cyber Defense; Department of Defense (DoD); Patriotic Hacking

Further Reading

Bryen, Stephen D. *Technology Security and National Power: Winners and Losers.* New Brunswick, NJ: Transaction Publishers, 2016.
Carr, Jeffery. *Inside Cyber Warfare.* 2nd ed. Sebastopol, CA: O'Reilly Media, 2012.

DEPARTMENT OF DEFENSE (DOD)

The Department of Defense (DoD) is one of the three major cyber actors in the U.S. government. The others are the Department of Homeland Security (DHS) and Department of Justice (DOJ). The DoD's mission is to secure the nation's freedom of action in cyber space and help mitigate risks to national security resulting from America's growing dependence on cyber space. Specific mission sets include directing, securing, and defending the DoD Information Network (DODIN) operations (including the dot.mil domain); maintaining freedom of maneuver in cyber space; executing full-spectrum military cyber-space operations; providing shared situational awareness of cyber-space operations, including indications and warning; and providing support to civil authorities and international partners. DoD articulates its cyber policy through *The DoD Cyber Strategy*, from April 2015, and Joint Publication 3-12, *Cyberspace Operations*, from February 2013. DoD's operations are designed to achieve and maintain cyber-space superiority, defined as "the degree of dominance in cyberspace by one force that permits the secure, reliable conduct of operations by that force, and its related land, air, maritime, and space forces at a given time and place without prohibitive interference by an adversary."

DoD organizations are allowed to perform defensive cyber operations; however, full-spectrum cyber operations (including offensive cyber operations) must be approved by the president and directed by the secretary of defense. Combatant commands provide operation instructions and command and control to the armed forces and have a significant impact on how they are organized, trained, and resourced—areas over which Congress has constitutional authority. Combatant commands share cyber information, largely through U.S. Cyber Command (USCYBERCOM) and their own joint cyber centers, but various personnel also meet periodically to share information in collaboration sessions.

The National Security Agency (NSA) is the nation's cryptologic organization that coordinates, directs, and performs highly specialized activities to protect U.S. information systems and to produce foreign signals intelligence information. It supports military customers, national policy makers, and the counterterrorism and counterintelligence communities as well as key international allies. The NSA also shares information about software vulnerabilities with vendors and users in any commercial product or system (not just software) used by the United States and its allies, with an emphasis on risk mitigation and defense.

The Defense Information Systems Agency (DISA) provides, operates, and assures command and control, information-sharing capabilities, and a globally accessible enterprise information infrastructure in direct support to joint warfighters, national-level leaders, and other mission and coalition partners across the full spectrum of operations. They are overall responsible for DODIN. Each service also has its own equivalent to DISA that operates its part of DODIN. The DoD Cyber Crime Center (DC3) delivers superior digital forensics and multimedia laboratory services, cyber technical training, research, development, testing and evaluation, and cyber-analysis capabilities supporting cyber counterintelligence and counterterrorism, criminal investigations, intrusion forensics, law enforcement, the Intelligence Community, critical infrastructure partners, and information operations for the DoD.

USCYBERCOM was formed in 2010 by consolidating two U.S. Strategic Command (USSTRATCOM) subordinate organizations: the Joint Functional Component Command–Network Warfare and Joint Task Force–Global Network Operations. It is a subunified command under USSTRATCOM. USCYBERCOM plans, coordinates, integrates, synchronizes, and conducts activities to direct the operations and defense of specified DODIN. It also prepares, when directed, to conduct full-spectrum military cyber-space operations to enable actions in all domains, ensure U.S. and allied freedom of action in cyber space, and deny the same to adversaries.

USCYBERCOM's main instrument of power consists of the Cyber National Mission Force, which conducts cyber-space operations to disrupt and deny adversary attacks against national critical infrastructure. It is the U.S. military's first joint tactical command with a dedicated mission focused on cyber-space operations. It plans to create 133 cyber mission teams by the end of fiscal year 2018.

The plan is for these 133 teams to consist of 13 national mission teams to defend the United States and its interests against cyber attacks of significant consequence by performing full-spectrum cyber operations; 68 cyber protection teams to defend priority DoD networks and systems against priority threats; 25 support teams to provide analytic and planning support to the national and combat mission teams; and 27 combat mission teams to provide support to combatant commands by generating integrated cyber-space effects in support of operational plans and contingency operations. They are similar to the national mission teams, but rather than serving at the national level, they conduct cyber-space operations to achieve combatant commanders' objectives and are geographically and functionally aligned under one of four Joint Force Headquarters–Cyber (JFHQ-C) in direct support of geographic and functional combatant commands:

- JFHQ-C Washington supports U.S. Special Operations Command, U.S. Pacific Command, and U.S. Southern Command.
- JFHQ-C Georgia supports U.S. Central Command, U.S. Africa Command, and U.S. Northern Command.
- JFHQ-C Texas supports U.S. European Command, USSTRATCOM, and U.S. Transportation Command.
- JFHQ-DODIN defends DoD information networks at USCYBERCOM.

The services provide component commands under CYBERCOM that also function as the cyber organization for each service. Under their Title 10 U.S. Code role as force providers to the combatant commanders, the services recruit, train, educate, and retain the military cyber force. These are Second Army/Army Cyber Command; Tenth Fleet; 24th Air Force; and U.S. Marine Corps Forces Cyber Command.

DoD conducts operations through the combatant commands. The services provide forces for the combatant commands. Each combatant command has component commands representing each service, for example, Central Command has Army Central Command (ARCENT) and Air Forces Central Command (AFCENT). Cyber operations are planned either at the national level or in a combatant command. The Cyber National Mission Force conducts national-level operations, while combatant commands and their subordinate units plan and conduct operations at the regional and local levels. Combatant commands have joint cyber centers that are responsible for planning cyber operations, and the forces in their respective JFHQ-Cs execute the plans. Although there are stand-alone cyber operations, most cyber operations are designed to be a part of an integrated holistic plan designed to achieve a certain effect.

G. Alexander Crowther

Portions of this entry have been previously published as G. Alexander Crowther and Shaheen Ghori, "Detangling the Web: A Screenshot of U.S. Government Cyber Activity." Joint Force Quarterly 78, July 1, 2015.

See also: Cyber Defense; National Cyber Security Strategy; National Security Agency (NSA); Second Army/Army Cyber Command; 24th Air Force; U.S. Cyber Command (USCYBERCOM); U.S. Tenth Fleet

Further Reading

Clarke, Richard A., and Robert K. Knake. *Cyber War: The Next Threat to National Security and What to Do about It.* New York: HarperCollins, 2010.

Kramer, Franklin D., Stuart H. Starr, and Larry K. Wentz, ed. *Cyberpower and National Security.* Washington, D.C.: National Defense University Press, 2009.

Reveron, Derek S., ed. *Cyberspace and National Security: Threats, Opportunities, and Power in a Virtual World.* Washington, D.C.: Georgetown University Press, 2012.

Singer, P. W., and Allan Friedman. *Cybersecurity and Cyberwar: What Everyone Needs to Know.* New York: Cambridge University Press, 2014.

DEPARTMENT OF ENERGY (DOE)

The Department of Energy (DOE) was founded on August 4, 1977, bringing together the nuclear weapons program of the U.S. military with federal energy programs. The DOE is responsible for the energy infrastructure of the United States, including the nuclear energy program as well as coal, solar, and other forms of energy production. They are also responsible for protecting the nuclear arsenal of the U.S. military and the material needed to ensure its continued operation. The DOE is also tasked with the security of nuclear materials at civilian, naval, and nuclear weapons complex facilities. The DOE must also support policy makers in all national security agencies in regard to nuclear security, providing information and expertise on energy-related issues. They provide important information on threats to the power grid, both physical and cyber, and to the nuclear weapons with other intelligence agencies to coordinate resources.

The security of these programs is an important part of the DOE's day-to-day activities. DOE's intelligence branches are required to handle both the cyber and physical security of the U.S. energy infrastructure. As the centers of energy production have become increasingly reliant on information technology for daily operations, cyber security must be continually monitored. The power grid can be shut down for days because of a cyber attack, and important equipment can take months to fix or replace. Preventing attacks before they begin is critical, as any downtime of the power grid could have large political, economic, and military effects on the United States.

The DOE has its own intelligence and counterintelligence branch. The Office of Intelligence and Counterintelligence collects and analyzes information in the fields of nuclear terrorism, counterintelligence, cyber threats, nuclear proliferation, strategic surprise, and energy and environmental security. It specializes in longer term, strategic perspectives on energy issues and their security. The need for an intelligence agency to monitor American energy concerns began with the Manhattan Project during World War II. It continued by tracking the Soviet atomic weapons program and evolved to track other nations and groups in their attempts to build nuclear weapons or obtain the materials needed to make nuclear weapons. Exports of nuclear material is tightly controlled by the DOE, along with other federal departments, to prevent the material from going to potentially dangerous state and nonstate actors. They also track foreign threats to the economic and military elements of the power grid, such as e-commerce.

Brad St. Croix

See also: Cyber Defense; Cyber Terrorism; Infrastructure

Further Reading

Kerschischnig, Georg. *Cyberthreats and International Law.* The Hague, Netherlands: Eleven International Publishing, 2012.

Kraft, Michael B., and Edward Marks. *U.S. Government Counterterrorism: A Guide to Who Does What.* Boca Raton, FL: CRC Press, 2012.

DEPARTMENT OF HOMELAND SECURITY (DHS)

The Department of Homeland Security (DHS) was established on November 25, 2002, by the Homeland Security Act of 2002 (Public Law 107-296). Composed of all or part of 22 different federal agencies, DHS became operational on March 1, 2003, under the leadership of former Pennsylvania governor and homeland security adviser Tom Ridge. Its headquarters are at the Nebraska Avenue Complex in Washington, D.C.

DHS has the lead for the federal government in securing civilian government computer systems, and it works with industry and state, local, tribal, and territorial governments to secure critical infrastructure and information systems. DHS works to analyze and reduce cyber threats and vulnerabilities, distribute threat warnings, and coordinate the response to cyber incidents to ensure that our computers, networks, and cyber systems remain safe.

The following DHS operational and support components perform key cyber missions: National Protection and Programs (NPPD) Directorate; Science and Technology (S&T) Directorate; U.S. Coast Guard (USCG); U.S. Immigration and Customs Enforcement (ICE); U.S. Secret Service (USSS); U.S. Customs and Border Protection (CBP); the Federal Emergency Management Agency (FEMA); and the Transportation Security Administration (TSA).

NPPD leads DHS's efforts to protect and enhance the resilience of the nation's physical and cyber infrastructure and is headed by the under secretary for the

National Protection and Programs Directorate. Cyber components of NPPD include the Office of Cybersecurity and Communications (CS&C) and the Office of Cyber & Infrastructure Analysis (OCIA).

DHS's S&T Directorate formally established the Cyber Security Division (CSD) within S&T's Homeland Security Advanced Research Projects Agency (HSARPA) in 2011. CSD's mission is to enhance the security and resilience of the nation's critical information infrastructure and the Internet by (1) developing and delivering new technologies, tools, and techniques to enable DHS and the United States to defend, mitigate, and secure current and future systems, networks, and infrastructure against cyber attacks; (2) conduct and support technology transition; and (3) lead and coordinate research and development (R&D) among the R&D community, which includes department customers, government agencies, the private sector, and international partners.

The USCG protects maritime critical infrastructure from online threats through the Coast Guard Cyber Command (CGCYBER). To operate effectively within the cyber domain and to counter and protect against maritime cyber threats over the next decade, the Coast Guard's 2015 Cyber Strategy emphasizes three strategic priorities: defending cyber space, enabling operations, and protecting infrastructure.

ICE's Cyber Crimes Center (C3) delivers computer-based technical services to support domestic and international investigations into cross border crime. C3 is made up of the Cyber Crimes Unit, the Child Exploitation Investigations Unit, and the Computer Forensics Unit. This state-of-the-art center offers cyber-crime support and training to federal, state, local, and international law enforcement agencies. C3 also operates a fully equipped computer forensics laboratory, which specializes in digital evidence recovery, and offers training in computer investigative and forensic skills.

The USSS maintains Electronic Crimes Task Forces (ECTFs), which focus on identifying and locating international cyber criminals connected to cyber intrusions, bank fraud, data breaches, and other computer-related crimes. The ECTFs also bring together not only federal, state, and local law enforcement but also prosecutors, private industry, and academia. The Secret Service's Cyber Intelligence Section has directly contributed to the arrest of transnational cyber criminals responsible for the theft of hundreds of millions of credit card numbers. The Secret Service also runs the National Computer Forensic Institute, which provides law enforcement officers, prosecutors, and judges with cyber training and information to combat cyber crime.

CBP's cyber mission is to protect U.S. businesses from intellectual property theft, while FEMA's cyber mission is to maintain the Ready.gov Web site, which provides tips about cyber and all hazards preparedness. FEMA also facilitates National Level Exercises (NLEs), some of which have cyber components, to test emergency readiness. TSA's cyber mission is to assess and update cyber-security protocols and programs to ensure the protection of both public and private data sources.

Jim Dolbow

See also: Cyber Crime; Cyber Terrorism; National Infrastructure Protection Plan (NIPP); U.S. Coast Guard Cyber Command (CGCYBER)

Further Reading

Reveron, Derek S., ed. *Cyberspace and National Security: Threats, Opportunities, and Power in a Virtual World*. Washington, D.C.: Georgetown University Press, 2012.

U.S. Department of Homeland Security. *Blueprint for a Secure Cyber Future: The Cybersecurity Strategy for the Homeland Security Enterprise*. Washington, D.C., 2011.

U.S. Coast Guard. *United States Coast Guard Strategy*. Washington, D.C., 2015.

DEPARTMENT OF JUSTICE (DOJ)

The Department of Justice (DOJ) is one of the three major cyber actors in the U.S. government. They investigate, attribute, disrupt, and prosecute cyber crimes; lead domestic national security operations; conduct domestic collection, analysis, and dissemination of cyber threat intelligence; support the national protection, prevention, mitigation of, and recovery from cyber incidents; and coordinate cyber-threat investigations.

The department's goals are articulated in the 2014–2018 strategy. The number one goal is to "prevent terrorism and promote the nation's security consistent with the rule of law," which contains the department's cyber efforts. They combat cyber-based threats and attacks through the use of all available tools, strong public-private partnerships, and the investigation and prosecution of cyber-threat actors.

The Federal Bureau of investigation (FBI) leads the national effort to investigate high-tech crimes, including cyber-based terrorism, espionage, computer intrusions, and major cyber fraud by gathering and sharing information and intelligence with public- and private-sector partners worldwide. Its Cyber Division brings together various FBI cyber initiatives and missions and has placed cyber task forces in all 56 field offices.

The Cyber Action Team (CAT) is the investigative rapid response team that can be on scene anywhere in the world within 48 hours, bringing in-depth cyber-intrusion expertise and specialized investigative skills to bear. The CAT provides support to local field offices. The FBI is also the executive agent for the National Cyber Investigative Joint Task Force (NCIJTF), the focal point for government agencies to coordinate, integrate, and share information related to domestic cyber-threat investigations. Partners include the National Security Agency (NSA), Central Intelligence Agency (CIA), Secret Service, DHS, and U.S. Cyber Command (USCYBERCOM). Its mission areas include coordinating whole-of-government campaigns against known cyber threats, exploiting valuable cyber data, analyzing and reporting on that data, applying traditional financial investigative approaches to the cyber domain, and maintaining an around-the-clock cyber incident management watch.

The Justice Department's National Security Division and Criminal Division each concentrate on their own cyber issues. The division deals with cyber-based threats to national security. It created the National Security Cyber Specialist network that is a new tool in the government's cyber toolkit and a critical part of the department's efforts to better address cyber intrusions and attacks carried out by nation-states or terrorist organizations.

The Computer Crime and Intellectual Property Section (CCIPS) implements Justice's national cyber strategy. CCIPS prevents, investigates, and prosecutes computer crimes by working with other government agencies, the private sector, academic institutions, and foreign counterparts. CCIPS attorneys regularly run complex investigations; resolve unique legal and investigative issues raised by emerging computer and telecommunications technologies; litigate cases; provide litigation support to other prosecutors; train federal, state, and local law enforcement personnel; comment on and propose legislation; and initiate and participate in international efforts to combat computer and intellectual property crime.

The Offices of the U.S. Attorneys is the last major part of Justice that works cyber issues. One of their ten priority areas is cyber crime. Their four areas of concentration are Internet stalking, computer hacking, intellectual property rights, and forensics. They also assist the National Computer Forensics Institute.

G. Alexander Crowther

Portions of this entry have been previously published as G. Alexander Crowther and Shaheen Ghori, "Detangling the Web: A Screenshot of U.S. Government Cyber Activity." Joint Force Quarterly 78, July 1, 2015.

See also: Cyber Crime; Department of Homeland Security (DHS); Federal Bureau of Investigation (FBI); U.S. Cyber Command (USCYBERCOM)

Further Reading

Brenner, Joel. *America the Vulnerable: Inside the New Threat Matrix of Digital Espionage, Crime, and Warfare.* New York: Penguin Press, 2011.

U.S. Department of Justice. *Department of Justice Strategic Plan Fiscal Years 2014–2018.* www.justice.gov/about/strategic-plan-fiscalyears-2014-2018.

DISTRIBUTED DENIAL-OF-SERVICE (DDOS) ATTACK

Distributed Denial of Service (DDoS) attacks are an attack against system or resource availability. They can be thought of as a form of intentional "flash crowd," whereby a large number of entities simultaneously seek access to a limited resource, thereby causing it to become temporarily unavailable for everyone. The most common version, a network DDoS, seeks to saturate a target's network links such that there is insufficient bandwidth for legitimate communications. The attackers take advantage of the fact that modern packet-switched networks (such as the Internet) rely on statistical multiplexing and best-effort communications, which means that there are no guarantees provided on the timely or eventual delivery of data.

Many communication protocols, including the Transmission Control Protocol (TCP), have mechanisms to detect congestion in the network and take measures to alleviate it (typically by reducing the data transmission rate), under the implicit assumption that congestion is a naturally occurring event. Such mechanisms make it significantly easier for a DDoS attack to achieve the desired effect.

The difference between a flash crowd and a DDoS attack primarily lies in that the latter is coordinated by a single malicious entity, whereas a flash crowd is the manifestation of uncoordinated, and usually benign, actors acting independently toward the same (but not shared) objective, such as accessing a popular piece of content (news article, song, etc.). Although it is possible to coordinate large numbers of human users toward launching a denial-of-service attack, the most common form of such attacks involves the use of botnets.

The precise resource that is exhausted depends on the specifics of the underlying network infrastructure and the attack itself and may involve link capacity, router buffers, router processing and forwarding capacity or memory, or end host processing or memory resources. In all cases, exhaustion of that resource causes service degradation (e.g., through dropped packets) for all clients. The simplest version of a DDoS attack involves a large number of end hosts sending packets as fast as they can toward the target, exhausting one or more of the previously mentioned resources. One challenge with defending against DDoS attacks is that the exhausted resource may lie outside the target's network (e.g., in the upstream Internet service provider's infrastructure), which requires coordination between the entity affected (target) and the entity that can potentially mitigate the attack (ISP).

DDoS attacks are perhaps the easiest type of attack to launch; they often do not even require that the target be contacted, as the exhausted resource may be outside its network or firewall perimeter. The main difficulty in launching such attacks lies in acquiring a large number of hosts that can be induced to send packets to the target. However, the emergence of DDoS-as-a-service in recent years has reduced the barrier to entry, at least for the most common attacks. DDoS services are a form of malicious cloud computing, whereby the service providers are responsible for acquiring and managing a large number of compromised computers, which are then rented out to their customers for the purpose of launching DDoS attacks.

DDoS attacks often make use of source address spoofing so that simple packet filtering becomes infeasible. Even when spoofing is not used, the use of a large number of attack hosts means that it is difficult to easily distinguish and filter malicious traffic from legitimate traffic. Given a large enough botnet, it may in fact be impossible to differentiate between attack and legitimate traffic, as all remote hosts may appear to faithfully adhere to network protocol behavior (including backing off due to congestion). For attacks involving fewer hosts that are transmitting more aggressively, it may be possible to filter out attack traffic using behavioral heuristics.

Mirroring the emergence of DDoS-as-a-service, there exist DDoS-protection-as-a-service providers that act as intermediaries between legitimate sites and their users (including potential attackers). Such providers use a number of mitigation techniques, including network address reputation management, Completely Automated Public Turing test to tell Computers and Humans Apart (CAPTCHA), and various heuristics, to determine which network connections are legitimate (or at least are tightly coupled with a human user) and to drop or rate limit all others. These providers have a number of distributed data centers with very good connectivity to make DDoS attacks against them impractical. Other defenses against DDoS attacks include the use of TCP cookies and content delivery networks (CDNs).

Angelos D. Keromytis

See also: Anonymous; Botnet; Cyber Attack; Estonian Cyber Attack (2007); Georgian Cyber Attack (2008); Malware; Spoofing

Further Reading

Libicki, Martin. *Cyberspace in Peace and War.* Annapolis, MD: U.S. Naval Institute Press, 2016.

Springer, Paul J. *Cyber Warfare: A Reference Handbook.* Santa Barbara, CA: ABC-CLIO, 2015.

DOMAIN NAME SYSTEM (DNS)

The Domain Name System (DNS) is a distributed collection of servers containing databases of host and user identifications and their corresponding Internet Protocol (IP) addresses. DNS enables users to perform such actions as finding Web sites or sending e-mail messages using domain names (such as [name].com) rather than a string of numerals representing an IP address (such as 162.11.24.17).

The idea for DNS developed in the early 1980s, when the development of Transmission Control Protocol/Internet Protocol (TCP/IP) enabled computer networks to communicate with one another. The rapid growth of the *Internet* complicated the ability of host computers to locate other hosts. For instance, hosts on two different networks may have had the same name, so it would be difficult to determine which IP address was the correct one. Now that the networks were connected, there needed to be a way to differentiate such hosts.

In August 1982, Zaw-Sing Su of the Stanford Research Institute (SRI) and Jon Postel of the Information Sciences Institute (ISI) at the University of Southern California (USC) published Request for Comments (RFC) 819, in which they proposed an *Internet naming convention* to establish an administrative hierarchy for Internet names. Instead of simply identifying a destination host computer, data would be sent to addresses based on a *domain*, which would include different layers of information indicating the precise location of the recipient.

In November 1983, Paul Mockapetris of ISI developed this idea further. In RFC 882, he laid out the concept of a distributed database of name servers and a consistent naming structure. He elaborated on the concept in RFC 883, proposing the development of programs called *resolvers*. These resolvers would respond to user queries by searching various name servers until they located the appropriate address. The name servers would update their databases periodically, based on locally stored *master files*, and store search information in caches to assist in future queries.

An informal committee of network designers discussed and debated what the top-level domains should be. Seven were eventually selected: com (commercial organization); edu (educational institution); int (international agency); gov (U.S.

government agency); mil (U.S. military agency); net (network organization); and org (other organization). In 1986, with the endorsement of the Defense Advanced Research Projects Agency (DARPA), whose network (ARPANET) was the original central hub of the Internet, DNS became the locating system for the major computer networks.

Today, DNS typically operates in a seamless manner. When a user searches for a Web site by typing in a domain name in the universal resource locator (URL) of a Web browser, the resolver sends out a query to the local name server, which may either access the site or forward the query on to another name server until the site is located. Occasionally, an IP address is changed before the DNS cache has been updated, resulting in an error message.

Christopher G. Marquis

See also: ARPANET; Defense Advanced Research Projects Agency (DARPA); Hardware; Internet; Server; Transmission Control Protocol/Internet Protocol (TCP/IP)

Further Reading

Abbate, Janet. *Inventing the Internet.* Cambridge, MA: The MIT Press, 2000.
Hafner, Katie, and Matthew Lyon. *Where Wizards Stay Up Late: The Origins of the Internet.* New York: Simon & Schuster, 1996.

E-COMMERCE

E-commerce is a loosely defined term that denotes the conduct of business by electronic means, chiefly via the Internet. E-commerce is a recent invention that has rapidly become one of the most important sectors of the modern economy, restructuring financial and business infrastructure. Billions of dollars are exchanged every day around the globe in purely electronic transactions, both legal and illegal.

E-commerce proper dates to the 1980s. When networks became available to the public via phone lines, businesses quickly began to move into the digital realm to sell products and services, both to each other and to customers. However, the major advance in the field took place in the following decade, as online banking profited from the development of the SSL protocol that enabled online transactions to be encrypted. This caused an explosion in e-commerce as millions of customers began to purchase goods and services online rather than in person, including from electronic versions of physical stores.

During the 1990s and 2000s, most significant e-commerce companies appeared, representing different forms of the medium. Amazon and Alibaba are traditional one-stop stores that sell physical and electronic products. EBay is an online auction house for conducting business directly between buyer and seller. Apple's iTunes Store sells digital music via its iTunes app and is now the world's largest music retailer. E-commerce also provides the possibility of entirely new forms of commerce, particularly on-demand services. Netflix, which launched in 1998, is the best example of such a business. The company functioned much like a traditional video-rental service until 2008, when it opened a streaming video service. Similarly, streaming radio and music services such as Pandora and Spotify developed to allow users to stream music partially or wholly on demand. All of these companies offer subscriptions to pay licensing and infrastructure costs, but many also offer free ad-based streaming as well, mimicking both the cable-subscription and broadcast-revenue models.

The transition to electronic commerce has naturally produced a shift away from traditional payment methods. Smartphones equipped with electronic wallets began to replace debit and credit cards after 2010. Online banking has eliminated much of the need to visit the physical location; for example, checks can be deposited via app rather than physically being deposited in the bank. Electronic currencies have also appeared, with varying degrees of success. The most famous is Bitcoin, a digital currency system developed around 2008.

The rise of e-commerce has also taken place outside traditional and legal channels. As e-commerce exploded in the 1990s, so did illegal and quasi-legal forms. One of the first that the general American public became aware of was the peer-to-peer network called Napster, which launched in 1999. It allowed its users to digitally share files. This often took the form of music files, which violated copyright laws and led to Napster's closure.

The Napster issue launched an international debate about piracy, ownership, and commerce in the digital era. Music piracy was merely one element of the new illegal e-commerce. The ability to conceal or falsify identities drew many criminals to e-commerce for every variety of crime. Entire portions of the Internet, called the deep web and the dark web, are unavailable to traditional users because they do not appear in search indexing. While law enforcement authorities have become more savvy to e-commerce methods, like shutting down the many versions of Silk Road, the proliferation of the field has led to a sharp increase in such crimes.

The proliferation of e-commerce has influenced cyber warfare in indirect but important ways. E-commerce has connected billions of people and businesses to each other, providing trillions of opportunities for theft, espionage, and other forms of mayhem. For example, the TJX Corporation attack of 2006–2007 compromised millions of T.J. Maxx customers' financial and identity information. Defense against cyber attacks remains difficult at best, considering that the defensive force must act against all possible threats, while the offensive only needs a single vulnerability. E-commerce provides such vulnerabilities: identity theft, espionage, direct influences on kinetic operations, and others. The most important is likely the sale and exchange of illegal weapons and technology via e-commerce. Domestic terrorists in America could buy automatic weapons or biological or chemical agents via dark web retailers. Perhaps more threateningly, terrorist groups such as the Islamic State could do the same. They could also use such methods, traditional and nontraditional, to conduct legal business, steal money, gather espionage, and dozens of other activities. Cyber criminals can easily become cyber terrorists or cyber mercenaries. As a result, nonstate actors and even individuals now have power once reserved to states to wreak havoc, digitally and physically.

Jonathan Abel

See also: Bitcoin; Cyber Attack; Cyber Crime; Cyber Security; Dark Web; Deep Web; Google; Hacker; Identity Theft; Silk Road; The Onion Router (TOR); TJX Corporation Hack

Further Reading

Bartlett, Jamie. *The Dark Net: Inside the Digital Underworld.* New York: Melville House, 2015.
Brenner, Susan W. *Cyberthreats and the Decline of the Nation-state.* New York: Routledge, 2014.
Laudon, Kenneth, and Carol Traver. *E-commerce 2016: Business, Technology, Society.* New York: Pearson College Division, 2016.

EINSTEIN (CYBER SYSTEM)

EINSTEIN is a conglomeration of cyber-security systems managed by the Department of Homeland Security (DHS). Its purpose is to protect federal executive branch information systems. EINSTEIN has developed incrementally, first to observe network traffic and assist in investigating hacks, later adding traffic-blocking functionality, and recently layering commercial-security measures on top of existing infrastructure. It is not meant to mitigate all possible attacks, but rather provide an effective baseline perimeter defense.

EINSTEIN was created under the purview of the Department of Homeland Security's computer emergency response team (US-CERT) in 2003 to fulfil obligations imposed by the Federal Information Security Management Act (FISMA) of 2002. FISMA sought to create a minimum level of information-security controls and provide a mechanism for oversight into the protection of federal information and information-security programs. Its baseline configuration in 2003 was as a confederation of intrusion detection systems (IDS—EINSTEIN 1) to scan and log traffic. When malicious traffic was detected, the US-CERT coordinated the investigation with responsible government agencies. Since its creation in 2003, EINSTEIN has undergone two major changes: federating the enterprise (EINSTEIN 2) and then adding both signature-based blocking as well as commercially sourced malware blocking (EINSTEIN 3). In 2008, President Bush launched the Comprehensive National Cybersecurity Initiative (CNCI) through National Security Policy Directive (NSPD) 54/Homeland Security Policy Directive (HSPD) 23. This directive sought to unify the disparate federal network system into one enterprise managed by DHS. Additionally, it directed implementation of traffic blocking by signature. Essentially, signature-based intrusion prevention systems (IPS) use the data gathered by the IDS to fingerprint the malware, gathering indicators of its use and subsequently blocking all traffic that appears malignant.

In 2014, changes to FISMA and the EINSTEIN concept led to the implementation of the EINSTEIN 3 Accelerated (E3A) architecture. As part of a new National Cybersecurity Protection System (NCPS), E3A adds commercial malicious traffic blocking to existing government-managed architecture and is thought to afford flexibility in capabilities, as the contracts are renegotiated periodically. Generally, the system is deployed in the Border Gateway Protocol (BGP) backbone of the Internet between autonomous systems. This position allows the sensors that comprise EINSTEIN to observe "over 90 percent of all federal civilian Internet traffic." Despite this statistic, DHS secretary Jeh Johnson pointed out that implementation remains a challenge, as DHS may not mandate its use by other agencies or departments. According to Johnson, before the Office of Personnel Management (OPM) hack in January 2015, only 20 percent of the federal executive enterprise was covered by E3A. In 2016, this number is still only approximately 50 percent.

In 2014, an amendment to FISMA reinforced the roles of both the Office of Management and Budget (OMB) as well as DHS in setting policy and ensuring federal information security. This amendment also established the role of the Government Accountability Office (GAO) in assisting all parties in auditing cybersecurity practices. In 2015, operating under its responsibilities delineated in the amended FISMA, GAO conducted an assessment of the NCPS and the EINSTEIN system. Ultimately, it determined that the system was not meeting its stated objectives. GAO identified several key concerns with its technical efficacy, including its ability to detect known exploits and prevent intrusions into federal computer systems. GAO also highlighted that DHS had not implemented a bulk of its stated information-sharing mechanisms, leaving gaps in confederated architecture.

The recommendations of the GAO report focused on expanding the efficacy of EINSTEIN. As noted in the GAO report, EINSTEIN does not have any contextual understanding of appropriate network behavior, nor does it have visibility of other key technologies such as industrial control systems (ICS) or Internet Protocol version 6 (IPv6). GAO also recommended that EINSTEIN focus on rapid collaboration with industry and customer federal agencies to effectively share threat intelligence and understand risks posed. Addressing the first point will most likely be challenging in the near term, as behavioral malware detection is not mature. The second point, though, is being addressed by DHS via its System Engineering and Development Institute (SEDI). SEDI is working with the broader community of interest to create a robust framework of mechanisms and standards to address this foundational issue. Structured Threat Information eXpression (STIX), Trusted Automated eXchange of Indicator Information (TAXII), and Cyber Observable eXpression (CybOX) are the three DHS projects aimed at increasing technical efficacy of information sharing in response to the challenges facing EINSTEIN.

As part of its mandate to secure the nation, DHS, via US-CERT, has begun providing resources for state, local, tribal, and territorial (SLTT) governments to assist with local cyber security. As part of this effort, DHS has offered EINSTEIN as a template for other governmental cyber-security efforts under the auspices of the Critical Infrastructure Cyber Community Voluntary Program (C^{3}VP). DHS, partnered with the Center for Internet Security (CIS), has established managed security services (MSS) as a service to SLTT governments. This has led to the establishment of the Multi-State Information Sharing and Analysis Center (MS-ISAC) and the locally focused "Albert System."

Spencer Calder

See also: Comprehensive National Cybersecurity Initiative (CNCI); Computer Emergency Response Team (CERT); Cyber Defense; Department of Homeland Security (DHS); National Cyber Security Strategy; Office of Personnel Management Data Breach

Further Reading

Hayden, Michael V. *Playing to the Edge: American Intelligence in the Age of Terror.* London: Penguin Press, 2016.

Kaplan, Fred. *Dark Territory: The Secret History of Cyber-war.* New York: Simon and Schuster, 2016.

Savage, Charles, et al. "Hunting for Hackers, N.S.A. Secretly Expands Internet Spying at U.S. Border." *New York Times,* June 4, 2015.

ELECTROMAGNETIC PULSE (EMP)

The term *electromagnetic pulse* is wide-ranging in its definition and scope. Generally, the term refers to a short burst of electromagnetic energy. This energy can be generated by nature or through man-made means. When it comes to man-made EMP effects, they can be generated by nuclear and nonnuclear means. EMP can further be broken down into the types of energy generated: electric, magnetic, electromagnetic radiation, and electric conduction. With each of these, there is an associated effect on electrical devices that can range from short dwell distributions to widespread outages of electrical systems. Common natural occurrences of EMP range from low-level static discharges up to lightning strikes. While lightning strikes generate high-current pulses that can damage electric equipment, low-level static discharges can also be devastating, such as when a discharge from a cell phone ignites gasoline vapors.

In 1962, the United States had its only direct experience with a man-made EMP derived from a nuclear weapon. A nuclear detonation in the Pacific Ocean generated electrical outages in Hawaii, which at the time had antiquated electronics. In today's world, with the prevalence of the Internet, cell phones, and tablets, a nuclear-generated EMP would have more devastating effects. The worst and most far-reaching effects would come from a high-altitude EMP (HEMP) with effects that can attenuate throughout the atmosphere. EMP effects can also come from the gamma rays released in a nuclear explosion, which can strip electrons from atoms, leaving those atoms free to attach to electric devices, rendering the devices useless. Protecting important equipment from an EMP can involve heavy shielding, such as the use of a Faraday cage, or mechanisms to ground electrical currents before they cause damage.

Melvin G. Deaile

See also: Infrastructure; Weapons of Mass Disruption

Further Reading

Glasstone, Samuel, and Philip J. Dolan. *The Effects of Nuclear Weapons.* Washington, D.C.: U.S. Department of Defense, 1977.

ENCRYPTION

Encryption is the transformation of information into a form that is only readable by those it is intended for to prevent interception, loss, or theft. Encryption predates electronic computing, but with the advent of increasing information transfer over computer networks, encryption increasingly features in public debate on individual privacy and civil liberties. There are numerous types of encryption.

Symmetric encryption takes plaintext and transforms it so that it is unreadable and then decrypts it back into a readable form. As with all techniques, a key (password, special file, or device) facilitates an algorithm to achieve encryption and decryption. In symmetric encryption, both the encrypter and the decrypter require access to the same key. A fundamental drawback of symmetric encryption is the need to store a key and make it available only to the software that needs it; if the key is transmitted unprotected over a network and intercepted, the encryption is compromised. Symmetric encryption is commonly utilized in cloud backup services that transfer the decryption key to the end user.

In asymmetric encryption, a different key is used for each end. Encrypters use a public key (literally available to the public; accordingly, this technique is referred to as *public key encryption*) to encrypt the data, with a matching private key on the other end to decrypt the data into readable form. Similar to symmetric encryption, the private key must be protected, but the advantage is that only one party ever needs access to the private key; thus, the encryption is less prone to interception, loss, or theft. A further feature of asymmetric encryption is the ability to cryptographically sign data; that is, the private key is used to create a signature, and the public key is used to verify it, thus confirming its authenticity. Asymmetric encryption is used to establish secure connections between browser and Web site, to secure log-in sessions to remote servers, and to verify software updates are from a trusted party. One drawback of using asymmetric encryption is the necessity of trusting the public key and avoiding a man-in-the-middle attack. In a man-in-the-middle attack, a user unwittingly accepts a key from a third party who then supplies the other end user with a further false key, in the pretense that it is the victim who has supplied that key. In this attack, the man in the middle can decrypt protected data, reencrypt it with the real public key, and then use a similar process in the other direction to gain access to unprotected plaintext data. As a consequence, public keys should only be accepted when distributed as part of trusted software or by having authenticated third parties sign or certify new keys. For example, HTTPS sites send signed public keys to browsers that they can then trust to secure the connection.

Hashing is not strictly a form of encryption; instead, it takes data and creates a string of data out of it (a hash) that includes three properties: the same data always produces the same hash, the hash cannot revert back to its original form, and it is impossible to create another string of data capable of repeating the same hash (provided the user only has knowledge of the original hash). Hashing is the process referred to when a password is encrypted; it is commonly used to protect passwords and to check passwords that are entered into a system by hashing them and comparing them. Another use of hashing is to authenticate plaintext using a shared key. The hash is generated from the plaintext data and the key. Once sent, only the data and the hash are visible; the key is not transmitted, and it thus becomes difficult to modify either the data or the hash without its being detected.

Notwithstanding the above, it is possible, with access to the hashes and the brute force of resources, to find data that hashes identically to the password; this is known as a collision in cryptography. Therefore, it is important to select the best possible password-hashing algorithm that raises the costs (in terms of time and effort) of attempting to overcome encryption.

Graem Corfield

See also: Cyber Attack; Cyber Defense; Cyber Security; Internet; Spoofing; Spyware; Transmission Control Protocol/Internet Protocol (TCP/IP)

Further Reading

Bryen, Stephen D. *Technology Security and National Power: Winners and Losers.* New Brunswick, NJ: Transaction Publishers, 2016.

Rosenzweig, Paul. *Cyber Warfare: How Conflicts in Cyberspace Are Challenging America and Changing the World.* Santa Barbara, CA: Praeger, 2012.

ESCALATION DOMINANCE

Escalation dominance in the cyber realm refers to the ability to control what occurs as a result of a cyber attack or cyber crisis and is derived from theories on escalation dominance in the physical realm vis-á-vis state-on-state military attacks. Given that cyber escalation refers to the possibility that a cyber attacker (or belligerent) may increase their efforts to include more damaging cyber attacks, kinetic violence, or nuclear war—the escalation ladder—the attacked (or status quo entity) must assess its capabilities with these levels of violence in mind. Thus, to maintain escalation dominance, a status quo entity must be willing to maintain the capacity to thwart a belligerent's actions at every level of the escalation ladder to include nuclear war at the extreme.

Escalation dominance as a deterrent to potential aggression also requires a status quo entity to maintain the will and ability to escalate rather than simply respond to a belligerent's actions. Escalation in the cyber domain may move from hacking to glean information to spoofing so as to masquerade one's efforts and make it appear that another entity is the culprit (whether either is escalatory is based on perceptions of intent and effect). Escalation may also take a form similar to spreading a computer virus, with the end result being physical damage such as that seen with Stuxnet. For an entity to undertake such activity, it must be confident in its ability to dominate across the spectrum and potentially into the physical or kinetic realm.

For example, entities X and Y are involved in a cyber war, and X has escalated by amassing infantry troops on Y's borders. Entity Y responds by moving artillery batteries to its border region, challenging X's action, which provokes an all-out attack by X's infantry troops that overwhelm and destroy Y's artillery defenses. Arguably, X had accurately assessed its will and possessed the ability to dominate up the escalation ladder. This rudimentary scenario does not adequately address the myriad nuances of escalation dominance such as the potential for third-party intervention or the deterrent effect of escalation on the same.

Calculating the effects of escalation and considerations of escalation dominance are particularly difficult in cyber space. In theory, an entity carrying out a cyber attack on legitimate targets during a conflict is not necessarily escalating. It is conceivable that such attacks may indeed be limited to the cyber realm as a means to convey intent and the fact that an entity is confident in its ability to dominate up the escalation ladder. However, it is important to remember that an entity's actions are often judged as escalatory based on what was done or intended rather than how the actions were carried out. For example, targeting a civilian facility with the intent to make people pressure their government to sue for peace may be seen as escalatory even if perpetrated at the low end of cyber operations. Notwithstanding debate over means versus ends, consideration must be given to the potential that laws of armed conflict may be violated, an issue especially problematic as there are few if any protocols expressly addressing cyber operations or cyber war.

Ronald N. Dains

See also: Cyber Attack; Cyber Escalation; Cyber War; Hacker; Spoofing; Stuxnet

Further Reading

Clarke, Richard A., and Robert K. Knake. *Cyber War: The Next Threat to National Security and What to Do about It.* New York: HarperCollins, 2010.

Kramer, Franklin D., Stuart H. Starr, and Larry K. Wentz. *Cyberpower and National Security.* Dulles, VA: NDU Press and Potomac Books, Inc., 2009.

Libicki, Martin C. *Crisis and Escalation in Cyberspace.* Santa Monica, CA: RAND Corporation, 2012.

Libicki, Martin C. *Cyberdeterrence and Cyber War.* Santa Monica, CA: RAND Corporation, 2009.

ESTONIAN CYBER ATTACK (2007)

Sandwiched between heightened cyber-attack threats to U.S. government networks in December 2006 (NASA) and June 2007 (Pentagon), on April 27, 2007, the Baltic state of Estonia suffered a widespread distributed denial-of-service (DDoS) cyber attack that lasted three weeks. At the time, it was the largest DDoS attack ever to take place and employed hundreds of thousands of computers against Estonian government and commercial Web sites, slowing down some of the functions and services of these Web sites and shutting down others. Primary targets included communications and banking networks. As multiple servers collapsed under the burden of request for access hits, online government services were unreachable in many instances, and basic consumer goods such as bank cards and mobile phones became unusable. Estonian officials and citizens reeled as the realization of the DDoS attack's massive scale grew. Then they changed their focus to a host of questions, followed by accusations.

At the forefront of the Estonian outcry were the escalating tensions with Russia that had peaked in the spring of 2007, ostensibly over a World War II monument. That February, the parliament in Tallinn had passed legislation prohibiting the display of structures on Estonian soil related to the 49-year (1940–1989) Soviet occupation of Estonia. Especially at issue was a statue known as the *Bronze Soldier* of Tallinn, a six-and-a-half-foot bronze sculpture of a Red Army regular standing in front of a section of stone wall vaguely resembling a mausoleum. The work was completed in 1947 in honor of the Soviet "liberators of Tallinn" from the Nazis.

Originally located in a park in central Tallinn, the monument sat atop the buried remains of several Soviet World War II soldiers. Local sentiment led to a call not to destroy it, but to relocate the monument away from the city center. Elements from the ethnic Russian population in Estonia (estimated at 26 percent of the country's inhabitants) generated an outcry of protest, matched by similar protests in Moscow, setting the stage for a standoff. Probably seeking to de-escalate the tensions, Estonian president Toomas Ilves vetoed the legislation but failed to undermine the standoff, which peaked on April 27, also known as "Bronze Night."

On Bronze Night, protestors on both sides rioted, prompting police intervention. Concurrent with the rioting, the DDoS attack began to strike Estonian servers and quickly assumed a character well beyond previous DDoS attacks, which had typically taken aim at one or two Web sites. Tallinn called for help from international partners, who sent over experts to assist with network rehabilitation. As the attack began to take down government and banking sites over the next several days, Tallinn leveled accusations at Russia and also appealed to NATO allies, attempting to evoke a ruling from NATO that the DDoS merited an Article V response—the stipulation that an attack on a NATO member is a matter of common defense requiring an Alliance counterattack. Direct Alliance involvement would have widened, and perhaps complicated, the effects of the attack.

Moscow denied any involvement in the DDoS attack, but they also refused to assist the Estonians in investigating the source of the attack. As Estonian authorities worked to restore servers and services, they also began to shift away from further antagonism of Russia and from urging a full-blown NATO condemnation of Russia. Russian public statements also began to change, admitting the possibility of the involvement of private Russian patriots acting on their own initiative. The Estonians repeated their demands for investigative assistance, pointing to a bilateral agreement on legal matters (MLAT, or Mutual Legal Assistance Treaty), which the Russians had persisted in ignoring, leading some observers to declare this as proof of direct Russian government responsibility for the DDoS. This line of reasoning is incomplete, however, as it relies on Western preferences in the practice of geopolitics and warfare, which tends to miss crucial elements of Russian strategic thinking.

An underlying factor was Estonia's high degree of vulnerability to this sort of attack in 2007. The country's limited cyber byways out of Estonia increased the threat and magnified the potential for extended shutdowns. Estonian network architecture facilitated, rather than blocked, the spread of damage from a DDoS. These factors made such an attack more likely as well as increasing the range of possibilities as to the likely suspects behind the attack. Better protection means more sophisticated attackers, which would have narrowed the field considerably on who was responsible. In the context provided by the shaky reality of Estonian network security at the time, one must add the lack of utility in a costly pursuit of the party directly responsible for the attack.

Whereas it costs the Russians nothing to deny responsibility for something almost impossible to prove, given the inherent challenges in the success rate of cyber forensics from the inception of the Internet to the present day, the victim is theoretically pinned between high potential costs. It is costly to be attacked and appear impotent in one's ability to prevent attacks and prosecute attackers, and it is similarly costly to expend resources in a lengthy and ultimately fruitless (barring a complete and unadulterated admission of guilt) search for bona fide state-level perpetrators who generally do not want to be caught. Combined with the tenuous state of fixing direct blame in the cyber universe is the historical Russian preference for ambiguity.

Russian consciousness includes a vital, defining topographic feature, namely, the sense of the vastness of the land, blurring any sense of lines between its own territory and that of neighbors, and over the centuries, this feature has informed tsarist strategic thinking of the past as well as the modern Kremlin's strategic thinking. For example, Russia and Estonia have yet to finalize agreements over a precise border between their territories. Russia participates in developing treaties to resolve the remaining disputes, but they have resisted ratifying them. This type of policy suggests a view of borders at extreme odds with Western conceptions, namely, that such borders only exist when they threaten to move inward.

In the same sense with which Russia appears to be content to allow its border with Estonia to remain unresolved as long as it gives nothing away, and, turning to another example, to allow the Transdniestrian crisis to molder Moldovan and Ukrainian sovereignty and international credibility, the inherent ambiguities of the cyber domain would seem to be well aligned with Russian international behavior patterns. This resonance between the gray of cyber and the gray of Russia's foreign policy calculus would explain the apparently contradictory Russian behavior of denying responsibility for the DDoS and yet refusing to cooperate in the investigation. The same resonance would help account for several of the other frustrating outcomes of the 2007 DDoS against Estonia.

After the rioting and the restoration of Internet sites and services, Tallinn moved the statue later in 2007 to a military cemetery, resisting ethnic Russian demands that it stay as well as Estonian voices calling for its defacement or destruction. The *Bronze Soldier* persists in its new location as a symbol of Tallinn's struggle to improve its domestic unity across its resident ethnic groups. Combined with other policies, such as its approach to citizenship questions, Russia's pattern of stalling and avoiding definitions cripples neighbors from effectively integrating their ethnic Russian populations. Any Russian admissions on the cyber attack have similarly muddied the waters as opposed to providing clarification and improved bilateral relations.

Soon after the attack, investigators traced a link in the attack back to a computer within President Vladimir Putin's administrative bureaucracy, which the Kremlin simply never acknowledged. In 2008, Estonian authorities prosecuted one ethnic Russian living in Estonia for involvement in the DDoS. In the months following the attack, Russian officials suggested that criminal elements may have been involved, including some possibly operating from within Russia. Later, a Russian nationalist youth group claimed responsibility, citing its motivation as Estonian bigotry against Russia and its ethnic Russians. More recently, Russian member of parliament Sergei Markov claimed that an aide of his may have done it operating on his own and from outside of Russia. These contradictory and deniable allegations and suspicions can become part of the problem, particularly when parties choose to emphasize them at the expense of developing more effective statecraft in dealing with the cyber domain. More progress by Estonia has been made in recovering from the attack in the area of cyber defenses.

In addition to receiving significant international assistance, Tallinn has made solid progress in inoculating Estonian cyber pathways through use of increased numbers of routers, hosting sites on well-protected outside networks, and the redesign of its networks by private high-tech companies. Other countries tended to follow suit, learning from Estonia's victimization to bolster their own defenses. In the end, Estonia's days of suffering a massive DDoS resulted in the loss of 97 percent of its banking transactions during that time, the threat of loss of Estonian power and water grids, the defacement or temporary shutdown of government and political party Web sites and e-mail servers, and, finally, in the realization that the

Estonia of 2007 was extraordinarily vulnerable to this kind of attack. The biggest remaining question regarding the DDoS attack on Estonia is whether Internet-reliant countries have learned all of the lessons it offers.

Daniel Connelly

See also: Botnet; Cyber Attack; Cyber War; Georgian Cyber Attack (2008); NATO Cooperative Cyber Defence Centre of Excellence (CCDCOE); North Atlantic Treaty Organization (NATO); Patriotic Hacking; Putin, Vladimir; Russia Cyber Capabilities; Russian Business Network (RBN); Rustock Botnet; *Tallinn Manual*

Further Reading

Clarke, Richard A., and Robert K. Knake. *Cyber War: The Next Threat to National Security and What to Do about It.* New York: HarperCollins, 2010.

Libicki, Martin C. *Crisis and Escalation in Cyberspace.* Santa Monica, CA: RAND Corporation, 2012.

Myers, Stephen Lee. *The New Tsar: The Rise and Reign of Vladimir Putin.* New York: Alfred A. Knopf, 2015.

ETHERNET

The Ethernet is a family of technologies in computer networking, particularly among local area networks (LANs). Based on a physical cable, Ethernet enormously expanded bandwidth compared to earlier experimental systems. The radio transmission method used in Alohanet, part of the Advanced Research Projects Agency Network (ARPANET) studies, transmitted thousands of bits of information per second. Coaxial-based Ethernet transmitted in the millions of bits, and refinements in Ethernet to fiber-optic materials allowed further increases, into rates exceeding 100 gigabits per second.

Developed in the early 1980s, Ethernet created practical networking options for the owners of personal computers, and both the timing of its introduction and its continual refinements in capability led to its establishment as a standard method for local area networking. The niche of local area networking emerged in the mid-1970s when early ARPANET users employed interface message processors (IMPs), intended to link distant computers via telephone lines, to instead also exchange information among computers already sharing an IMP. In the 1980s, purpose-build LANs using Ethernet succeeded these arrangements.

Ethernet systems rely heavily on hosts, and to facilitate communication between hosts and enable the creation of the Internet, Transmission Control Protocol/Internet Protocol (TCP/IP) were created in the early 1980s. Ethernet, whose standards are maintained by the Institute of Electrical and Electronics Engineers, remains crucial in supporting Internet communication.

Nicholas Michael Sambaluk

See also: ARPANET; Internet; Transmission Control Protocol/Internet Protocol (TCP/IP)

Further Reading
Abbate, Janet. *Inventing the Internet.* Cambridge, MA: MIT, 2008.
von Burg, Urs. *The Triumph of Ethernet: Technological Communities and the Battle for the LAN Standard.* Stanford, CA: Stanford University, 2001.

EVRON, GADI

Gadi Evron is CEO and founder of Cymmetria, a cyber-deception start-up focused on changing cyber security by switching the traditional security routine so that hackers are vulnerable. Cymmetria does this by creating decoys embedded in networks to draw hackers to them. This makes it quicker and easier for a business to detect and mitigate a security breach. Cymmetria's focus is advanced persistent threats (APTs) in which attackers aim to enter a network and lie in wait undetected to steal large amounts of data. Evron was previously vice president of Cybersecurity Strategy for Kaspersky Lab and led Pricewaterhouse Cooper's (PwC) Cyber Security Center of Excellence, located in Israel. Prior to that, Gadi was chief information security officer (CISO) for the Israeli government's Internet operation and founder of the Israeli government computer emergency response team (CERT). He is a research fellow at the Yuval Ne`eman Workshop for Science, Technology and Security at Tel Aviv University. He is recognized for his work in Internet-security operations and global incident response and is considered the first botnet expert. Evron coauthored *Botnets: The Killer Web Applications and Open Source Fuzzing Tools* and authored *Battling Botnets and Online Mobs: Estonia's Defense Efforts during the Internet War* as well as a host of pertinent cyber-security items.

Lisa Beckenbaugh

See also: Botnet; Computer Emergency Response Team (CERT); Cyber Defense; Cyber Security; Israel Cyber Capabilities; Kaspersky Lab

Further Reading
Lifeboat Foundation. "Gadi Evron." http://lifeboat.com/ex/bios.gadi.evron.
Lomas, Natasha. "YC-Backed Cymmetria Uses Virtual Machines to Decoy and Detect Hackers." *TechCrunch*, June 27, 2015. http://techcrunch.com/2015/06/27/cymmetria.

F

FEDERAL BUREAU OF INVESTIGATION (FBI)

The FBI began as a force of special agents created in 1908 by Attorney General Charles Bonaparte during the presidency of Theodore Roosevelt, with a force of 34 agents as a permanent part of the Department of Justice (DOJ). Attorney General George Wickersham, Bonaparte's successor, named the force the Bureau of Investigation on March 16, 1909. In turn, the Bureau of Investigation was renamed the United States Bureau of Investigation on July 1, 1932. When the Department of Justice experimented with a Division of Investigation and its Bureau of Prohibition, public confusion between Bureau of Investigation special agents and Prohibition agents led to a permanent name change for the Department of Justice's investigators to the Federal Bureau of Investigation in 1935.

Initially, there were few federal crimes. The agency primarily investigated violations of laws involving national banking, bankruptcy, naturalization, antitrust, peonage, and land fraud. The first major expansion in its jurisdiction came in June 1910 when the Mann Act was passed, making it a federal crime to transport women over state lines for immoral purposes. It also provided a tool for the federal government to investigate criminals who evaded state laws but had no other federal violations. Contributing to its forensic expertise, the Bureau established a Technical Laboratory in 1932. Initially, the small laboratory operated strictly as a research facility. However, with the expansion of federal funding, specialized equipment and reference collections enhanced their capabilities. Additionally, its highly skilled and inventive staff cooperated with engineers, scientists, and cryptographers in other agencies to enable the United States to penetrate and sometimes control the flow of information from belligerents. Consequently, the investigation of fascist and communist groups came in 1936 with President Roosevelt's authorization through Secretary of State Cordell Hull. A 1939 Presidential Directive further strengthened the FBI's authority to investigate subversives in the United States, and Congress reinforced it by passing the Smith Act in 1940, outlawing advocacy of violent overthrow of the government.

With the outbreak of war, the responsibilities of the Bureau escalated even more. Subversion, sabotage, and espionage became major concerns, and it participated in intelligence collection. The FBI's role in fighting crime expanded in the postwar period through its assistance to state and local law enforcement and increased jurisdictional responsibility. Continuing advances in forensic science and technical development enabled the FBI to devote a significant proportion of its resources to assisting state and local law enforcement agencies. In 1982, following an explosion of terrorist incidents worldwide, counterterrorism became a fourth national priority.

As computers and access to the Internet became commonplace in homes across the United States, the FBI initiated measures to address crime in cyber space. It created the Computer Investigations and Infrastructure Threat Assessment Center (CITAC) to address physical and cyber attacks against U.S. infrastructure. The Bureau has also played a crucial role in the investigation and prevention of computer crimes. In 1991, the FBI's Computer Analysis and Response Teams (CART) began to provide investigators with the technical expertise necessary to obtain evidence from suspect's computers. Seven years later, the Bureau's National Infrastructure Protection Center (NIPC) was created to monitor the dissemination of computer viruses, worms, and other malicious programs as well as to warn government and business computer users of these dangers.

When the September 11 terrorist attacks hit New York and Washington, D.C., Director Robert S. Mueller led the FBI's investigative efforts in partnership with all U.S. law enforcement, the federal government, and allies overseas. On October 26, 2001, President George W. Bush signed into law the USA PATRIOT Act, which granted new provisions to address the threat of terrorism. Seven months later, the attorney general issued revised investigative guidelines to assist the Bureau's counterterrorism efforts. To support the Bureau's change in mission and to meet newly articulated strategic priorities, Director Mueller reengineered FBI structure and operations to focus on the prevention of terrorist attacks, countering foreign intelligence operations against the United States, and addressing cyber-crime attacks as well as other high-technology crimes. A Cyber Division was formed in 2002, with the responsibility to investigate and prosecute Internet crimes, including cyber-based terrorism, espionage, computer intrusions, and major cyber fraud.

As the second decade of the new millennium unfolds, the FBI stands dedicated to its core values and ethical standards. Commitment to these ensures the FBI effectively carries out its mission: protect and defend the United States against terrorist and foreign intelligence threats; uphold and enforce the criminal laws of the United States; and provide leadership and criminal justice services to federal, state, municipal, and international agencies and partners.

Roy Franklin Houchin II

See also: Bush, George W.; Computer Emergency Response Team (CERT); Cyber Crime; Cyber Espionage; Infrastructure; National Infrastructure Protection Plan (NIPP); USA PATRIOT Act

Further Reading

Federal Bureau of Investigation and the Department of Justice. *FBI: A Centennial History 1908–2008*. Washington, D.C.: U.S. Government Printing Office, 2008.

Jeffery-Jones, Rhodri. *The FBI: A History*. New Haven, CT: Yale University Press, 2007.

Kessler, Ronald. *The Secrets of the FBI*. New York: Crown Forum, 2011.

Weiner, Tim. *Enemies: A History of the FBI*. New York: Random House, 2012.

FIREEYE

FireEye is a public network-security company that provides protection against malware and other cyber threats, provides threat forensics and risk analysis, and conducts investigations of prior cyber attacks. Combining their data with crowd-sourced information, FireEye maintains a database that provides a real-time picture of current cyber-crime threats that is distributed globally. Based in Milpitas, California, the company was founded in 2004 by Ashar Aziz, formerly of Sun Micro-systems. FireEye's key investors include Sequoia Capital and In-Q-Tel, which is associated with the U.S. Central Intelligence Agency (CIA). In 2012, Dave DeWalt, the former CEO and president of McAfee, became FireEye's chairman and later its CEO. In 2013, FireEye purchased Mandiant Corporation, and its president, Kevin Mandia, became the CEO of FireEye in 2016.

FireEye has over 4,400 customers in 67 countries, including the U.S. federal government, universities such as Harvard and Berkeley, and large global corporations such as Yahoo, eBay, and Adobe Systems. FireEye has partnered with Microsoft, the U.S. government, and the University of Washington, which included efforts to take down botnets such as Mega-D (also known as Ozdok) and Rustock, which was responsible for over 47 percent of global spam e-mail. FireEye investigated cyber attacks against high-profile targets such as Target, JPMorgan Chase, and Sony Pictures. In 2015, FireEye became the first cyber-security company to be certified under the SAFETY Act by the U.S. Department of Homeland Security (DHS).

Michael Hankins

See also: Botnet; Cyber Crime; Cyber Security; Department of Homeland Security (DHS); JPMorgan Hack; Mandia, Kevin; Mandiant Corporation; Rustock Botnet; Sony Hack; Target Corporation Hack

Further Reading

Steer, Jason. "The Gaping Hole in Our Security Defenses." *Computer Fraud and Security*, January 2014: 17–20.
Stewart, Christopher S. "FireEye: Botnet Busters." *Bloomberg Businessweek*, June 16, 2011. http://www.bloomberg.com/news/articles/2011-06-16/fireeye-botnet-busters.

FIREWALL

Passenger vehicles with combustion engines are manufactured with a protective barrier between the engine and passenger compartment called a *firewall*. This concept has been adopted in network security, where a software barrier is constructed to prevent anything harmful from outside of a network from entering into the network.

These software barriers function through various devices. For example, some firewalls are packet filters that prevent communications streams from entering the network unless the data identifying the stream matches certain criteria (such as coming from a specific IP address or adhering to specific data standards). These work at the most basic layer of Internet functionality and are said to be *network layer* firewalls. Other firewalls work on the software application layer and screen incoming traffic for certain suspect file types, subject lines, or other previously encountered warning signs.

Because spam and all types of malicious software (malware) are constantly evolving, effective firewalls require frequent updates. Firms that specialize in firewall software are constantly surveying the Internet for new methods of introducing new types of spam and malicious software and often notify their software user base (sometimes for a premium fee) when the list of offending sources, file types, or content changes. The firewall filters are then remotely updated and are effective until a new generation of offending spam or malware is detected. This ongoing competition between attackers and filters is worldwide in scope and impact, and it is experienced by even the most infrequent Internet user.

Jeffrey R. Cares

See also: Cyber Security; Malware; Software

Further Reading

Graham, James, Richard Howard, and Ryan Olson. *Cyber Security Essentials.* Boca Raton, FL: Auerbach Publications, 2011.

FLAME WORM

The Flame worm is a piece of highly advanced malware for targeted cyber espionage. It is also known as Da Flame, Flamer, and Skywiper. Cyber-security experts consider Flame one of the most complex examples of malware ever discovered. Flame was identified in May 2012 by a cooperative of cyber-security institutions led by Kaspersky Lab while investigating a virus infecting Iranian Oil Ministry computers. In 2012, it was primarily detected in countries in the Near and Middle East, with the majority of targets in Iran.

Flame can spread to other systems via a local network or a USB stick. It can copy data and record audio, video, Skype calls, screenshots, keyboard activity, and network traffic. Flame can turn computers into beacons that attempt to download information from nearby Bluetooth devices. Flame sends data to one of several servers scattered around the world where it can be downloaded, then it awaits further instructions from those servers. Flame also possesses a "kill" command that wipes all traces of itself from infected computers.

Flame shares code with the Stuxnet worm that targeted Iranian nuclear centrifuges in 2010, and both exploit the same zero-day vulnerabilities in Microsoft operating systems. Flame is 20 megabytes in size—40 times larger than Stuxnet. Experts believe Flame is the work of nation-states, with some indications pointing to a United States–Israeli cyber-espionage cooperative.

Steven B. Davis

See also: Cyber Espionage; Cyber Weapon; Kaspersky Lab; Malware; Stuxnet; Worm

Further Reading

Kushner, David. "The Real Story of Stuxnet." *IEEE Spectrum* 50, 2013: 48–53.

Zettner, Kim. *Countdown to Zero Day: Stuxnet and the Launch of the World's First Digital Weapon*. New York: Broadway Books, 2015.

FOREIGN INTELLIGENCE SURVEILLANCE ACT (FISA)

The Foreign Intelligence Surveillance Act (FISA) is a law enacted by President Jimmy Carter in 1978 to provide a legal framework for the use of electronic surveillance in the context of gathering foreign intelligence. In 1972, the Supreme Court case *United States v. U.S. District Court*, which is more commonly referred to as the *Keith* case, held that the Fourth Amendment forbids warrantless surveillance against domestic threats to national security. As a result of civil liberty violations, FISA was signed into law following congressional hearings conducted by the Church Committee, named for Senator Frank Church (D-ID), who chaired the U.S. Senate Select Committee to Study Governmental Operations with Respect to Intelligence Activities. This committee investigated the National Security Agency (NSA), Central Intelligence Agency (CIA), and Federal Bureau of Investigation (FBI) for legality of operations. With the backdrop of the Watergate Scandal, antiwar protests, and Martin Luther King Jr. being targeted by President Richard Nixon's Counter Intelligence Program (COINTELPRO), the committee determined that these intelligence agencies had committed civil liberty violations, which were the direct result of the uncertain nature of law regarding the subject. The subsequent legislation was an attempt to find a delicate balance between national security interests and civil liberties.

In providing a framework for government agencies to collect intelligence, FISA established that electronic surveillance in the United States was only permitted for the collection of foreign intelligence and counterintelligence against agents of foreign powers. Two important court rulings, *United States v. Troung Dinh Hung* and *United States v. Pelton*, ruled that in domestic criminal cases, government agencies were able to use FISA only if the "primary purpose" of the investigation was foreign intelligence gathering. Additionally, FISA also established a standard of needs to be met before probable cause could be demonstrated. To ensure that these laws were upheld, FISA created the Foreign Intelligence Surveillance Court (FISC) to ensure that the legality of surveillance operations was upheld. Since the enactment of FISA, several subsequent pieces of legislature have expanded federal laws dealing with but not limited to physical searches, wiretapping, pen registers, trap and trace devices, and access to private business records.

Following the terrorist attacks on September 11, 2001, Congress rushed to pass legislation to improve national security measures. On October 26, 2001, President George W. Bush signed into law the United and Strengthening America by Providing Appropriate Tools Required to Intercept and Obstruct Terrorism Act (USA PATRIOT Act). Many of the provisions within this law either changed or amended FISA. For instance, the USA PATRIOT Act expanded the number of district court judges on FISC. FISA language was also amended, which changed the required certification deemed necessary of federal officers when applying for electronic surveillance and physical search documentation. The changes to FISA were an effort to enable more efficient information sharing between law enforcement agencies and the intelligence community.

Not all changes to FISA were well received by the general population, as opposition to the PATRIOT Act focused on elements within the law that facilitated indefinite detentions of noncitizens, increased search and seizures by law enforcement agents without consent, and the expanded use of National Security Letters, which allowed the FBI to search telephone, financial, and business records without a court order. Since the inception of the law, several legal challenges occurred rendering some portions of the law unconstitutional. With the growing emphasis on the Global War on Terror (GWOT), Congress has continued to place more emphasis on the need for expanded surveillance capabilities, and as a result, further modifications to FISA occurred in the Homeland Security Act of 2002, the Intelligence Reform and Terrorism Prevention Act of 2005, the USA PATRIOT Act Additional Reauthorizing Amendments of 2006, the Protect America Act of 2007, and the FISA Amendments Act of 2008. The changing enemy of the 21st century has required a balancing act of civil liberties and national security by Congress to ensure the military and federal intelligence agencies remain one step ahead.

John J. Mortimer

See also: Bush, George W.; Central Intelligence Agency (CIA); Federal Bureau of Investigation (FBI); National Security Agency (NSA); USA PATRIOT Act

Further Reading

Bazan, Elizabeth B. *The Foreign Intelligence Surveillance Act: Overview and Modifications.* New York: Nova Science Publishers, 2008.

Musch, Donald J. *Civil Liberties and the Foreign Intelligence Surveillance Act.* Vol. 14, Second Series. *Terrorism: Documents of International and Local Control.* Dobbs Ferry, NY: Oceana Publications, 2003.

Wills, Brett J., ed. *Foreign Intelligence Surveillance Act and Its Ramifications.* New York: Nova Science Publishers, 2010.

4CHAN

4chan is a popular English-language image board Web site. It was created by Google employee Christopher "Moot" Poole in 2003, while he was still in high school. Poole got the idea from the Japanese image board Web site Futaba Channel, or 2chan, and decided to create an English-language counterpart. It was originally conceived of as a place where English-language speakers could discuss and trade images of Japanese manga and anime. 4chan started with just two boards, anime-original (/a/) and anime-random (/b/). Later, the /b/ board dropped the anime moniker and just became a board where users could post about anything.

4chan currently has over 60 boards on which users can post about anything from anime to cooking. Each board has its own specific guidelines as to what is allowed to be posted. Volunteer moderators patrol the boards to ensure postings do not violate guidelines. A unique characteristic of 4chan is that users are not required to register to post on the Web site. Users may create an alias or can simply post under the title "anonymous." Boards are limited to 14 pages, and old posts beyond that are not stored on 4chan Web servers; they simply "evaporate" as new posts are added. While 4chan encourages anonymity, 4chan administrators do have access to user Internet Protocol (IP) addresses if they are not hidden.

The most highly trafficked board is the random, or /b/, board, where most anything is allowed as long as it does not violate U.S. law. The /b/ board is infamous, as it is home to a variety of Internet memes, including "Rickrolling" and viral videos such as "Chocolate Rain." In general, the /b/ board is meant to shock and disturb, and users are encouraged to post anonymously. However, child pornography, animal abuse, and other violations of U.S. law are banned, and the IP addresses of violators are generally reported to the local authorities. This has led to a few arrests of individuals who have either posted or downloaded child pornography or have made school-shooting threats on 4chan.

4chan is perhaps most famous for its association with the hacktivist group Anonymous. The group took its name directly from 4chan and planned one of its first Internet pranks, or "tricks," by communicating through the /b/ board. Anonymous planned and coordinated the Habo Hotel prank on 4chan's /b/ board. Anonymous continues to use 4chan's /b/ board to recruit participants and publicize upcoming activities.

4chan users have also been linked to variety of denial-of-service (DDoS) attacks against AT&T; as a result, AT&T temporarily blocked access to the site. 4chan users have also used the site to coordinate attacks or pranks against Republican politician Sarah Palin, celebrity Justin Bieber, and Mountain Dew. It continues to function as a popular discussion-based board and records millions of users each day. In 2015, Poole sold the infamous Web site to the founder of 2chan, Hiroyuki Nishimura.

Barbara Salera

See also: Anonymous; Hacktivist; LulzSec

Further Reading

Coleman, Gabriella. *Hacker, Hoaxer, Whistleblower, Spy: The Many Faces of Anonymous.* London: Verso, 2014.

Olson, Parmy. *We Are Anonymous: Inside the Hacker World of LulzSec, Anonymous and the Global Cyber Insurgency.* New York: Back Bay Books, 2012.

GATES, BILL

William Henry "Bill" Gates III (1955–) is a technology entrepreneur who cofounded Microsoft and wrote much of the early software that became the foundation for the company's success. Gates is known for his immense fortune; he has consistently been ranked in the top-five richest people in the world since the late 1980s. He is also arguably the single individual most responsible for the ubiquity of computers, largely by making them affordable and accessible to individuals and businesses rather than simply to the wealthy, hobbyists, and businesspeople.

Gates was born on October 28, 1955, in Seattle, near childhood friend Paul Allen. The two developed an interest in computers, and when Gates attended Harvard in the early 1970s, Allen convinced him to drop out to pursue a career. In 1975, Gates and Allen cofounded Microsoft. By 1980, the company had partnered with IBM to write MS-DOS, which became the basic operating system (OS) for Microsoft computers. Over the next five years, Gates and Microsoft followed the lead of Apple to create a graphic user interface (GUI) for their OS, which became Windows. Microsoft and IBM split in 1985, allowing Microsoft to begin to create its own workstations to compete in the "Workstation Wars" of the 1980s. During the 1990s, Microsoft emerged as the premier computer company in the world.

Gates played a pivotal role in the ascendancy of Microsoft, serving as its CEO until 2000. Until at least the early 1990s, he personally reviewed the source code of the company's products, often making his own changes to it. MS-DOS remained the basis for most computer workstations until the late 1990s. His vision also drove the company's corporate strategy: unlike Apple, which concentrated on higher-end products, Gates's company focused on powerful but low-cost software that would prove highly adaptable to many different hardware and software formats. While it gained a reputation for stodginess and vulnerability to cyber attacks as a result, Microsoft grew to dominate the market, particularly in businesses, with low-cost, powerful products such as Windows and Office.

Gates maintains a highly public presence, particularly in the tech and philanthropic communities. He has funded the tech think tank bgC3 and the networking site ResearchGate and has a stake in the nuclear power company TerraPower. After 2010, he became a futurist. Gates has addressed much of his punditry to the future of robotics, noting that robotic intelligence will become ubiquitous over the next few decades. In 2009, he compared the contemporary state of robotics to that of the computer in 1980, poised to take great leaps. He has also expressed concern about the concept of superintelligence. Like Elon Musk and others, Gates worries that superintelligence may one day overtake human capabilities and rebel against its creators, an event often called the *singularity*. This would create a new form of cyber warfare, not against enemy individuals and states, but rather against the tools of cyber warfare themselves.

Jonathan Abel

See also: Apple Inc.; Cyber Attack; Intel Corporation, Microsoft Corporation; Microsoft Windows

Further Reading

Becraft, Michael. *Bill Gates: A Biography.* Santa Barbara, CA: Greenwood, 2014.
Gates, Bill. *The Road Ahead.* New York: Viking, 1995.

GATES, ROBERT M.

Robert M. Gates was born on September 25, 1943, in Wichita, Kansas. He attended the College of William and Mary, where he received a BA in history in 1965. He subsequently received an MA in history from Indiana University in 1966 and a PhD in Russian and Soviet history from Georgetown University in 1974. Prior to serving as the secretary of defense, Gates spent 27 years at the Central Intelligence Agency (CIA), where he became the only officer to begin at an entry-level position and rise to oversee the entire agency. He also served briefly as a U.S. Air Force intelligence officer.

While serving as secretary of defense, from December 2006 to July 2011, Gates instituted centralizing organizational changes to help prepare the United States to wage cyber war. He also declared cyber warfare to be the fifth domain of warfare, in addition to land, sea, air, and space. In June 2009, Gates announced the formation of the U.S. Cyber Command (USCYBERCOM), which integrated the individual cyber arms of the air force, army, navy, and marine corps. In that same year, the Department of Defense (DoD) also published its first cyber strategy.

Gates unsuccessfully attempted to forge an agreement between DoD and the Department of Homeland Security (DHS) in 2010 to break down communication and information barriers between the National Security Agency (NSA) and DHS. Gates hoped to share NSA's resources with DHS to prevent cyber attacks. As such a merger had the possibility of violating civil liberties, Gates attempted to limit the risk by using a legal team for oversight.

In 2011, Gates announced that the United States would consider responding to cyber attacks as acts of war. Since resigning from DoD in 2011, Gates has continued to speak out about cyber-war threats. He argues that the United States does not have the luxury of agonizing about civil liberties to the extent that some would like given the serious threats faced by the country.

Heather Pace Venable

See also: Department of Defense (DoD); Department of Homeland Security (DHS); National Security Agency (NSA); Obama, Barack; U.S. Cyber Command (USCYBERCOM)

Further Reading

Clarke, Richard A., and Robert K. Knake. *Cyber War: The Next Threat to National Security and What to Do about It.* New York: HarperCollins, 2010.

Gates, Robert M. *Duty: Memoirs of a Secretary at War.* New York: Vintage, 2015.

Gates, Robert M. "Establishment of a Subordinate Unified US Cyber Command under US Strategic Command for Military Cyberspace Operations." *Memorandum for Secretaries of the Military Departments.* Washington, D.C.: Office of the Secretary of Defense, 2009.

GAUSS WORM

The Gauss worm is a special variant of malware worm that collects users' credentials (i.e., authentication information) for a handful of specific banking systems, social networks, and e-mail accounts via the Windows operating systems. Kaspersky Labs first detected the worm in June 2012, but they were unable to determine its origin. However, its code base, architecture, and communications to its command and control server share similarities with the Flame worm. Once installed, the worm creates some files to store information, while other modular files perform specific functions. These modules collect system information, browsing history, passwords, text, and cookies from a handful of targeted banks, credit companies, and social media sites. The information is then encrypted, saved to a temporary file, and sent to command and control servers.

The worm creators named the modular files after famous mathematicians, such as Gauss, Lagrange, Gödel, and Taylor. The Gauss module collects the user's credentials, hence the worm's name. Two unique features, supplied by the Gödel and Lagrange modules, install a custom Palida Narrow font and decrypt the worm only on target systems. Investigators have not found the worm's self-replication functionality, so the worm's intended targets remain an open question. Nonetheless, roughly 2,500 infections have been detected, which have occurred mainly in Israel, Lebanon, and the Palestinian Territory.

Paul Clemans

See also: Authentication; Cyber Crime; Malware; Worm

Further Reading

Bencsáth, Boldizsár, Gábor Pék, Levente Buttyán, and Márk Félegyházi. "The Cousins of Stuxnet: Duqu, Flame and Gauss." *Future Internet*, November 6, 2012. http://www.mdpi.com/1999-5903/4/4/971/htm.

GReAT. "Gauss: Abnormal Distribution." *SecureList*, August 6, 2012. https://securelist.com/analysis/publications/36620/gauss-abnormal-distribution.

GEORBOT

Georbot is both the name of a Trojan designed to steal data from infected computers and a fast-growing botnet made up of computer systems infected with the Georbot Trojan. The Georbot Trojan targeted Georgian nationals and stole information from their systems. It could steal documents and certificates, create audio and video recordings, and browse the local network for information. The botnet targeted Georgian financial and governmental Web sites in 2008 by launching a series of distributed denial-of-service (DDoS) attacks. The number of computers comprising the zombie army numbered around 400 systems.

Speculation attributed the attacks to the Russian government because they preceded Russian military actions against the Georgian government. Georgia's computer emergency response team (CERT) determined that one of the sites used to control infected systems belonged to the Russian Business Network (RBN), and another domain linked to that network was directly written into the malware itself. In addition, a domain registered using the address of Russia's Secret Service (FSB) was used to send e-mails spreading Georbot.

CERT identified the hacker who created the botnet by using his own malware against him. CERT set a trap by creating a zip file named "Georgian-NATO Agreement" that was another version of Georbot. When the hacker downloaded the document, he infected his system, allowing CERT access to his system. Once inside the system, CERT was able to take a picture of the hacker, and researchers could access the control panel to learn the extent and intent of the operation. They determined that Georbot targeted specific keyword strings and document types related to nongovernmental organizations' (NGO) activities and government offices.

Lori Ann Henning

See also: Botnet; Computer Emergency Response Team (CERT); Cyber Crime; Cyber War; Georgian Cyber Attack (2008); Trojan Horse

Further Reading

Libicki, Martin. *Cyberspace in Peace and War.* Annapolis, MD: U.S. Naval Institute Press, 2016.
Springer, Paul J. *Cyber Warfare: A Reference Handbook.* Santa Barbara, CA: ABC-CLIO, 2015.

GEORGIAN CYBER ATTACK (2008)

One year after the 2007 cyber attack on Estonia, allegedly conducted and supported, or at least approved, by Russia, the Georgian military opened fire from artillery positions on Russian and pro-Russian Ossetian forces in the South Ossetian town of Tskhinvali, initiating the more organized, wider-scale kinetic combat phase of the Russian-Georgian War of 2008. The August 7 attack spurred counterattacks from Russian and Ossetian troops, whose combat edge in weapons and numbers helped decisively end the open combat phase five days later, with Georgian forces breaking off the ground maneuver and departing Ossetian territory. The primary physical clash between forces occurred over control of Tskhinvali, and although it lasted less than a week, it produced a months-long refugee crisis, further destabilized the Georgian government, and, despite a cease-fire, provided a debilitating brake against normalized bilateral relations. Moreover, the scope of the conflict extends over far more than the battle for Tskhinvali. It reflects years of high tensions and multiple skirmishes and encompasses a sophisticated cyber component.

Despite the establishment of NATO's first cyber-defense center in Tallinn, Estonia, earlier in 2008, cyber attacks rocked Georgia on multiple fronts weeks before the war opened in Ossetia. These attacks followed years of tension that reached back to the dissolution of the Soviet Union. Repeating its push for independence from Russia in 1918, during the civil war that erupted after the October Revolution of 1917, Georgia again declared its independence from Russia in 1991. In response, the Kremlin underwrote two pro-Russian secessions from Georgia accompanied by combat violence and the forced expulsion of many ethnic Georgians—South Ossetia in 1992 and Abkhazia in 1993. Since then, despite the lack of formal recognition internationally, both regions have operated as de facto self-governing regimes.

In addition to the destabilizing effects of the status of these two regions, Russian-Georgian relations plummeted further in the spring of 2008 when NATO issued a promise (without a timeline) of eventual Alliance membership to the Georgian government in Tbilisi. Following several violent skirmishes between Georgian military and Ossetian militia forces that July, unknown parties, presumably either South Ossetians opposed to Tbilisi or Russians, conducted small-scale missile attacks against Georgian villages near the Ossetian territory. Georgian forces then responded with artillery and ground assaults into Ossetia, starting on August 7. However, the significant factor that set apart this instance of Russian aggression along its borderlands is the unprecedented succession and scope of cyber attacks that accompanied the more traditional forms of military violence in physical combat.

The cyber-space assault against Georgia appears to have begun as early as mid-July, timed to coincide with the provocative missile attacks against Georgian villages, and included a variety of techniques that mainly produced two effects: distributed denial-of-service (DDoS) attacks and Web site defacement. Attacks began with a DDoS against the Georgian presidential Web site that was similar in nature to previous attacks, presumably involving the infection of a large number of host computers that, co-opted as "zombies," worked as botnets run by a smaller number of controlling computers to flood the target site with so many requests for access that bona fide Web users could not open the site. However, the nature of the attacks did not remain at that level for long.

Simultaneously with the Russian ground assault to repel Georgian forces from South Ossetia, cyber attacks expanded to include multiple government Web sites, including the parliament and several ministries, as well as commercial finance and communications Web sites, particularly media Web sites—some 54 Internet sites in all. Of special note, specific attacks targeted the Web sites of known Georgian hackers, presumably to eliminate them as an effective cyber counterforce during the hostilities. During this phase, more sophisticated DDoS methods such as SQL injections and cross-site scripting (XSS) blocked legitimate access to some of these sites. These methods can be more effective in some cases because they bypass the need for wielding large numbers of computers as botnets and directly assault the target servers. They also require more intelligence information on those servers and more planning, which is why they tend to indicate state-level complicity and resources.

The defacement attacks were also significant in their scope and extent as well as in their timing, running simultaneous with the Russian ground maneuvers and the DDoS attacks. The thrust of the defacement attacks was often to discredit the actions and motivations of Tbilisi while bolstering pro-Russian sentiment, such as the provocative attempts to compare President Mikheil Saakashvili with Adolf Hitler. At the same time as these attacks were taking place, other reporting suggested that attackers had achieved some measure of control over the Internet byways across the border that Georgian networks depended on, such as connections to Armenia and Turkey. The threat to cross border Internet connections, combined with the timing of these attacks, occurring simultaneously with the Russian ground assault, indicate a deep level of coordination between the military and the hacker community as well as a concerted attempt to completely control the flow of electronic information in and out of Georgia.

This coordination had severely degrading effects on Georgian sovereignty. Despite a limited attempt by pro-Georgian hackers to combat Russian cyber attacks, ultimately unsuccessful due to the massive scope of the enemy cyber attacks, credit card transactions, mobile phone use, and government processes relying on the Internet were driven to a standstill for days. Perhaps more important strategically, Russia effectively denied Georgia a voice in the international community to publicize its story and version of events during the critical moments of the war. In sum, cyber forces seem to have been effectively employed as virtual shock troops to unseat Georgian government, financial, and media organs, rendering them ineffective and unable to translate the crisis to international partners. In addition to Georgia's crippling loss of Internet service and gagging of its ability to strategically communicate, Georgian interests were haunted by ease of deniability.

Proof of actual Russian complicity, that perennial complication of cyber warfare, centered around three circumstances of the conflict. First, some cyber forensic evidence has implicated the underworld group known as the Russian Business Network. Many have alleged the organization at times performs services for Moscow. Second, the seeming synchronization of the cyber attacks with the Russian aerial and ground assaults appears to many observers to be inconceivable as coincidence and the product of sympathy. Much of this reporting has focused on the Russian assault against the Georgian town of Gori, which received an onslaught of cyber attacks on its government and media sites directly preceding the military kinetic attacks. Third, noting the attackers' attempts to eliminate known Georgian hackers likely to be sympathetic to Tbilisi before the simultaneous cyber and military assaults on Georgia, others see state-level and military thinking behind this kind of threat-reducing approach. Given this possibility of government-hacker collusion and the combination of cyber and military kinetic attacks, the following implications of the 2008 cyber attack on Georgia are important to consider.

The use of cyber space to create confusion and blunt recovery and an effective government response by specifically targeting the location of an impending military attack can have devastating consequences, and it can also provide crucial information on the intentions of involved parties. Second, closely linked to these elements of cyber warfare is the role and vulnerability of hackers sympathetic to the victim. What role will hacker-on-hacker combat play in future conflicts? Third, to what extent was the attack on Georgia, with its unique combination of cyber and military kinetic force, "practice"? What does this portend for the future of Russian behavior as well as other actors, or did it portend the Crimean annexation and other events of the 2014–2016 crisis in Ukraine? Fourth, there would appear to be from the evidence and outcomes of this attack a profusion of potential tip-offs, some playing the part of cyber tip-offs of military activity and others the part of pre-cyber attacks as preemptive maneuvers before cyber activity. Finally, observers can closely consider the strategic effects of, in this case, what at first glance looks like a five-day hot war. In addition to analyzing the extended benefits for Russia in continuing the ambiguity of many of its bilateral relationships, what has been the connection between this expensive stalemate, in which South Ossetia simply retained its secessionist status, and the relative multinational interests in the energy sector in the region?

Part of the effects of cyber warfare is that the attacker can provide a cyber "show of force," demonstrating what it is capable of without actually following through. For example, the 2008 crisis revealed Georgian vulnerabilities on multiple fronts. Understandably, economic partners in the energy sector tend to require a certain amount of stability as a *sine qua non* of future transactions. Russia appears to have sought in the conflict at least the following: a firmer grip on the breakaway South Ossetia and Abkhazia; more distance from its wounded past including the 1991 breakup of the Soviet Union; and more stature in the regional energy sector.

Feints and ploys are just as possible in cyber warfare and hybrid conflicts, including messaging to parties not even involved in the conflict of the moment. Perhaps the most significant lesson from the 2008 cyber attack on Georgia is the requirement to fold the objectives and nature of the attack into a larger tapestry, to determine the relevance of the behavior to the higher strategic purposes that may be behind it.

Daniel Connelly

See also: Botnet; Cyber Attack; Cyber War; Distributed Denial-of-Service (DDoS) Attack; Estonian Cyber Attack (2007); Georbot; Patriotic Hacking; Russia Cyber Capabilities; Russian Business Network (RBN); SQL Injection

Further Reading

Berdyaev, Nicolas. *The Russian Idea.* New York: Macmillan, 1948.

Clarke, Richard, and Robert Knake. *Cyber War: The Next Threat to National Security and What to Do about It.* New York: HarperCollins, 2010.

Kalb, Marvin. *Imperial Gamble: Putin, Ukraine, and the New Cold War.* Washington, D.C.: Brookings Institution Press, 2015.

Libicki, Martin. *Crisis and Escalation in Cyberspace.* Santa Monica, CA: RAND Corporation, 2012.

Mankoff, Jeffrey. *Russian Foreign Policy: The Return of Great Power Politics*. Lanham, MD: Rowman & Littlefield, 2009.

Myers, Stephen Lee. *The New Tsar: The Rise and Reign of Vladimir Putin*. New York: Alfred A. Knopf, 2015.

GHOSTNET

GhostNet is the name given by researchers to one of the most well-known examples of an advanced persistent threat (APT), or a cyber attack by which an unauthorized user acquires access to a network and maintains access for a significant period of time to steal information. The term *ghost net* refers to the tendency of fishermen to leave or lose their nets in the ocean, where they appear to be almost invisible in dim light. In this case, the casting of virtually invisible nets through cyber networks resulted in the infection of more than 1,200 high-profile computers, including those of many prominent diplomats, in 103 countries.

GhostNet sought to extract sensitive information from the Tibetan government-in-exile, the Office of the Dalai Lama, and Tibetan nongovernmental organizations (NGOs), many of which are located in Dharamsala, India. The Dalai Lama fled the People's Republic of China (PRC) in 1959, and he and other organizations have increasingly turned to the Internet as a means of communication as well as a way to gain support for Tibetan causes, which has often embarrassed the PRC.

Much of what is known about GhostNet comes from a Canadian-based organization known as Information Warfare Monitor (IWM), which released its findings in 2009 in a report titled *Tracking GhostNet: Investigating a Cyber Espionage Network*. IWM wanted to focus on this particular incident because of the unique level of access the Tibetan organizations willingly provided. IWM subsequently followed up this investigation with a report titled *Shadows in the Cloud: Investigating Cyber Espionage 2.0*, with its title highlighting how cyber espionage increasingly relies on the cloud as well as social networking for command and control. The report shows how the cloud provides attackers with the ability to hide while offering more redundancy and reliability. The report further voiced concerns with a trend toward cyber privateering, or the process by which a government approves of individuals engaging in cyber attacks. IWM also worried that the line between cyber crime and cyber espionage was becoming increasingly blurred.

GhostNet functions very similarly to other APTs. Attackers become familiar with the target's background to craft an e-mail most likely to seem perfectly normal because it comes from a known recipient about an expected topic of conversation. This type of social engineering is often referred to as the "information acquisition phase," or a spear-phishing e-mail. Then the recipient clicks on a Word, PDF, or other type of file. Again, the attachment is made to appear extremely relevant. Upon opening the file, malware becomes embedded in the system. As recipients continue to use the unknowingly infected computer, they spread the virus within the network as well as to other users from different networks. Simultaneously, the malware establishes connections with the attacker's servers, which communicate and allow for the transmission of information back to the attacker. Once established, this malware often remains in the computer for as long as a year, as antivirus software generally fails to detect it. The Office of the Dalai Lama, for example, only became alert to the possibility that its information had been compromised when it contacted diplomats to schedule interviews and subsequently learned that the Chinese government had recently pressured those same diplomats not to meet with it.

To gain access to Tibetan files, attackers had trailed the online discussions of Tibetan monks, which helped them discover their e-mail addresses. They then sent seemingly legitimate e-mails using the names of other monks and included attachments with names like "Translation of Freedom Movement ID Book for Tibetans in Exile.doc." They were also able to steal e-mail as it was being sent and replace the original attachments with malware. Having obtained an initial foothold, they then proceeded to target higher-ranking staff members. Once they had access to the system, the malware spread via e-mail to the contacts in their e-mail accounts, thus leading to the infection of over 1,200 computers in organizations around the world.

Not only did GhostNet enable its attackers to gain access to information, but it allowed them to control the victims' computers, including activating microphones and cameras to surveil them. This resulted from the type of Trojan placed on the system, known as a RAT, or remote access tool. Researchers have traced the origin of this tool to Hainan Island, People's Republic of China. With this information, the Chinese government could acquire information to imprison Tibetans or to stop them from reentering the country. One Tibetan woman, for example, returned to the country claiming to have been away at school. Challenging her claim, interrogators showed her copies of her online chats.

Despite detailed research, IWM has not established a definitive link between the Chinese government and the compromise of Tibetan computers. In fact, it is insistent that it would be erroneous to claim the government is involved. It particularly urges a careful consideration of the issue in light of the difficulty of attributing attacks. For example, another nation could be using a "false flag scenario" by which another entity could be making China appear to be the culprit. Similarly, although many of the domain names used in GhostNet have been registered to the same person, they could have been stolen. Scholars point to the existence of a strong and large constituency of patriotic hackers in China as well as criminal operators who could also be behind this. IWM's measured conclusions are in contrast to a more vocal but similar report made by Mandiant Corporation in regard to PRC's Unit 61398.

Heather Pace Venable

See also: Attribution; Cloud Computing; Cyber Attack; Cyber Espionage; Malware; Mandiant Corporation; People's Liberation Army Unit 61398; People's Republic of China Cyber Capabilities; Social Engineering; Spear Fishing; Spyware; Trojan Horse

Further Reading

Adair, Steven, Ron Deibert, Rafal Rohozinski, Nate Villeneuve, and Greg Walton. *Shadows in the Cloud: Investigating Cyber Espionage 2.0.* Toronto: A Joint Report of the Information Warfare Monitor and Shadowserver Foundation, 2010.

Deibert, Ron, and Rafal Rohozinski. *Tracking GhostNet: Investigating a Cyber Espionage Network*. Toronto: Centre for International Studies, University of Toronto, 2009.

Lin, Xue, and Rocci Luppicini. "Socio-technical Influences of Cyber Espionage: A Case Study of the GhostNet System." In *Moral, Ethical, and Social Dilemmas in the Age of Technology: Theories and Practice*. Edited by Rocci Luppicini. Hershey, PA: Information Science Reference, 2013: 112–124.

Nagaraja, Shishir, and Ross Anderson. *The Snooping Dragon: Social-malware Surveillance of the Tibetan Movement*. Cambridge: Computer Laboratory, University of Cambridge, 2009.

Poindexter, Dennis F. *The Chinese Information War: Espionage, Cyberwar, Communications Control and Related Threats to United States Interests*. Jefferson, NC: McFarland, 2013.

GOOGLE

Google is a software giant known for revolutionizing Internet navigation and applications, including its eponymous search engine, innovative advertising technology, cloud computing, and e-mail. Google's main focus has been the development of cross-platform organizational applications for personal and corporate users. The conglomerate's key competitors include Apple and Microsoft. With its unofficial motto, "Don't be evil," Google's business philosophy champions open access to information while working to safeguard its consumers—and proprietary technology—from cyber attacks.

In 1997, while doctoral students at Stanford University Larry Page and Sergey Brin used a research project as the basis for a search engine whose unique algorithm utilized a Web site's links to other sites. The next year, the duo registered google.com, and the company Google was formally established in Menlo Park, California, in 1998. Later that year, the search engine was an indomitable force on the Web, largely because of consumer word of mouth. From 2000 until 2004, Google was Yahoo's client search engine, a further boost to the company's growth and profile. Eric Schmidt, CEO of software firm Novell Inc., became Google's first CEO and chair in 2001. Google went public in 2004, and it reorganized in 2015, establishing Alphabet as an umbrella company with Google as a subsidiary. Page became Alphabet's CEO and Brin its president.

Much of Google's revenue is produced through advertising generated by consumer searches. This abundant revenue source permitted it to prioritize research and development (and experimentation). To this end, Google turned to developing groundbreaking Web-based applications. Google Earth, a sophisticated mapping service that provides interactive satellite imagery and localized statistics, was released in 2005. Google Apps debuted in 2006 and included a free calendar and word-processing programs, albeit with advertisements. After enhanced security features were incorporated, Google Apps increased its popularity with corporate consumers. Launched publicly in 2007, Gmail, Google's free cloud-based e-mail application, offered an unprecedented 1 gigabyte of free storage. The Web browser Chrome launched in 2008. Google moved into mobile operating systems when it acquired Android Inc., the creator of wireless device operating systems, in 2005, leading to innovation in cloud services, smartphones, and tablet development.

After the disappointing performance of Google Video, the company purchased its biggest video-streaming market competitor, YouTube, in 2006. Google+, a social network rival for Facebook, went live in 2011. As of 2016, the conglomerate's driverless car was being readied for market.

Google has had a number of issues due to a perceived lack of sensitivity regarding personal data privacy. Google's use of targeted advertising has produced an effective revenue stream, yet the methodology has drawn criticism. Targeted advertising involves mining user data via tracking searches and scanning e-mail. Consumer watchdogs see this as a privacy violation and contend its accepted use as a corporate tool has bled into Google's product development, whereby innovation comes before privacy and obtaining permission. This has resulted in investigations and legal action over application data mining and privacy encroachment; for example, Google's Street View's potentially intrusive photographic mapping project drew international ire, and amassing data on millions of students through Google Apps for Education resulted in a lawsuit filed by University of California, Berkeley, students and Harvard alumni. In 2011, Google Health, a medical record application permitting company servers access to sensitive private information, was canceled.

Despite Google's shaky history stretching user privacy boundaries, it has been a fierce advocate for cyber security. The company guards its code closely, with particular concern over software vulnerabilities, going so far as to financially reward hackers who revealed flaws. In July 2014, Google established Project Zero, a unit of security researchers assembled to find possible weaknesses in open-source applications, which present opportunities to criminals, state-sponsored hackers, and government intelligence organizations. These countersurveillance initiatives increased after Edward J. Snowden's revelations showed National Security Agency (NSA) surveillance had captured Google user information.

In response to its own hacking incidents, Google has taken up a position of corporate social responsibility, moving to protect human rights activists and combat repressive forces threatening cyber space. This has brought it into direct conflict with authoritarian states. To access the vast Chinese market, Google agreed to follow government-censorship protocols. In January 2010, Google announced that Chinese hackers were spying on users who had searched for information on Chinese dissident organizations. These hackers also explicitly targeted human rights activists, foreign journalists, and the Dalai Lama, and they passed Google's intellectual property to its Chinese-based competitors. Hackers had broken into Google's source code and network servers. As a result of Operation Aurora, Google announced it would not abide censorship policies and directed Chinese searches to its Hong Kong servers, where they would be unfiltered. This precipitated a withdrawal from the mainland Chinese market, though Google's (censored) Chinese services gradually came back online. As of 2016, Google was preparing to reenter China, working with authorities to establish an Android store offering only government-approved applications.

Google's experience in China led to a tentative cyber-security alliance with U.S. government intelligence agencies, which, as the Snowden leaks disclosed, has been tenuous. Google participated in talks with President Barack Obama's Commission on Enhancing National Cybersecurity, a series of public-private sector conferences to develop recommendations for improving the American position on cyber security. In June 2016, Google joined executives from other tech firms, such as IBM, in pushing a commission agenda based on consumer data privacy, threat sharing between government agencies and industry, and transparency. Google has argued that the relationship between the government and tech firms has been badly damaged by agency secrecy, especially the use of national security letter (NSL) gag orders, documents to secretly compel customer information disclosure. Indeed, Google has been an industry leader in public advocacy over government data collection, publishing NSL transparency reports and data demands since 2010.

Anna Zuschlag

See also: Apple Inc.; Baidu; Microsoft Corporation; National Security Agency (NSA); Obama, Barack; Operation Aurora; People's Republic of China Cyber Capabilities; Snowden, Edward J.

Further Reading

DeVos, Stephanie A. "The Google-NSA Alliance: Developing Cybersecurity Policy at Internet Speed." *Fordham Intellectual Property, Media, and Entertainment Law Journal* 21:1 (2011): 174–227.

Hughes, Christopher R. "Google and the Great Firewall." *Survival* 52(2), April–May 2010: 19–26.

Stross, Randall E. *Planet Google: One Company's Audacious Plans to Organize Everything We Know.* New York: Free Press, 2008.

Tan, Justin, and Anna E. Tan. "Business under Threat, Technology under Attack, Ethics under Fire: The Experience of Google in China." *Journal of Business Ethics* 110(4), November 2012: 469–479.

HACKER

The earliest use of *hacker* referred to an unorthodox problem solver and master programmer. Many of these original hackers made the machines and programs that are vital to modern society. There is no one universal meaning for the term *hacker* due to the many terms that have been created to define the different types of hackers, such as *computer cracker* and *black hat* to describe criminal hackers. The widespread, popular belief is that hackers are bad people who do bad things, but this oversimplifies the concept.

The original hackers typically did not hack with the intention of doing harm to others but because they lacked the necessary resources on their own. These hackers who received recognition for their contributions disputed the criminalization of the word *hacker*. The origin of the term *hacker* comes from the Massachusetts Institute of Technology (MIT), where students engaged in elaborate pranks dubbed *hacks*. When students first applied *hacker* to computer hackers, there was a serious amount of respect implied because the feat involved innovation, style, and technical virtuosity. As a result, hacking was most closely associated with overcoming the limitations of early computers with creative, unorthodox problem solving. Due to the limited number of computers available, hackers took special care not to harm them while hacking the programs.

The concept of hacking persisted into the 1960s as computers shifted from university to military applications. This angered many programmers, despite the significant funding of their work by the military and the federal government. At the center of this backlash was the belief that information should be free to all to understand how things work and can be improved. It was at this time that a hacker ethic developed and formed the core of hacker culture. This ethic included the following tenets: access to computers; free access to information; a mistrust of authority; the idea that hackers should be judged on their hacking, not formal degrees; that one can create art and beauty on a computer; and that computers can change one's life for the better.

Breaking computer laws between the 1950s and 1970s never concerned hackers because there were no laws to break. Criminal hacking emerged and generated a significant impact on society in the 1980s and 1990s with the increased use and prominence of the Internet and IBM's new stand-alone personal computer. By the start of the year 2000, most computers were interconnected through the Internet, including the ability to find government and other sensitive data. Due to the access of so much information on the Internet, hackers' actions began to become more malicious in nature.

Hackers use terms to draw distinctions between themselves, and understanding these different types allows insight into the hacker community. A first differentiation is between hackers and cyber criminals. A "pure" hacker is harder to prosecute because the laws are designed around financial damages. Most of hacker online activity is perfectly legal; however, the hacker subculture does accept some actions that violate laws. It is when the actions of hackers overlap with computer crime that criminal hacking occurs. Cyber criminals, on the other hand, engage in acts more often associated with criminality, such as fraud, scamming, and embezzlement.

There are numerous terms for different types of hackers in the larger subculture. Crackers are malicious hackers, though there is no final authority who determines when a hacker crosses this line. Script kiddies are mischievous hackers often primarily concerned with bragging and attacking each other or anyone who draws their wrath. They tend to have limited programming skills, instead relying on downloaded attack programs. White hat hackers are often termed "ethical" hackers because they have reformed and entered the computer-security field. One example of white hat hackers is "tiger teams" who test organizations' cyber defenses by attacking their own employer's site. Gray hat hackers generally behave in an ethical manner, but they sometimes violate accepted ethics. Their intrusions are typically recreational, and they do not profit or cause harm as a result of their actions. At times, they even inform the system administrators of security flaws.

Black hat hackers are essentially a cracker or malicious hacker, although this term does not apply to all computer criminals. Only when hackers' actions violate or conflict with hacker ethics are they considered black hat hackers. These hackers tend to have a great deal more skill than script kiddies and, in contrast with popular perceptions, are quite open about their beliefs and actions. There are even black hat conferences where hackers gather to share ideas, concepts, and even train with new methodologies and tactics.

Finally, hacktivists are hackers who have come together to challenge the treatment of their peers by the government. These hacktivists often focus on political ends rather than the standard goals of the hacker subculture. Due to the fact that most hacktivist activities are legal, they are one of the most accessible of hacker types.

The hacker subculture appears to provide some justification for behavior, information, and skills to engage in hacking as well as beliefs about the nature of their actions. There are several subcultural norms that hackers use to shape the understanding of their actions. First, the relationship between technology and hackers represents a deep connection that structures hackers' interests and activities. Second, hackers pursue knowledge; they have a devotion to learning about and understanding technology. Third, they possess a level of commitment to their belief system; true hackers that move beyond script kiddies have devoted time and effort in progressing their skills to an advanced level. Fourth, hackers categorize their actions; commitment, knowledge, and technology clearly affect how hackers construct their meaning and definition of *hacker*. Finally, hackers are aware of the law; they regularly discuss the legality of hacking and information sharing in both the cyber and real worlds. Hackers are acutely aware of the legal codes because they want to know whether their activities are legal. It is important to understand the hacker subculture because the hackers themselves are acutely aware of their own history and subcultural hierarchy. Understanding these aspects allows society to better adapt to their increased presence in society.

Christopher Menking

See also: Anonymous; Black Hat; Hacktivist; LulzSec; Mitnick, Kevin; Patriotic Hacking; Tenenbaum, Ehud "Udi"; White Hat

Further Reading

Haerens, Margaret, and Lynn M. Zott, eds. *Hacking and Hackers.* Detroit: Greenhaven Press, 2014.
Holt, Thomas J., and Bernadette H. Schell. *Hackers and Hacking: A Reference Handbook.* Santa Barbara, CA: ABC-CLIO, 2013.
Levy, Steven. *Hackers: Heroes of the Computer Revolution.* Beijing: O'Reilly, 2010.
Taylor, Robert W., Eric J. Fritsch, and John Liederbach. *Digital Crime and Digital Terrorism.* 3rd ed. Upper Saddle River, NJ: Pearson, 2015.

HACKTIVIST

A hacktivist refers to an individual who practices a form of digital civil disobedience known as *hacktivism*. Hacktivism is the practice of using computer hacking as a form of political activism (hacking + activist = hacktivist). Hacktivism can be perpetrated by an individual or a group. Notable hacktivists include Julian Assange (1971–) and Aaron Schwartz (1986–2013). Notable hacktivist groups include Anonymous, LulzSec, Cult of the Dead Cow (cDc), and Hacktivismo. All these individuals and groups have used their hacking skills for explicitly political purposes. The term *hacktivism* itself is credited to cDc member Omega, who first used the term in an e-mail. The first known instance of hacktivism, that is, computer hacking with an explicitly political aim, dates to 1989, when hackers unleashed a computer worm on computers at NASA to protest nuclear weapons.

Hacktivist activities are rooted in hacktivists' culture of "tricksterdom," or conducting online pranks; yet, they also share a common purpose with other forms of civil disobedience. Hacktivism is a direct action meant to bring attention to a political cause or issue. Commonly used tactics include using malware, defacing Web sites, distributed denial-of-service (DDoS) attacks, constructing mirror sites, or diverting Web traffic. The cDc computer-hacking group is widely recognized as the first with a specific political cause, namely, supporting human rights, in particular free speech. The group cDc partnered with the Hong Kong Blondes to hack into Chinese networks for the purpose of overriding censorship filters. From there, other groups, such as the Electronic Disturbance Theater and the Legions of the Underground (LoU) began to use computer-hacking skills to attack government Web sites and networks as a form of protest.

Like other forms of civil disobedience, it is not without controversy. Critics equate hacktivism with cyber terrorism, or the use of targeted computer attacks to cause harm or violence to unsuspecting individuals for political purposes. Governments argue that hacktivist tactics can be easily co-opted by terrorist groups to cause widespread harm or violence to populations. However, governments, such as the United States and Canada, have been known to draft hacktivists, specifically to attack Chinese and Iranian Internet censorship.

There are also disagreements among hacktivists as to what can be considered acceptable forms of digital disobedience. Members of the cDc argue that groups like Anonymous, who engage in DDoS attacks or who shut down access to Web sites, are not practicing hacktivism, as they are themselves violating norms of free speech. In a DDoS attack, Web sites that hackers find distasteful are essentially shut down. Oxblood Ruffin, a cDc hacktivist, likens attacks such as these to the digital equivalent of "shouting someone down at a town hall meeting." For these hacktivists, there are definite limits as to what actions qualify as hacktivism. According to many hacktivists, any activity meant solely to silence a message that one may find distasteful does not qualify as hacktivism.

Barbara Salera

See also: Anonymous; Assange, Julian; 4chan; LulzSec

Further Reading

Coleman, Gabriella. *Hacker, Hoaxer, Whistleblower, Spy: The Many Faces of Anonymous.* London: Verso, 2014.
Olson, Parmy. *We Are Anonymous: Inside the Hacker World of LulzSec, Anonymous and the Global Cyber Insurgency.* New York: Back Bay Books, 2012.
Stryker, Cole. *Hacking the Future: Privacy, Identity, and Anonymity on the Web.* New York: Overlook Duckworth, 2012.

HARDWARE

Hardware is a general term for the physical parts of a computer, but the specific instances of hardware differ between handheld, laptop, desktop, mainframe, or supercomputers. In fact, even a computing chip contained in digital watch or automobile computer has elements similar to the hardware components found in a laptop or desktop computer. The main distinction is not between different types of hardware, but between the software that provides operating instructions to hardware and the hardware itself.

The basic hardware components of a desktop personal computer are a case, a monitor, a motherboard (integrated circuitry that connects most of the components together), a central processing unit (CPU), random-access memory (RAM), a power supply, an optical disc drive, a hard disk drive, a keyboard, and a mouse. Laptops are quite similarly constructed and usually have all the hardware components contained in the same case, unlike a desktop, which connects many of the components, such as the keyboard, monitor, mouse, and (often) an optical disc drive, by a variety of cables through ports on the outside of the case.

Data is stored by a computer using a variety of media hardware, both hardwired and removable. Peripherals are input and output devices typically housed externally to the main computer case; they can include a mouse, keyboard, touch-pad, Web cam, microphone, joystick, image scanner, printer, monitor, or speakers.

Jeffrey R. Cares

See also: Software

Further Reading

Graham, James, Richard Howard, and Ryan Olson. *Cyber Security Essentials.* Boca Raton, FL: Auerbach Publications, 2011.

HAYDEN, MICHAEL V.

Michael V. Hayden (1945–), a retired four-star U.S. Air Force general, is a controversial figure in U.S. intelligence for his views on civil liberties in pursuing counterterrorism and interrogation. He is the only person to have led both the National Security Agency (NSA) and the Central Intelligence Agency (CIA).

Born in Pittsburgh, Pennsylvania, Hayden attended Duquesne University, where he earned a BA in history in 1967. After receiving a commission as a U.S. Air Force officer, he then received his MA in modern American history in 1969. Subsequently, he spent over 41 years in the air force as a career intelligence officer.

Hayden served as director of the NSA from 1999 to 2005 and revitalized the agency, replacing its Cold War mentality with a focus on counterterrorism. He sought to increase the NSA's openness, even inviting journalists to dine with him at his home. However, he also battled vocally with them, including in one notable exchange where he claimed that the Constitution's Fourth Amendment makes no mention of probable cause.

He also markedly expanded the collection of data, often controversially. Initially very concerned with the protection of civil liberties, he changed his mind after the attacks on 9/11. In light of that terrorist attack, he instituted a domestic-surveillance program that listened to conversations between American citizens and terrorists abroad without warrants. Similarly, he began a program of massive metadata collection, largely revealed by Edward J. Snowden's leak of classified sources. The program, known as PRISM, allowed the government to obtain personal information from key communication companies such as Google, Yahoo, and Facebook.

As director of the CIA from 2006 to 2009, Hayden helped further the transition of the agency from one of intelligence gathering to carrying out covert military operations, in large part through drone strikes. Hayden also called for the loosening of targeting restrictions on these drone operations. While the practice of "enhanced interrogation techniques" was already entrenched before his arrival, he continued to support the practice. Many argue that these techniques did not produce any real intelligence.

Hayden retired from the air force in 2008, and he now teaches as a distinguished visiting professor at George Mason University. He is also employed by the Chertoff

Group, where he provides subject matter expertise on intelligence, especially cyber issues. In the wake of the data breach at the Office of Personnel Management, Hayden proclaimed that if the NSA had been able to break into a similar Chinese office, it would have gladly taken analogous data, characterizing this as the typical behavior of powerful nations. He has also warned that the U.S. government is ill-prepared to handle cyber attacks and that U.S. technological corporations must pioneer the means of protecting the nation. In regard to Stuxnet, Hayden worried that the use of a cyber attack to cause physical destruction may have established a dangerous precedent.

In 2016, Hayden profiled his experiences with the NSA and CIA in *Playing to the Edge*. The title expresses his philosophy of pushing his intelligence operations as far as possible without actually breaking the law.

Heather Pace Venable

See also: Central Intelligence Agency (CIA); National Security Agency (NSA); Office of Personnel Management Data Breach; Snowden, Edward J.

Further Reading

Hayden, Michael V. *Playing to the Edge: American Intelligence in the Age of Terror.* New York: Penguin Press, 2016.

Kaplan, Fred. *Dark Territory: The Secret History of Cyber War.* New York: Simon & Schuster, 2016.

HONEYPOT

A honeypot is an isolated early warning security device or system used to gather information on outside intruders attacking a network system while safely protecting the more critical information on the network. The system or device acts like an additional layer of protection over the current Internet security systems in place. The honeypot is a decoy system to entice outside malicious attackers or spammers with false critical information that can be easily compromised while on a separate but similar safe network. Once the intruder enters the system, the system will detect, monitor, and record information on the intrusion. The system can be taken off-line to analyze and research the system's vulnerabilities. The old school of thought is that once the intruders have compromised the system they will return for more visits, which will allow the system to gather more information about each of the intrusions. The purpose of the honeypots allows one to gain a better insight into the attacker's methodologies of probing and gaining access into the system while better protecting and securing the real critical systems within a network.

The origin of honeypots can be linked back to the 1980s. One of the first recorded uses was by the military around 1986. They used fake military records as bait to entice intruders into the system. A more recent example came from the collective effort to battle the Conficker worm, when network defenders managed to divert the particularly dangerous malware into a honeypot, both as a preventive measure and to study its design.

Steven A. Quillman

See also: Conficker Worm; Cyber Security

Further Reading

Andress, Jason, and Steve Winterfield. *Cyber Warfare: Techniques, Tactics and Tools for Security Practitioners.* Waltham, MA: Syngress, 2011.
Bowden, Mark. *Worm: The First Digital World War.* New York: Grove Press, 2011.
Graham, James, Ryan Olson, and Richard Howard. *Cyber Security Essentials.* Boca Raton, FL: CRC Press. 2010.

IDENTITY THEFT

Identity theft is the practice of stealing and assuming a person's identity to use it for nefarious purposes, including financial gain, espionage, and disruption. Identity thieves target private information, such as Social Security numbers, passwords, log-in credentials, and credit card numbers. Identity theft is likely as old as humanity, but the advent of the cyber age transformed it. The invention of charge cards in the 1950s opened up new avenues for mayhem, and the combination of charge-card and check fraud created the modern definition of *identity theft*, which was coined in 1964. The networking of computer systems and the proliferation of e-commerce over the next several decades provided the opportunity for identity theft to take place partially or wholly by digital means, and identity theft now costs companies and financial institutions billions of dollars per year.

Methods of identity theft generally fall into three categories: physical, electronic, and hybrid. Physical methods involve the material theft of identifying credentials, such as stealing trash marked with them or forging documents. Electronic methods include the use of keylogging software on a target computer and phishing and pharming schemes. Hybrid methods involve a combination of the two methods, such as physically manipulating a radio-frequency identification (RFID) or Wi-Fi system to gain access to electronic information. *Ghosting* is the assumption of a dead person's identity, often for financial gain.

Phishing is one of the more popular forms of online identity theft, involving the sending of seemingly trustworthy messages designed to trick a target into revealing identifying information. Several specific forms of phishing exist, including *spear phishing*, where the target is a known quantity, and *whaling*, where the target is a high-level or wealthy person. *Pharming* is an evolution of the phishing techniques that redirects a target to a different Web site than intended to obtain identifying information. The above attacks and others are often used in conjunction with each other to accomplish the goal of identity theft. Taken together, they are referred to as *social engineering*.

In the realm of cyber warfare, identity theft plays a significant role. The same methods of social engineering and theft for financial gain are also used for espionage and warfighting. Identity theft can grant access to military databases, for example. Often, such intrusions will be combined with other intrusion methods, such as leaving a backdoor in the network to return. Identity thieves can also conceal themselves with remarkable ability in the modern cyber age by routing a network intrusion through multiple locations or proxies to conceal the original location of the intruder, as in the case of the 2014 Sony Pictures attack.

Kinetic operations can also be influenced by identity theft. The 2007 Israeli incursion into Syria, dubbed Operation Orchard; the likely Russian-based attacks Georgia in 2008; and NATO operations in the Balkans in the late 1990s all used identity theft to redirect enemy efforts on the battlefield. In each, attackers infiltrated enemy networks and misdirected antiaircraft and other defensive capabilities of the target states, allowing kinetic operations to proceed with little to no resistance in each case. Identity theft and concealment proved vital to each—although the United States avowed its role in the Balkans operations, neither the Operation Orchard nor Georgian attacks have been claimed by Israel or Russia.

Jonathan Abel

See also: Attribution; Authentication; Cyber Attack; Cyber Crime; Cyber Security; E-commerce; Georgian Cyber Attack (2008); Hacker; North Atlantic Treaty Organization (NATO); Operation Orchard; Phishing; Social Engineering; Spear Phishing; Spoofing

Further Reading

Biegelman, Martin. *Identity Theft Handbook: Detection, Prevention, and Security.* Hoboken, NJ: Wiley, 2009.

Kaplan, Fred. *Dark Territory: The Secret History of Cyber Warfare.* New York: Simon & Schuster, 2016.

Warren, Peter, and Michael Streeter. *Cyber Crime and Warfare.* London: Hodder & Stoughton, 2013.

ILOVEYOU VIRUS

While often called a virus, ILOVEYOU was technically a worm transmitted through Microsoft Outlook e-mail. E-mail was a popular method of electronic communication used by businesses to pass information and, for many, to stay in touch with others prior to the invention of many of today's popular social media sites. On May 4, 2000, two Filipino men took advantage of the need for information and social interconnectivity when they launched the worm via e-mail with the subject line "ILOVEYOU". When a recipient clicked on the "LOVE-LETTER-FOR-YOU.txt.vbs" e-mail attachment, it activated the Visual Basic script. The script sent copies of the virus to all Outlook addresses and damaged the host computer by overwriting random files. Ultimately, over 45 million people worldwide were affected, as the virus infected over 1 million computers per day, resulting in an estimated $5.5 billion in damage. At the time, the ILOVEYOU virus was the biggest malware event to date. All charges against the men responsible, Onel de Guzman and Reomel Ramones, were dropped by prosecutors, as there were no laws in the Philippines against malware writing at the time.

Brandee J. Harral

See also: Cyber Security; Malware; Worm

Further Reading

Bowden, Mark. *Worm*. New York: Grove Press, 2011.
Seltzer, Larry. "'I Love You Virus' Turns Ten: What Have We Learned?" *PCMag.com*, April 28, 2010. http://www.pcmag.com/article2/0,2817,2363172,00.asp.

INFORMATION WARFARE WEAPONS TREATY

An international debate over the necessity, feasibility, form, and desirability of an information warfare weapons treaty is ongoing between nations. There are several subjects for possible agreements and forms that a treaty could take. The subjects include treaties that would suppress private misconduct and treaties to restrict state action. The forms of such agreements could include multilateral conventions, bilateral agreements, UN General Assembly Resolutions, or a codification of existing customary international law.

Among the most basic issues complicating the ability to create such a treaty is in the definition of terms. There is a lack of consistent terminology and clear understanding of the possible types of weapons. For example, the term *information weapons* is used by some participants in the debate; others use *cyber weapons*. Are the terms interchangeable? What kinds of technologies qualify as weapons? Are any or all of these technologies dual use? The very nature of the technology under discussion makes creating a treaty problematic.

Perhaps the largest hurdle to the creation of a treaty regulating information warfare weapons is the ideological differences between the nations involved in the discussions. The United States and some European countries have articulated the desire to improve international cooperation in the investigation and prosecution of computer crimes and terrorism. Russia and a few other countries would like a treaty to focus on protecting international information security with multilateral arms control treaties.

It is also not clear to what extent a treaty is even needed. Some scholars contend that portions of the law of armed conflict apply, and others have suggested that the 1967 Outer Space Treaty may contain relevant principles. Scholars agree that it may be premature for the development of overarching principles concerning information warfare weapons.

There has been some successful international cooperation, however, in battling cyber crime and cyber terrorism. Researchers contend that it is less likely that an international agreement broadly prohibiting or regulating state action involving information warfare techniques will be created because the issues involved are not clearly understood by any of those involved. Nations do not know what is in their best interests. Even if such a treaty was supported and ratified by nation-states, regulating it would require a massive undertaking, if it could be achieved at all. Much of the discussion lacks the specificity needed for legal regulation. Instead of a treaty, it is more likely that international law will develop slowly, based on the actions and statements of nations in response to events as they happen.

Lori Ann Henning

See also: Cyber Attack; Cyber Crime; Cyber Weapon; Informatization; Laws of Armed Conflict

Further Reading

Arimatsu, Louise. "A Treaty for Governing Cyber-weapons: Potential Benefits and Practical Limitations." In *2012 4th International Conference on Cyber Conflict*. Edited by Christian Czosseck, Rain Ottis, and Katharina Ziolkowski. Talinn, Estonia: NATO CCD COE Publications, 2012.

Johnson, Phillip A. "Is It Time for a Treaty on Information Warfare?" In *Computer Network Attack and International Law*. Edited by Michael N. Schmitt and Brian T. O'Donnell. Newport, RI: Naval War College, 2002.

Johnson, Thomas A., ed. *Cybersecurity: Protecting Critical Infrastructures from Cyber Attack and Cyber Warfare*. Boca Raton, FL: CRC Press, 2015.

Kaplan, Fred M. *Dark Territory: The Secret History of Cyber War*. New York: Simon and Schuster, 2016.

INFORMATIZATION

Informatization is a total integration concept that refers to the application of informatics to a function, such as economics or national security. The informatization of society is a global movement. Some countries, such as Finland and the Republic of Korea, lead the way with almost universal Internet penetration. The United States as a society has been partially informatized. Google and Amazon have a presence in almost every home in the country and are aggregating and analyzing huge amounts of data. Approximately 64 percent of Americans have a smartphone in 2016, and 60 percent have personal computers. Other countries are following rapidly.

Informatization has huge implications for personal and national security. As billions of sensors provide metadata to the cloud, everyone gains the ability to personalize services and related purchases. As an example, people can now monitor and control certain aspects of their home security, such as cameras and locks, from their smartphones. However, this potentially allows hackers to use these same systems to determine that the house is empty and to unlock the door at will.

These opportunities and challenges also concern organizations and states. The United States has enjoyed a tremendous advantage in cyber operations, information warfare, logistics, and intelligence. This advantage is eroding as others seek to harness information for their own advantage. The Chinese and the Russians have both integrated informatization into their military concepts, particularly manifested in China's Military Strategy from May 2015 and the Military Doctrine of the Russian Federation from June 2015. There are two reasons for this. First, they have noted U.S. tactical battlefield prowess in modern conventional combat and have derived lessons from it. Second, they both fear their populations and seek to control all information that their people have access to. They both feel that the United States has fomented the "color revolutions" and are determined that they will not succumb to their own version.

Russia uses information as part of what they call "political warfare," which George Kennan described as "the employment of all the means at a nation's command, short of war, to achieve its national objectives." Others at the National Geospatial-Intelligence Agency call it Russia's "new generation warfare," which has five component elements: political subversion, proxy sanctuary, intervention, coercive deterrence and negotiated manipulation. Indeed, one set of authors uses all the terms—political warfare, hybrid-war, asymmetric warfare, and new-generation warfare—to describe the modern Russian approach. This is often referred to as the Gerasimov Doctrine, after Russian chief of the general staff Valery Gerasimov, who argues that nonmilitary means of achieving military strategic goals have grown. Others say there is no model, but that Moscow has instead shaped its operations upon careful analysis of the operational environment. The Russians themselves say that the characteristics of current military conflicts are the integrated employment of military force and the other elements of national power (e.g., political, economic, informational, or other nonmilitary measures). Regardless of the label, Russian efforts in Estonia in 2007, Georgia in 2008, and Ukraine in 2014–2015 are all manifestations of this Russian approach to warfare and were greatly enhanced by Russian cyber efforts.

Russia combines deniable operations with robust information capabilities that simultaneously legitimize their operations while delegitimizing those of their opponents. Their cyber efforts gather intelligence and perform operational preparation of the environment in case they want to develop cyber attacks in the future or disseminate propaganda on a global level. One tool that the Russians use are proxies. Proxies allow some sort of anonymity or deniability when performing offensive cyber operations. Analysts at the Center for Naval Analysis comment that powers will use proxies to achieve political and military effects in a deceptive and confusing manner to obscure the belligerent's direct participation. This all reflects their concept of informatization and their use of information warfare.

The Chinese seek to leverage information in support of their economy, as has the United States. The Alibaba Group was the world's largest retailer as of April 2016 and has functions similar to both Amazon and eBay. The Chinese military sees information as a domain, as does the U.S. military. Where the two differ is that China sees the network, electromagnetic, psychological, and intelligence domains as part of the information domain. Others include space, command and control, and physical operations (which would be similar to the Western concept of kinetic operations). China has even activated a new Strategic Support Force that commands all People's Liberation Army (PLA) cyber and space forces. This command reports directly to the Central Military Committee, which allows the government in Beijing to use these forces as national assets in the quest for information dominance. This may well increase the capability of the Chinese to achieve this goal.

The United States does not have a concept like informatization. The Department of Defense (DoD) stovepipes each of those communities within special groups. The commander is responsible for the integration of all effects in an operation, including information effects. Cyber operations are done by U.S. Cyber Command (USCYBERCOM); information operations and psychological operations both operate as part of information operations. The electronic warfare community is separate, as is the signals intelligence community. The U.S. Navy is the only DoD organization that has conceptualized information as something similar to the Chinese perspective by creating the Information Warfare Community (formerly the Information Dominance Corps), which contains intelligence, cyber, networks, space, oceanography, meteorology, and electronic warfare. They have also expanded the position of the chief of naval intelligence to encompass the role of the vice chief of naval operations for information warfare.

G. Alexander Crowther

See also: Cyber War; Patriotic Hacking; People's Liberation Army Unit 61398; People's Republic of China Cyber Capabilities; Russia Cyber Capabilities; *Unrestricted Warfare*

Further Reading

Libicki, Martin. *Cyberspace in Peace and War.* Annapolis, MD: U.S. Naval Institute Press, 2016.
Singer, P. W., and Allan Friedman. *Cybersecurity and Cyber War: What Everyone Should Know.* New York: Oxford University Press, 2014.
Springer, Paul J. *Cyber War: A Reference Handbook.* Santa Barbara, CA: ABC-CLIO, 2015.
Stiennon, Richard. *Surviving Cyber War.* Lanham, MD: Government Institutes, 2010.

INFRASTRUCTURE

The term *infrastructure* has multiple meanings in regard to cyber space. At a simplistic level, infrastructure in cyber space describes the connection between the physical world and the virtual world, but which specific part of that connection varies widely in each definition. The use of the term in cyber security stems from the more traditional use of the word to describe the critical systems, roads, and industries that society relies on to conduct the core of governance and commerce. Each of the following three terms has significant meaning in U.S. cyber-security policy and the U.S. cyber-security industry: critical infrastructure, cyber infrastructure, and hacking infrastructure.

In U.S. policy, *critical infrastructure* describes the core sectors required for governance and commerce. If disrupted, these industries could have a significant effect on the national security or economic security of the United States. Presidential Policy Directive (PPD) 21 established 16 critical infrastructure sectors: chemical, commercial facilities, communications, critical manufacturing, dams, defense industrial base, emergency services, energy, financial services, food and agriculture, government facilities, health care and public health, informational technology, nuclear, transportation, and water and waste. By identifying critical infrastructure, the U.S. government prioritizes efforts to protect these sectors through operational and cyber-security efforts. Each sector has a lead government agency responsible for ensuring its defense, and this extends to cyber space as well. The Department of Homeland Security (DHS) is responsible for the whole of the critical infrastructure protection program under PPD-21.

The focus of government effort to protect critical infrastructure stems from the vulnerability of how reliant much of that infrastructure is on cyber space. Networks and connectivity comprise a great deal of critical infrastructure management, especially in regard to public utilities. In 2003, President Bush focused his cyber-security strategy on this interdependency of critical infrastructure and cyber space and critical infrastructure's perceived vulnerability to sophisticated cyber threats.

Cyber infrastructure is a term used to describe routers, switches, servers, and cables that exist somewhere in the physical world. Usually this infrastructure of cyber space refers to the Internet backbone, but it may be used to apply to similar physical devices in corporations and governments. The backbone of the Internet is owned by a small handful of very large corporations, usually referred to as tier 1 Internet service providers (ISPs). Depending on the source, sometimes infrastructure is used to describe the physical devices and cables below the tier 1 ISP level, but cyber infrastructure almost always refers to physical devices that connect to cyber space. Tier 1 cyber infrastructure is considered a part of critical communications infrastructure.

Hacking infrastructure is used by cyber-security experts to describe the pathways adversaries use or create to conduct hacking activity. The purpose of building hacking infrastructure is to obfuscate the point of origin of the hacker and to enable hacking activity. Most cyber-security tactics are heavily dependent on defensive perimeters and host-based antivirus programs. To circumvent these defensive practices, a hacker uses computers throughout the world that will obfuscate the location of the hacker and frustrate attribution efforts. In some cases, hacking infrastructure can include thousands of computers available to a single threat actor.

Hacking infrastructure comprises the necessary components threats must build to support their hacking activity. Hacking infrastructure consists of three categories: infrastructure owned by the threat, infrastructure compromised by the threat, and infrastructure leased by the threat. Hackers need infrastructure to conduct successful penetrations because network defenders will block inbound addresses that are perceived to be hostile. Blocking actions by defenders can include large sections of Internet real estate, even entire countries. Hacking infrastructure is put together by hackers to circumvent these blocks to create successful network penetrations. Each piece of hacking infrastructure serves a different purpose for the hacker, and all these parts have cyber-security slang to describe them, such as hop points, malware repositories, and so on. When combined, hacking infrastructure forms the critical links in the way that hackers execute their activities.

To obfuscate their point of origin, hackers build or purchase hacking infrastructure to put distance between themselves and their targets. The source of the infrastructure is the computer or network that is usually owned by the hacker. Very rarely do sophisticated threats directly access victims from their source computers, and usually only by mistake. Most form an intermediary group of computers in between that are commonly referred to as *hop points* that relay commands between the source infrastructure and the target. Hop points are sometimes called *bots* or *zombies* as well. Depending on the threat, these hop points can completely frustrate network defenses. According to Mandiant Corporation, the APT1 espionage threat operated nearly 1,000 distinct and different hop points.

Each piece of hacking infrastructure is used for a specific purpose for hacking activity. Some function as simple relays that do nothing more than relay commands from one piece of infrastructure to another. Basic hacking infrastructure functions support command and control, relays, spear phishing, exfiltration, beaconing, Web hosting, and more. Each of these pieces of infrastructure are critical links to how a hacker exploits a target, but they are often disposable if they are blocked by the victim.

The primary purpose of infrastructure is to defeat the victim's attempts to easily identify hostile activity, but it will also complicate foreign policy and domestic laws. The location of hacking infrastructure throughout the world will greatly affect the legal and policy structures used to pursue or combat cyber threats. Greater foreign policy concerns will always supersede cyber-space operational considerations in attempting to pursue cyber threats through hacking infrastructure. Additionally, surveillance of domestic hacking infrastructure used by foreign adversaries compounds privacy concerns for governments. Countries that lack cyber-security cooperation are safe havens for hackers to build infrastructure and avoid pursuit. Additionally, governments often struggle to pursue cyber threats when hackers build infrastructure in cooperating nations, causing a delay while governments coordinate pursuit operations. Adversaries often cause geographic operational problems by rapidly moving through numerous countries to attack targets. Hacking infrastructure allows an adversary to exploit this complicated policy and legal structure.

Zachary M. Smith

See also: Cyber Defense; Hacking; Hardware; National Cyber Security Strategy; National Infrastructure Advisory Council (NIAC); National Infrastructure Protection Plan (NIPP)

Further Reading

Brenner, Joel. *America the Vulnerable: Inside the New Threat Matrix of Digital Espionage, Crime, and Warfare.* New York: Penguin, 2011.

Carr, Jeffrey. *Inside Cyber Warfare: Mapping the Cyber Underworld.* Sebastopol, CA: O'Reilly Media, 2009.

Clarke, Richard A., and Robert K. Knake. *Cyber War: The Next Threat to National Security and What to Do about It.* New York: HarperCollins, 2010.

Libicki, Martin. *Cyberspace in Peace and War.* Annapolis, MD: U.S. Naval Institute Press, 2016.

INTEL CORPORATION

Intel Corporation is an American manufacturer of semiconductor circuits for computers that is based in California. Intel was founded in 1968 by Robert Noyce (1927–1990) and Gordon Moore (1929–). Initially, the company was named Integrated Electronics, before it was shortened to the more commonly recognized moniker, Intel. Other noted contributors to the success of the business are Arthur

Rock (1926–) and Andy Grove (1936–2016). Intel is also known for producing random-access memory (RAM) chips, microprocessors, and integrated circuits.

Noyce, a graduate of the Massachusetts Institute of Technology (MIT) with a doctorate of physics in 1953, and Moore, holding a PhD in chemistry from the California Institute of Technology in 1954, left Fairchild Semiconductor to begin Intel. Fairchild was noted for being a leader in the creation of integrated circuits and transistors. Both Noyce and Moore used lessons learned from their days at Fairchild Semiconductor to build their new company. Gordon Moore is also famous for coining what became known as "Moore's Law," the belief that the number of transistors that could fit on integrated circuits would double approximately every 18 months. In other words, Moore recognized a pattern in past development and the advancement of technology, and he predicted that such growth would continue.

Rock is the founder of the term *venture capitalism* and is a noted investor who helped secure the $2.5 million that was used to start Intel. Grove joined the corporation and is credited with elevating the company to the status of world leader in microprocessors. Grove was another initial member of the Intel Corporation who received a PhD in chemical engineering from the University of California, Berkley, in 1963. Grove began as head of research and development with the firm and was tasked with finding ways for the newly formed enterprise to continually move forward. Eventually, Grove became president and also served as chief executive officer.

Intel is recognized for developing the first commercially available microprocessors and microcomputers. A microprocessor condenses the tasks on an integrated circuit board, thereby streamlining the internal processes of the computer. The company next developed dynamic random-access memory chips during the 1980s, an upgrade from static-memory chips. Eventually, Intel was able to establish their brand identity behind the revolutionary technology in Pentium processors, released in 1993.

The Pentium line of processors continued to elevate the status of Intel as a household name in computing. Ultimately, Intel became synonymous with producing high-quality computing products. In 2006, there was an announcement that the Pentium line of products would be discontinued. However, instead of fading away, Pentium processors endured and were improved as dual-core processors, meaning the chip contained two independent cores, or processing units, which sped up processing capabilities.

Overall, Intel Corporation is known for pushing the industry as a whole forward. Fast and reliable computing has become an essential component in the modern age of technology. Business is expected to be conducted with the aid of computers and the Internet. It has become a necessity to keep up with the leading edge of evolving technology so as not be caught behind the competition.

Jason R. Kluk

See also: Hardware; Moore's Law

Further Reading

Colwell, Robert P. *The Pentium Chronicles: The People, Passion, and Politics behind Intel's Landmark Chips.* Hoboken, NJ: Wiley-Interscience, 2006.

Jackson, Tim. *Inside Intel: Andy Grove and the Rise of the World's Most Powerful Chip Company.* Oakland, CA: University of California Press, 1998.

Malone, Michael S. *The Intel Trinity: How Robert Noyce, Gordon Moore, and Andy Grove Built the World's Most Important Company.* New York: HarperBusiness, 2014.

INTELLECTUAL PROPERTY

Intellectual property (IP) is the expression used to denote a series of legal principles and domains that create exclusive rights in intangible "properties of mind." These properties of mind are designated "intangible" because they emerge as aspects of human creativity that defy simple physical description or substance. The law of intellectual property is thought to provide an incentive to authors and inventors to produce works for the benefit of the public. In turn, intellectual property law regulates the public's use of such works to ensure that authors and inventors are fairly compensated for their efforts. The various aspects of intellectual property are usually classified into the following six categories: (1) copyright; (2) patents; (3) trade secrets; (4) trademarks; (5) unfair competition; and (6) right of publicity. Federal statutes establish and regulate copyrights, patents, and trademarks. Trade secrets, rights of publicity, and aspects of unfair competition fall under the jurisdiction of states.

Copyright laws protect works of authorship, such as books, magazine articles, computer programs, drawings, movies, and the like. Copyright does not protect the ideas and information themselves, but only the form in which those ideas are conveyed (e.g., art, writing, music). The author's rights are usually protected for the duration of the author's life plus 70 years. Patents, issued by governments only protect creations for 20 years, but they also protect ideas and inventions that are not covered by copyright. Trade secrets are defined as a secret that (1) gives its owner an actual or potential advantage in business and (2) the owner exercises reasonable measures to maintain. Trade secret laws protect commercially valuable ideas, such as the formula for Coca-Cola or particular research processes used by a company to develop products.

Trade secret laws are particularly relevant in the software development world, especially when software designers move to competitors' companies. This issue of trade secret misappropriation and noncompete clauses was most famously taken up in the *IBM v. Papermaster* case, after Mark Papermaster moved from IBM to Apple in 2008. Celebrity rights, sometimes also called rights of publicity, generally protect the commercial persona of well-known athletes, singers, and actors. Trademarks are not used to protect ideas, creations, or persons, but rather to protect brands that indicate where a product comes from, for example, Apple's apple logo. Finally, the laws of unfair competition largely parallel trademark law but have a broader scope. For example, they are often used to protect information that has been costly to gather or produce from misappropriation by competitors.

Intellectual property issues have taken on a whole new character since the development of the Internet and World Wide Web. Not only is it difficult to control information, but manipulating information and "pointing" to information can also be done with ease and a lack of accountability. Additionally, compression, streaming, and MP3 technologies now make the packaging and distribution of music and video much easier. For example, the 1999 landmark case of the *Recording Industry Association of America (RIAA) v. Napster*, an online peer-to-peer file-sharing service that allowed millions of computer users to get free access to copyrighted music, highlights the challenges of dealing with intellectual property issues in the digital age.

With respect to intellectual property and the military, the landscape is becoming increasingly complex. For example, weapons technologies are usually developed by both the government and private sector. Delineating who owns what is often the subject of complex contract and licensing agreements. Additionally, some countries are often reluctant to export weapons systems to allied countries who have weak intellectual property laws. Finally, as the technical sophistication of military weapons systems has increased, and these systems derive an increasing proportion of their value from intellectual property, it is not unlikely that in the future there will be an increase in cyber attacks on states, companies, and the law firms that protect patents.

Deonna D. Neal

See also: Cyber Crime; Cyber Espionage; Cyber Ethics

Further Reading

Hunter, Dan. *The Oxford Introduction to U.S. Law: Intellectual Property.* Oxford: Oxford University Press, 2012.

McJohn, Stephen M. *Examples & Explanations: Intellectual Property.* 5th ed. New York: Wolters Kluwer Law and Business, 2015.

Menell, Peter S., and Mark A. Lemley. *Intellectual Property in the new Technological Age.* 6th ed. New York: Aspen Publishers, 2012.

INTERNET

The Internet is a worldwide community of linked computer networks operating through a common protocol. Originally, there was a distinction between the capitalized "Internet," which referred to the system built on the U.S. government's network "backbone," and the lowercase "internet," which referred to the generic linkage of two or more networks. Today, both versions of the word are used interchangeably.

The idea of a network of computers became feasible soon after the advent of computer science in the post–World War II era. The concept of *packet-switching* envisioned a system of blocks of data (packets) being sent over links in a network through various nodes, which could change the route (switching) of the packets, allowing them to reach their destination by multiple paths. Telephone systems were too rigid for this type of network, so a digital network of computers became the preferred method.

The Advanced Research Projects Agency (ARPA), a U.S. Department of Defense (DoD) organization dedicated to scientific research, established a large-scale computer network based on the packet-switching concept in 1969. ARPANET connected computer laboratories across the country and enabled the laboratories to share capabilities and information. Host computers at each location were connected to large interface message processors (IMPs) that were programmed to communicate with other IMPs on the network. This "subnet" allowed hosts with otherwise incompatible hardware and operating systems to send data to one another. These IMPs would also serve as packet-switches, allowing for messages to be routed and rerouted through various lines to their destinations.

Soon after ARPANET became operational, an informal group of designers (who were also users) met regularly to discuss ways to improve and expand the network. Group members captured their ideas in modestly titled "Requests for Comments" (RFC). One of their first tasks was to establish a common method for the IMPs to communicate with one another, which they completed in 1970 and named the Network Control Protocol (NCP.)

ARPANET's public debut came in October 1972, at the First International Conference on Computer Communications (ICCC) in the Washington, D.C., Hilton. It was there that attendees from the computer and communications industries were introduced to the packet-switching network and were allowed to experiment with it on one of 40 terminals. Visitors could play chess games, read news, converse with a simulated psychiatrist program, and access other programs and information. The exhibit not only convinced the communications technology community that packet-switching networks were feasible, but it also brought about the establishment of the International Network Working Group (INWG), which sought to spread and combine network technology beyond the United States.

Although it was officially a DoD network designed for the performance of government contracts, users soon utilized ARPANET for other unofficial purposes. The introduction of electronic mail (e-mail) in July 1972 as part of the File Transfer Protocol (FTP) dramatically changed the manner and frequency of usage. By 1973, three-fourths of all traffic on ARPANET was through e-mail. This set the stage for the arrival of the first virtual community, Message Services Group (MsgGroup), where users could conduct conversations, and even arguments, on a variety of issues, purportedly to establish standards for network usage but often ranging on a wide-variety of topics. The concept of *flaming*, or sending a hostile message over e-mail, arose during this time—as did the introduction of *emoticons*. One of the more popular unofficial lists was SF-LOVERS, for the well-represented cohort of science-fiction enthusiasts on the network. In 1975, operational responsibility for ARPANET was transferred to the Defense Communications Agency (DCA), which established a more rigid administration and prohibited several of these frivolous customs.

In the years after the ICCC, other networks arose independent of ARPANET, and computer scientists began to consider ways to enable communications between them. This led to the design of the Transmission Control Protocol/Internet Protocol (TCP/IP), which established a standard set of rules to send data between networks through "gateway" computers. The concept was successfully tested in 1977, and in 1983, ARPANET adopted TCP/IP. This action is considered to be the official establishment of the Internet.

During the 1980s, Internet usage grew exponentially with the increased availability of local area networks (LANs) and personal computers (PCs). This demand strained ARPANET's resources. Another government agency, the National Science Foundation (NSF), had established its own network, NSFNET, with a backbone of five supercomputers. ARPANET's connections were transferred to the more capable NSFNET, and the older network was decommissioned in 1990.

Who invented the Internet? It may seem like a rhetorical question, but there are some notable contributors. Paul Baran of the RAND Corporation compared technological development to the construction of a cathedral, built over many years by many hands, none of whom could claim full credit. What follows is a brief and incomplete summary of some of the architects and builders, in rough chronological order of their contributions:

- J.C.R. Licklider served as the director of ARPA's Command and Control Division and Behavioral Science Division in the early 1960s. He established research contracts with geographically distributed computer centers, which he named the "Intergalactic Computer Network," and wrote at length about the possibility of a network of computers communicating through a standardized set of conventions (later called *protocols*).
- Polish-born engineer Paul Baran and English scientist Donald Davies each developed the concept of packet-switching independently of one another. Baran, working for the RAND Corporation, called his idea "distributed communications," and he focused on redundant links between nodes as a way of establishing survivable communications in case of a major (possibly nuclear) attack. Davies, working for the National Physical Laboratory in Teddington, United Kingdom, coined the term *packet-switching*, the purpose of which was to utilize resource sharing as a way of making data communications more affordable.
- Robert Taylor served as the director of ARPA's Information Processing Technique Office (IPTO). In February 1966, he proposed to ARPA director Charles Herzfeld the establishment of a network-linking computer laboratories to enable resource sharing. Herzfeld agreed to fund the project.
- Lawrence Roberts of Lincoln Labs came to ARPA and served as program director for the establishment of ARPANET. In 1968, he wrote the solicitation and awarded the subnet contract to Bolt, Beranek and Newman (BBN) of Cambridge, Massachusetts.
- Frank Heart, and his team at BBN, built and monitored the subnet of IMPs for ARPANET.
- Ray Tomlinson, a BBN employee, designed e-mail for ARPANET in 1972. He also selected the "@" symbol for e-mail addresses.

- Robert Metcalfe of Xerox's Palo Alto Research Center (PARC) invented a random-access broadcast system, which enabled the establishment of LANs, in 1972. He called his invention "Ethernet," after a theoretical substance through which light travels.
- Vinton Cerf of Stanford University and Robert Kahn of the Defense Advanced Research Projects Agency (DARPA—the former ARPA) published a paper, in 1974, describing a concept for a new protocol to allow connections between networks. Their idea eventually became TCP/IP.
- Louis Pouzin and Hubert Zimmerman were architects of the French network Cyclades, which was specifically designed to facilitate internetworking and thus heavily influenced Cerf and Kahn's work.
- Paul Mockapetris of the Information Sciences Institute (ISI) at the University of Southern California (USC) researched the problem of locating host computers across the Internet. In 1983, he published a paper proposing a distributed database of name servers that would identify host computers by name rather than by IP address. This idea became known as the Domain Name System (DNS).
- Tim Berners-Lee, an English physicist at the European Organization for Nuclear Research (CERN), drafted an idea in 1989 for an application that would use hypertext links to locate files over computer networks. That idea would become the World Wide Web. He was assisted by his CERN colleague, Belgian electrical engineer Robert Cailliau.
- Marc Andreesson, an undergraduate at the University of Illinois at Urbana-Champaign, worked with his colleague Eric Bina at the National Center for Supercomputing Applications (NCSA) to develop the X Mosaic 0.5 browser with a graphical user interface (GUI). In January 1993, he introduced the browser, before earning his bachelor's degree and later cofounding Netscape.

As the "official" Internet (those networks connected through TCP/IP) grew in parallel with a proliferation of private networks and internets, NSF officials determined it appropriate and necessary to terminate government operation and open it to the private sector. Their plan was to allow competitive Internet service providers (ISPs) to assume operational responsibilities and connect to one another through exchanges. This went into effect in 1995, when the NSF backbone was dismantled, and commercial ISPs were allowed access to the TCP/IP connections.

In the meantime, an application designed to simplify the sharing of data across networks emerged from the European Organization for Nuclear Research (CERN). This application, known as the World Wide Web (WWW—the name was almost rejected because the pronunciation of the abbreviation was longer than the pronunciation of the full name), utilized a uniform resource locator (URL) built on the Domain Name System (DNS) and browsers utilizing Hypertext Transfer Protocol (HTTP) to locate servers with documents printed in a common format, known as Hypertext Markup Language (HTML). The first Web browser was designed in 1991 and allowed anyone with Internet access the ability to search the WWW. However, overall Web usage was still a barely discernible trickle by the end of 1992.

In 1993, a browser named Mosaic included a feature that allowed users to load images to the Web. Web pages now resembled print media. The ease of use and viewing caused Web usage to surge. In the last quarter of the year, Web traffic more than doubled and Web servers increased tenfold.

Global Internet usage has expanded drastically in the last two decades. According to a UN International Telecommunication Union (ITU) report in 2015, 3.2 billion people throughout the world use the Internet. This equates to a sevenfold increase in 15 years. People use the Internet for all types of activities, both for legitimate reasons such as research, financial planning, socializing, shopping, and news, as well as for controversial or even illegal activities. Regardless, the Internet's impact on the lives of its users is immeasurable, just as it is inconceivable for many to live without it.

Christopher G. Marquis

See also: ARPANET; Defense Advanced Research Projects Agency (DARPA); Department of Defense (DoD); Domain Name System (DNS); Ethernet; Internet Service Provider (ISP); Transmission Control Protocol/Internet Protocol (TCP/IP)

Further Reading

Abbate, Janet. *Inventing the Internet.* Cambridge, MA: The MIT Press, 2000.

Gillies, James, and Robert Cailliau. *How the Web Was Born.* New York: Oxford University Press, 2000.

Hafner, Katie, and Matthew Lyon. *Where Wizards Stay Up Late: The Origins of the Internet.* New York: Simon & Schuster, 1996.

Moschovitis, Christos J. P., Hilary Poole, Tami Schuyler, and Theresa M. Senft. *History of the Internet: A Chronology, 1843 to the Present.* Santa Barbara, CA: ABC-CLIO, 1999.

INTERNET CORPORATION FOR ASSIGNED NAMES AND NUMBERS (ICANN)

The Internet Corporation for Assigned Names and Numbers (ICANN) is a private international nonprofit corporation that manages the governance of the Internet by administering the Internet Assigned Numbers Authority (IANA) functions. These functions include management of protocol parameters, Internet number resources, and domain names. This includes the codes and numbers used in Internet Protocols (IPs); the global coordination of the Internet Protocol addressing systems, or IP addresses; the allocation of blocks of autonomous system numbers to regional Internet registries; and the management of the root zone through the assignment of top-level domains such as .uk and .com.

In the 1960s, the U.S. Department of Defense's Advanced Research Projects Agency (DARPA) began developing packet-switching technology and communications networks that evolved into a network of networks. When this happened, DARPA developed the IANA functions as a list of technical parameters for protocol developers of the emerging Internet. In the early 1990s, the National Science Foundation (NSF) began to manage the nonmilitary portion of the Internet infrastructure and facilitated the first commercial activity on the Internet. However, as the Internet grew, the management of the IANA functions became too much for either DARPA or the NSF to coordinate effectively. In 1997, President Bill Clinton directed the secretary of commerce to privatize the management of the growing Internet to increase competition and facilitate international participation in its management. Although ICANN is a private corporation, the U.S. Department of Commerce's National Telecommunications and Information Administration retained oversight of ICANN's operations.

To effectively manage the IANA functions and the ever-increasing Internet infrastructure, ICANN is made up of a number of supporting organizations and advisory committees. These include the Address Supporting Organization (ASO); the At-Large Advisory Committee (ALAC); the Country Code Domain Name Supporting Organization (CCNSO); the Generic Names Supporting Organization (GNSO); the Governmental Advisory Committee (GAC); the Root Server System Advisory Committee (RSSAC); and the Security and Stability Advisory Committee (SSAC). ICANN is governed by a board of directors made up of 15 voting members that includes the president and CEO, who is also a voting member. Seven board members are nominated by ICANN's supporting organizations and committees. The remaining eight members, to include the CEO and president, are selected by the ICANN Nominating Committee (NomCom). NomCom is supposed to be independent of ICANN so that it can select volunteer board members in the best interests of the Internet, although there have been allegations that because the majority of the NomCom board members are from the domain name industry, ICANN is not at all independent.

ICANN manages the IANA functions mentioned above in addition to sponsoring technology research; developing architecture to ensure system security, stability, and resiliency; improving information system function and innovation; and coordinating the efforts of the Global Domains Division technical team. ICANN also influences Internet policy through the recommendations of the supporting organizations and committees and a wide variety of volunteer working groups. In this way, ICANN is responsive to grassroots suggestions and stakeholder comments through a consensus-driven process.

Michael A. Bonura

See also: Defense Advanced Research Projects Agency (DARPA); Internet; Internet Protocol (IP) Address; Transmission Control Protocol/Internet Protocol (TCP/IP)

Further Reading

Abbate, Janet. *Inventing the Internet.* Cambridge, MA: The MIT Press, 2000.
DeNardis, Laura. *The Global War for Internet Governance.* New Haven, CT: Yale University Press, 2014.

INTERNET GOVERNANCE

Internet governance is the idea that the cyber domain requires some degree of established norms and expectations for it to continue to function and serve a wide variety of stakeholders. Despite its singular origin in the U.S. Defense Advanced

Research Projects Agency's (DARPA) ARPANET in 1973, the Internet grew up as a confederation of systems. The National Science Foundation (NSF), building upon DARPA's work, set out in the mid-1980s to create an "inter-net," or network of networks, to connect research sites. Establishment of connections between the research centers at Cornell, Princeton, the University of Colorado, and the University of California, San Diego, set the tone for decades to come. This network was, however, largely devoid of deliberate governance. The confederation was still posed with challenges that required some form of collaboration. This problem of confederated collaboration was what spurred Sir Tim Berners Lee, then working at the European Organization for Nuclear Research (CERN), to sketch out a proposed method of collaboration in 1989—the "World Wide Web." Berners Lee's sketched what would become the Hypertext Markup Language (HTML).

It is in these protocols that the first methods of Internet governance dawned. As Professor Lawrence Lessig said in his treatise on law in cyber space, "Code [became] law." By virtue of creating foundational protocols, Berners Lee set in motion the methods of governing the Internet, and he and others had begun framing the constitution of the Internet, as Lessig said, "an architecture—not just a legal text but a way of life—that structures and constrains social and legal power, to the end of protecting fundamental values." Despite that lack of explicit sovereign borders in this new social space, these early pioneers established systems that advanced their core values.

Berners Lee went on to found the World Wide Web Consortium (W3C). Vint Cerf and Robert Kahn, two of the original programmers of the ARPANET, founded the Internet Society in the 1990s. Both of these organizations are critical to establishing standards on the Internet. Cerf and Kahn's Internet Society is the organization that charters the Internet Engineering Task Force (IETF). This organization provides the foundational systems design and venue for eventual acceptance of core Internet technologies. The mission of IETF is to produce high-quality, relevant technical and engineering documents that influence the way people design, use, and manage the Internet in such a way as to make the Internet work better. These documents include protocol standards, best current practices, and informational documents of various kinds.

It is through such institutions as IETF, which created the Border Gateway Protocol—core to Internet routing—and W3C and the use of HTML that the Internet began to self-regulate. In conjunction with these entities, several others have been influential in shaping Internet technologies as well. Internet Protocol version four (IPv4) is ubiquitous to the Internet; for more than 30 years it has been the foundation of Internet technology. To resolve IPv4 addressing, however, the Internet needed to assign numbers to networks and to translate those numbers to human language.

By virtue of its heavy use in U.S. academia, the U.S. Department of Commerce funded a central authority to do both. The Internet Assigned Numbers Authority (IANA) was funded by the U.S. National Telecommunications and Information Administration (NTIA) and run by the University of Southern California's Information Sciences Institute. This organization established the addressing allocations of IP addresses worldwide. After this initial allocation, the IANA handed regional allocation responsibilities to five regional Internet registries (RIRs): the American

Registry for Internet Numbers (ARIN); the Regional Internet Registry for Europe (RIPE); the Asia Pacific Network Information Center (APNIC); the Latin American and Caribbean Internet Addresses Registry (LACNIC); and the African Network Information Center (AFRINIC).

Since its creation, IANA has been the steward of registered numbers and domain name resolution. In 1998, a public nonprofit international organization was chartered to transition the IANA functionality further away from the U.S. government—seeking "a bottom-up, transparent process involving all necessary constituencies and stakeholders in the Internet Community." The Internet Corporation for Assigned Names and Numbers (ICANN) was awarded the contract from the NTIA to execute this function in February of 2000 and continues that function.

Even with execution of the IANA function performed in this neutral forum, however, several key stakeholders asserted that ownership of the process should be more neutral. Indeed, despite Cerf's recommendation in 1990 that this function continue with the U.S. government, in 2013, Cerf's Internet Society joined with others in calling for a shift out of U.S. government control. Largely, this was a response to the joint United Nations/International Telecommunications Union, World Conference on International Telecommunications (WCIT). During this landmark conference, delegates and sympathizers expressed deep antipathy to the way ICANN was administering the IANA function for the U.S. government. Currently, to address both these concerns and the equities of the United States, the NTIA is working with ICANN to relinquish ownership of the IANA process to the nonprofit. It is unclear whether this will address international concerns, but what is clear is that these standards-based institutions and their creations are the law of the Internet.

Spencer Calder

See also: Internet; Internet Corporation for Assigned Names and Numbers (ICANN)

Further Reading

DeNardis, Laura. *The Global War for Internet Governance.* New Haven, CT: Yale University Press, 2014.

Knake, Robert K. *Internet Governance in an Age of Cyber Insecurity.* New York: Council on Foreign Relations, 2010.

Mueller, Milton. *Networks and States: The Global Politics of Internet Governance.* Cambridge, MA: MIT Press, 2010.

INTERNET PROTOCOL (IP) ADDRESS

An Internet Protocol (IP) address is a specific set of numbers or characters assigned to every device connected to a computer network. The address is based on a set of established Internet Protocol standards that allow computers to communicate with one another. The first three versions of the Internet Protocol were used briefly in the late 1970s during the early, experimental years of the Internet. In 1978, engineers working on ARPANET first outlined Internet Protocol version 4 (IPv4) that would use 32-bit characters; they eventually implemented this standard in 1983.

IPv4 remained in use as of 2016, but the 32-bit characters naturally limited IPv4 to only 4.3 billion Web addresses, the last of which was released in 2011.

In the early 1990s, the Internet Engineering Task Force (IETF) had recognized that the exponential growth of the Internet would eventually exhaust the supply of IPv4 addresses. To remedy this situation, the IETF developed a new standard by 1996 known as IPv6 (IPv5 was an experimental system never in wide use) based on 128-bit characters. IPv6 can accommodate up to 3.4×10^{38} unique addresses. Both IPv4 and IPv6 remained in use as of 2016, with no clear plan in place to phase out the older standard.

Ryan Wadle

See also: ARPANET; Internet; Internet Corporation for Assigned Names and Numbers (ICANN); Transmission Control Protocol/Internet Protocol (TCP/IP)

Further Reading

Rosenzweig, Paul. *Cyber Warfare: How Conflicts in Cyberspace Are Challenging America and Changing the World.* Santa Barbara, CA: Praeger, 2013.

Singer, P. W., and Allan Friedman. *Cybersecurity and Cyberwar: What Everyone Needs to Know.* New York: Oxford University Press, 2014.

INTERNET RELAY CHAT (IRC)

Internet Relay Chat Protocol (IRCP) is a communication standard that allows person-to-group text communications. The group is typically called a *chat room*, and individual users enter the chat room to post text messages that appear in the sequence in which they arrive at the Internet Relay Chat server. Some IRC networks allow users to include attachments, such as pictures or audio files, and some allow person-to-person private chats (often mutually arranged in the chat room).

One of the peculiarities of Internet Relay Chat in chat rooms is that many people in the group can have simultaneous two- or multiperson chats in the room at the same time, even participating in many discussions simultaneously. This can make it quite difficult to track a particular conversation, discern who is talking with whom, and understand the context in which chats are occurring. In addition, the same people who are having a multiperson chat may also be involved in person-to-person chats without the rest of the group's knowledge. Finally, a user might have a "chat" with no one at all and simply be ranting about a topic or carrying on an electronic soliloquy. Many Internet Relay Chat platforms attempt to clarify these multithreaded conversations with color-coding or photographic or cartoonish avatars in addition to the usual username identifications.

Chat rooms and IRC platforms exist for a vast array of different communities of interest, as diverse as there are human interests. Many IRC platforms exist for a single category (such as pet owners) or, like America Online (AOL), as a common area for users with specific interests to start their own chat rooms. In recent years, military and first-responder command centers have employed IRC platforms to augment other forms of command and control communications. IRC chat rooms, users, and servers are subject to the same spam and malware threats that other Internet users are vulnerable to, including social engineering and phishing.

Jeffrey R. Cares

See also: Anonymous; Dark Web; 4chan; Internet; LulzSec

Further Reading

Isaacson, Walter. *The Innovators: How a Group of Hackers, Geniuses, and Geeks Created the Digital Revolution.* New York: Simon & Schuster, 2014.

INTERNET SERVICE PROVIDER (ISP)

An Internet service provider (ISP) is a company or organization that provides Internet access to customers or users. An ISP can make Internet access available using many technologies, including dial-up service from a touch-tone telephone over conventional telephone lines; a digital subscriber line (DSL, a technology to make conventional telephone lines transmit data faster); cable modem (with coaxial or fiber-optic cabling); wireless broadcast; or dedicated high-capacity cabling. Typically, ISPs also provide their customers with the ability to communicate with one another through electronic mail (e-mail) accounts, and other services, such as telephone and television services, may be bundled with the data service as well.

There are many types of ISPs, including access providers that provide basic Internet access; mailbox providers that provide only e-mail services and mail storage (such as Yahoo Mail or Gmail); hosting ISPs that provide e-mail, Web-hosting, or online storage services; transit ISPs that serve as ISPs to ISPs; virtual ISPs (VISPs) that purchase services from another ISP (sometimes called a wholesale ISP) to allow the VISP's customers to access the Internet using services and infrastructure owned and operated by the wholesale ISP; free ISPs that provide service free of charge; and wireless ISPs.

Jeffrey R. Cares

See also: Google; Internet; Wi-Fi

Further Reading

Graham, James, Richard Howard, and Ryan Olson. *Cyber Security Essentials.* Boca Raton, FL: Auerbach Publications, 2011.

INTERPOL

The International Criminal Police Organization (ICPO) is an international and intergovernmental policing body. The idea was conceived at the First International Criminal Police Congress in 1914. However, Interpol was not established until 1923, as the International Criminal Police Commission. By 1956, the ICPO was officially recognized by the common name of Interpol. Additionally, at this time, the organization became autonomous from control of individual nations. Interpol is the largest such organization with 190 member nations. Currently based in Lyon, France, it strives to provide 24-hour service across the globe every day of the year. Its mission statement declares its goal: "Preventing and fighting crime through enhanced cooperation and innovation on police and security matters."

Interpol was created with the idea of allowing police departments around the world to work together within a seamless system of information and resource sharing. Furthermore, Interpol attempts to provide high-level training, expert investigative techniques, and secure communication and information pools. A key aspect of Interpol is the concept of neutrality. The organization does this by collecting dues from each of its member nations and remaining free from influence by a particular governing body or country. Moreover, Interpol conducts investigations so as not to overstep a particular nation's existing laws.

Interpol works with partners in both the public and private sectors. Additionally, Interpol is recognized by both the United Nations and the European Union. Although there is an office in the United States, located in Washington, D.C., Interpol Washington had been limited by legislation passed under the administration of President Ronald Reagan. In 2009, however, President Barack Obama signed Executive Order 13524, which grants Interpol privileges, exemptions, and immunities while operating within the United States.

The concept of international crime was one that developed following the creation of Interpol. Previously, nations focused internally and did not do much in the way of international cooperation. Yet, with the creation of this intergovernmental organization, new questions arose on defining what was taking place in a changing world.

Interpol is constantly evolving to keep up with a developing world. An example of this mode of thinking is that every three years a new strategic framework is advanced to help guide its direction. The priorities that Interpol has chosen to work on in this current plan include developing a global police information system, continuing to provide 24-hour support to law enforcement, and assisting to identify crimes and criminals.

Since its inception in 1923, some individuals and organizations have questioned the validity and overall success of Interpol. There are arguments made that claim Interpol is not as effective as originally designed. Despite such claims, the international policing body has contributed to bringing international criminals to justice. This is done by compiling and sharing information with local or national police forces who then can carry out arrests.

Jason R. Kluk

See also: Cyber Crime; Federal Bureau of Investigation (FBI); Internet Governance

Further Reading

Fooner, Michael. *Interpol: Issues in World Crime and International Justice.* New York: Plenum Press, 1989.

Sandler, Todd, Daniel G. Arce, and Walter Enders. "An Evaluation of Interpol's Cooperative-based Counterterrorism Linkages." *The Journal of Law & Economics* 54(1), February 2011: 79–110.

IRAN CYBER CAPABILITIES

Although relatively late in developing significant cyber capabilities, Iran has created a respectable presence in the cyber domain. Iran's cyber army is used to censor social media Web sites and suppress regime opponents. Since 2002, various councils under the command of the Islamic Revolutionary Guard Corps (IRGC), which is the country's primary military unit responsible for the regime's overall survival, have been created to operate in cyber space. These cyber warriors have been known to commit cyber attacks domestically and internationally. A cyber attack is a computer-generated attack on other computer systems intended to obstruct data, disrupt services, steal information, or disable the targeted systems. Iranian cyber attacks range from blacklisting Web sites in Iran to damaging systems abroad.

After the 2010 Stuxnet virus, Iran's supreme leader Ayatollah Ali Khamenei strengthened the country's cyber division. Originally known as "Olympic Games" from President George W. Bush's administration, the 2010 cyber attack targeted Iran's nuclear facility in Natanz in an effort to slow down uranium enrichment. President Barack Obama continued the operation, which experts later renamed "Stuxnet." A computer worm believed to be developed by joint cooperation between the United States and Israel, Stuxnet successfully penetrated the nuclear facility and was operational for 17 months. The virus interrupted the operations of 1,000 of the 5,000 centrifuges by deceiving Iranian operators into believing the systems were working properly.

The Ashiyande Digital Security Team, created in 2002, and the Sun Army, which was commissioned in 2010, are hacking groups affiliated with the IRGC. Though these groups' primary objective is to monitor social media Web sites, their most notable cyber attack against the United States occurred in February 2012 against the National Aeronautics and Space Administration (NASA). This attack, among others committed by these groups, was a defacement in which the attackers changed the appearance of the NASA Web page.

On August 15, 2012, a group known as the Cutting Sword of Justice executed a cyber attack against Saudi Arabia's national oil and gas firm, Aramco. The virus was identified as Shamoon, and it infected at least 30,000 computers with the intent to delete or overwrite data from hard drives while simultaneously sending information to the attacker. A display of a burning American flag appeared upon completion. Shamoon not only affected the daily tasks and processes of the company but proved to be a costly repair.

Also in August and September 2012, a number of U.S. financial institutions were the victims of Iranian hackers, known as the Izz ad-Din al-Qassam Cyber Fighters. U.S. officials believed the group was operating under the command of the Iranian government and were likely retaliating for either the Stuxnet virus or these banks' fulfillment of international sanctions against Iran. Known as Operation Ababil, the hacker group used distributed denial-of-service (DDoS) against 46 U.S. institutions, many of which were financial institutions, between late 2011 and mid-2013. A DDoS attack attempts to make Web sites inaccessible. Customers of the financial institutions could not use their online accounts or other online services. Therefore, the cyber attack served as a disruption rather than an effort to steal confidential information or money.

Between August 28, 2013, and September 18, 2013, the Iranian hacker Hamid Firoozi covertly penetrated the Bowman Avenue Dam in Rye Brook, New York, and gained access to its operational controls. Though he did not take over the dam, the cost of the cyber intrusion was over $30,000. In September 2013, Iranian hackers even managed to gain access to the U.S. Navy's unclassified administrative network, the Navy Marine Corps Intranet (NMCI), for nearly four months before being discovered. Vital information was not compromised, and no data was stolen. But the disruption cost roughly $10 million to repair. Much like the New York dam interruption, the NMCI attack was an indication from Iranian hackers that they were capable of infiltrating U.S. networks.

Months later, in February 2014, the Sands Casino in Las Vegas, Nevada, was targeted by Iranian hackers by effectively obstructing many of their daily logistical functions. This included wiping a significant number of their hard drives and stealing confidential information, posting some of it online. The cyber attack was specifically aimed at the owner of the casino, Sheldon Adelson, for his 2013 remarks on attacking Iran with nuclear weapons.

It is difficult to determine the exact amount Iran spends on cyber-related programs in the country. However, the budget for the Ministry of Information and Communications Technology for fiscal year (FY) 2014–2015 was about $1.36 billion, up 95 percent from the previous FY. The Norse Intelligence Network has provided data that reveals the number of cyber attacks emanating from Iran have grown and become more sophisticated between January 2014 and March 2015.

There are strong links between the Iranian government; their information technology (IT) schools, such as Shariff University and the Imam Hussein University (IHU); and the IRGC. In 2010, the IRGC established another cyber-warfare division that develops advanced computer software, such as wireless data communications jammers, viruses and malware, data collection tools, and stealthy cyber-network tools for spying. Iran encourages enrollment by improving university curriculum and computer systems to better equip current and prospective hackers. Iran's cyber army ultimately seeks to impose an economic, political, or psychological strain on victims.

Alma Keshavarz

See also: Air Gapping; Aramco Attack; Cyber War; Cyber Warriors; Distributed Denial-of-Service (DDoS) Attack; Malware; Operation Ababil; Shamoon Virus; Stuxnet

Further Reading

Carr, Jeffrey. *Inside Cyber Warfare: Mapping the Cyber Underworld*. Sebastopol, CA: O'Reilly Media, Inc., 2010.

Collins, Sean, and Stephen McCombie. "Stuxnet: The Emergence of a New Cyber Weapon and Its Implications." *Journal of Policing, Intelligence and Counter Terrorism*, March 21, 2012: 80–91.

Kaplan, Fred. *Dark Territory: The Secret History of Cyber War.* New York: Simon & Schuster, 2016.

Lindsay, Jon R. "Stuxnet and the Limits of Cyber Warfare." *Security Studies*, August 1, 2013: 365–404.

Rid, Thomas. *Cyber War Will Not Take Place.* New York: Oxford University Press, 2013.

Singer, P. W., and Allan Friedman. *Cybersecurity and Cyber War: What Everyone Should Know.* New York: Oxford University Press, 2014.

ISLAMIC STATE IN IRAQ AND SYRIA (ISIS)

In June of 2014, a little-known organization of Sunni jihadists shocked the world as it moved swiftly across Iraq, wresting control of such key cities as Mosul. The Islamic State in Iraq and Syria (ISIS) quickly became a household name. ISIS goes by alternative names and acronyms, including ISIL and IGIL (the use of Daish or Daesh signifies that the Arabic rather than the English acronym is being used). In harkening back to the earliest days of Islam, ISIS seeks to purify Islam and institute a legitimate government in the form of a Muslim caliphate. Millenarianism, or a preparation for the end of the world, also infuses its actions.

ISIS traces its beginnings to Al Qaeda and, more closely, to Al Qaeda in Iraq. Its founder is considered to be the Jordanian Abu Musab al-Zarqawi. Unlike much of Al Qaeda's senior leadership, al-Zarqawi had humble roots. Yet, he demonstrated his strategic brilliance by inciting a civil war between Sunnis and Shiites after attacking a Shiite shrine. Killed in July 2006 by an American airstrike, his followers declared the Islamic State of Iraq in October 2006 but struggled to gain a territorial foothold in Iraq. Still, support grew as fervent Sunnis interacted with former Ba'ath Party members in Iraqi prisons during the U.S. occupation.

Unlike Al Qaeda's Osama bin Laden, who never dreamed of governing his own caliphate, ISIS made the formation of a caliphate an essential goal, which requires it to control physical territory. As borders around Syria have tightened and U.S. airstrikes have intensified in 2014 and 2015, ISIS has sought to expand into new power vacuums, such as Libya. It is impossible to know how many fighters have flocked to ISIS from around the world, but it is estimated that it has about 35,000 fighters. The caliphate itself controls between 3 million and 8 million Muslims.

ISIS emerged out of a sect known as Salafism, which seeks to emulate Muhammad and his earliest followers. Its followers are far more radical than their well-known rival Al Qaeda because they believe that any Muslim who does not adhere to their vision of Islam should be killed. This includes Shiites, who practice an alternate form of Islam, and any Muslim leaders who do not govern according to sharia, or Islamic, law. As Islam began in the seventh century, ISIS holds to an early medieval worldview. This includes punishments many find barbaric, such as punitive amputations and crucifixions.

However, this does not mean that ISIS's followers are not thoroughly modern when it comes to exploiting the cyber world and social media. The growth of cyber warfare as a threat is coming not only from the world's strongest nations but from nonstate actors as well, including terrorist groups. ISIS is no exception. Even the notorious executioner Jihadi John–who gained prominence through his grisly online videos—had received a degree in computer science from an English university.

ISIS has demonstrated an increasing ability to launch cyber attacks. In January 2015, ISIS humiliated U.S. Central Command after it temporarily gained control of its YouTube and Twitter accounts. It launched a similar attack against *Newsweek's* Twitter account the following month. It even temporarily knocked a French TV station off the air.

ISIS's online presence helps to distinguish it from Al Qaeda. Where Al Qaeda depended heavily on physical training camps to indoctrinate and train its recruits, ISIS seeks in part to recruit independent operators who do not require training or oversight. After inspiring terrorist acts, ISIS simply claims responsibility for them.

To support these increasing cyber activities, ISIS is turning to Eastern Europe's so-called dark Web market, which provides a vast array of necessary tools for waging cyber warfare, such as encrypted cell phones and malware. The United States has recently admitted launching cyber attacks against ISIS to include denial-of-service (DDoS) attacks and attacks designed to confuse and break down ISIS communication networks.

Even as nation-states such as France and the United States consider ways to wage kinetic operations against ISIS, other nonstate actors are waging their own cyber wars against the group. Most notably, the organization Anonymous has launched attacks around the world at targets ranging from governments to credit card companies. After ISIS claimed responsibility for the November 2015 attack in Paris, Anonymous declared war on ISIS. It is believed that Anonymous' strategic focus will be shutting down ISIS's online recruiting efforts. Others suggest that Anonymous' attacks might be counterproductive and unnecessary. Twitter, for example, has employees who are fluent in Arabic who are responsible for shutting down ISIS accounts.

Heather Pace Venable

See also: Anonymous; Cyber Attack; Cyber Terrorism; Dark Web; United States Cyber Capabilities; U.S. Cyber Command (USCYBERCOM)

Further Reading

Freedberg, Sydney J. "Cyber War against ISIL Hones Weapons vs. Russia, China." *Breaking Defense*, February 29, 2016. http://breakingdefense.com/2016/02/cyber-war-against -isil-is-model-for-other-threats.

Gerges, Fawaz A. *ISIS: A History.* Princeton, NJ: Princeton University Press, 2016.

Weiss, Michael, and Hassan Hassan. *ISIS: Inside the Army of Terror.* New York: Regan Arts, 2015.

Wood, Graeme. "What ISIS Really Wants." *The Atlantic*, March 2015. http://www.theatlantic .com/magazine/archive/2015/03/what-isis-really-wants/384980.

ISRAEL CYBER CAPABILITIES

The rapid technological changes that have occurred in recent years have affected the priorities of decision makers in Israel in various ways. These changes have far-reaching consequences in almost all areas of life, including the military and defense spheres. Many changes have occurred in the nature of warfare and the design of military forces, owing, among other things, to developments in strategic thinking and the formulation of military doctrines that are tailored to a changing reality.

Israel has been extremely efficient in intensifying its cyber activities. While this activity constitutes a source of strength for the nation, it also exposes its weak points; this is because the infrastructures essential for the functioning of each country have become dependent on computers. Discovering the optimal way of handling the threat posed by the technological development of cyber warfare has been a key challenge that has troubled Israel in recent years.

Israel's national interest focuses on maintaining its security against those seeking to harm it and undermine its very existence. This interest, along with Israel's geopolitical location, necessitates superiority in cyber space as an integral part of its ability to defend itself against conventional and cyber attacks, and it is an integral part of its deterrent attack capability in the Middle East theater and beyond.

Israel is considered a global leader in handling cyber attacks. A comprehensive report revealed that out of 23 countries in the cyber-war sphere, Israel holds the highest rating. The report also indicates that at any given moment, Israel is subject to about 1,000 cyber attacks. This shows the strength of Israel's defense system and demonstrates that Israel is well prepared to deal with a cyber attack against it under almost any situation.

The development of Israel's operational capabilities in the field of cyber warfare is a key element in maintaining its national strength. Its economy, industry, security, education, and preservation as a democratic, open, and established society mainly depend on its ability to protect its essential computer networks against an attack liable to disrupt its way of life. The increasing reliance on computer systems in Israel and throughout the world has brought new challenges with it that demand immediate solutions at the national level.

In strengthening its cyber capabilities, Israel has developed unique methods by formulating a regular strategy for handling the threat posed by the development of cyber technology. Israel is constantly using its homegrown capabilities to combat the threat posed by cyber-warfare technology. This is known as "start-up nation" to young people living in Israel. Israel has been able to identify the diverse features of the cyber threat and subsequently applied corresponding changes. The armed forces of Israel have been reframed, and a National Information Security Authority has been established to deal with protecting Israeli infrastructures. The Cyber Bureau of Israel Defence Force (IDF) was set up in Unit 8200, and the C4I Corps has begun to develop a special cyber-training program. The most important among these was the establishment of the National Cyber Bureau, whose objective is to integrate cyber defense into both the various defense agencies and the civilian sector. In addition, a Law, Information, and Technology Authority has been set up to take responsibility for maintaining Internet privacy and the security of personal information. These have been created in accordance with current cyber-security practices to make Israel's cyber capabilities state of the art.

Manas Dutta

See also: Evron, Gadi; Operation Orchard; Stuxnet; Tenenbaum, Ehud "Udi"

Further Reading

Green, James A., ed. *Cyber Warfare: A Multidisciplinary Analysis.* New York: Routledge, 2015.
Richards, Julian. *Cyber-war: The Anatomy of the Global Security Threat.* London: Palgrave, 2014.
Springer, J. Paul. *Cyber Warfare.* Santa Barbara, CA: ABC-CLIO, 2015
Tabansky, Lior, and Isaac Ben Israel. *Cybersecurity in Israel.* New York: Springer, 2015.

J

JPMORGAN HACK

One of the largest cyber attacks ever carried out against an American corporation, the JPMorgan hack, constituted a major data breach of JPMorgan Chase that affected approximately 83 million accounts. Specifically, the breach exposed some 76 million household and 7 million small business accounts to hackers. Around two-thirds of American households were possibly impacted. Disclosure of the attack came in September 2014, after JPMorgan Chase's security teams realized that a data breach had occurred that July. Hacks continued from July to August 2014. Although the hackers did not apparently gain access to Social Security numbers or passwords, JPMorgan Chase reported that information such as names, telephone numbers, and addresses were compromised. The attack extended beyond JPMorgan Chase, hitting at least nine other financial institutions, such as Citigroup, HSBC Holdings, Regions Financial Corporation, and E Trade, but only managed to breach the systems of JPMorgan Chase and Fidelity Investments.

The 2014 hack was not the first example of cyber crime directed against JPMorgan Chase. Cyber attacks against economic targets have been a growing concern because it is feared that the economic impact of such attacks could ultimately prove as damaging in terms of financial impact and fear as a physical attack. In 2012, a group called the Izz ad-Din al-Qassm Cyber Fighters executed a series of attacks that sought to deny service to customers of American banks, such as Bank of America, PNC Financial Service Group, SunTrust, and JPMorgan Chase. The online services for these institutions were off-line for several minutes or even hours in some cases. Thus, JPMorgan Chase was already cognizant of the reality of the cyber threat. It remains unclear exactly who carried out the 2014 attacks, yet a Federal Bureau of Investigation (FBI) report indicated the possibility of Russian involvement. Ultimately, in November 2015, the FBI indicted four men: Gery Shalon, Joshua Samuel Aaron, Zic Orenstein, and an unidentified hacker. Shalon and Orenstein, both Israelis, were extradited in May 2016, following a request by the U.S. government.

The JPMorgan hack occurred during a period of dramatic increase in cyber attacks, with the American public increasingly alert to the threat of hackers. In addition to the attack on JPMorgan Chase, 2014 saw several prominent American companies fall victim to cyber crime. These included retail companies such as Target and Home Depot and entertainment corporations such as Sony. Hackers quickly put stolen data for sale on the black market. The attacks focused public attention on the vulnerability of information systems and their private information, most of which was held by at least one corporation or another.

The U.S. government responded not only by prosecuting the hackers involved in the attack but by calling for greater vigilance on the part of the American public to practice safer methods to ensure online security. In addition, U.S. companies were called on to invest in their security protocols and to work with the public sector to enhance U.S. cyber security, including working closely with law enforcement agencies. Yet, the U.S. government did not mobilize a major national effort specifically in response to the JPMorgan hack beyond initiating criminal investigations. The first time the United States led such an effort was in response to the North Korean attack on Sony, which occurred shortly after the JPMorgan hack, in response to the American film *The Interview*. Nonetheless, the incident revealed continuing gaps in America's cyber security, particularly in the private sector and pertaining to the personal information of American citizens.

Jordan R. Hayworth

See also: Cyber Crime; Sony Corporation Hack; Target Corporation Hack; TJX Corporation Hack

Further Reading

Ablon, Lillian, and Martin Libicki. "Hackers' Bazaar: The Markets for Cybercrime Tools and Stolen Data." *Defense Counsel Journal* 82(2), April 2015: 143–152.

Bossler, Adam M., and Thomas J. Holt. *Cybercrime in Progress: Theory and Prevention of Technology-enabled Offenses.* Basingstoke: Routledge, 2016.

Libicki, Martin. *Cyberspace in Peace and War.* Annapolis, MD: U.S. Naval Institute Press, 2016.

JUST WAR

The term *just war* refers to the body of ethics that governs the conduct of war. The just war tradition can trace its lineage to the writings of various ancient philosophers, such as St. Augustine, St. Thomas Aquinas, and Hugo Grotius. The purpose of the just war tradition is to provide criteria on the use of war as a morally justifiable action. The concept of just war refers to two different but related concepts, *jus ad bellum*, the right to go to war, and *jus in bello*, the right conduct in war. Lately, some scholars have advocated introducing the concept of *jus post bellum*, or the conduct of nations after war has ceased.

Though different theorists may have different exact criteria, most require that the country pursuing war have a just cause, such as self-defense or to prevent an even greater atrocity. In addition, the action of war must be thought of as the last resort, conducted only after all other options to stop aggression have been attempted. There must be some reasonable idea that the war will be successful in achieving its goal, as stated by the just cause. War must be waged by the "proper political authority," leaving a debate as to whether this only refers to recognized governments. The entity going to war must also have the intention to right a wrong and not to punish the enemy or for economic gain. In addition, the anticipated good outcome of war must outweigh the expected evil done by war.

Once war has begun, the conduct of war is governed by the criteria of *jus in bello*. The criteria include guidelines on how combatants should act and must be treated. First, there is the recognition of the distinction between combatants, those actively engaged in fighting war, and noncombatants or civilians. Acts of war, in general, should be directed toward combatants as opposed to noncombatants. Next, the nation conducting the war should use the minimum required level of force to achieve success. Measures should be taken to avoid excessive harm to civilians and noncombatants. All attacks should be deemed militarily necessary to defeat the enemy only. Prisoners of war should not be tortured or subject to acts of revenge. Certain weapons or acts are so heinous as to be banned. These include genocide, rape, and the use of weapons of mass destruction (WMDs). Finally, all sides to the conflict must adhere to already established international obligations, treaties, and laws.

Scholars argue that the rise of new technology and new ways of fighting have always challenged the proper application of just war principles. This is of particular concern in the area of cyber war. Questions raised include what constitutes a proper act of cyber war, what criteria is used to determine whether harm has been caused by the cyber attack, and how the attacker can be legally and definitively identified. Without answers to these basic questions, it becomes difficult to apply the concept of just war within the realm of cyber warfare.

Barbara Salera

See also: Cyber Ethics; Cyber War; Laws of Armed Conflict

Further Reading

Dunlap, Charles. J., Jr. "Some Reflections on the Intersection of Law and Ethics in Cyber War." *Air & Space Power Journal.*27(1), 2013: 22–43.

Farrell, Michael. *Modern Just War Theory: A Guide to Research.* Scarecrow Press: Toronto, 2013.

Walzer, Michael. *Just and Unjust War: A Moral Argument with Historical Illustrations.* New York: Basic Books, 1977.

JWICS NETWORK

The Joint Worldwide Intelligence Communications System (JWICS), is the Top Secret/Sensitive Compartmented Information (TS/SCI) network operated by the U.S. Department of Defense (DoD). It is administered by the Defense Information Services Agency (DISA) and is also used by the Department of Homeland Security (DHS), Department of Justice (DOJ), and Department of State (DOS) to transmit extremely sensitive, highly classified information. JWICS was created to replace DSNET2 and DSNET3, earlier classified networks that had relied on decades-old ARPANET technology.

Because of the highly sensitive nature of information transmitted on JWICS, access to the network is extremely limited. The most frequent users of JWICS are members of the intelligence community and the Federal Bureau of Information (FBI), both of whom have need for extremely secure communications in everyday activities. The bulk of defense communications are carried out using SIPRNet and NIPRNet.

JWICS can utilize satellite network connections, and the traffic moving across the network can be sent in prioritized premarked packets, meaning that the most important and sensitive information can be sent on the fastest and most secure routes. JWICS is capable of supporting video teleconferencing and voice over Internet Protocol (VOIP) audio.

Information taken from JWICS was allegedly part of the classified material leaked by Private Bradley Manning, who in 2010 orchestrated one of the largest such leaks in history, demonstrating the vulnerability of even the most classified networks to human agents.

Jeffrey R. Cares

See also: ARPANET; Defense Information Systems Agency (DISA); Department of Defense (DoD); Department of Homeland Security (DHS); Manning, Bradley; National Security Agency (NSA); NIPRNet; SIPRNet

Further Reading

Brenner, Joel. *America the Vulnerable: Inside the New Threat Matrix of Digital Espionage, Crime, and Warfare.* New York: Penguin Press, 2011.

K

KASPERSKY LAB

Kaspersky Lab is an international software-security group operating in nearly 200 countries. It was founded in 1997 by cyber-security specialist Eugene Kasperky and is headquartered in Moscow, Russia. It is the world's largest privately held vendor of endpoint protection. It employs over 3,000 software professionals and protects over 400 million users and 270,000 corporations worldwide. Kaspersky Lab's security products include antivirus, antimalware, and firewall applications as well as security systems designed for small businesses, corporations, and large enterprises. Kaspersky Lab ranks among the top antivirus vendors globally and competes with such companies as Symantec Corporation (Norton) and McAfee.

Kaspersky Lab is a global leader in identifying and understanding recent sophisticated cyber-espionage attacks. The company is credited with discovering the Flame worm in 2012, first detected on Iranian Oil Ministry computers. In 2015, Kaspersky Lab announced the discovery of the Equation Group—a highly advanced computer-espionage and cyber-attack group responsible for over 500 malware infections in at least 42 countries since 2001. It is linked to Flame and the Stuxnet worm that targeted Iranian nuclear centrifuges in 2010. Kaspersky Lab attributes to the Equation Group the first known ability to reprogram hard disk drive firmware via Trojan horse that cannot be removed with disk reformatting or wiping.

Steven B. Davis

See also: Flame Worm; Kaspersky, Yevgeniy "Eugene" Valentinovich; McAfee; Stuxnet; Symantec Corporation

Further Reading

Bradley, Tony. "In Their Own Words: Kaspersky Lab Cofounder and CEO Eugene Kaspersky." *Forbes*, September 23, 2013.

Zettner, Kim. *Countdown to Zero Day: Stuxnet and the Launch of the World's First Digital Weapon.* New York: Broadway Books, 2015.

KASPERSKY, YEVGENIY "EUGENE" VALENTINOVICH

Yeveniy "Eugene" Valentinovich Kaspersky (1965–) is a Russian specialist in information security and cofounder and chairman of the global cyber-security company Kaspersky Lab. Born October 4, 1965, in Novorossiysk, Soviet Union, Kaspersky developed an early interest in mathematics and spent his final two years in high school taking advanced courses for gifted students at Moscow State University. In 1987, he graduated from the technical faculty of the Dzerzhinsky Higher School of the Committee for State Security (KGB).

Kaspersky began developing disinfection utilities for computer viruses in 1989 after discovering a virus on his personal computer. This collection of utilities became the foundation of the Kaspersky Anti-Virus database. He joined the KAMI Information Center in 1991 and worked with colleagues to develop the AVP antivirus project, which gained international recognition in 1994 after winning a contest on computer virus neutralization programs conducted by Hamburg University.

In 1997, Kaspersky and his colleagues founded Kaspersky Lab. Kaspersky Lab is the world's largest privately held vendor of endpoint protection, employing over 3,000 professionals and protecting over 400 million users worldwide. Kaspersky has written articles on computer virology and speaks regularly at security conferences. He has earned a number of international awards, including an honorary doctorate of science from Plymouth University. He was named one of *Foreign Policy* magazine's 2012 Top Global Thinkers for his contributions to information technology (IT) security awareness.

Steven B. Davis

See also: Kaspersky Lab

Further Reading

Fischer, Paul. "100 Top Global Thinkers: Eugene Kaspersky, #40." *Foreign Policy* 197, 2012: 78–80.

Schachtman, Noah. "Eugene Kaspersky: Virus Hunter." *Wired* 20, August 2012: 86.

LAWS OF ARMED CONFLICT

The United Nations Charter specifically forbids member states from engaging in warfare against other members, except in a defensive fashion, and theoretically requires all members to come to the assistance of an aggrieved party. This has probably prevented or at least mitigated some disputes from growing into armed conflicts, but it has also served to push some wars into less traditional forms of conflict. These irregular wars often involve an unconventional aspect and include insurgencies and civil wars. The cyber warfare of the future is far more likely to resemble the small wars of irregular conflict than the major engagements of open warfare.

International law has developed over centuries to establish who can legally carry out acts of warfare and who must remain apart from engaging in conflict. To be considered a lawful combatant, a belligerent must bear arms openly, wear a uniform or recognizable device, belong to an organization with a clear hierarchy of leaders responsible for the actions of subordinates, and obey all of the laws of armed conflict (LOAC). To fail on any of these points is to relinquish legal standing as a lawful combatant and, by extension, to lose any of the protections extended by the LOAC.

The LOAC also include a prohibition on inflicting unnecessary suffering and a requirement that an offer of surrender be accepted. These laws also require participants in a conflict to avoid deliberately targeting noncombatants, to engage in the minimum amount of violence to achieve ends of military necessity, and to keep the use of violence proportionate to the objectives at hand. Cyber attacks might allow a nation to achieve its objectives with substantially less violence, death, and destruction than conventional attacks and, at least in some cases, the damage they inflict might be completely reversible. In this regard, cyber attacks might easily be covered by the LOAC and even encouraged over other forms of engagement. However, cyber attacks are capable of causing massive indirect, and possibly unintended, effects by targeting key elements of a nation's infrastructure. Shutting down the electrical grid in the city, for example, might cause a massive increase in traffic accidents, a rise in violent crime, and the collapse of the city's medical systems, all in relatively short order.

Civilians, at least in theory, are largely protected from the direct violence of conflict. In exchange for that protection, they are expected to refrain from direct engagement in combat and to consent to peaceful occupation should their uniformed defenders vacate their area. Thus, civilians are not allowed to launch guerrilla attacks and then return to their everyday lives. They must remain aloof from combat at all times. Those working in direct support of a war effort are in a bit of a legal gray area—for example, civilians working at a factory producing military equipment may be considered a legitimate target and placed in danger of enemy attacks.

In the cyber domain, it is difficult to distinguish between the uniformed representatives of a nation and other participants acting on their own motives. As such, there is at the very least a gap in the LOAC that requires modifications if they are to cover the entire range of potential cyber conflicts. Cyber attacks might not discern between legitimate warfare targets, such as government and military entities, and illegitimate targets, such as civilians not directly related to the war effort, due to the uncontrolled nature of some cyber attacks.

The question of whether a state of warfare can exist without a physical component is largely a red herring. Cyber capabilities are a powerful tool in the hands of national actors and certain subnational organizations, and they are a part of conflict in the world of the 21st century. Just as military commanders of the Cold War could not imagine engaging in a major ground offensive without at least some modicum of air support, modern military leaders cannot ignore the role of cyber attacks in modern conflicts. Nations simply cannot consider engaging in conflict without taking steps to secure their own networks and will not attack an enemy with physical forces without also seeking to disrupt that enemy's cyber systems. Further, if the effects created by cyber war are essentially the same as those caused by physical attacks, the debate is largely moot; to the victims of attacks, the method of inflicting punishment will be largely irrelevant. Cyber war is thus a part of the modern notion of war, whether it can stand alone or not.

Perhaps most importantly, Secretary of Defense Leon E. Panetta announced in 2012 that the United States reserved the right to classify cyber attacks as acts of war and to retaliate by any appropriate means. Panetta remained deliberately ambiguous about what type of attacks might provoke a retaliation and whether retaliation would be confined to the cyber realm.

Paul J. Springer

See also: Attribution; Cyber Attack; Cyber Ethics; Cyber War; Panetta, Leon E.; People's Republic of China Cyber Capabilities; Russia Cyber Capabilities; United States Cyber Capabilities

Further Reading

Arquilla, John, and David Ronfeldt. *The Advent of Netwar.* Santa Monica, CA: RAND, 1996.

Carr, Jeffrey. *Inside Cyber Warfare: Mapping the Cyber Underworld.* Sebastopol, CA: O'Reilly Media, 2009.

Clarke, Richard A., and Robert K. Knake. *Cyber War: The Next Threat to National Security and What to Do about It.* New York: HarperCollins, 2010.

Darnton, Geoffrey. "Information Warfare and the Laws of War." In *Cyberwar, Netwar and the Revolution in Military Affairs.* Edited by Edward Halpin, Philippa Trevorrow, David Webb, and Steve Wright. New York: Palgrave Macmillan, 2006.

Libicki, Martin. *Cyberdeterrence and Cyberwar.* Santa Monica, CA: RAND, 2009.

Reveron, Derek S., ed. *Cyberspace and National Security: Threats, Opportunities, and Power in a Virtual World*. Washington, D.C.: Georgetown University Press.

Rid, Thomas. *Cyber War Will Not Take Place*. New York: Oxford University Press, 2013.

Ventre, Daniel, ed. *Cyberwar and Information Warfare*. Hoboken, NJ: John Wiley & Sons, 2011.

LIBICKI, MARTIN C.

Martin C. Libicki has been a senior management scientist at the RAND Corporation since 1998. He is also a professor at the Pardee RAND Graduate School, a distinguished visiting professor at the U.S. Naval Academy, and an adjunct professor with the Center for Security Studies (CSS) at Georgetown University. Prior to working at RAND, Libicki spent 12 years at the National Defense University, 3 years with the U.S. Navy as a program sponsor for industrial preparedness, and 3 years as a policy analyst for the U.S. General Accounting Office's (GAO) Energy and Minerals Division. Libicki has also worked as a consultant for the U.S. Department of Justice (DOJ), the Defense Advanced Research Projects Agency (DARPA), and the Federal Bureau of Investigation (FBI). Libicki received his PhD in city and regional planning from the University of California, Berkeley.

Libicki's most recent research has involved net assessments of Russia and China in cyber space; modeling cyber-security decisions, cyber-war strategy, and demographic change for the U.S. Air Force and organizing it for cyber war; exploiting cell phones in counterinsurgency; developing a post-9/11 information technology strategy for the DOJ; and using biometrics for identity management. He is one of the foremost global theorists regarding cyber warfare and an extremely active author. Among his most notable works are *Cyberspace in Peace and War*; *Conquest in Cyberspace: National Security and Information Warfare*; and *Cyberdeterrence and Cyberwar*.

Lisa Beckenbaugh

See also: Arquilla, John; Brenner, Joel; Clarke, Richard A.; Cyber War; RAND Corporation

Further Reading

Libicki, Martin. *Conquest in Cyberspace: National Security and Information Warfare*. New York: Cambridge University Press, 2007.

Libicki, Martin. *Cyberdeterrence and Cyberwar*. Santa Monica, CA: RAND Corporation, 2009.

Libicki, Martin. *Cyberspace in Peace and War*. Annapolis, MD: U.S. Naval Institute Press, 2016.

LIVE FREE OR DIE HARD

Live Free or Die Hard is a 2007 action film directed by Len Wiseman that stars Bruce Willis and Timothy Olyphant. In this fourth installment of the popular *Die Hard* films, Willis reprises his character, New York Police Detective John McClane, who becomes involved in the investigation to hunt down a former Department of Defense (DoD) employee turned rogue cyber terrorist Thomas Gabriel (Olyphant).

Gabriel enlists the support of unwitting hackers to unleash a series of cyber attacks, referred to as a "fire sale," designed to disrupt the nation's infrastructure, including the stock market, transportation, telecommunications, and the power grid. In a motif common to the series, Gabriel's publicly professed motive of demonstrating the weakness of American cyber networks is a cover for an elaborate robbery intending to steal billions of dollars from a secret facility designed to store financial records in case of attack.

The film's plot is inspired by the 1997 article "A Farewell to Arms," authored by John Carlin, that appeared in *Wired* magazine. Carlin's article raises the specter of "cyber Pearl Harbors" that Richard A. Clarke and other national-security experts warned could pose a major threat to national security due to the increasing reliance on networked computer systems in key sectors.

Ryan Wadle

See also: Clarke, Richard A.; Cyber Attack; Cyber Terrorism

Further Reading

Carlin, John. "A Farewell to Arms," *Wired*, May 1997. https://www.wired.com/1997/05/netizen-2.

Demchak, Chris. *Wars of Disruption and Resilience: Cybered Conflict, Power, and National Security*. Athens: University of Georgia Press, 2011.

LOGIC BOMB

A logic bomb is malware, either a program or a partial program, that when placed lies dormant until a specific preprogrammed time and date is reached. Then the logic bomb activates, executing its programing. Another activating factor could be a certain message sent on a regular basis. When the logic bomb stops seeing the message, it will activate and execute its code. Other applications may be included at a programmer's discretion.

In its most dangerous form, this computer virus or Trojan horse activates when something does not happen. If the creator of the logic bomb does not log-in after a specific time, it might wipe out all of an infected server's data. The logic bomb is unique in that it does not replicate itself, it is easy to write, and it will not spread to unintended parties. It is specifically targeted.

A logic bomb is widely used to trigger payment for software after a trial period. If payment is not received by a certain date, the logic bomb activates and the software deletes itself. More nefarious logic bomb attackers, in combination with spyware, will attempt to steal one's identity by capturing keystrokes, and when certain Web sites are visited, they secure usernames and passwords.

In defense against logic bombs, an updated antivirus program can detect and eliminate this malware with periodic computer file scans. Auto-protect and e-mail screening should be used whenever a computer is online. Network administrators usually provide added protection. There is no known absolute protection against sophisticated logic bombs.

There have been numerous logic bomb applications. In June 2006, Roger Duronio of USB AG, based in Zurich, planted a logic bomb to drive down the company's stock. He failed and was convicted of securities fraud, receiving eight years in prison and a $3.1 million fine. Another attack was launched against South Korea on March 20, 2013. Three banks and two media companies' master boot records were wiped out.

In 2008, an information technology (IT) contractor for Fannie Mae's Urbana, Maryland, facility, Rajendrasinh Babubhai Makwana, was terminated, but prior to losing his access to the network, he planted a logic bomb that could have wiped out 4,000 servers. Upon discovery, Makwana was sentenced to 41 months in prison. Douglas Duchak was terminated from his data analyst job at the TSA Colorado Springs Operations Center. He tried to plant a logic bomb but was caught on camera. He was sentenced to two years in prison and fined over $60,000.

Logic bombs on the extreme level could initiate cyber wars. In theory, a sophisticated cyber user might sprinkle logic bombs throughout a nation's infrastructure, to be activated in the event of a future conflict. The U.S. infrastructure is dependent on computer networks, which also makes it vulnerable to this level of attack. To counter the possibility, cyber-security experts, working with the Department of Homeland Security (DHS), have sought to upgrade the cyber defenses of the nation's infrastructure.

Raymond D. Limbach

See also: Cyber Attack; Cyber Crime; Infrastructure; Malware

Further Reading

Clarke, Richard A., and Robert K. Knake. *Cyber War: The Next Threat to National Security and What to Do about It.* New York: HarperCollins, 2010.
Rosenzweig, Paul. *Cyber Warfare: How Conflicts in Cyberspace Are Challenging America and Changing the World.* Santa Barbara, CA: Praeger, 2013.

LOW ORBIT ION CANNON (LOIC)

The Low Orbit Ion Cannon (LOIC) is a program designed to allow multiple linked users to overwhelm targeted Web sites with requests that ultimately cause the site to crash. A number of hackers affiliated with the anonymous imageboard Web site 4chan first developed the LOIC in 2004. Praetox Technologies refined the tool to stress test networks and eventually released the LOIC to the public as a free download.

Once downloaded onto a computer, the LOIC is extremely easy to use and only requires that users know the name of the Web site they wish to attack. Once a site is targeted, the LOIC sends a large number of UDP, TCP, or HTTP communications requests as part of a distributed denial-of-service (DDoS) attack. The LOIC also allows its users to turn over control of the program via Internet relay chat servers that link hundreds or thousands computer to completely overwhelm even large, well-supported Web sites, causing them to crash and go off-line.

In 2010, the hacktivist groups Anonymous and LulzSec used the LOIC to attack Web sites as part of Operation Payback, a series of retaliatory hacks. Initially, the groups focused their attacks against the Recording Industry Association of America, the Motion Picture Association of America, and other copyright enforcement groups. Later, the focus shifted to several banks and financial services, such as PayPal and MasterCard, after those companies ceased allowing individuals to donate money to WikiLeaks after the site published numerous classified State Department cables leaked by Private Bradley Manning.

The LOIC fell out of favor with Anonymous and LulzSec in 2011 after the arrest of hackers in the wake of a series of DDoS attacks both groups launched against the Department of Justice (DOJ) and other Web sites in retaliation for the FBI and international authorities closing the popular file download site megaupload.com. The arrests proved that authorities possessed the means to trace LOIC attacks, a critical factor that led to the 2012 release of a more advanced hacking tool, the High Orbit Ion Cannon (HOIC). Like its predecessor, the HOIC is free for public download and easy to use, but the HOIC can initiate up to 256 simultaneous attacks. Still, because HOIC attacks can also be traced, other more sophisticated programs, such as Hping, which can spoof tracking measures, found favor with Anonymous and other hacking collectives.

Ryan Wadle

See also: Anonymous; Distributed Denial-of-Service (DDoS) Attack; 4chan; Hacktivist; Internet Relay Chat (IRC); LulzSec; Manning, Bradley; Operation Payback; WikiLeaks

Further Reading

Coleman, Gabriella. *Hacker, Hoaxer, Whistleblower, Spy: The Many Faces of Anonymous.* New York: Verso, 2014.

Olson, Parmy. *We Are Anonymous: Inside the Hacker World of LulzSec, Anonymous, and the Global Cyber Insurgency.* New York: Little, Brown, and Co., 2012.

Stryker, Cole. *Hacking the Future: Privacy, Identity, and Anonymity on the Web.* New York: Overlook Duckworth, 2012.

LULZSEC

LulzSec (full name Lulz Security) is an offshoot of the organization Anonymous. Like Anonymous, its membership includes hackers and hacktivists worldwide, though most are from the United States or the United Kingdom. LulzSec was created in 2011 by a small group of hackers known by their online aliases, Tflow, Topiary, Sabu, and Kayla. The group later expanded to about six core members and various associates, most of whom have been identified by their real name and subsequently arrested and charged with computer crimes. The name comes from combining the term *lulz*, itself a reference to the text shorthand "lol," or "laugh out loud," and the word "security". It was originally created to launch lulz, or Internet pranks, against various corporations for fun as opposed for purely principled reasons, like the activities undertaken by Anonymous. The group's motto is "Laughing at your security since 2011." The group is known by the symbol of a figure wearing a black top hat and monocle.

While still working with Anonymous, a small group of hackers later known as LulzSec first hacked into the Web site of the computer-security firm HBGary, its affiliate HBGary Federal, and its CEO Aaron Barr. Members of the group Anonymous happened to stumble on a plan proposed by HBGary Federal to smear and spy on WikiLeaks on behalf of Bank of America. The group easily hacked into the company Web site and downloaded thousands of company files and e-mails as well as remotely controlled Barr's iPhone and iPad. After the success of this infiltration, the group splintered from Anonymous and began to scour the Internet looking for security holes on the Web sites of many different corporations and government entities. The group started to gather the usernames and passwords of thousands of individuals connected to various databases, including Great Britain's National Health Service Web site, Sony's PlayStation Network, the American Public Broadcasting System, and Fox.

The goal of this new group was not just to steal information but to widely distribute it as a form of "lulz." It was not interested in supporting social justice causes per se, but in exposing the security vulnerabilities in the Web sites of many corporations to raise public awareness. LulzSec also targeted so-called white hat computer hackers who charged corporations thousands of dollars to expose security vulnerabilities and help fix them.

The group's most active year was 2011, during which they expanded their attack list to include various governments, the U.S. Senate, and a nonprofit organization affiliated with the Federal Bureau of Investigation (FBI) known as InfraGard. The attack on the Senate and InfraGard was in direct response to the Obama administration's statement that cyber attacks could be considered an act of warfare. Through a distributed denial-of-service (DDoS) attack, the group also brought down the CIA. gov Web site. Soon after, they were contacted by Julian Assange of WikiLeaks to help infiltrate the Web sites of several Icelandic government and corporate Web sites. By the end of 2011, members of LulzSec had released a statement titled "50 Days of Lulz," in which the group founder Topiary stated that LulzSec would cease operations.

Barbara Salera

See also: Anonymous; Assange, Julian; Cyber Crime; 4chan; Hacktivist

Further Reading

Coleman, Gabriella. *Hacker, Hoaxer, Whistleblower, Spy: The Many Faces of Anonymous*. London: Verso, 2014.

Olson, Parmy. *We Are Anonymous: Inside the Hacker World of LulzSec, Anonymous and the Global Cyber Insurgency*. New York: Back Bay Books, 2012.

M

MALWARE

Malware, short for "malicious software," is a broad term that applies to any software designed to disrupt the function of a computer or network. It encompasses everything from state-sponsored cyber attacks to intrusive advertising on otherwise benign Web sites. The term was coined in 1990, replacing "computer virus," when it became apparent that there were many forms of intrusive and dangerous software that did not technically conform to the proper definition of a virus.

Malware can be divided into several main categories, depending on the type of program and the intent of the user. *Computer viruses* seek to replicate on other hosts and then cause some form of damage, such as data corruption or rerouting of Internet traffic. *Worms* are a subspecies of computer virus that primarily seek to spread as rapidly as possible, often damaging systems in the process. *Trojan horses* appear to be useful but instead contain harmful code hidden inside. *Spyware* is a term referring to software that attempts to copy and extract data from a computer system. *Adware* is an annoying form of intrusive advertising that bombards the user with unwanted images and links to other network sites. *Ransomware* is software that attempts to seize control of a computer and prevent the user from regaining control until a ransom is paid to a third party. *Scareware* attempts to frighten a user into purchasing software to confront a phony threat to the system, and often installs worse programs if the user panics and agrees to download further malware. Malware is primarily combated through the use of antivirus and antimalware software and through firewalls.

Malware, like any other form of software, can take many forms, including active content, executable code, and scripts. It may be designed to evade detection (particularly spyware), or its presence might be overt (ransomware and scareware) as part of its function. Some malware has been discovered embedded into otherwise beneficial programs, including spyware concealed within Web sites that tracks a user's online behavior after the user has left the host Web site.

One prominent example, the Sony rootkit, was embedded on CDs sold by the Sony Corporation. When those CDs were copied onto a computer, the rootkit was also installed, allowing the Sony Corporation to track users' listening habits, ostensibly as a means of combating piracy. Unfortunately, this malware created vulnerabilities that were exploited by new malware released by unrelated programmers, meaning that Sony had compromised its customers' computer networks without their consent.

Jeffrey R. Cares

See also: Antivirus Software; Cyber Crime; Cyber Espionage; Cyber Security; Spyware; Trojan Horse

Further Reading
Libicki, Martin. *Cyberspace in Peace and War.* Annapolis, MD: U.S. Naval Institute Press, 2016.

MANDIA, KEVIN

Kevin Mandia (1972–) is the founder and former president of Mandiant Corporation, which provided cyber security to businesses from its headquarters in Alexandria, Virginia. In 2013, Mandiant Corporation caught the world's attention when it released a 60-page report detailing Chinese espionage. Mandia had made the personal decision to release the report, only informing one of his board members of his intention. He had determined that it was his patriotic duty to make Americans aware of the massive amount of intellectual information that the Chinese military had stolen from U.S. companies.

Unlike other similar reports issued around the same time by other organizations, Mandia had no hesitation in attributing these attacks to the Chinese military. Mandiant's report emboldened the United States to become more vocal about Chinese cyber attacks. Later that year, Mandia sold Mandiant to another cyber-security company, FireEye, Inc., for $1.05 billion. He initially served as its chief operations officer and senior vice president until February 2015, when he was appointed president of FireEye.

After growing up in Pottstown, Pennsylvania, Mandia received a BS in computer science from Lafayette College in 1992 and an MS in forensic science from George Washington University in 1995. It is Mandia's dual background in computers and forensic science that made Mandiant Corporation so distinctive. Unlike many business models that stress firewalls, Mandiant emphasizes detecting cyber attacks and then responding to them to shut out the hackers rather than focusing on preventing them. Mandia also served in the U.S. Air Force as a computer-security officer until he became frustrated with its bureaucracy.

Heather Pace Venable

See also: Advanced Persistent Threat (APT); Attribution; Cyber Attack; Cyber Espionage; Firewall; GhostNet; Malware; Mandiant Corporation; People's Republic of China Cyber Capabilities

Further Reading
Easton, Nina. "The CEO Who Caught the Chinese Spies Red-handed." *Fortune,* July 8, 2013. http://fortune.com/2013/07/08/the-ceo-who-caught-the-chinese-spies-red-handed.

Luttgens, Jason T., Matthew Pepe, and Kevin Mandia. *Incident Response & Computer Forensics.* 3rd ed. New York: McGraw-Hill, 2014.

Mandiant Corporation. *APT1: Exposing One of China's Cyber Espionage Units.* Alexandria, VA: Mandiant Corporation, 2013.

MANDIANT CORPORATION

Kevin Mandia established Mandiant Corporation in 2004 to provide cyber security to businesses. Headquartered in Alexandria, Virginia, Mandiant had more than 300 employees at its peak, including some in Dublin, Ireland, and others in Redwood, California. Mandia primarily hired former military intelligence officers (Mandia served in the U.S. Air Force) and experts in computer forensics.

In 2013, Mandiant Corporation released a 60-page report detailing Chinese espionage. The report attributed massive theft of U.S. corporate secrets to a secretive Chinese military unit known as People's Liberation Army Unit 61398. Mandia's dual background in computer science and forensics explains the company's business model. Believing that attacks are impossible to prevent, Mandia focuses on identifying attacks and responding to them in a manner analogous to an alarm company.

Mandiant Corporation's growing reputation resulted in prominent companies and the government increasingly turning to them when they learned they had been victims of cyber attacks. Mandiant then sent in teams of three to five specialists, who might spend months identifying every piece of malware before removing it. In 2012, the company served 30 percent of Fortune 100 companies, which earned it more than $100 million in revenue. Another cyber-security company, FireEye, Inc., acquired Mandiant in December 2013 for $1.05 billion. FireEye's complementary focus is on the detection of malware. It had worked extensively with Mandiant prior to purchasing the company, using it to remove malware it had detected.

Heather Pace Venable

See also: Cyber Attack; Cyber Defense; Cyber Espionage; Cyber Security; Firewall; GhostNet; Malware; Mandia, Kevin; People's Liberation Army Unit 61398; People's Republic of China Cyber Capabilities

Further Reading

Easton, Nina. "The CEO Who Caught the Chinese Spies Red-handed." *Fortune,* July 8, 2013. http://fortune.com/2013/07/08/the-ceo-who-caught-the-chinese-spies-red-handed.

Stone, Brad, and Michael Riley. "Mandiant, the Go-to Security Firm for Cyber-espionage Attacks." *Bloomberg Business,* February 7, 2013. http://www.bloomberg.com/bw/articles/2013-02-07/mandiant-the-go-to-security-firm-for-cyber-espionage-attacks#p3.

MANNING, BRADLEY

Bradley Manning (1987–) is the former name of the U.S. Army private responsible for the biggest data leak in U.S. military history. Manning was convicted in July 2013 of various violations of the Espionage Act of 1917 for leaking over 700,000 government files, including videos. He released these government files through the Web site WikiLeaks. The various documents that he leaked went on to be known as the video "Collateral Murder," the "Iraqi War Logs," and the "Afghan War Diary."

Bradley Manning was born on December 17, 1987, to Brian and Sue Manning. He spent most of his childhood in a small town in rural Oklahoma. However, after his parents divorced, Manning and his mother moved to his mother's hometown in Wales, United Kingdom. At the age of 17, he returned to the United States to live with his father in Oklahoma City. Family life was rough, and soon after, Manning was kicked out. Manning moved from city to city until finally staying with his aunt in a suburb outside of Washington, D.C. He enrolled in a local community college but left after one semester. In the fall of 2007, at the age of 19, Manning decided to join the military.

Manning enlisted in the U.S. Army in early October 2007. He began basic training on October 7, 2007, at Fort Leonard, Missouri. After first failing basic training, Manning finally completed it in April 2008. He went on to train as an intelligence analyst in Fort Huachuca, Arizona. After his training, he was assigned to be an all-source intelligence analyst with the 10th Mountain Division, 2nd Brigade. His unit was deployed to Iraq. While in Iraq, his position as intelligence analyst meant he spent anywhere from 12–14 hours per day on a computer on base in a room known as a sensitive compartmented information facility (SCIF). Manning was charged with mining data from a variety of sources on the Iraqi insurgency, including the State Department's Net-centric Diplomacy database. This database was maintained by the State Department to facilitate communication between government agencies and thus was connected to the Department of Defense's Secret Internet Protocol Router Network (SIPRNet).

By Manning's own admission, like other soldiers, he spent most of his deployment both miserable and bored. To pass the time, soldiers often watched videos, some dubbed "war porn," which consisted of anything from live feeds from drones to video clips shot from Apache helicopters engaged in combat. Manning was particularly troubled at watching a clip showing an Apache helicopter fire at what appeared to be unarmed civilians. In this clip, it appeared that the crew and pilot were making wisecracks while also shooting those who tried to crawl away. The clip was later released in April 2010 by WikiLeaks, dubbed "Collateral Murder."

A turning point for Manning was when Iraqi Federal Police arrested Iraqi citizens for printing "anti-Iraqi literature." When the U.S. military was called to assist the investigation, Manning was assigned to the task. He found that the anti-Iraqi literature was a scholarly critique of the corruption within Iraqi Prime Minister Maliki's government. Manning informed his superior officers of this, but he was told to ignore the information and help the Iraqi police find more individuals to arrest.

After this event, Manning began to question U.S. occupation policies in Iraq. By late November 2009, he began to use his data-mining skills to investigate events surrounding WikiLeaks' released information on the DoD's SIPRNet. In December,

Manning contacted WikiLeaks, and he received a message to contact its founder, Julian Assange. By January 2010, Manning had begun collecting classified information to turn over to WikiLeaks.

In May 2010, Manning was designated for discharge due to "adjustment disorder." By this time, he was struggling with a gender-identity disorder and knew his only hope of being able to transition to living as a female was outside of the military. He punched a female superior officer and was demoted back to private first class. It was at this time that he made the fateful decision to reach out to well-known hacker Adrian Lamo, on May 21, 2010. On May 26, 2010, Manning was arrested while still in Iraq and sent to the brig at Camp Arifjan, in Kuwait. Later, he was transferred to Quantico, Virginia.

Supporters of Manning protested the harsh treatment he received in prison, sparking a UN investigation. He was then transferred to Fort Leavenworth, Kansas, and court martialed after being deemed mentally fit to stand trial. He was sentenced to 35 years in Fort Leavenworth, but his sentence was commuted by President Obama. A transgender woman, he has changed his name to Chelsea Manning.

Barbara Salera

See also: Assange, Julian; Snowden, Edward J.; WikiLeaks

Further Reading

Madar, Chase. *The Passion of Bradley Manning.* London: Verso, 2013.

Nicks, Denver. *Private Bradley Manning, WikiLeaks, and the Biggest Exposure of Official Secrets in American History.* Chicago: Review Press, 2013.

MATRIX, THE

The Matrix is a 1999 film directed by Andy and Lana Wachowski that stars Keanu Reeves and Laurence Fishburne. In the film, Reeves plays Thomas "Neo" Anderson, a hacker who thinks he is living in the late 1990s. With the help of Fishburne's Morpheus, he discovers that the world he knows is merely an elaborate simulation. Instead, human body heat and energy serves as a power source for the machines controlling Earth sometime in the 22nd century.

The Matrix depicts a future where combat between machines and humans occurs in two realms: The first is the real world, where robots known as Sentinels hunt humans traveling aboard hovercraft ships in a postapocalyptic wasteland. The second realm is inside the simulation known as the "Matrix." The film's human heroes tap into the Matrix via plugs that connect directly to their nervous systems and receive guidance from "operators" who can read the machines' code. Once inside the Matrix, they are hunted by self-aware programs known as Agents. Death while inside the Matrix results in the death of the physical body in the real world.

The Matrix is one of the most prominent examples of "cyberpunk" culture that combines noir and technological anxieties in a dystopian future. It also includes elements of postmodern theory and Eastern philosophy. The film's financial and creative success led to the production of two sequels, video games, and other media.

Ryan Wadle

See also: Neuromancer; Terminator, The

Further Reading
Clover, Joshua. *The Matrix*. New York: British Film Institute, 2007.

MCAFEE

McAfee is the largest dedicated computer-security technology company in the world and is headquartered in Santa Clara, California. It was one of the first companies to produce antivirus software. The company was founded by John McAfee in 1987 as McAfee Associates and is best known for its antivirus and antispam product lines. Controversies led to McAfee's resignation from the company in 1994. In 2010, it was bought by the Intel Corporation for over $7 billion and is now part of the Intel Security Group. Intel continues to use the McAfee name and brand for products. McAfee's digital-security products are mostly designed for personal computers and server devices, but Intel is beginning to expand into mobile device protection.

Lori Ann Henning

See also: Antivirus Software; Cyber Defense; Cyber Security; Intel Corporation; Kaspersky Lab; Malware

Further Reading
Springer, Paul J. *Cyber Warfare: A Reference Handbook*. Santa Barbara, CA: ABC-CLIO, 2015.
Vacca, John R., ed. *Computer and Information Security Handbook*. Burlington, MA: Morgan Kaufmann Publishers, 2009.

MICROSOFT CORPORATION

Microsoft Corporation is a titan in the computer software sector. Its programming innovations revolutionized the industry, particularly the Windows operating system and Office suite. Founded in 1975 by Bill Gates and Paul Allen in Albuquerque, New Mexico, Microsoft's main focus has been software creation for personal and commercial devices, though it has diversified by entering the hardware and gaming console markets. As the world's largest software development company, Microsoft has confronted cyber-security issues for much of its existence.

In the mid-1970s, longtime friends Gates and Allen developed the BASIC programming language for the MITS Altair 8800, an early personal computer. Allen joined U.S.-based Micro Instrumentation and Telemetry Systems (MITS), and Gates left his studies at Harvard University. Microsoft was officially established on April 4, 1975, under MITS's auspices. Gates was its first CEO. Microsoft separated from MITS in 1976. IBM contracted Microsoft to create an operating system in July 1980. Microsoft retained the licensing rights to the highly successful system, MS-DOS (Microsoft disk operating system). In 1981, the Microsoft mouse made a small piece of hardware a requisite computer accessory. Allen left the company in 1983, keeping his stock holdings. Microsoft went public in March 1986 and was the world's largest personal computer (PC) software company by 1988.

In 1985, Microsoft debuted its revolutionary Windows operating system, which gave users a graphical interface. Microsoft introduced its Office software suite in 1989, which bundled applications such as Word and Excel with Windows. Both became industry standard-bearers. Developing software that is preinstalled on devices produced by PC manufacturers such as Acer and Lenovo, or licensed directly to users, has generated much of Microsoft's revenue. It also found success in the highly competitive game console market with the 2001 Xbox launch. Its search engine, Bing, went live in 2009. The Windows Phone, Microsoft's first smartphone, was released in 2011. Forty years after its founding, Microsoft launched its first laptop, the Surface Book, in 2015.

Microsoft's progressive approach to the Internet was propelled by Gates's belief that the Internet should take precedence in computer research and development. The company's Web portal, MSN, debuted in August 1995. Microsoft's embrace of the Internet was underscored by Gates's announcement on December 7, 1995, that the company would create a free Web browser, albeit in a Windows bundle. Internet Explorer 3.0, released in August 1996, was Microsoft's breakthrough Internet application.

Microsoft's reliance on licensing and application bundling resulted in clashes with government agencies. The Department of Justice (DOJ) investigated Microsoft's business practices in the late 1990s, prompted by complaints that the company's bundling was anticompetition. In 2000, a judge ruled that Microsoft was a monopoly. Microsoft agreed to a settlement that did not require divestiture. The European Commission brought a similar suit in 2004, resulting in the largest fine handed out by the commission at the time.

Over the 2000s, Gates moved to spend more time on his global philanthropic initiative, the Bill and Melinda Gates Foundation, which has donated billions to various humanitarian causes. He stepped down as CEO in 2014, replaced by longtime Microsoft executive Satya Nadella. Microsoft redefined its development path, rethought licensing, and made its products cross-platform friendly (including its Azure cloud service). In 2016, Microsoft purchased the business-directed social network LinkedIn.

Microsoft has been active in combating security issues related to its products. Its approach has revolved around protecting consumers, detecting and responding to threats, and preventing piracy of its products. The company's business strategy was initially criticized for eschewing security for product innovation. Pushing to have every product Internet-oriented meant they often launched before being wholly secure. Microsoft products are vulnerable to cyber attacks, in part, due to design flaws. Windows has been particularly susceptible because of its size; errors in millions of lines of code are difficult to detect and present hacking opportunities. Integrating Windows with Internet Explorer across Microsoft platforms also enticed attacks.

After facing increasing complaints from elite business consumers, security was prioritized in the 2000s. The Digital Crimes Unit works with international legal and cyber-security experts to investigate and analyze cyber crime and hacking behavior. Microsoft's Cyber Defense Operations Center opened in 2015 as a war room for its global cyber-security team. Microsoft has also developed relationships with benevolent hackers, who are hired to test product defenses.

One of Microsoft's methods for combating cyber conflict has been to take legal action against those running malware through its systems. This includes filing actions under the Computer Fraud and Abuse Act (1986) and the CAN-SPAM Act (2003). Using stealthy legal maneuvering, Microsoft essentially seizes private assets, such as servers, obtaining restraining orders to shut down botnets (an infected group of remotely, often criminally, controlled computers) based on the premise that the company's trademark is harmed by this malicious activity. The company has been commended and criticized for its tactics. While largely successful, this strategy often impacts real users on authentic network services and disrupts legitimate businesses.

A component of Microsoft's cyber-security awareness is the recognition of its role in protecting consumers from government surveillance. In April 2016, the company filed a lawsuit against the U.S. government, arguing it has the right to notify users when government agencies request access to personal documents located on its remote servers. This is in addition to Microsoft's promise to inform e-mail users when their accounts have been accessed by the government.

Microsoft contends that cyber security, national security, and privacy rights must find balance. It participated in President Barack Obama's 2016 Commission on Enhancing National Cybersecurity, through which high-tech industry leaders and government officials worked to improve the U.S. position on cyber security. Recommendations included protecting consumer data, sharing threat intelligence, and transparency. Microsoft is tangentially involved in the National Guard's cyber squadron, which participates in offensive cyber missions and includes Microsoft employees. Moreover, in 2015, Microsoft signed an information-sharing agreement with the North Atlantic Treaty Organization's (NATO) Communications and Information Agency. The agreement allowed for the sharing of technical information and threat intelligence to establish a stronger cyber-defense network in the European Union. Indeed, Microsoft has similar relationships with dozens of governments around the world.

Anna Zuschlag

See also: Apple Inc.; Botnet; Department of Justice (DOJ); Gates, Bill; Google; Malware; National Security Agency (NSA); North Atlantic Treaty Organization (NATO); Obama, Barack; Software

Further Reading

Allen, Paul. *Idea Man: A Memoir by the Cofounder of Microsoft.* New York: Penguin Group, 2012.

Andrews, Paul. *How the Web Was Won: How Bill Gates and His Internet Idealists Transformed the Microsoft Empire.* New York: Broadway Books, 1999.

Hiller, Janine S. "Civil Cyberconflict: Microsoft, Cybercrime, and Botnets." *Santa Clara High Technology Law Journal* 31(2), January 2014: 163–214.

Stross, Randall E. *The Microsoft Way: The Real Story of How the Company Outsmarts Its Competition.* New York: Basic Books, 1997.

MICROSOFT WINDOWS

Microsoft Windows is a computer operating system (OS) first released by the Microsoft Corporation in 1985. In the decades that followed, successive versions of Windows dominated the personal computer (PC) market. Microsoft also adapted Windows for use by commercial servers and handheld devices such as smartphones.

Windows improved on Microsoft's first operating system, MS-DOS, which it designed for IBM and released in 1980. MS-DOS had relied on a text interface for users to input commands, but Microsoft overlaid a more intuitive and user-friendly graphical user interface (GUI) over MS-DOS. First announced in 1983, Microsoft finally released Windows 1.0 in late 1985. Windows 1.0 set a trend followed by all of its successors whereby Microsoft "bundled" other programs with the OS, including a drawing program and a word processor. Microsoft's engineers, including cofounder Bill Gates, used their experience with Apple's Macintosh to construct the first Windows program.

Windows 2.0 (1987) became the first version of Windows that was compatible with other companies' software. Although Microsoft had grown significantly in the late 1980s, Windows had yet to truly catch on in the market.

Windows 3 (1990), followed by Windows 3.1 (1992), were extremely popular, selling over 10 million copies in the first two years of release. Windows 3 appeared just as personal computers were becoming common household items. The success was not without controversy, as Apple accused Microsoft of infringing on the copyrights of its operating systems. The lawsuit was first filed in 1988. In 1994, the Ninth Circuit Court of Appeals rejected Apple's argument that Microsoft's aping of the "look and feel" of Apple's operating systems constituted copyright infringement.

By the mid-1990s, Microsoft had parallel lines of operating systems, one for consumers and one for servers and business computers. For consumers, Microsoft introduced Windows 95 in 1995, followed by Windows 98 (1998) and Windows ME (2000). While each was a distinct operating system, they shared many traits. Windows 95 was a success, and Windows 98 further refined the OS. But the instability of Windows ME resulted in a commercial disaster. Meanwhile, Windows NT first appeared in 1993 for use in servers. The Windows NT family continued to evolve through the decade, culminating with the popular Windows 2000.

In 2001, Microsoft merged its consumer and commercial software together with the release of Windows XP. The new operating system grew out of the Windows NT line and abandoned the MS-DOS underpinnings of previous consumer versions of Windows. Initially disliked, XP became the most popular and long-lived version of Windows due to its stability and low hardware requirements. In fact, Microsoft continued to provide updates and support for some XP users until 2014. Unfortunately, XP proved susceptible to viruses and malware, and the software's ubiquity only exacerbated that tendency.

Not until 2007 did Microsoft unveil XP's successor, Windows Vista. The new OS attempted to remedy the security deficiencies of Windows XP, but fixing these issues came at the cost of slow boot times and frequent permission requests. In addition, Microsoft incorporated features to limit the spread of pirated media. Consumer dissatisfaction with Windows Vista led to a much shorter release cycle for its successor, Windows 7. Released in 2009, Windows 7 built on the strengths of Vista while correcting the previous software's numerous inefficiencies.

With the release of Windows 8 in 2012, Microsoft attempted to adapt the venerable platform to work on touchscreen-enabled computers. Users heavily criticized the changes made in Windows 8, especially for its new touch-friendly "Metro" home screen, and a significant update known as Windows 8.1 did little to stem the criticism. Microsoft released Windows RT alongside Windows 8 to serve as the operating system for low-power computers such as Microsoft's Surface, a computer-tablet hybrid, but the incompatibility of programs between Windows 8 and RT led to the latter's failure and rapid demise.

The 2015 release of Windows 10 saw a number of significant changes to the OS. First, Windows 10 partially rolled back the changes made to Windows 8 while simultaneously integrating better touchscreen functionality. Second, whereas Microsoft had previously required users to purchase each version of Windows, Microsoft allowed users of older versions of Windows to upgrade for free for up to one year. This move matched Apple's release strategy for its iOS, but it also allowed Microsoft to more rapidly cease support for the older versions. Third, Microsoft integrated a number of new features, including the personal assistant Cortana—similar to Apple's Siri—that incorporated cloud capabilities. Privacy advocates have criticized Windows 10 because of the default sharing of significant amounts of user data with Microsoft.

As the personal computer market stagnated and contracted in the 2010s, Microsoft looked to expand the Windows brand into new devices. As early as 2000, Microsoft started producing a series of operating systems designed for palm PCs and other smaller devices that shared some of Windows' basic functions. PocketPC 2000 and PocketPC 2002 were followed by Windows Mobile 2003, Windows Mobile 5 (2005), and Windows Mobile 6 (2007). Subsequent to Windows Mobile 6, Microsoft switched the focus of these operating systems to the burgeoning smartphone market to compete with Apple's iOS and Google's Android. Windows Phone 7 appeared in 2010, followed by Windows Phone 8 in 2012. Microsoft partnered with Swedish phone manufacturer Nokia in 2011 to develop Windows-based Lumia smartphones and eventually bought Nokia outright in 2014. Microsoft released the first Lumia phones with Windows Mobile 10 in late 2015. Despite the significant effort Microsoft invested in the smartphone market, only approximately 3 percent of global smartphones ran a variant of Windows Phone/Mobile as of 2015.

Ryan Wadle

See also: Apple Inc.; Gates, Bill; Google, Microsoft Corporation

Further Reading

Allen, Paul. *Idea Man: A Memoir of the Cofounder of Microsoft.* New York: Portfolio, 2011.

Isaacson, Walter. *The Innovators: How a Group of Hackers, Geniuses, and Geeks Created the Digital Revolution.* New York: Simon and Schuster, 2014.

Swaine, Michael, and Paul Freiberger. *Fire in the Valley: The Birth and the Death of the Personal Computer.* 3rd ed. Raleigh, NC: Pragmatic Bookshelf, 2014.

Zachary, G. Paschal. *Showstopper: The Breakneck Pace to Create Windows NT and the Next Generation at Microsoft.* New York: Open Road Media, 2014.

MINIMUM ESSENTIAL EMERGENCY COMMUNICATIONS NETWORK (MEECN)

The Minimum Essential Emergency Communications Network (MEECN) is designed to maintain communications between the National Command Authority (the president and the military chain-of-command) and the fielded nuclear-capable forces of the United States. It was initially proposed in 1994 as a means to upgrade emergency transmissions in the event of a nuclear war. As such, it requires a robust transmission and receiving capability as well as the ability to withstand enemy attempts at disruption should a nuclear war become a realistic possibility.

The U.S. nuclear arsenal requires a series of code authentications before nuclear weapons can be made operable. The codes reside with the president of the United States and must be transmitted to individual fielded forces before a nuclear attack can be launched. This need for communication represents a potential vulnerability for a sophisticated opponent, as it theoretically could be jammed or otherwise cut off, rendering the nuclear arsenal unusable. Other nations have considered this problem and created a series of fail-safe mechanisms to utilize at least a portion of their nuclear arsenal in the event of total communications loss, on the theory that such an event could only occur during a major nuclear exchange. The United States has shown no inclination to create such a system, often called a "dead hand switch," as it carries the risk of accidental deployment. Instead, American systems rely on maintaining at least a one-way communication capability.

Although the exact specifications of the MEECN are classified, certain aspects of it have been released to the public. It requires a miniature receive terminal, a specialized piece of equipment that is capable of transmitting and receiving on the Extremely High Frequency (EHF) and Very Low Frequency/Low Frequency (VLF/LF) sections of the electromagnetic spectrum. It relies on both satellites and airborne relays, creating redundant paths for a message to get through. These terminals guarantee a high data rate for transmissions, even in the face of enemy attempts at signals jamming, and are capable of functioning even in the immediate area of an electromagnetic pulse (EMP). Because the MEECN does not rely on a cyber network, it is at least theoretically immune to cyber attack, and guarantees that the key element of U.S. deterrence policies remains functional, while minimizing the possibility of an accidental nuclear attack.

Paul J. Springer

See also: Cyber War; Electromagnetic Pulse (EMP); Infrastructure; Weapons of Mass Disruption

Further Reading

Hoffman, David E. *Dead Hand: The Untold Story of the Cold War Arms Race and Its Dangerous Legacy.* New York: Doubleday, 2009.
Schlosser, Eric. *Command and Control.* New York: Penguin, 2009.

MITNICK, KEVIN

Kevin Mitnick (1963–) is an American computer-security consultant, author, and hacker best known for his high-profile 1995 arrest and imprisonment for computer and communications-related crimes. Mitnick was born August 6, 1963, in Los Angeles, California. His first unauthorized computer access took place in 1979 at age 16, for which he was sentenced to 12 months' imprisonment and 3 years' probation in 1988. In 1992, Mitnick became a fugitive from the Federal Bureau of Investigation (FBI), facing a host of hacking and software theft allegations at some of the nation's largest cellular telephone and computer companies. He gained national notoriety after a 1994 *New York Times* article claimed he hacked into NORAD's computer system at age 17 and was the inspiration for the 1983 film *WarGames*, allegations Mitnick denies.

Mitnick was arrested February 15, 1995, after a highly publicized pursuit. In 1999, he accepted a plea bargain agreement and was sentenced to five years' imprisonment, including time served. He spent eight months in solitary confinement and was released January 21, 2000. Mitnick wrote in a 2002 book that he had compromised computers solely by using passwords gained through social engineering, not software programs. Since 2002, Mitnick has been a paid computer-security consultant, performing penetration-testing services and teaching social-engineering classes to dozens of corporations and government agencies.

Steven B. Davis

See also: Cyber Crime; Federal Bureau of Investigation (FBI); Hacker; Social Engineering; *WarGames*

Further Reading

Mitnick, Kevin. *The Art of Deception: Controlling the Human Element of Security.* Indianapolis, IN: Wiley Publishers, 2002.
Mitnick, Kevin. *Ghost in the Wires: My Adventures as the World's Most Wanted Hacker.* New York: Little, Brown and Company, 2011.

MOONLIGHT MAZE

Moonlight Maze was a large-scale cyber attack that began in March 1998. Still mostly classified, the attack consisted of hundreds of cyber-espionage attacks, mainly targeting the National Aeronautics and Space Administration (NASA), the Pentagon, other government agencies, universities, and research laboratories. The thousands of stolen files included maps of military installations, troop manifests and configurations, and military hardware designs. The Joint Task Force for Computer Network Defense (JTF-CND) and the Federal Bureau of Investigation (FBI) combined their efforts to locate the source of these multiple intrusions. They were able to trace the source to a mainframe in Russia. The attackers remained unknown, and Russia denies any involvement. These attacks are still being investigated by U.S. intelligence and law enforcement agencies.

This event was a wake-up call for cyber security and a sign of the increasing role of state-sponsored attacks. Today, there is little unclassified information available on what was compromised. The FBI investigation was made public in 1999, which spread shockwaves through the cyber-security industry. Moonlight Maze made them aware that there was no easy way to ascertain the source, dynamics, or goals of this form of espionage. In defending cyber space, the government now needed new and different tools, concepts, and organizations to fight this threat.

The government response to prior threats was the creation of the Joint Task Force for Computer Network Defense (JTF-CND). On May 22, 1998, President Bill Clinton signed Presidential Decision Directive 63 (PDD 63), which called for an interagency department that would secure the nation's governmental and civilian infrastructure from cyber attack, the National Incident Protection Center (NIPC). Moonlight Maze brought to focus that security of cyber space required larger focus with different tools, organizations, and concepts. It also brought into focus that the Russians were capable of "system on system" military operations and recognized the importance of the "military-technical revolution."

Institutions with critical infrastructures now needed to be protected. Various agencies were formed, including a national coordinator for security, infrastructure protection, and counterterrorism, who also chairs the Critical Infrastructure Coordination Group (CICG); the National Infrastructure Assurance Council (NIAC) was composed of the private sector combined with state and local government officials to protect critical infrastructures. Information and analysis centers were created in the United States and on the international level, and the United Nations and Geneva began debating the integration of cyber warfare to existing laws.

The cyber intrusions for Moonlight Maze were not conducted solely through the Internet. They included attacks on the DoD's scientific and industrial contract providers. The attackers employed sophisticated hardware and computer power, and their operational skills were able to counter all attempts to shut them down. The attackers used thousands of servers to overwhelm a single server, called *distributed coordination approach*, which disguised their identities and made it difficult for the server to realize that it was under attack.

Targeting the attackers and disabling their operations were contemplated, but curtailed, because the United States feared these measures might be considered an act of war if sponsored by the Russian government. Also, a lack of understanding of who the adversaries were, coupled with Russian denial, hindered the response. The Pentagon rerouted its communications through eight expanded gateways to better monitor and cut down the attackers' focus. Encryption of passwords was forced on the DoD, and $200 million was invested in new firewalls, encryption development, and intrusion technology. The Chinese espionage cases in October 1999 also hindered the U.S. response, as they depleted manpower resources.

The attack was traced to Internet servers located 20 miles from Moscow. Their pattern of attack revealed that they had regular office hours, 8:00 a.m. to 5:00 p.m., and they never attacked on Russian holidays. This implied that if the attacks were not conducted by the Russia, they were state-enabled. The intrusions also showed that they had an unusually high-speed connection that linked research facilities in Moscow to the United States, hiding an offensive command and control network within civilian research facilities. It was not until 2000 that the United States formally complained to Russia, providing the attackers' telephone numbers. In response, Russia denied any prior knowledge and claimed the numbers were all nonoperational. The United States also went to Moscow to reach out to the Russian government to investigate the source, with no success. Russia consistently denied any involvement in Moonlight Maze. In 2001, the attackers were continuing to operate within the system through code or instructions that would let them gain access to a previous compromised system.

While considered an espionage incident, it was also a hostile military cyber-war act. It was a warning of what was to occur in future, recurring cyber-attack methods and investigations. It took years to attribute the attackers to Russia, and no one knows how long they had access prior to detection. Moonlight Maze showed that even though a government agency can be protected, its dependence on outside institutions is still a cyber-security problem. It raised the concept of *defense in depth*, which began reorganizational innovations under a counterintelligence czar implementing policy shifts.

Raymond D. Limbach

See also: Advanced Persistent Threat (APT); Cyber Espionage; Operation Aurora; Operation Shady RAT; Russia Cyber Capabilities

Further Reading

Brenner, Joel. *America the Vulnerable: Inside the New Threat Matrix of Digital Espionage, Crime, and Warfare.* New York: Penguin, 2011.

Carr, Jeffrey. *Inside Cyber Warfare: Mapping the Cyber Underworld.* Sebastopol, CA: O'Reilly Media, 2009.

Clarke, Richard A., and Robert K. Knake. *Cyber War: The Next Threat to National Security and What to Do about It.* New York: HarperCollins, 2010.

MOORE'S LAW

Moore's Law refers to an observation published in the trade journal *Electronics* in April 1965 by chemist Gordon Moore (1929–), then employed by Fairchild Semiconductors. Moore noted that the surface area of a transistor, as etched on an integrated circuit, was being reduced by approximately 50 percent every 18 months and that the subsequent computing power increased at an exponential rate. In 1968, Robert Noyce and Moore founded the corporation that would later become Intel, eventually the world leader in the production of microprocessors. Moore revised his previous observations in 1975, postulating that this doubling of semiconductor power was actually happening every 2 years. This observation has widely been expanded to include virtually all aspects of computer memory and performance, especially semiconductor memory, disk storage, and other aspects of digital microelectronics. As of this writing, Moore's Law is still holding. In general, this means that computers double in speed and computing power for roughly the same price every 2 years. In many ways, recognition of this phenomena drives both consumer expectations and manufacturing goals for computers and their subcomponents.

Although recognition of the growth in computing power specifically in regard to integrated circuits spurred the concept, others have projected the growth in information-processing power more broadly over the history of all mechanical, electromechanical, and digital information-processing devices. One notable theorist in this regard is computer scientist and futurist Ray Kurzweil, who describes this as "The Exponential Growth of Computing, 1900–1998" in his book *The Age of Spiritual Machines*.

John G. Terino

See also: Hardware; Intel Corporation

Further Reading

Brock, David C., ed. *Understanding Moore's Law: Four Decades of Innovation*. Philadelphia: Chemical Heritage Press, 2006.

Thackray, Arnold, David C. Brock, and Rachel Jones. *Moore's Law: The Life of Gordon Moore, Silicon Valley's Quiet Revolutionary*. New York: Basic Books, 2015.

MS BLASTER WORM

MS Blaster Worm is a computer worm released on August 11, 2003, that infected approximately 100,000 computers, including those belonging to government agencies in the United States, operating Microsoft Windows XP and Windows 2000. MS Blaster Worm is also commonly referred to as Lovsan, Lovesan, MSBlast, MSBlaster, the Blaster Worm, and simply, Blaster. MS Blaster Worm was able to infect computers through a vulnerability and security flaw in the Microsoft Distributed Component Object Model (DCOM) remote procedure call (RPC) service. The computer worm caused computers to reboot, have blank screens, and become inoperable. Microsoft released two patches, the MS03-026 and MS03-039, to fix the security flaw.

MS Blaster Worm is able to spread to other computers through networked computers that are already affected by the worm. MS Blaster Worm illustrated the importance of network and computer security for governments, networks, companies, universities, organizations, and businesses due to the volume of Internet and computer users in such institutions and because the worm highlighted the ease of spreading computer infections among institutionally networked machines. The attack from the MS Blaster Worm cost millions of dollars in damages, interfered with network traffic, and prevented organizational transactions.

Even though the identity of the original author of the MS Blaster Worm is still unknown, U.S. law enforcement officers arrested an 18-year-old Minnesota teenager who pleaded guilty to spreading a version of the MS Blaster Worm that infected approximately 50,000 computers in August 2003.

Roger J. Chin

See also: Antivirus Software; Malware; MyDoom Virus; SQL Slammer Worm; Worm

Further Reading

Bowden, Mark. *Worm: The First Digital World War.* New York: Grove Press, 2011.
Schultz, E. Eugene. "The MSBlaster Worm: Going from Bad to Worse." *Network Security* 10, 2003: 4–8.

MYDOOM VIRUS

The MyDoom virus was a computer worm sent via e-mail that was first detected on January 26, 2004. The worm targeted Microsoft Windows–based systems. MyDoom was transmitted through an e-mail with an infected attachment. Once the recipient opened and thus executed the attachment, the virus located the user's address lists and sent itself to other unsuspecting users. The virus also created a backdoor by use of a Trojan horse program to allow a remote computer to assume control, which was then used to launch distributed denial-of-service (DDoS) attacks as part of a botnet.

MyDoom launched DDoS attacks on Microsoft and SCO Group by accessing the Web sites simultaneously from infected computers. The attack on the SCO Web site occurred on February 1, 2004, with an estimated 25,000 to 50,000 computers involved. SCO Group and Microsoft offered a $250,000 reward for information leading to the arrest of the malware's creator.

Approximately 500,000 systems were affected worldwide by MyDoom. At its height, it was infecting roughly 1 in 12 e-mail messages. According to Jaikumar Vijayan, MyDoom became "one of the fastest-spreading viruses in history" during that time period. The creator of the worm remains a mystery.

Steven A. Quillman

See also: Botnet; Distributed Denial-of-Service (DDoS) Attack; Microsoft Corporation; MS Blaster Worm; SQL Slammer Worm; Worm

Further Reading

Metz, Cade. "Havoc from MyDoom: A Fast-spreading Virus Teaches Lessons." *PC Magazine*, March 16, 2004: 21.

Springer, Paul J. *Cyber Warfare: A Reference Handbook*. Santa Barbara, CA: ABC-CLIO, 2015.

Vijayan, Jaikumar. "Mydoom Lesson: Take Proactive Steps to Prevent DDos Attacks." *Computerworld*, February 9, 2004.

NATIONAL CYBER SECURITY STRATEGY

The U.S. National Cyber Strategy is a strategy shaped and formed by a collection of presidential directives, executive orders, and legislation that traces its origins to the 1980s with the collective goal of securing and protecting the federal, state, and local governments; private sector; and civilian population from increasing threats to the disruption of operational information systems for critical infrastructures. The aim of the National Cyber Security Strategy is not to end attacks and disruptions to informational systems, but instead to limit their consistency and improve recovery time.

The U.S. National Cyber Security Strategy has evolved over the last 30 years and traces its roots to the Reagan administration. In 1987, Congress passed the first law of its kind regarding computer security with the Computer Security Act (CSA), which was signed into law by President Ronald Reagan. At the most basic level, the CSA required every federal institution to inventory its information technology (IT) systems and to create security plans for said systems and review these plans annually. This act also confirmed that the National Institute of Standards and Technology (NIST) was responsible for nonmilitary government computer systems, and it limited the National Security Agency (NSA) to providing assistance in the civilian-security sector. By 2002, Congress had passed the E-Government Act, which includes Title III, more commonly known as the Federal Information Security Management Act (FISMA), and this was created to replace the CSA. As a result of the terrorist attack on September 11, 2001, FISMA was created in response to congressional demands for increased security. FISMA upgraded informational security and provided the framework for federal agencies to secure their IT systems with a risk-based approach.

As technology advanced and critical military, government, and economic systems became more reliant on technology, the need for increased security became an important factor of national security. Continued efforts were made to increase the security of private and government IT systems. Major headway in this area occurred in 2003 when the Department of Homeland Security (DHS), as part of their national strategy, produced the *National Strategy to Secure Cyberspace*. Though not a mandate or presidential directive, the suggestions offered within came from three strategic objectives: to prevent cyber attacks against critical infrastructure, to reduce vulnerability to attacks, and to limit recovery time and damage from attacks that do occur. Based on these three objectives, DHS detailed five priorities for future and improved security that focused on the public, private, and government spheres of cyber space: a national cyber-space security response system, a security threat and vulnerability reduction program, a security awareness and training program, securing governments' cyber space, and a national security and international cyber-space security cooperation.

In 2008, the Comprehensive National Cybersecurity Initiative (CNCI) was created by *Presidential Directive 23*. The directive outlines further cyber-security goals and extends across multiple federal agencies, including the National Security Agency (NSA) and DHS. The goals of this directive were to enhance situational awareness of vulnerabilities and threats within the federal government. Also included were tasking objectives to improve counterintelligence, to secure of the supply chain for key technologies, to improve education, and to strengthen research and development.

When President Barack Obama took office, he requested a review of cyber-space policy, which resulted in the production of the "Cyber Policy Review." This review examined current policies and methods to improve weaknesses it found. Following the review's publication, Obama announced cyber security as a national challenge and important part of national security. This policy review also advised the president to create a government cyber-security official that would recommend policy for future security. The recognition of cyber security as significant to national security encouraged several executive orders, reviews, and legislation that produced the International Strategy for Cyberspace, Prosperity, Security, and Openness in a Networked World (2011) and the Department of Defense Strategy for Operating in Cyberspace (2011). These all culminated with a presidential executive order entitled Improving Critical Infrastructure Cybersecurity (2013), which ordered the improvement of the country's cyber infrastructure—physical and virtual assets—and communication and sharing of information with public and private companies. It also requires these organizations to maintain that civil liberties violations do not occur.

John J. Mortimer

See also: Bush, George W.; Comprehensive National Cybersecurity Initiative (CNCI); Department of Homeland Security (DHS); Infrastructure; National Institute of Standards and Technology (NIST); National Security Agency (NSA); Obama, Barack

Further Reading

Andress, Jason, and Steve Winterfeld. *Cyber Warfare: Techniques, Tactics, and Tools for Security Practitioners.* 2nd ed. Waltham, MA: Syngress, 2014.

Department of Homeland Security. *The National Strategy to Secure Cyberspace.* Washington, D.C.: U.S. Government Printing Office, 2003.

Grama, Joanna Lyn. *Legal Issues in Informational Security.* 2nd ed. Burlington, MA: Jones and Bartlett Learning, 2015.

Reveron, Derek S., ed. *Cyber Challenges and National Security: Threats, Opportunities, and Power in a Virtual World.* Washington, D.C.: Georgetown University Press, 2012.

NATIONAL INFRASTRUCTURE ADVISORY COUNCIL (NIAC)

The National Infrastructure Advisory Council (NIAC) provides advice on issues related to the security and resilience of the critical infrastructure of the United States, focusing on their functional systems, physical assets, and cyber networks, to the president through the secretary of homeland security.

President George W. Bush created the NIAC in 2001 as part of a wider effort to protect critical infrastructure in the information age. It was formally established by Executive Order 13231. This executive order established several focus areas for the NIAC to include the security of information systems for critical infrastructure supporting the banking, finance, transportation, energy, and manufacturing sectors of the economy and for emergency government services. To provide the best advice for securing both governmental and private critical infrastructure, the NIAC consists of 30 members of the private sector, academia, and state and local governmental officials appointed by the president. Executive branch employees are prohibited from becoming members of the NIAC.

The NIAC meets quarterly to enhance the partnership of the public and private sectors for the protection of information systems for critical infrastructure, to propose and develop the private sector's ability to perform risk assessments of critical information systems, and to advise lead agencies with critical infrastructure responsibilities. The NIAC is led by a chair and a vice chair designated by the president and is managed by a Designated Federal Officer (DFO) appointed by the Department of Homeland Security's under secretary for national protection and programs. While the chair and vice chair lead the advisory functions of the NIAC, the DFO manages the operations of the NIAC, such as approving and calling NIAC meetings, approving meeting agendas, adjourning NIAC meetings, executing NIAC business transactions, and fulfilling all reporting requirements according to the Federal Advisory Committee Act.

The NIAC provides advice on the security and resiliency of national infrastructure by presenting the president and responsible federal agencies with formal reports and recommendations. These reports and recommendations are the products of a NIAC working group. NIAC working groups are formed in response to either a White House or congressional request for information or from a focus area determined internally by the NIAC membership. Once a research topic is approved by the NIAC, a working group is formed that ultimately produces a report or recommendation. Over the course of its history, the NIAC has produced reports on transportation-sector resilience; the creation of a critical infrastructure security resilience research and development plan; the implementation of EO 13636 and PPD-21, which ordered an increase in cyber security across the country; intelligence information sharing; the optimization of resources for mitigating infrastructure disruptions; a framework for disaster mitigation, insider threats to critical infrastructure, and chemical, biological, and radiological events; and the critical infrastructure workforce.

Michael A. Bonura

See also: Bush, George W.; Department of Homeland Security (DHS); National Infrastructure Protection Plan (NIPP)

Further Reading

Brenner, Joel. *America the Vulnerable: Inside the New Threat Matrix of Digital Espionage, Crime, and Warfare.* New York: Penguin, 2011.

Carr, Jeffrey. *Inside Cyber Warfare: Mapping the Cyber Underworld.* Sebastopol, CA: O'Reilly Media, 2009.

Clarke, Richard A., and Robert K. Knake. *Cyber War: The Next Threat to National Security and What to Do about It.* New York: HarperCollins, 2010.

Department of Homeland Security. "The National Infrastructure Advisory Council." https://www.dhs.gov/national-infrastructure-advisory-council.

NATIONAL INFRASTRUCTURE PROTECTION PLAN (NIPP)

The National Infrastructure Protection Plan (NIPP) is issued by the U.S. Department of Homeland Security (DHS). It provides a coordinated and collaborative approach to help public- and private-sector partners understand and manage all risks to critical infrastructure and key resources (CI/KR), including cyber risks.

The Homeland Security Act; other statutes and executive orders; the National Strategies for Homeland Security, for the Physical Protection of CI/KR, and for Securing Cyberspace; and Homeland Security Presidential Directive 7 (HSPD-7) provided the authority for the component elements outlined in the NIPP. These documents worked together to provide a coordinated national approach to homeland security that is based on a common framework for CI/KR protection, preparedness, and incident management.

The NIPP also formally defined the CI/KR protection components of the homeland-security mission. Implementing CI/KR protection requires partnerships, coordination, and collaboration among all levels of government and the private sector. Many CI/KR functions and services are enabled through cyber systems and services; if cybersecurity is not appropriately addressed, the risk to CI/KR is increased. The responsibility for cyber security spans all CI/KR partners, including public- and private-sector entities.

The first NIPP was released by DHS in June 2006, with subsequent revisions released in 2009 and 2013. The June 2006 NIPP provided the first approach for integrating the nation's 18 CI/KR sectors. The 2009 NIPP revised the 2006 NIPP and stated that CI/KR protection planning involved special consideration for unique cyber elements that support CI/KR operations and complex interpersonal relationships. It also addressed the protection of the cyber elements of CI/KR in an integrated manner rather than as a separate consideration. As a component of the sector-specific risk assessment process, cyber infrastructure components would now be identified individually or included as cyber elements of a larger asset's, system's, or network's description, if they are associated with one. This identification process included information on international cyber infrastructure with cross border implications, interdependencies, or cross sector ramifications.

NIPP 2013 was issued by DHS on December 20, 2013, in response to the February 2013 Presidential Policy Directive-21 (PDD-21) signed by President Barack Obama on Critical Infrastructure Security and Resilience. NIPP 2013 promoted cyber security by facilitating participation and partnership in CI/KR protection initiatives, leveraging cyber-specific expertise and experiences, and improving information exchange and awareness of cyber-security concerns. It also provided a framework for public- and private-sector partner efforts to recognize and address the similarities and differences among the approaches to cyber risk management for business continuity and national security. This framework enabled CI/KR partners to work collaboratively to make informed cyber risk management decisions, define national cyber priorities, and address cyber security as part of an overall national CI/KR protection strategy.

Jim Dolbow

See also: Cyber Terrorism; Department of Homeland Security (DHS); Infrastructure

Further Reading

Clarke, Richard A., and Robert K. Knake. *Cyber War: The Next Threat to National Security and What to Do about It.* New York: HarperCollins, 2010.
Department of Homeland Security. *National Infrastructure Protection Plan 2009: Partnering to Enhance Protection and Resiliency.* Washington, D.C., 2009.
Department of Homeland Security. *NIPP 2013: Partnering for Critical Infrastructure Security and Resilience.* Washington, D.C., 2013.

NATIONAL INSTITUTE OF STANDARDS AND TECHNOLOGY (NIST)

The National Institute of Standards and Technology (NIST) is a nonregulatory agency of the U.S. Department of Commerce that focuses on the development of measurement standards with the goal of enhancing economic security, improving quality of life, and promoting innovation and industrial competitiveness. The institute was created in 1901 as the National Bureau of Standards, with the mandate of overseeing weights and measures, and served as the national physical laboratory for the United States.

During World War I, the bureau aided with production of war materiel and military research and development. In 1948, with funding from the U.S. Air Force, the bureau built the Standards Eastern (or Electronic) Automatic Computer (SEAC), the first stored-program electronic computer in the United States. In 1988, the bureau became the National Institute of Standards and Technology. The institute is headquartered in Gaithersburg, Maryland, and maintains a facility in Boulder, Colorado, that is known for housing an atomic clock that serves as the nation's official time. NIST is involved in developing a diverse array of technologies, including building design, aircraft, global communications networks, and nanomachines, in addition to a grant program that shares the cost of high-risk technologies with industry partners.

NIST became involved with cyber security beginning in the 1990s through a series of special publications emphasizing the importance of computer security by listing and continually updating best security practices. These were initially aimed at assessing and protecting government networks, but the best practices were equally applicable to private security efforts. In February 2013, President Barack Obama issued Executive Order 13636: Improving Critical Infrastructure Cybersecurity, which directed NIST to develop a voluntary cyber-security framework—a system of best practices to protect critical infrastructure sectors and organizations and limit cyber-security risks as well as foster communication regarding cyber-security practices. The framework was completed after a yearlong process of collaboration between NIST, industry, government organizations, and academia. The Cybersecurity Enhancement Act of 2014 further strengthened NIST's role of facilitating voluntary, industry-led cyber-security standards to ensure the safety of critical infrastructure.

Because various organizations have unique threats and risk-tolerance levels, the framework is intended to be an adaptable set of general guidelines to be implemented differently by adopting institutions. At the same time the framework was released, NIST also released the "Roadmap for Improving Critical Infrastructure Cybersecurity," which identifies high-priority areas in need of development for future versions of the framework. This project involved a partnership with infrastructure operators and the U.S. Department of Homeland Security (DHS) known as the Critical Infrastructure Cyber Community (C^3) Voluntary Program. The Framework Core is publicly available, although it is considered a living document and is subject to continual updates as the result of cooperation and coordination with stakeholders.

Michael Hankins

See also: Cyber Defense; Cyber Security; Department of Homeland Security (DHS); Infrastructure; National Infrastructure Advisory Council (NIAC); National Infrastructure Protection Plan (NIPP)

Further Reading

Andress, Jason, and Steve Winterfeld. *Cyber Warfare: Techniques, Tactics and Tools for Security Practitioners.* 2nd ed. Waltham: Syngress, 2014.

Lopez, Javier, et al. *Critical Infrastructure Protection: Information Infrastructure Models, Analysis, and Defense.* New York: Springer, 2012.

Singer, P. W., and Allan Freidman. *Cybersecurity and Cyberwar: What Everyone Needs to Know.* Oxford: Oxford University Press, 2014.

NATIONAL SECURITY AGENCY (NSA)

The National Security Agency (NSA) is the premier U.S. intelligence agency operating in the cyber domain. It holds primary responsibility for overseeing the nation's cyber defense and, when authorized by the president, conducting offensive cyber operations. It has been heavily criticized in recent years for apparent intrusions into American citizens' private lives.

The NSA was created in 1949 under the name Armed Forces Security Agency (AFSA). Its initial mission was to bring American code-breaking assets under a single umbrella. In 1952, the name was changed to the National Security Agency, and the organization began a much closer relationship with its military counterparts. The NSA was one of the earliest government agencies to adopt computing technology as a means to enhance its cryptological capabilities. The first decade of the NSA was characterized by efforts to improve the security of the national communications infrastructure and determine means to compromise the networks utilized by other nations. Despite the expectation that the Allied victory in World War II would usher in an era of prolonged peace, President Harry S. Truman and his successors understood that maintaining an internal ability to break the encryption used by other nations would enhance the intelligence-collection efforts of the federal government and hence make a major contribution to the security of the United States.

As the nature of the Cold War emerged, with a growing rivalry between the United States and the Soviet Union, the NSA shifted its primary focus toward the erstwhile ally. The victory of the Chinese Communist Party in the Chinese Civil War, completed in 1949, underscored the notion that communism, rather than fascism, had become the most aggressive political philosophy on the planet. When the United States announced a policy of containment toward the expansion of communism, the NSA became a key player in the intelligence community for its ability to intercept foreign communications and decrypt them. Eventually, the NSA assumed responsibility for the communications security (COMSEC) of the nation, under the auspices of the National Security Council. Unifying the responsibility for secure communications ensured that there would be standardization in American components and a centralized authority to respond to any detected threats.

In 1955, the NSA purchased an IBM computer, dubbed "HARVEST," as part of a program to create a general-use computer that could be reprogrammed to suit new purposes. By the end of the 1950s, the NSA had fully embraced the use of computers as a means to both create and break sophisticated codes. This early adoption provided a significant advantage to their cryptologic efforts. The NSA established partnerships with research universities working on the next generation of computers and was able to offer suggestions and advice regarding design architecture, thus creating a perpetual government-academic partnership for the development of increasingly powerful computers.

While many government agencies adopted a wait-and-see approach to computers, the NSA set aside increasing portions of its budget for the purchase and improvement of computers. The agency had grasped the fundamental principle that computers improved so rapidly as to make models obsolete within a few years. If the agency wished to remain at the top of the cryptological hierarchy, it needed to continually update its technology, regardless of how wasteful such spending might appear to other agencies. In 1963, the agency purchased a UNIVAC, a computer that could process enormous volumes of communications from a widely dispersed array of interception stations, and the agency's reach became truly global. By the end of the 1960s, NSA could boast it had over 100 computers, covering five acres of floor space, serving both defense and national signals intelligence (SIGINT) and COMSEC customers. By the 1970s, computers had emerged into a full-fledged industry, with university support not just of experimental models but also of computer science and engineering courses to assist in the design and operation of continually improving models. The NSA tapped into this new field of expertise and began to recruit the top graduates of computer programs across the country.

In 1971, President Richard Nixon combined the NSA with its military counterparts into a unified command, keeping the NSA's name for the new agency. The following year, he directed the establishment of the Central Security Service (CSS). Although separate organizations, the director of the NSA served as the chief of the CSS. This "dual-hat" concept allowed the top cryptological commander to oversee both military and nonmilitary initiatives. As communications and computing speeds increased, the private sector and scientific community grew concerned about the security of their communications. This concern led to the rise of publicly available encryption programs. The NSA contributed to the field by improving cipher machines that could be integrated with radio transmitters. The NSA also purchased desktop terminals to speed its own internal communications. As more offices began relying on computers, disparate groups of users emerged, each favoring different, and often incompatible, systems. In 1974, the NSA established an interconnecting system, known as PLATFORM, that centered computer operations on four core host complexes. The new system allowed for the use of a variety of interactive systems around the agency.

During the 1980s, the Soviet Union, and by extension the Communist Bloc, continued to be the major focus of the cryptologic community, although other national-security threats, such as the rise of mass-casualty terrorism, began to occupy significant amounts of the NSA's capabilities. Recognizing the rising number of responsibilities held by the agency, President Ronald Reagan secured a major increase in financial resources for the NSA, which in turn allowed the agency to continue its policy of pushing the technological capabilities of the computing industry to their utmost limits. Of course, expanded capabilities required a corresponding increase in the size of the NSA workforce, as the agency began to employ fixed stations, airborne platforms, ground-based communications satellite dishes, geosynchronous and orbiting satellites, and other assets to achieve its mission.

The 1990s saw the end of the Cold War, a development that caused many political leaders to believe that the nation's intelligence-collection efforts could be safely scaled back as a cost-saving measure. Military drawdowns also occurred, leading to a significant decline in the intelligence agencies' abilities to detect and respond to emerging threats, particularly from nonstate actors. At the same time, computer technology continued to expand at an exponential rate, and the costs of maintaining a technological edge required sacrifices in the number of outposts and the personnel staffing of the agency. An assumption that the NSA should provide enhanced computer security to the private sector contributed to the complexity of the agency's mission.

Rather than waiting to have the nation's computer systems attacked, the NSA adopted a highly aggressive "red team" approach to network security. NSA employees sought to penetrate U.S. computer networks to discover vulnerabilities that might be exploited by foreign agents. In the process, they discovered an unprecedented number of security flaws in a wide array of software and found that these same flaws might be exploited in foreign networks if those entities utilized the most ubiquitous computer software in the world, in particular Microsoft Windows. In most instances, the NSA notified Microsoft and other software designers of potential vulnerabilities and assisted in the creation of patches to close the weaknesses. In other cases, though, the NSA almost certainly held back its knowledge of a new potential exploit until it had the opportunity to use it as a means to infiltrate foreign networks.

With the dawn of the 21st century, media sources began to claim the NSA was failing in its efforts to maintain a significant technological edge over rivals. Perhaps most embarrassing, on January 24, 2000, a software anomaly caused a massive computer failure within the agency's networks at its Fort Meade facility. NSA computer networks experienced significant degradation for three full days. When the crisis was past, the agency issued a public statement designed to maintain American citizens' confidence that the agency's functions had continued and no intelligence had been leaked—but the very issuance of the statement confirmed that the NSA was not invulnerable to cyber attacks.

During the War on Terror, the NSA played a crucial role in tracking down Al Qaeda leaders, largely through massive intelligence-collection efforts that involved computers sifting through huge reams of data searching for telltale signs of terrorism links. To maintain the security of the American homeland, the NSA also began collecting metadata from U.S. telephone service providers and running the data through its computer systems to search for relationships between potential terrorist agents on American soil. When details of the collection efforts emerged, the American public was infuriated to discover that its own government had essentially been spying on private citizens without any judicial oversight. Promises to halt the program did little to assuage the public rage against an agency that few understood or fully trusted.

In 2010, President Barack Obama directed that the NSA should be incorporated into a new unified military organization, U.S. Cyber Command (USCYBERCOM). The NSA director, General Keith B. Alexander, was named to command the new military unit while also retaining his official role as the director of the NSA. Alexander called for an aggressive response to cyber attacks, recommending that the NSA be the lead agency for offensive operations in retaliation for enemy activities. This proactive stance directly countered previous NSA approaches to cyber security.

In 2013, NSA contractor Edward J. Snowden leaked thousands of internal NSA documents to several journalists. Fearing prosecution for his activities, Snowden fled the country, stopping first in Hong Kong and then seeking asylum in Russia. Snowden has been called both a patriotic whistle-blower and a traitor to the nation and has been charged with violating the Espionage Act for releasing classified information. The Snowden revelations rocked the intelligence community, as they demonstrated that the NSA had developed far more capabilities to break into computer networks and eavesdrop on computer users than had previously been thought possible. Worse, Snowden demonstrated not only how easily the NSA could infiltrate even secured systems but also that the agency had been systematically engaging in a massive invasion of American citizens' privacy in its never-ending quest to obtain information about potential threats to the nation. Snowden became the feature of a number of documentary films and books and a frequent guest for technological interviews carried out via teleconference. He remains in Russia, where he has sought without success to obtain permanent asylum.

The NSA remains the foremost offensive cyber-operations organization in the United States. In the aftermath of the Snowden revelations, the Obama administration took pains to curtail the activities of the agency, and it is now hindered from launching cyber attacks without explicit approval from the president. The NSA is an enormous intelligence agency that has gone to great lengths to avoid significant public scrutiny of its activities while still holding responsibility for the security of U.S. communications systems. It retains an active presence on American universities, assisting in research efforts and the training of future cyber warriors. Its current commander, Admiral Michael S. Rogers, is still the commander of USCYBERCOM, although there have been several proposals to return the NSA to complete independence.

Roy Franklin Houchin II

See also: Alexander, Keith B.; Bush, George W.; Comprehensive National Cybersecurity Initiative (CNCI); Defense Advanced Research Projects Agency (DARPA); Defense Information Systems Agency (DISA); Gates, Robert M.; Red Team; United States Cyber Capabilities; U.S. Cyber Command (USCYBERCOM)

Further Reading

Budiansky, Stephen. *Code Warriors: NSA's Codebreakers and the Secret Intelligence War against the Soviet Union.* New York: Knopf, 2016.

Hayden, Michael V. *Playing to the Edge: American Intelligence in the Age of Terror.* London: Penguin Press, 2016.

Kaplan, Fred. *Dark Territory: The Secret History of Cyber-war.* New York: Simon & Schuster, 2016.

Wallace, Robert, H. Keith Melton, and Henry R. Schlesinger. *Spycraft: The Secret History of the CIA's Spytechs, from Communism to Al-Qaeda.* New York: Dutton Adult, 2008.

NATO COOPERATIVE CYBER DEFENCE CENTRE OF EXCELLENCE (CCDCOE)

NATO Centres of Excellence (COE) are international military organizations that train and educate officers and civil servants from NATO members and partner countries. They assist in doctrine development, identify lessons learned, improve interoperability and capabilities, and test and validate concepts through experimentation. Centres of Excellence offer recognized expertise and experience, and they support the transformation of NATO. They embody "pooling and sharing" by avoiding the duplication of assets and resources. Centres of Excellence were first proposed by Allied Command Transformation following the 2002 Prague Summit. However, they are not part of the NATO Command Structure, nor do they receive any funding from NATO.

Estonia, a NATO member since 2004, proposed a Cooperative Cyber Defence Centre of Excellence (CCDCOE), located in Estonia's capital, Tallinn, in 2005. Estonia believed a CCDCOE would enhance Estonia's value to the alliance and ensure a better defended Estonia. Cyber security was crucial to Estonian defense because Estonia had responded to the challenges of reindependence (1991) by prioritizing information technology infrastructure (Project Tiger Leap). This created a digital society, commonly called E-Estonia. E-Estonia made the former Soviet republic bordering Russia extremely vulnerable to cyber attacks, as it lacked many of the analog redundant systems found in nations whose technology infrastructure had developed over time. The need for and importance of a Cooperative Cyber Defence Centre of Excellence was driven home in 2007, when the government of Estonia decided to move a Soviet war memorial called the *Bronze Soldier* from the center of Tallinn to a military cemetery. The move triggered the first large-scale ethnic riots since reindependence, which were followed by a large-scale cyber attack, widely suspected to have been orchestrated by Russia. Government Web sites and the Web sites of banks, media outlets, businesses, and universities were targeted by a massive and effective denial-of-service (DDoS) attack that lasted for three weeks and effectively isolated Estonia from the world. Estonia's political leadership was deeply shaken by the *Bronze Soldier* riots and the cyber attack, which indicated that Russia could seriously imperil the Estonian economy and society without even sending troops across the border.

The cyber attack on Estonia following the *Bronze Soldier* riots also convinced other NATO members of the need for such a COE and of the benefits of committing to its support. This support was vital, as a COE cannot be established without at least seven NATO members committing support for funding and staffing. In the aftermath of the *Bronze Soldier* riots, the Cooperative Cyber Defence Centre of Excellence was officially established by seven sponsoring nations: Estonia, Germany, Italy, Latvia, Lithuania, the Slovak Republic, and Spain, who signed a Memorandum of Understanding on May 14, 2008, with the aim to enhance the cooperative cyber-defense capabilities of NATO and individual NATO nations. The current sponsoring nations are the Czech Republic, Estonia, France, Germany, Greece, Hungary, Italy, Latvia, Lithuania, the Netherlands, Poland, Slovakia, Spain, Turkey, the United Kingdom, and the United States. In addition, Austria and Finland have joined the CCDCOE as contributing participants.

The CCDCOE is guided by an international steering committee consisting of the representatives from the sponsoring nations. Day-to-day business is coordinated and led by the organization's directorate, consisting of the director and chief of staff. The CCDCOE consists of five branches: law and policy, strategy, technology, education and exercise, and support. The law and policy branch has issued the *Tallinn Manual on the International Law Applicable to Cyber Warfare,* which is the guiding document for cyber warfare within NATO. *Tallinn 2.0* is the follow-on project to the *Tallinn Manual*. The strategy branch supports the development of NATO cyber strategy and the cyber strategies of member states, allies, and partners. The education and exercise branch provides resources, including subject matter experts on cyber security, to professional military education institutions, ministries, and headquarters and provides expertise to NATO and member state exercises in addition to hosting cyber exercises. The support branch ensures necessary host support is provided by Estonia and that non-Estonian personnel have been assigned to the CCDCOE.

Augustine Meaher IV

See also: Cyber War; Estonian Cyber Attack (2007); Patriotic Hacking; *Tallinn Manual*

Further Reading

Libicki, Martin. *Crisis and Escalation in Cyberspace*. Santa Monica, CA: RAND Corporation, 2012.

Schmitt, Michael N. *Tallinn Manual on the International Law Applicable to Cyber Warfare*. New York: Cambridge University Press, 2013.

NET-CENTRIC WARFARE (NCW)

Since the 1990s, the United States has sought to obtain an asymmetric advantage through network-centric warfare (NCW). This theory of war, when implemented in practice, is referred to as *network-centric operations* (NCO). NCO enables joint forces to link their devices to communicate faster and more effectively. The sharing of important information has the ultimate goal of improving situational awareness on the battlefield to see through the fog of war as much as possible.

In its essence, NCW is the military's conceptual response to the information age. It anticipates moving away from industrial warfare—and its platform-centric approach (different types of airplanes, tanks, or ships)–to one of linked networks as a way to counter opponents relying on a quantitative material superiority. The ability to obtain and apply relevant information quickly results in a de-emphasis on massed firepower. Although less force might be applied than in a platform-centric approach, a network-centric approach has a greater warfighting effect.

The U.S. Navy pioneered NCW, borrowing from transformations within the computer industry. In 1996, Admiral William Owens first published a paper titled "The Emerging U.S. System-of-Systems" that morphed into what came to be known as *net warfare*, with its goal of obtaining information superiority. Owens wanted to emulate the transformation made in the computer industry in which connecting individual computers, despite possible geographical dispersion, worked as a force multiplier.

Navy intellectuals married the computer industry's transformation to Air Force Colonel John Boyd's vision of an OODA loop, which consists of four phases: observe, orient, decide, and act. Boyd argued that whomever could complete this thought process first would win an engagement. Thus, the goal of net-centric warfare is to allow the U.S. military to complete its OODA loop faster than its adversaries. In operationalizing this concept, the military envisioned the interaction of three domains. Information would be obtained from the physical domain and then transferred through the information domain to be processed and acted on in the cognitive domain. Much of this operationalization occurred while Arthur K. Cebrowski served as the director of the Office of Force Transformation for the Department of Defense.

NCW moves the U.S. military away from attrition-style warfare, or trying to exhaust one's opponent, to an efficient way of waging war that speeds up the pace of operations. It brings together the "sensors"; the "command and control" (C2) or decision makers; and the "shooters." Information does not just flow in one direction from the sensors to C2 to the shooters, as it might in a more traditional organization. Rather, the flow of information is intertwined, with each feeding information to the other, even as the sender of information continues to receive it. This provides a powerful form of situational awareness, which is commonly referred to as C4ISR. C4ISR reflects the transformation from the more traditional concept of C2 (command and control) to one of command, control, communications, computers, intelligence, surveillance, and reconnaissance.

NCW enables effects-based approach to operations (EBAO). Developed in large part by the U.S. Air Force, EBAO seeks to evaluate an opponent's system holistically by managing vast amounts of information and considering a range of kinetic and nonkinetic options. Once the end goals are determined, the way of achieving those objectives comes under consideration.

As an offsetting advantage for the United States, NCW is increasingly coming under threat as the increasing affordability of this technology allows others to develop similar concepts. Another problem is that NCW relies in part on satellite-enabled communications; yet, near-peer competitors such as China and Russia are actively seeking to challenge U.S. space superiority.

Heather Pace Venable

See also: Cebrowski, Arthur K.; Department of Defense (DoD); Informatization; United States Cyber Capabilities

Further Reading

Blaker, James R. *Transforming Military Force: The Legacy of Arthur Cebrowski and Network Centric Warfare Army.* Westport, CT: Praeger, 2007.

Cebrowski, Arthur K. *The Implementation of Network-centric Warfare.* Washington, D.C.: Office of the Secretary of Defense, 2005.

Cebrowski, Arthur K. "Network-centric Warfare: An Emerging Military Response to the Information Age." *Military Technology*, May 2003: 16–22.

NET NEUTRALITY

Net neutrality is the principle under which all Internet users are equally able to access the network where they want, when they want. The U.S. Federal Communications Commission (FCC) argues that net neutrality fosters open competition between Internet service providers (ISPs) and can create consumer demand for faster, better communication. Conversely, a number of technology companies, including Amazon, Netflix, Google, AT&T, and Verizon, have voiced opposition to legislating for net neutrality and, instead, that ISPs should actively manage the network to provide better services. ISPs argue that by controlling the download speeds of particular users or types of data, they can ensure that every user has an optimized service, and they can also prevent illegal file swapping over their networks. Controversially, they also advocate for privileged special services that require heavy, uninterrupted bandwidth consumption, but at an additional premium price for consumers.

On June 12, 2015, the FCC introduced the Open Internet rules to protect and maintain open, uninhibited access to legal online content without ISPs being allowed to block, impair, or establish fast and slow lanes; the rules also included measures intended to sustain and encourage further commercial investment in U.S. broadband networks. The FCC's Open Internet rules apply to both fixed and mobile broadband networks equally and incorporate multiple sources of authority, including Title II of the Communications Act and Section 706 of the Telecommunications Act of 1996. Despite criticism that the use of Title II constituted a regressive monopoly regulation, the FCC emphasized that broadband would thereafter be treated as a telecommunications service instead of as a utility, thereby avoiding the latter's regulatory regime and thus encouraging investment in broadband networks. The FCC's regulations are summarized by the Bright Line Rules:

- Broadband providers may not block access to legal content, applications, and services.
- Broadband providers may not impair or degrade lawful Internet traffic on the basis of content, applications, or services.
- Broadband providers may not favor some lawful Internet traffic over other lawful traffic in exchange for consideration of any kind.

Following the adoption of the Digital Single Market (DSM) strategy by the European Union (EU) in 2015, the European Parliament, Council, and Commission reached agreements on the rules of net neutrality that apply from April 30, 2016. Although the rules state that every European must have access to the Open Internet and that all content and service providers must be able to provide their services, there are a number of exceptions: if a judge or the police have ordered blocking of specific illegal content or to preserve the security of the network by combating viruses, malware, or distributed denial-of-service (DDoS) events. Unlike the U.S. legislation, privileged services can be provided if there is sufficient additional network capacity to provide them, and they must not be to the detriment of the availability or quality of access services for end-users. However, these privileged services cannot be provided for additional compensation to the ISP.

Graem Corfield

See also: E-commerce; Internet; Internet Service Provider (ISP)

Further Reading

Federal Communications Commission. *Report and Order on Remand, Declaratory Ruling, and Order. FCC 15-24.* GN Docket No. 14-28. Washington, D.C. Released March 12, 2015.

Libicki, Martin. *Cyberspace in Peace and War.* Annapolis, MD: U.S. Naval Institute Press, 2016.

NEUROMANCER

Neuromancer is a 1984 novel by William Gibson that is credited with popularizing the term *cyber space* and is widely considered a seminal work in the literary cyberpunk genre. The book was the first to garner the triple crown of science fiction by earning the Nebula, Hugo, and Philip K. Dick Awards. Set in a dystopian future, the main characters exist in a reality where boundaries between computers, machines, and humanity are supple and flexible. Computers are networked, consciousness and experience are easily shared, and reality can be completely augmented or constructed. The vast network of machines and "jacked-in" people described as cyber space in the novel in turn became the default popular description for the World Wide Web a few years after publication.

Elements of the novel are influenced by and, in turn, have influenced perceptions of cyber, computers, and technology in many parts of popular culture and media since the 1980s. Among the most prominent examples, a line from the 1981 John Carpenter movie *Escape from New York* purportedly stimulated Gibson's writing of the book. The movies *Blade Runner* and *Tron* (1982), in some respects, resemble aspects of the book. The movie *The Matrix* (1999) draws on elements of the work in its depictions of the future of both computers and humanity. Gibson also wrote the screenplay for the film *Johnny Mnemonic* (1995), which was adapted from one of his other short stories and has characters from *Neuromancer* in it.

John G. Terino

See also: Matrix, The

Further Reading

Edwards, Paul N. *The Closed World: Computers and the Politics of Discourse in Cold War America.* Cambridge, MA: The MIT Press, 1996.
Gibson, William. *Neuromancer*. New York: Ace Books, 2000.

NIMDA WORM

Nimda is a self-propagating worm that infects computer files though mass e-mailings. The computer worm was first discovered on September 18, 2001, and affects both Microsoft Windows computers and servers. The name *Nimda* derives from "admin" spelled backward. Nimda was listed at the top of the reported attacks on the Internet within 22 minutes of Nimda hitting the Internet. Computers can be infected one of two ways, either by opening an infected attachment or browsing on an infected server. The worm's primary targets are Internet servers, but it can also infect personal computers.

According to F-Secure Labs, Nimda's life cycle can be broken into four parts: infecting files, mass e-mailing, Web worm, and local area network (LAN) propagation. File infection consists of Nimda locating the .exe file from a local user's system and infecting the host by assimilating that file. The worm locates e-mail addresses in the user's e-mail client and searches for additional address lists on the computer. Nimda then sends an infected file called "README.exe" to each e-mail address collected. Web worm allows Nimda to scan the Internet for servers and then attempts to infect these servers via known security holes. The infected file server will then modify the site's Web pages for future infection by Web surfers browsing the site. LAN propagation is when the worm to searches for file shares within the computer system. Once the file shares are located, Nimda will then drop a hidden file within the directories containing DOC and EML files. The PC then becomes infected once the user's programs open and execute these types of files.

Steven A. Quillman

See also: Code Red Worm; Malware; Worm

Further Reading

Libicki, Martin. *Cyberspace in Peace and War.* Annapolis, MD: U.S. Naval Institute Press, 2016.
Singer, P. W., and Allan Friedman. *Cybersecurity and Cyber War: What Everyone Should Know.* New York: Oxford University Press, 2014.

NIPRNET

NIPRNet (Non-classified Internet Protocol Router Network) is the primary computer network of the U.S. Department of Defense (DoD). It is used by millions of DoD employees, particularly those engaged in telework, as well as partner agencies, for the bulk of Internet connections and usage. It evolved from MILNET, an all-encompassing computer network originally built on the same architecture as ARPANET. Use of NIPRNet is limited to unclassified materials, as it is considered a nonsecure Internet Protocol (IP) data service. In addition to providing communications through e-mail and file transfers, NIPRNet also serves as the primary means for DoD personnel to access the public Internet. This access is routed through a centralized access system, which improves the defense of the network but slows down its performance as a result.

One primary function of NIPRNet is to provide common IP services to the entire DoD community. This guarantees that all DoD computer systems will be able to communicate in a seamless fashion and is largely the result of earlier communication breakdowns between the various services, each of which created its own radio and telephone networks. Data rates on NIPRNet vary widely, as it can be utilized in field situations via satellite connections or through direct connections to a NIPRNet router.

The NIPRNet Federated Gateway system creates a DoD-wide common approach to protecting against malware, dangerous protocols, and loss of connections to the larger Internet. This makes NIPRNet capable of quick reactions to new cyber threats. NIPRNet has its own Domain Name System (DNS), and hence does not rely upon outside agencies to maintain its contacts.

Jeffrey R. Cares

See also: ARPANET; Cyber Defense; Department of Defense (DoD); Domain Name System (DNS); JWICS Network; SIPRNet

Further Reading

Brenner, Joel. *America the Vulnerable: Inside the New Threat Matrix of Digital Espionage, Crime, and Warfare.* New York: Penguin Press, 2011.

NORTH ATLANTIC TREATY ORGANIZATION (NATO)

The North Atlantic Treaty Organization (NATO) is the world's most successful political-military alliance. It consists of 28 member countries—26 from Europe plus Canada and the United States. The political headquarters is in Brussels, Belgium. Allied Command Operations (ACO, also known as the Supreme Headquarters for Allied Powers Europe, or SHAPE) commands all NATO operations and is located in Mons, Belgium. Allied Command Transformation (ACT) provides for education, research and development, and doctrine and is located in Norfolk, Virginia, in the United States.

These two headquarters have subordinate organizations all around the globe, from the United States to Afghanistan. The main subordinates are the two Allied Joint Force Commands in Brunssum, Netherlands, and Naples, Italy; Allied Maritime Command in Northwood, United Kingdom; Allied Air Command in Ramstein, Germany; and Allied Land Command in Izmir, Turkey. They provide command and control for daily operations in Afghanistan, the Indian Ocean, the Mediterranean, the Balkans, the Baltic Sea, and the North Atlantic. Because of the global dispersion of NATO operations, their command and control requirements (as well as the need to safeguard them) are substantial. NATO cyber efforts are mainly oriented on providing for and securing those command and control systems, although their efforts have expanded recently in the face of Russian political warfare (which has a strong cyber element). Other actors also seek to weaken NATO. Anyone seeking to weaken NATO would use a variety of cyber techniques. As NATO Headquarters stated, "The growing sophistication of cyber attacks makes the protection of the Alliance's communications and information systems (CIS) an urgent task."

The U.S. Department of Defense (DoD) identifies four types of cyber actions: cyber-space defense; cyber-space intelligence, surveillance, and reconnaissance (ISR); cyber-space operational preparation of the environment (OPE); and cyber-space attack. Any actor facing NATO will perform at least two of them on a daily basis: cyber-space ISR and cyber-space OPE. In the case of emergency or conflict, NATO will face cyber-space attack. NATO has to constantly defend against both ISR and OPE while simultaneously preparing to defend their networks.

NATO has been focusing on cyber activities since the Prague Summit of 2002. In the wake of the 2007 Russian attacks on Estonia, the North Atlantic Council (NAC) activated the Cooperative Cyber Defence Centre of Excellence (CCDCOE). Interest continued to intensify in 2012 when Allied leaders reaffirmed their commitment to improve the Alliance's cyber defenses by bringing all of NATO's networks under centralized protection and upgraded the NATO Computer Incident Response Capability (NCIRC) under the NATO Communications and Information

Agency (NCIA). In 2014, the Allies created the Cyber Defence Committee, the NCIRC achieved full operational capability, the Allies approved a new action plan at the Wales Summit, and they also created the NATO Industry Cyber Partnership. In 2016, NATO signed the Technical Arrangement on Cyber Defense with the European Union. These evolutions will continue into the future as Russia and others continue to challenge NATO.

G. Alexander Crowther

See also: Estonian Cyber Attack (2007); NATO Cooperative Cyber Defence Centre of Excellence (CCDCOE); Riga Summit (2006); *Tallinn Manual*

Further Reading

Duffield, John S. *Power Rules: The Evolution of NATO's Conventional Force Posture.* Stanford, CA: Stanford University Press, 1995.

Schmitt, Michael N. *Tallinn Manual on the International Law Applicable to Cyber Warfare.* New York: Cambridge University Press, 2013.

NORTH KOREA CYBER CAPABILITIES

Several recent major cyber attacks have been attributed to the Democratic People's Republic of Korea (DPRK), commonly known as North Korea. These attacks included attacks on South Korean television stations and a bank in March 2013 as well as on Sony Pictures Entertainment in November 2014. Since North Korea is a totalitarian state that spends a lot of energy isolating itself from the rest of the world, information on such secretive activities as those related to cyber warfare are especially hard to obtain. Given this, the little open-source information that is known about the DPRK's cyber capabilities has to be regarded as at least partially speculative, though the following is what most experts agree on.

In general, North Korea is not a high-tech, advanced economy. However, its cyber capabilities are very good. They are even better than those of the Republic of Korea (commonly known as South Korea), which is known for its cutting-edge technology. The fact that the DPRK is, for the most part, a conventional nation centered around its military makes its advanced cyber capabilities particularly dangerous. While the DPRK could potentially cause great damage to a technologically advanced economy in cyber warfare, its enemies could not cause equal damage in retaliation because the DPRK does not have an extensive technological infrastructure for them to target. For example, only a few more than 1,000 Internet addresses exist in the DPRK.

The DPRK's agencies tasked with cyber-warfare operations are mainly located in its military's General Bureau of Reconnaissance (GBR) and the General Staff Department (GSD). Different agencies are concerned with various aspects of cyber warfare. Within the GBR, the Korean People's Army (KPA) Joint Chiefs Cyber Warfare Unit is the main cyber-warfare agency. This agency has existed since 1998, but it became more important to the DPRK in the late 2000s. Bureau 121 has also been identified as the one that caused the high-profile cyber attacks mentioned above, which received a great deal of attention in the media. In this cyber unit alone, more than 3,000 experts are employed.

There are several other relevant units within the GBR: Office 91 directs principal hacking tasks. Office 3132 is tasked with electronic cyber warfare. Bureau 110 (Technology Reconnaissance Team) conducts cyber attacks against strategic targets. Finally, the Document Investigation room conducts cyber attacks on civilian organizations.

The main organization responsible for general cyber capabilities is the GSD, which is also responsible for every other aspect of the DPRK's army. The GSD is believed to play merely a supporting role in cyber infrastructure and projected wartime cyber operations, while the GBR and its Bureau 121 are focused on cyberwarfare operations, especially during peacetime. Within GSD's Command Automation Bureau, there are three units—Units 31, 32, and 56—that are responsible for software development and enhancing the networking within the KPA. Unit 31 is responsible for hacking software, Unit 32 is responsible for military software, and Unit 56 is responsible for developing communication and command software.

Within the GSD's Operations Bureau, the Enemy Secret Department Cyber Psychological Warfare Unit (Unit 204) has a more active operating role—compared to the more passive one of the above-mentioned three units. It is responsible for the psychological aspects of cyber warfare (cyber propaganda) and the acquisition of cyber intelligence. However, Bureau 121 and the other units in the GBR remain the key peacetime units that conduct cyber warfare in the DPRK.

Because the DPRK is a totalitarian state, it recruits its cyber experts in an unusual way compared to many other countries. Talented people are identified at a very young age, and an education with a focus on information technology is planned for them. This includes a domestic university education as well as being sent for further study abroad. Within this system, an estimated 100 new cyber experts are added each year to the existing cyber-warfare units.

Strategically, North Korea's cyber strategy fits seamlessly into its general military strategy. Its main goal is to emphasize its asymmetric capabilities. Because the DPRK does not provide much of a target for cyber warfare, enhancing its cyber capabilities is a cost-effective way for the country to reinforce its military strategy in both peacetime and wartime. There are also two additional explanations for the increased importance of developing cyber capabilities in the DPRK. First, it is difficult to identify the origin of a cyber attack, which may help to protect the DPRK from retaliation by its enemies. Second, the KPA appears to believe that its enemies are unlikely to retaliate in response to a cyber attack with a conventional use of force.

Lukas K. Danner

See also: Cyber Attack; Cyber Espionage; Sony Hack

Further Reading

Haggard, Stephan, and Jon R. Lindsay. "North Korea and the Sony Hack: Exporting Instability through Cyberspace." *AsiaPacific Issues* 117, May 2015: 1–8.

Hewlett-Packard Security Research. "Profiling an Enigma: The Mystery of North Korea's Cyber Threat Landscape." *HP Security Briefing* 16, August 2014: 1–75.

Jun, Jenny, Scott LaFoy, and Ethan Sohn. *North Korea's Cyber Operations: Strategy and Responses*. Lanham, MD: Rowman & Littlefield, 2016.

Siers, Rhea. "North Korea: The Cyber Wild Card." *Journal of Law & Cyber Warfare* 4, Winter 2014: 1–12.

OBAMA, BARACK

On January 20, 2009, Barack Obama became the 44th president of the United States. Immediately after taking office, he met with Defense Secretary Robert M. Gates and the Joint Chiefs of Staff concerning cyber security. This led to the Cyberspace Policy Review released on May 30, also known as "60 Day Cybersecurity Review." It called for a comprehensive "clean slate" to assess U.S. policies and structures for strategies, policy, and standards for the future. Directed toward the U.S. State Department, Commerce Department, Department of Homeland Security (DHS), and Department of Defense (DoD), the review encompassed a full range of threat reduction, deterrence, vulnerability reduction, international engagement, response, resiliency, and recovery policies on computer network operation security on global communications information and infrastructures. These cyber experts also received information from industrial, academic, private, and civil liberties communities.

By March 2010, the administration had declassified limited material from the Comprehensive National Cybersecurity Initiative (CNCI). They established a number of mutually reinforcing goals for a front-line defense against network intrusion and for defense against threats through counterintelligence. They called for education, coordination, and research to strengthen future cyber security. By January 6, 2011, the National Security Agency (NSA) began building the Community Comprehensive National Cybersecurity Initiative Data Center (Utah Data Center) at Camp Williams, Utah.

Throughout his presidency, Obama issued cyber-security policy initiatives. On March 30, 2011, he signed Presidential Policy Directive 8 (PPD-8), "Structural Reforms to Improve the Security of Classified Networks and Responsible Sharing and Safeguarding of Classified Information." On February 12, 2013, the White House issued Presidential Policy Directive 21 (PPD-21) and Executive Order 13636, "Improving Critical Infrastructure Security, Resilience, and Cybersecurity." Finally, a "Cybersecurity National Action Plan," dated February 9, 2016, requested $19 billion for cyber security in 2017, a more than 35 percent increase from 2016.

Raymond D. Limbach

See also: Cyber Security; Department of Homeland Security (DHS); National Security Agency (NSA); United States Cyber Capabilities; U.S. Cyber Command (USCYBERCOM)

Further Reading

Clarke, Richard A., and Robert K. Knake. *Cyber War: The Next Threat to National Security and What to Do about It.* New York: HarperCollins, 2010.

Libicki, Martin. *Cyberspace in Peace and War.* Annapolis, MD: U.S. Naval Institute Press, 2016.

Springer, Paul J. *Cyber Warfare: A Reference Handbook.* Santa Barbara, CA: ABC-CLIO, 2015.

OFFICE OF PERSONNEL MANAGEMENT DATA BREACH

In April and May 2015, the Office of Personnel Management (OPM) detected a large breach of personal information from background investigation records that affected 22.1 million current, former, and prospective U.S. federal government employees due to a lack of security measures on numerous older information systems.

The Office of Personnel Management is responsible for all human resources actions for employees of the U.S. federal government. As such, the OPM maintains records on all current, former, and prospective federal government employees. This makes the OPM a valuable target for hackers interested in large quantities of personal information on federal employees. The OPM was created in 1978 as a result of the recommendations of the Civil Service Commission, and it has been managing the federal workforce ever since. This has led to the coexistence of a large number of legacy information databases.

In February 2014, the director of OPM, Katherine Archuleta, issued a *Strategic Information Technology Plan* that established a strategy for streamlining OPM's information technology to make the hiring, retention, and retirement of federal government employees more efficient and to increase information security for the millions of records entrusted to OPM's care. During the implementation of the strategy, OPM discovered a large data breach of background and security investigation records in April 2014. Not 30 days later, OPM discovered an additional data breach of investigation records, prompting Director Archuleta to resign under pressure.

On April 15, 2015, OPM discovered malicious software on a server with access to the security clearance database. The malware was a never-before-seen variant of the programs PlugX and Sakula. PlugX and Sakula are remote administration tools (RATs) used by hackers to gain control over computer systems; they allow them to either disable the systems or steal information. OPM investigators then discovered data traffic between the secure OPM servers and Web sites deliberately designed to appear legitimate, or faux infrastructure. Hackers use a faux infrastructure in conjunction with a RAT to gain access and control over secure systems and export secure data. One of the faux Web sites was opmsecurity.org. It was registered in April 2014, went active in December 2014, and then went inactive on June 3, 2015, the day before OPM officially announced the data breach. The other was opm-learning.org, which was registered to Tony Stark in July 2014. It went active using an Internet Protocol (IP) address of a California company with excellent network access to Asian networks and China. The detection of malware RATs and faux infrastructure are all signs of deliberate hacking.

Information from the OPM investigation in April–May 2015 began to explain what had until that time seemed to be unrelated security issues. In June 2014, OPM contractor United States Investigation Services disclosed a breach of 25,000 federal employees' records. This breach was most likely connected to a wider effort by the OPM hackers to gain access to OPM information systems. In September 2014, hackers compromised 390,000 Department of Homeland Security employees' records from another OPM contractor for background investigations, KeyPoint Government Solutions. In December 2014, a second data breach occurred at Key-Point Government Solutions that compromised another 48,000 federal employees' records. It is believed that during this data breach the hackers stole security credentials to access the OPM systems directly. The hackers used these credentials to access the OPM servers and perpetrate the largest data breach in U.S. history.

Information technology security experts continue to consider the OPM hack an act of state-sponsored espionage, even though the Obama administration chose not to officially accuse the Chinese government of direct involvement. Experts cite information from the investigation that points to the use of the two RATs, PlugX and Sakula, built by Chinese hackers. The use of this malware is similar to a series of other high-profile data breaches that have been linked to China, including the Wellpoint/Anthem, Premera, Empire, and CareFirst hacks. All of these companies provided health care to federal employees. Additionally, all of these hacks used faux infrastructure to hide the data breaches and to facilitate the movement of data out of the companies' secure databases.

The *Washington Post* reported in December 2015 that China was investigating the OPM hack as a criminal case and had arrested several suspects linked to the hack. The Chinese government has continued to deny involvement in the hack, stating instead that it was the work of a cyber-criminal gang for purposes of commercial espionage. However, the investigation and the arrests have as yet been unconfirmed by sources outside the *Washington Post*.

Most jobs in the federal government require some form of security clearance or background investigation. It is highly likely that anyone who went through a background investigation from 2000 through 2014 is affected by the breach. Specifically, people who filled out the Standard Forms 85, 85P, or 86 were vulnerable as these are the forms used for new investigations and periodic reviews. Although in the past these forms and the supporting documentation were collected in hard copy, OPM has used the Electronic Questionnaires for Investigations Processing (e-QIP) since 2003. The e-QIP questionnaire requires applicants to include information about personal finances, family members, previous addresses, criminal records, mental health information, Social Security numbers, and digital copies of fingerprints. Stealing these questionnaires provides comprehensive records on federal employees and their families.

Investigators concluded that in the December 2014 breach, 21.5 million employee records were compromised, which included 5.6 million sets of fingerprints. The second hack of background investigation records, discovered in May

2015, affected 4.2 million current and former employees. Because many of these people were affected by both breaches, it is estimated that 22.1 million total Americans had their government records compromised, which included 19.7 million people who applied for clearances as well as 1.8 million nonapplicants, such as spouses and cohabitants. OPM sent notifications to all those affected and offered identity theft monitoring and restoration services through the end of 2018.

Michael A. Bonura

See also: Cyber Crime; Cyber Espionage; Identity Theft; Malware; People's Republic of China Cyber Capabilities; Remote Administration Tool (RAT); Trojan Horse

Further Reading

Libicki, Martin. *Cyberspace in Peace and War.* Annapolis, MD: U.S. Naval Institute Press, 2016.

Schmidt, Michael S., David E. Sanger, and Nicole Perlroth. "Chinese Hackers Pursue Key Data on U.S. Workers." *New York Times,* July 9, 2014.

Zetter, Kim, and Andy Greenberg. "Why the OPM Breach Is Such a Security and Privacy Debacle." *Wired,* June 11, 2015.

OPERATION ABABIL

Operation Ababil refers to a series of cyber attacks launched against American financial institutions in 2012. It was named after a Pakistani operation that failed in 1984. The attackers "justified" their attacks on Pastebin, criticizing Israel and the United States in response to a video they believed was an attack against the Prophet Muhammad and Islam called "Innocence of Muslims." The attackers, Izz ad-Din al-Qassam Cyber Fighters, were named after a Muslim preacher of the 1920s and 1930s who resisted French, British, and Jewish nationalists. They claimed to be volunteers from different parts of the Middle East, but they appear to be mainly based in Palestine and Iran. The distributed denial-of-service (DDoS) attacks began on September 18, 2012, and ended on October 23, 2012. Targets included the New York Stock Exchange and a number of banks, resulting in limited disruption of their Web sites.

Their first target was the Bank of America and the New York Stock Exchange on September 18, 2012. The next day, they targeted JPMorgan Chase banks. A week later, the targets included Wells Fargo (September 25); U.S. Bank (September 26); and PNC Bank (September 27). Attacks resumed in October: Capital One Financial Corporation on the 9th; Sun Trust Banks on the 10th; Regions Financial Corporation on the 11th; the Capital One Financial Corporation on the 16th; BB&T Corporation on the 17th; and HSBC Bank USA on the 18th. The attacks ended on October 23, 2012, coinciding with the Eid al-Adha holiday.

The attacks were at first believed to have come from the Iranian government, in response to Western economic sanctions. Senator Joseph Lieberman made this claim on C-Span, and later the *Washington Post* and *Reuters* published it on September 21, 2012. The size of the attacks, at 65 gigabits per second, was consistent with a state-sponsored action. Some found the attacks to be amateurish, as they depended on outmoded techniques. Others claimed that they had help from the hacker group Anonymous.

Phase 2 of Operation Ababil began on December 10, 2012, once again targeting banks and financial institutions. The Qassam Cyber Fighters denied the involvement of any nation, but the sophistication of the attacks increased focus on Iran. This phase ended on January 29, 2013, when YouTube removed the main copy of the offending video. But the attackers claimed other copies were still available on the site. A warning on February 12, 2013, followed by a "serious warning" and then an "ultimatum" promised that attacks would resume if the videos were not removed. On March 15, 2013, they began Phase 3, again disrupting several previously targeted financial institutions.

In response, the banking industry has developed "BankInfoSecurity" and "Packet Storm," which show fast and efficient sources for early warning of future attacks. Operation Ababil has an uncertain conclusion, for there is little real detail on the Qassam Cyber Fighters. Some observers considered it too convenient for the attackers to call for the U.S. government and the financial community to remove a video that they have no control over and believe the "cause" being offered was merely a red herring, used by Russian hacker syndicates to skim money from major banks while using the DDoS attacks as a distraction.

Raymond D. Limbach

See also: Anonymous; Cyber Crime; Distributed Denial-of-Service (DDoS) Attack; Hacker; Iran Cyber Capabilities

Further Reading

Ablon, Lillian, and Martin Libicki. "Hackers' Bazaar: The Markets for Cybercrime Tools and Stolen Data." *Defense Counsel Journal* 82(2), April 2015: 143–152.

Bossler, Adam M., and Thomas J. Holt. *Cybercrime in Progress: Theory and Prevention of Technology-enabled Offenses.* Basingstoke: Routledge, 2016.

Libicki, Martin. *Cyberspace in Peace and War.* Annapolis, MD: US Naval Institute Press, 2016.

OPERATION AURORA

An extended intrusion by Chinese hackers occurred during the second half of 2009. Operation Aurora was first publicly disclosed by Google on January 12, 2010. Its name derives from a reference in its code that was identified by McAfee security company executive Dmitri Alperovitch. The Operation Aurora hack is unrelated to the similarly named Aurora Project, which was a U.S. action to simulate remote degradation of supervisory control and data acquisition equipment used in electrical generation.

Operation Aurora relied on spear phishing against certain Google employees. Those who unsuspectingly followed a link in a received e-mail were directed to a Web site that contained malicious JavaScript code. The specific exploit, known as Trojan.Hydraq, specifically targeted users navigating the Internet through the popular Microsoft Internet Explorer Web browser. Those victims using Internet Explorer became subject to an unidentified zero-day exploit that established a remote administration tool (RAT), allowing hackers to collect information about the user's activities and files. Having gained access to the accounts of victims, hackers proceeded to send e-mail messages to new potential victims, drawing on contacts lists to spread further.

Even more seriously, Aurora hackers managed to access Google source code. This development enabled intruders to not only illicitly access information from hacked individuals' machines but also provided the opportunity to adjust corporate source code in various ways; this included the ability to create fresh vulnerabilities to espionage among customers and partners of the victim's system who trusted the source code of the victim. The potentially compromised source code involved the Gaia system that was built to enable users to sign into multiple Google services through the entry of a single password. Organized hacking efforts frequently involve a consolidation phase in which garnered information and successful methods are compiled for use in subsequent actions. The ability to access, and potentially manipulate, source code represents an extremely valuable tool in this respect.

Perhaps partly because the hack was able to insinuate access so widely, its range of targets was so diverse that the motivations and objectives of the action were difficult to definitively identify. Activists working on civil rights issues in the People's Republic of China (PRC) appeared to be a prime target. Remote access to victims' computers compromised both their stored files and their communications via Gmail accounts. PRC has demonstrated interest in maintaining domestic political stability, and information dominance is a useful element in these efforts.

However, many corporate entities in various business sectors were also affected, and this suggests that Operation Aurora's objectives may have been more complex than simply internal control. This included U.S. information technology companies such as Yahoo, Symantec Corporation, and Adobe; the U.S. aerospace company Northrop Grumman; and Dow Chemical. Three dozen U.S. companies were affected by the hack, suggesting that the effort may not have been solely intended for the purpose of countering individuals criticizing PRC human rights policies. It has been suggested that the total number of victimized companies worldwide ranges in the thousands.

The likelihood of an industrial and financial espionage component to the effort aligns closely with patterns in Chinese cyber activity and capabilities. It has furthermore been suggested that Aurora may have been linked to another hacking effort, Operation Shady RAT, which dates to 2006. As such, Aurora fits the description of an advanced persistent threat (APT).

Evidence points to PRC culpability in the Aurora hack. Researchers from the security company VeriSign traced the hack to Internet Protocol (IP) addresses that had been compromised and used in an earlier distributed denial-of-service (DDoS) action against South Korea and the United States in the summer of 2009, and they noted patterns in the operations that further suggested that the entity responsible for the 2009 DDoS effort had also undertaken Operation Aurora.

Experts believe that the hacks emanated from some of PRC's premier universities in the computer science field. Students at Jiaotong University in Shanghai have defeated rivals from over 100 international institutions in such competitions as the 1997 Battle of the Brains competition sponsored by IBM. The potential involvement of another institution in eastern China, Lanxiang Vocational School, has also been debated. Officials at the school have denied any connection to the hack and have argued that personnel at Lanxiang lacked the sophistication to perpetrate it. However, the school is closely linked to the People's Liberation Army (PLA). Some analysts also believe that Unit 61398, the most notorious of the hacking entities in the PLA, may be connected to Operation Aurora. Unit 61398, like Jiaotong University, is in Shanghai. Evidence does suggest the unit's culpability in a number of other efforts geared toward gaining strategically and sometimes economically valuable information through espionage directed against foreign entities.

Operation Aurora sparked responses by a number of parties. Google, which had previously agreed to comply with PRC strictures in the formation of its PRC engine, Google.cn, announced the retraction of its earlier policy and stated that it would instead operate its search engine without censorship or would end operations in China. Signs of spontaneous support for Google within PRC's borders emerged and were quickly stifled by the regime. One of the PRC politburo members, Li Changchun, has been linked not only with the Operation Aurora hacks but is also affiliated with the Chinese company Baidu, whose ventures include a national Internet search engine.

Nicholas Michael Sambaluk

See also: Advanced Persistent Threat (APT); Alperovitch, Dmitri; Baidu; Cyber Crime; Cyber Espionage; Google; Malware; Microsoft Corporation; Operation Shady RAT; People's Liberation Army Unit 61398; People's Republic of China Cyber Capabilities; Spear Phishing

Further Reading

Brenner, Joel. *America the Vulnerable: Inside the New Threat Matrix of Digital Espionage, Crime, and Warfare.* New York City: Penguin Press, 2011.

Rid, Thomas. *Cyber War Will Not Take Place.* Oxford: Oxford University, 2013.

Rosenzweig, Paul. *Cyber Warfare: How Conflicts in Cyberspace Are Challenging America and Changing the World.* Santa Barbara, CA: Praeger, 2013.

Segal, Adam. "From TITAN RAIN to BYZANTINE HADES: Chinese Cyber Espionage." In *A Fierce Domain: Conflict in Cyberspace, 1986 to 2012.* Edited by Jason Healey. Vienna, VA: Cyber Conflict Studies Association, 2013.

Shakarian, Paulo, Jana Shakarian, and Andrew Ruef. *Introduction to Cyber-warfare: A Multidisciplinary Approach.* Waltham, MA: Syngress, 2013.

Springer, Paul J. *Cyber Warfare: A Reference Handbook.* Santa Barbara, CA: ABC-CLIO, 2015.

OPERATION BABYLON

Operation Babylon, also known as Operation Opera, saw the State of Israel launch a surprise airstrike in June 1981 against an Iraqi nuclear reactor facility being constructed on the orders of Saddam Hussein. The Iraqi nuclear facility was located some 10 miles south of Baghdad. Iraq purchased a nuclear reactor from France in 1976, which the French sold to Iraq on the understanding that it would be used for a peaceful nuclear energy program. Israel opposed the sale of the reactor from the beginning and feared that it would be used to develop a nuclear weapons program. Israel's successful attack followed Operation Scorch Sword, an unsuccessful attempt by the Islamic Republic of Iran to destroy the same facility in 1980. Hussein commissioned French technicians to repair the facility during the first year of the Iran-Iraq War. While the Israelis did not favor the Iranians, they feared that allowing Hussein to acquire nuclear weapons would lead to nuclear proliferation throughout the Arab world, endangering the State of Israel. The attack was planned and ordered by Israeli prime minister Menachem Begin. As part of the so-called Begin Doctrine, "every future government in Israel" was prepared to take action to prevent nuclear proliferation in the Middle East. Controversial at the time and still today, Operation Babylon set an important precedent for Israeli foreign policy that remains especially relevant as Iran considers its own nuclear program.

Operation Babylon was executed on June 7, 1981, when a group of Israeli Air Force F-16A fighter jets escorted by F-15As hit the facility with bombs, inflicting severe damage on the reactor. Israeli Air Force commander David Ivry led the operation. Begin announced that Hussein was one month away from possessing the ability to build a nuclear weapon and asserted that the operation was an act of self-defense. The operation resulted in the deaths of 10 Iraqi soldiers and a French civilian.

The United Nations responded negatively to the Israeli operation, issuing a resolution against Israel for an act of aggression. Worldwide criticism was harsh, including from the United States and the administration of Ronald Reagan. Nonetheless, Operation Babylon has become a textbook example of a successful preventive strike. Iraq lost its nuclear reactor, and Israel suffered no significant consequences.

Jordan R. Hayworth

See also: Israel Cyber Capabilities; Operation Orchard

Further Reading

Feldman, Shai. *Nuclear Weapons and Arms Control in the Middle East.* Cambridge, MA: MIT Press, 1997.

Scott, Shirley V., and Anthony Billingsley. *International Law and the Use of Force: A Documentary and Reference Guide.* New York: Praeger, 2009.

Shue, Henry, and David Rhodin. *Preemption: Military Action and Moral Justification.* New York: Oxford University Press, 2010.

OPERATION BUCKSHOT YANKEE

Operation Buckshot Yankee was the U.S. Department of Defense's (DoD) reaction to the infiltration of computer malware throughout DoD classified and unclassified computer systems in late 2008. The incident forced the U.S. government to reconsider its approach to cyber warfare, leading to the creation of U.S. Cyber Command (USCYBERCOM) in 2009.

The incident probably began when a U.S. serviceman or contractor in Afghanistan found a flash drive and inserted it into a networked computer sometime in early 2008. The malware rapidly replicated itself and spread to a North Atlantic Treaty Organization (NATO) ally's network by June and then was picked up throughout various DoD networks. It was finally noticed by National Security Agency (NSA) Advanced Network Operations (ANO) team analysts in October after the malware penetrated the DoD and State Department's Secret Internet Protocol Router Network (SIPRNet) and began sending a beacon to its creator.

That malware, called Agent.btz, needed to communicate with its creator to receive instructions on what documents it needed to look for and on how to transmit them back home. To do that, Agent.btz sent a signal out on the World Wide Web, and it was that signal that NSA analysts discovered. After an intense investigation to determine the extent of the damage, the ANO team needed to come up with a way to either neutralize or remove the virus without damaging sensitive files or key programs. This was the genesis of Operation Buckshot Yankee.

The ANO team finally devised a way to counteract Agent.btz. The counterprogram searched for the beacon signal of Agent.btz and mimicked its creator, effectively putting the malware to sleep. Then the painstaking process of removing the Agent.btz malware from U.S. government computers began. Cooperating with DoD was another NSA group called the Tailored Access Operations (TAO) unit that went outside of the government on the World Wide Web to search for Agent.btz variants to help government defenders anticipate new threats and engage and defeat them before they could degrade the integrity of the network. This collaboration, and the realization for its need, was one of the key takeaways by the government from Operation Buckshot Yankee.

William J. Lynn III, the deputy secretary of defense, wrote a controversial article in the journal *Foreign Affairs* in 2010 that discussed the Agent.btz incident, the Pentagon's response to it, and the creation of U.S. Cyber Command (USCYBERCOM). Lynn discussed how the Agent.btz breach was the largest experienced by DoD up to that point. It forced the U.S. government to recognize the nature and scope of the threat, and Operation Buckshot Yankee provided a blueprint for dealing with those threats.

Terry L. Beckenbaugh

See also: Cyber Espionage; Cyber Security; National Security Agency (NSA); North Atlantic Treaty Organization (NATO)

Further Reading

Lynn, William J., III. "Defending a New Domain: The Pentagon's Cyberstrategy." *Foreign Affairs* 89(5), September/October 2010: 97–108.

Reveron, Derek S. *Cyberspace and National Security: Threats, Opportunities, and Power in a Virtual World*. Washington, D.C.: Georgetown University Press, 2012.

OPERATION CARTEL

Operation Cartel refers to a cyber quasi war between Anonymous and Los Zetas, a major drug cartel based in Northern Mexico. It exists within the context of a broader social media and Internet-based conflict that had been taking place between the Mexican cartels and various cyber vigilantes. This conflict roughly began when *Borderland Beat* (in English) and *Blog del Narco* (in Spanish) were founded in April 2009 and March 2010, respectively.

These informative blogs and the utilization of other forms of social media—such as Twitter messaging—emerged as a reaction to both the ongoing Mexican cartel's atrocities that were being committed and the fact that the traditional radio and television news media in many parts of that country had been both suppressed and co-opted by the cartels. While at first glance progressive, such cyber vigilantism actually trailed the cartel's use of such social media. These criminal groups, as early as 2005–2006, had already begun using YouTube and other Web media to transmit photos and videos of their killings, gunmen, group symbols, and messages.

Anonymous—the shadowy hacker collective—became directly involved in this conflict as early as August 2011 by means of Operation Paperstorm, which was a leaflet campaign denouncing Veracruz authorities for protecting Los Zetas while at the same time prosecuting Twitter users for posting cartel kidnapping reports. Later, on October 6, 2011, they stated that one of their members had been kidnapped by the Los Zetas cartel during a street protest in the Mexican port city of Veracruz. One of their members, wearing a Guy Fawkes mask, as seen in the 2006 movie *V for Vendetta*, delivered their online video message to Los Zetas in Old World–accented Spanish mixed with Mexican slang. In the message, they demanded that the Zetas release their member by November 5 or the collective would hack into their Web sites and protected accounts and release information pertaining to their members and journalists, politicians, police officers, and taxi cab drivers they had co-opted. As a show of force, Anonymous defaced the Web site of Gustavo Rosario Torres, a former Tabasco state prosecutor, changing it to a Halloween background. Anticrime activists earlier identified Torres as being linked to illicit narcotics-trafficking activity.

By the end of October and going into the first days of November, Anonymous members fell into disarray over whether to go ahead against Los Zetas with Operation Cartel as planned. Some members of the collective called for the operation to be called off, citing the danger to the group's membership. Some individuals and commentators questioned whether an Anonymous member had even been kidnapped and suspected that the collective was dangerously toying with Los Zetas, originally founded by ex-Mexican special forces personnel, for no valid reason. Additionally, the Stratfor group, a private intelligence organization, stated that Los Zetas was now in fact hiring mercenary hackers to track down Anonymous members that could then either be kidnapped or killed. This threat was not unfounded, given the deaths of a number of bloggers in Mexico who had earlier been tortured and killed by the cartels. Ultimately, Operation Cartel was called off by the collective prior to the November 5 deadline, although the IberoAmerica Anonymous site still continued to solicit anonymous tips concerning Los Zetas collaborators.

Robert J. Bunker

See also: Anonymous; Cyber Crime; Dark Web; Hacker

Further Reading

Arthur, Charles. "Anonymous Retreats from Mexico Drug Cartel Confrontation." *The Guardian*, November 2, 2011.

Bunker, Robert J. "The Growing Mexican Cartel and Vigilante War in Cyberspace." *Small Wars Journal*, November 3, 2011. smallwarsjournal.com/printpdf/11731.

Kan, Paul Rexton. "Cyberwar in the Underworld: Anonymous versus Los Zetas in Mexico." *Yale Journal of International Affairs*, February 26, 2013. http://yalejournal.org/article_post/cyberwar-in-the-underworld-anonymous-versus-los-zetas-in-mexico.

OPERATION CAST LEAD

Operation Cast Lead was a 22-day military assault on the Gaza Strip by the Israel Defense Forces (IDF), December 27, 2008 to January 18, 2009, in response to continued missile attacks originating from groups and individuals in the area. The name of the operation was taken from a poem by Chaim Nachman Bialik, the Hebrew national poet, titled "In Honour of Chanukah," in part because the attack occurred during the Jewish festival of Chanukah. The poem mentions a spinning top of the finest cast lead. The operation commenced at 11:30 a.m. on December 27, 2008, with a surprise aerial attack that lasted a week before ground forces entered the area. Israeli F-16 fighter jets, Apache helicopters, and unmanned drones hit over 100 locations across the Gaza Strip in minutes. Although some Palestinian civilians reported that they had received recorded messages, radio broadcasts, texts, and leaflets to evacuate structures adjacent to Hamas buildings, the initial loss of life and property damage was extensive.

On January 3, 2009, the Israeli army invaded Gaza from the north and east. The number of total causalities varies by source, and there are even bigger discrepancies between the published numbers of combatants killed. No foreign journalists were permitted to enter Gaza, and none were embedded with Israeli troops.

In response to the damage and casualties inflicted, cyber attacks were launched against Israeli Web sites and other related sites by members and supporters of the Arab and Muslim communities. Most of the hackers were believed to be Moroccan, Algerian, Saudi Arabian, Turkish, and Palestinian, based on the information left on hacked Web sites. Thousands of sites were attacked. Most of the attacks were Web site defacements containing images of victims and destruction in Gaza or appeals to Israel and the United States to stop the violence. Internet traffic was also redirected from legitimate sites to ones created by the hackers with similar images and messages and the apparent motivation of drawing the world's attention to the plight of the Palestinians.

Israel and its supporters tried to respond with their own cyber attacks, but they were less successful in winning international support for the incursion into Gaza. They used recruits to flood blogs with pro-Israel opinions and hacked a Hamas television station. Hackers supporting Israel also infiltrated pro-Palestinian Facebook groups and collected information about the group members. Israel also tried to pressure hosting companies to cut off service to hacker Web sites. A group of Israeli hackers also created the botnet Patriot to initiate distributed denial-of-service attacks against anti-Israel Web sites. Although Israel gained one of its major objectives, to reduce the number of rockets entering Israel from the Gaza Strip, it lost the battle for international public opinion. Under intense international pressure, Israel declared a unilateral cease-fire and withdrew its forces from Gaza. Armed Palestinian groups followed with a separate unilateral cease-fire.

Lori Ann Henning

See also: Distributed Denial-of-Service (DDoS) Attack; Hacker; Hacktivist; Israel Cyber Capabilities

Further Reading

Carr, Jeffrey, and Lewis Shepherd. *Inside Cyber Warfare.* Sebastopol, CA: O'Reilly Media, Inc., 2010.

Gavriely-Nuri, Dalia. *The Normalization of War in Israeli Discourse, 1967–2008.* Lanham, MD: Lexington Books, 2013.

Shindler, Colin. *A History of Modern Israel.* 2nd ed. Cambridge: Cambridge University Press, 2013.

OPERATION NIGHT DRAGON

Operation Night Dragon was a targeted and coordinated cyber-espionage campaign against global oil, energy, and petrochemical companies to exfiltrate competitive proprietary operations and project-financing information regarding oil and gas field bids and operations as well as collect data from automated industrial supervisory control and data acquisition (SCADA) systems. The main countries affected by Night Dragon included the United States, Taiwan, Kazakhstan, and Greece. The campaign, classified as an advanced persistent threat (APT), ran from at least 2007 through 2009.

Night Dragon attacks followed a consistent methodology:

1. Structured Query Language injection (SQLi) was used to gain access to an extranet server and then retrieve data from databases by injecting harmful SQL payloads. Targeted spear phishing and social engineering of mid- and senior-level executives was also used to trick individuals into compromising cyber-security procedures enabling access into systems.

2. Hash-dumping tools were uploaded to collect the underlying authentication protocol of user passwords along with password-cracking tools. These programs would harvest credentials in the Active Directory to gain access to sensitive servers and desktops.
3. Once access to servers and desktops was gained, they were scanned to access sensitive documents and material.
4. Remote administration tools (RAT) malware were used to provide cybercriminals with unlimited access to infected terminals, which enabled uninhibited conduct of cyber crime and freedom to create custom Trojans.
5. E-mail archives and sensitive information were exfiltrated out of systems laterally.

Night Dragon is similar to other cyber crimes, such as Operation Aurora, Operation Shady RAT, Elderwood, APT1, and Byzantine Candor, in that they all targeted companies in the oil and gas industries and focused on the large-scale theft of corporate data. The Night Dragon attacks were not sophisticated in nature, as they appeared to implement standard host administration techniques, which is why they were successful in avoiding detection through standard network policies and security software. McAfee did not begin to monitor Night Dragon until late 2009, and it is estimated that the attacks had been ongoing for two years, but likely up to four. Seminal to Night Dragon attacks is the released McAfee report providing an advanced persistent threat (APT) analysis and technical attribution.

No specific attribution for Night Dragon was made, but McAfee was able to provide circumstantial evidence based on observations and findings. One individual in Heze City, Shandong Province, China, was attributed as providing the command and control (C&C) infrastructure to hackers through his company and may have had knowledge of some of those involved in the cyber attacks. The individual's U.S.-based servers hosted the zwShell C&C application that was responsible for controlling machines across victim companies. Other factors also indicate the probability of China-based operations for the Night Dragon attacks.

McAfee was able to determine that a majority of the hackers operated during the hours of 9:00 a.m. to 5:00 p.m., Beijing time. This suggests that those involved in hacking were regular employees who were conducting operations as part of their normal job as opposed to being freelance or unprofessional hackers. Furthermore, it was found that the password to unlock the zwShell C&C Trojan, "zw.china," coupled with exfiltration activities occurring from identified Beijing-based Internet Protocol (IP) addresses to be compelling. Finally, many of the hacking tools that were employed were known to be of Chinese origin and common in Chinese underground hacking forums.

George L. Chapman

See also: Advanced Persistent Threat (APT); Cyber Attack; Cyber Espionage; Operation Aurora; Operation Shady RAT; People's Republic of China Cyber Capabilities; Social Engineering; Spear Phishing; SQL Injection

Further Reading

Brenner, Joel. *America the Vulnerable: Inside the New Threat Matrix of Digital Espionage, Crime, and Warfare.* New York: Penguin, 2011.

Libicki, Martin. *Cyberspace in Peace and War.* Annapolis, MD: U.S. Naval Institute Press, 2016.

Rid, Thomas. *Cyber War Will Not Take Place.* New York: Oxford University Press, 2013.

Singer, P. W., and Allan Friedman. *Cybersecurity and Cyber War: What Everyone Should Know.* New York: Oxford University Press, 2014.

OPERATION ORCHARD

Operation Orchard is the English name for an Israeli preemptive operation against a Syrian nuclear reactor in 2007. The operation adhered to Israel's "Begin Doctrine." Put forth by former Israeli prime minister Menachem Begin in 1981, the doctrine states that Israel will not allow a Middle Eastern nation to pose a threat to its national security from weapons of mass destruction, particularly nuclear ones. The doctrine was announced after Operation Opera, during which Israel preemptively destroyed an Iraqi nuclear facility in Osirak in that same year.

The Israeli government took many steps to ascertain Syria's nuclear weapons developments before the operation. U.S. intelligence had first discovered the Al-Kibar complex, located in the northern area of the Syrian desert in 2004. Passing the intelligence along to Mossad, Israel's intelligence and counterterrorism agency, the agency happened to also learn of a Syrian official's arrival in London. When the official left his laptop unaccompanied in a London hotel room, Mossad operatives entered the hotel room and installed a Trojan horse on the laptop. As a result, Israel obtained access to key intelligence on the complex, including building plans and photographs. This intelligence helped Mossad to begin confirming that the building was indeed a nuclear facility. In fact, Syria's reactor at the Al-Kibar complex was nearly identical to North Korea's Yongbyon Nuclear Scientific Research Center, which has processed nuclear material that could be used in nuclear bombs. Before making the decision to carry out a preemptive attack, Mossad also sent in a team of commandos to test the soil surrounding the complex as well as to gather reconnaissance. Despite being detected, the team returned to Israel safely with its evidence, which was found to contain trace results of nuclear material. In deciding to go forward with a preemptive attack, Israel alerted the United States to its intentions. Accounts differ of what occurred, but the United States seems not to have offered its formal support; but it also did not announce Israeli intentions as a way of precluding the operation.

The actual operation was so secretive that Israeli pilots did not know their intended target until after takeoff. Israeli Air Force (IAF) F-15 and F-16 escort fighters flew north from Israel, over the Mediterranean, and into Turkey accompanied by an electronic intelligence-gathering airplane, probably a modified Gulfstream G550. Upon entering Syrian airspace, they dropped precision bombs and conducted electronic warfare and cyber hacking against a Syrian radar site. This was key to defeating Syria's highly advanced Russian-made integrated air defense system (IADS). It is believed that the Israelis used something similar to the U.S. Suter program, about which little is known, except that it is a network airborne attack system manufactured by BAE Systems. The Israeli version enabled IAF to peer into Syrian communications as well as to provide false information to Syrian radar by temporarily administering the network system.

Eighteen minutes later, the jets arrived safely at their target. The F-15s dropped their bombs on the Al-Kibar complex, completely destroying it with the help of Israeli commandos on the ground, who used lasers to assist in targeting. In the wake of the attack, the Israeli prime minister used the Turkish prime minister to convey to the Syrian prime minister that no further attacks would be launched as long as Syria did not seek to reestablish a similar complex.

Despite Israel's blatant use of military force, the operation did not make many headlines. It should also be noted that Operation Orchard was far more preemptive than Operation Opera, where the Iraqi reactor had been nearing completion. This limited stage of development caused consternation among some U.S. officials, who worried about the ramifications of such a preemptive strike. Another key difference was that Operation Opera resulted in far more international condemnation than the aftereffects of Operation Orchard. Israel, Syria, the United States, and other Arab nations remained almost silent on the operation. Publicly, Syrian president Bashar al-Assad only commented that Israeli jets had targeted an incomplete nonmilitary building. The one nation to speak out loudly against the operation was the one that had provided key materials and personnel: North Korea. It is likely that some of that nation's citizens were killed in the strike, as they were highly involved with the facility. Given this general silence, along with other factors, there are varying reports and interpretations still circulating about this highly secretive operation.

Heather Pace Venable

See also: Cyber Espionage; Cyber War; Israel Cyber Capabilities; Spoofing; Trojan Horse

Further Reading

Federation of American Scientists. "A Sourcebook on the Israeli Strike in Syria, 6 September 2007: Version of 2015-01-09." https://fas.org/man/eprint/syria.pdf.

Follath, Erich, and Holger Stark. "How Israel Destroyed Syria's Al Kibar Nuclear Reactor." *Spiegel Online* 11, 2009. http://www.spiegel.de/international/world/the-story-of-operation-orchard-how-israel-destroyed-syria-s-al-kibar-nuclear-reactor-a-658663.html.

Spector, Leonard S., and Avner Cohen. "Israel's Airstrike on Syria's Reactor: Implications for the Nonproliferation Regime." *Arms Control Today* 38(6), July/August 2008: 15–21.

OPERATION PAYBACK

Operation Payback was an attempt by the activist group Anonymous to retaliate against a variety of actors and agents for shutting down file-sharing Web sites as well as trying to punish various entities that withheld services from WikiLeaks.

Operation Payback took place in the latter part of 2010. It is noteworthy as perhaps the first cyber war between nonstate actors.

The cyber attacks began in September 2010 as a result of the shutdown of the Swedish file-sharing Web site Pirate Bay. This site allowed users to share music and other files, some of which contained copyrighted material. When Pirate Bay was forced to close down, the collective group known as Anonymous claimed that these companies were restricting the freedom of the Internet and that they had decided to attack the institutions that had closed down Pirate Bay.

Anonymous' first attack was on the Motion Picture Association of America (MPAA) Web site on September 16, 2010. The group attacked the MPAA, and soon afterward other Web sites, by using a network stress test program titled, "Low Orbit Ion Cannon," or LOIC. The program was readily available and free to anyone with a computer and Internet access. LOIC increased the volume of Web traffic to a Web site. This is known as a distributed denial-of-service (DDoS) attack. One user would not be enough to stop the Web site from functioning, but a group of users coordinating their attacks on the site could overwhelm it with traffic to the point that the Internet user trying to use the attacked Web site found it nonfunctional. This is what Anonymous did: It encouraged users to download LOIC, and it set times and dates for specific coordinated DDoS attacks on specific Web sites. The effectiveness of the attacks varied with the ability of the targeted sites to resist the attacks. While in the midst of Operation Payback, Anonymous found another cause: WikiLeaks.

Anonymous shifted its targets to businesses and other entities that refused financial and other services to the whistle-blowing Web site WikiLeaks in early December 2010. WikiLeaks obtained secret government and business documents from around the world and posted them on its various Web sites. Several large corporations, including Amazon.com, MasterCard, Visa, and PayPal, refused their services to WikiLeaks. In retaliation, Anonymous targeted these Web sites with DDoS attacks of varying effectiveness.

The leaders of Operation Payback were indicted in federal court for a variety of crimes, and eventually they all took a plea bargain to, in most cases, avoid jail time. All were cited for misdemeanors and fined for the losses the attacked businesses incurred. Some of the entities attacked fought back with DDoS attacks of their own, and this is why at least one author argues that Operation Payback may be the first case of two nonstate actors engaging in cyber warfare.

Terry L. Beckenbaugh

See also: Anonymous; Hacktivist; Low Orbit Ion Cannon (LOIC); WikiLeaks

Further Reading

Coleman, Gabriella. *Hacker, Hoaxer, Whistleblower, Spy: The Many Faces of Anonymous.* London: Verso, 2014.

Olson, Parmy. *We Are Anonymous: Inside the Hacker World of LulzSec, Anonymous and the Global Cyber Insurgency.* New York: Back Bay Books, 2012.

Rosenzweig, Paul. *Cyber Warfare: How Conflicts in Cyberspace Are Challenging America and Changing the World.* Denver: Praeger, 2013.

OPERATION SHADY RAT

Operation Shady RAT was an extended data exfiltration project conducted by Chinese hackers, begun in 2006. Hackers used spear phishing to fool victims into opening electronic documents that were accompanied by malicious code. To sharpen the effectiveness of the e-mails, hackers frequently referred to actual people and events that would be of interest to victims, such as a national-security seminar hosted by the Center for Naval Analysis in the Washington, D.C., area. Including such information seemingly bolstered the credibility of the phishing message and increased the chances that a victim would unwittingly open a document with a command that simultaneously opened a remote administration tool (RAT).

Authors have pointed to Microsoft Windows' significant security vulnerabilities as a factor facilitating this hack. Users whose software patches were not thoroughly up-to-date found the nominal files opening with a slight delay, while the Trojan operated unnoticed in the background. The RAT navigated online in search of one of the command and control Web sites the hackers had established to remotely control victim computers and exfiltrate data. The addresses for these control sites typically appeared to be normal text files so that even an alert human user might see the Trojan and not identify it as abnormal. Command and control functions were unobtrusively hidden as HTML comments, and because HTML comments are often a part of normal and innocent code, the Trojan was relatively secure against discovery. Using the RAT, hackers could access files on the victim's machine and could also insert further malware onto the victim's computer, building further on their capabilities and access.

Operation Shady RAT was not publicly identified until the second half of 2011, after five years of operation. The report by McAfee vice president Dmitri Alperovitch also identified more than 70 victim organizations. By nationality, 49 of these were located in the United States, and the rest were mostly located either in Western Europe or the industrialized Pacific Rim. More than a dozen of the victim companies were defense contractors. Other companies suffering intrusions represented a variety of other sectors, including electronics and energy. Two think tanks were also targeted. Responders during the events noticed that policies intended to maintain security also led to inadvertent shortcomings in sharing information about the hack.

A puzzling factor, which ultimately became an additional clue for attribution, was that five Olympic committees and the World Anti-Doping Agency were also among the targeted entities. The hacks appear to have peaked as the 2008 Olympic Games were held in Beijing. The absence of obvious financial opportunity in targeting an antidoping body, a national security think tank, and a global democracy organization pointed to politically oriented motives. The sophistication of the hack, from the creation of plausible and enticing phishing messages to the way in which the Trojan was hidden, suggested that the perpetrators possessed significant talent and training and implied potential state sponsorship. The array of defense and economic entities that were targeted matched the pattern established at the time and since by hackers operating from the People's Republic of China (PRC).

The origins and even the scale of Operation Shady RAT have proven somewhat murky and contested. At McAfee, Alperovitch noted that the perpetrator appeared to have nation-state support and to be especially interested in Asian affairs, but he was reluctant to identify a particular nation-state. Others have since pointed to similarities between Operation Shady RAT and other actions, such as Operation Aurora, that emanate from the PRC. Different companies within the security field debate the scale of the hacks; as with many such actions, it is difficult to determine exactly what information and how much of it was illicitly accessed. Extensive data exfiltrations, such as Operation Shady RAT, Operation Aurora, and the Operation Night Dragon hacks against the energy sector in 2008 and 2009, have basically coincided with an apparent trend toward reporting on cyber activities involving economic espionage.

Nicholas Michael Sambaluk

See also: Alperovitch, Dmitri; Cyber Crime; Cyber Espionage; Malware; McAfee; Operation Aurora; Operation Night Dragon; People's Republic of China Cyber Capabilities; Spear Phishing

Further Reading

Lindsay, Jon R., Tai Ming Cheung, and Derek S. Reveron, eds. *China and Cybersecurity: Espionage, Strategy, and Politics in the Digital Domain.* New York: Oxford University Press, 2015.

Rid, Thomas. *Cyber War Will Not Take Place.* New York: Oxford University Press, 2013.

Rosenzweig, Paul. *Cyber Warfare: How Conflicts in Cyberspace Are Challenging America and Changing the World.* Santa Barbara, CA: Praeger, 2013.

Singer, P. W., and Allan Friedman. *Cybersecurity and Cyberwar: What Everyone Needs to Know.* New York: Oxford University Press, 2014.

OPERATION TITAN RAIN

Operation Titan Rain was the U.S. federal government designation for a series of cyber attacks against U.S. computer systems, beginning in 2003. Although the attacks appear to have originated from China, the actual identities of the attackers remain unknown. The attacks were classified as an advanced persistent threat (APT), but the use of zombie computers, proxy servers, virus- and spyware-infected sources, made it impossible to determine their nature, whether corporate- or state-sponsored espionage, or random hackers. They were able to gain access to U.S. defense contractor computer networks and their sensitive information, to include Lockheed Martin, Sandia National Laboratories, Redstone Arsenal, and NASA. Their main targets were the U.S. Defense Intelligence Agency (DIA) and the British Ministry of Defense (MoD).

The security SANS Institute claimed in December 2005 that the attackers were likely the result of Chinese military hackers. Some believed that the Chinese People's Liberation Army (PLA) was responsible. China has admitted no association to the attacks, instead claiming the possibility of hackers using Chinese computers. Many Chinese computers and Web sites are unsecured, and hackers use the Web site or system to attack a targeted system, making it look as if China were the source with relative ease. This concept protects the hackers, and the Chinese government cannot prove they were not responsible, causing tension between China and the United States, Great Britain, and Russia.

The attacks were first noted in September 2003 during a network break-in at Lockheed Martin. Several months later, they hit Sandia, but the threat became evident when the U.S. Army cyber intelligence also confirmed the methodical and deep intrusions by penetrating secure networks of the most sensitive military bases, defense contractors, and aerospace companies, getting all the files that they could find in the hidden section of hard drives. They were then transmitted to stations in South Korea, Taiwan, or Hong Kong, and from there to mainland China in the southern province of Guangdong. The attackers were traced to three Chinese routers that acted as the first connection point from a local network to the Internet. The attackers wiped their electronic fingerprints clean with undetectable beacons but retained the ability to reenter the attacked computer at will. Attacks took 10 to 30 minutes, and they never made overt mistakes, such as hitting the wrong keys, especially in government computers.

The quantity of compromised files was enormous. Titan Rain could be a point of departure for more serious assaults and might shut down or even take over several U.S. military networks, according to the Department of Defense (DoD). The compromised data were not classified as secrets, but they were sensitive, such as flight-planning software from the army, and subject to strict export control laws that required U.S. government licenses for foreign use. In 2006, the British House of Commons' computer system was shut down, exposing sensitive material from the Ministry of Defense. Other companies affected were Mitsubishi in Japan and Rio Tinto of Australia. Canada, France, and Germany reported APTs traced back to China, but they were cautious to not directly accuse the Chinese government.

Titan Rain also saw attacks on many countries. In 2008, BAE, Britain's biggest defense contractor, was compromised, and MI5 warned companies that do business with the Chinese that their networks were being attacked. After German government ministries, to include Chancellor Angela Merkel's office, were compromised, she complained directly to Chinese premier Wen Jiabao and labeled the attacks espionage. Canadian firms in the aerospace, agriculture, biotech, military, oil, and communication sectors were attacked. The collapse of Nortel, the telecom giant, after a decade of espionage attacks was linked to China. Mitsubishi in Japan reported cyber attacks on submarine manufacturing and research on guided missiles and rocket engines, power ships, and nuclear power stations. Japanese Agriculture, Forestry, and Fishery Ministries reported stolen files pertaining to trade negotiations over the Trans-Pacific Partnership.

In 2009, the Joint Strike Fighter project, known as F-35 Lightning II, was attacked, and diagnosing maintenance problems during flights was compromised. Lockheed Martin, Northrop Grumman, and BAE Systems had over 24,000 files concerning developmental systems stolen over a period of 18 months, including online meetings and technical discussions. When finally discovered in 2011, cyber analysts found that hackers gained access to the security tokens through aggressive espionage efforts. Software for the specialized communication and antenna arrays had to be rewritten.

China has repeatedly denied any involvement in the Titan Rain attacks, claims the accusations are an effort to destroy bilateral relationships, and argues that they are irresponsible and calculating. Despite denials, the United States accused China in October 2011 of "a massive and sustained intelligence effort by a government to blatantly steal commercial data and intellectual property" by the House Committee on Intelligence, and the Office of the National Counterintelligence stated that China was the "world's most active and persistent perpetrators of economic espionage."

At the Security and Economic Dialogue in 2012, cyber security was on the agenda and raised by Secretary of State Hillary Clinton during her meeting with Chinese Foreign Minister Yang Jiechi and by Secretary of Defense Leon E. Panetta with Chinese Defense Minister General Liang Guangjie in the United States. These dialogues have had no effect publicly. The difficulty is that the United States promotes cyber security, which protects communications and critical networks. China refers to information security, a broader category that includes controlling content. The United States tries to limit economic espionage, which China claims it does not engage in, while maintaining the ability to conduct operations against foreign governments, militaries, and terrorist groups. China makes no distinction and has no prohibition against economic espionage and sees itself vulnerable to U.S. computer operations.

Titan Rain attacks from China are massive. The NSA and U.S. Cyber Command (USCYBERCOM) have called espionage attacks on U.S. companies the "greatest transfer of wealth in history," at a cost of $250 billion per year through intellectual property theft. The U.S. reactions have been restrained due to the nature of demands for a positive relationship with China as well as for not wanting to reveal intelligence capabilities. It should be expected that the Chinese operations will continue, and in keeping the U.S.-China relationship intact, industries will have to learn to accommodate them until the U.S. government decides to raise the costs for Chinese hackers.

Raymond D. Limbach

See also: Advanced Persistent Threat (APT); Cyber Espionage; Operation Aurora; Operation Night Dragon; Operation Shady RAT; People's Republic of China Cyber Capabilities

Further Reading

Clarke, Richard A., and Robert K. Knake. *Cyber War: The Next Threat to National Security and What to Do about It.* New York: HarperCollins, 2010.

Lindsay, Jon R., Tai Ming Cheung, and Derek S. Reveron, eds. *China and Cybersecurity: Espionage, Strategy, and Politics in the Digital Domain.* New York: Oxford University Press, 2015.

Rosenzweig, Paul. *Cyber Warfare: How Conflicts in Cyberspace Are Challenging America and Changing the World.* Santa Barbara, CA: Praeger, 2013.

P

PANETTA, LEON E.

Leon E. Panetta served as the director of the Central Intelligence Agency (CIA) from 2009 to 2011 and the secretary of defense from 2011 to 2013. Born June 28, 1938, in Monterey, California, to Italian immigrant parents, Panetta graduated from Santa Clara University in 1960 and Santa Clara University School of Law in 1963. He served two years in the U.S. Army, received the Army Commendation Medal, and was discharged as a first lieutenant.

Panetta represented California in Congress (1977–1993). Then he became the White House chief of staff (1994–1997) under President Bill Clinton. As the director of the CIA, he conducted a review of CIA interrogation programs under President George W. Bush, increased the CIA's use of drones, and oversaw operations that resulted in Osama bin Laden's death on May 1, 2011. In 2012, he warned of the possibility of a cyber Pearl Harbor and outlined the three areas of focus for the Department of Defense (DoD): develop new capabilities for defense and attack, create new rules of engagement to strengthen U.S. Cyber Command (USCYBER-COM), and build stronger partnerships between the private and public sectors. Panetta retired from government service in 2013.

Mary Elizabeth Walters

See also: Central Intelligence Agency (CIA); Cyber Terrorism; Department of Defense (DoD); U.S. Cyber Command (USCYBERCOM)

Further Reading

Panetta, Leon, with Jim Newton. *Worthy Fights: A Memoir of Leadership in War and Peace.* New York: Penguin Publishing Group, 2015.
Springer, Paul J. *Cyber War: A Reference Handbook.* Santa Barbara, CA: ABC-CLIO, 2015.

PATRIOTIC HACKING

Patriotic hacking is the hacking of Web sites and Web-based services by individuals who believe that their actions are helping a particular country. These actors may sometimes be known as *hacktivists*, as they can be driven by patriotism or the wish to attack other states' governments. Hacktivists and patriotic hacking are not always the same, but as the definition is fluid, it may be difficult to know the true motivations of the hacker. Understanding hacking is essential to understanding this term. Hacking includes installing software on computers that allow others to spy on the computer and connected networks, to corrupt data, or to plant a back-door program. Such a program, also called a *trapdoor*, allows data to be stolen, and it can also change the entire system to allow for more uses of the backdoor program or even to shut the entire system down. The skills and wits of the administrators are often the only line of defense to protect a system and to stop hacking attempts.

Patriotic hackers may conduct their operations with or without government support or knowledge of their activities. These activities are often directed against other foreign governments, particularly in times of conflict. They are often viewed as guerillas or saboteurs operating in cyber space, particularly when receiving clandestine support from governments or other groups. Governments may choose not to prosecute the patriotic hackers in exchange for the benefits they receive from their actions. This certainly depends on the goals of the country where the hackers are present and the relations with the attacked country. Public opinion is also greatly affected by patriotic hacking. As the Internet is an information network, opinions and propaganda posted there can easily reach millions of people with little effort and time. This can be used by governments as attacks against enemies, but if the targeted government is particularly vulnerable to public opinion, patriotic hacking can do more than simply affect computer systems.

This form of hacking is an example of how nonstate actors can affect relations between two states, often negatively. If the government of the attacking nation does not halt the action, relations can become strained between nations. Proxy wars can also be fought by patriotic hackers. Certain nonstate actors can receive support from governments for attacks on groups or states. Doing this allows governments to deny any involvement in the attack while still being able to achieve its goals. Cyber attacks also allow smaller groups to have more impact than they normally would. Nonstate actors can achieve more through a cyber attack by being able to shut down an enemy's energy infrastructure or its e-commerce. This can be done with just one person, and the impacts can be much larger than what one person can do on a conventional battlefield. Patriotic hacking has allowed governments to attack their enemies with plausible deniability when they do not wish to be identified. They can also cause much more damage than conventional attacks, with minimal cost and public exposure.

There have been many examples of patriotic hacking in the 21st century. Numerous countries have used patriotic hacking, including the Russian Federation and the People's Republic of China (PRC), to achieve diplomatic or internal state control goals. On April 27, 2007, a cyber attack was launched on Estonia. It affected major banks, the telecommunications system throughout the country, and numerous media outlets. The attack lasted two weeks and is thought to be a Russian response over the relocation of a Soviet war memorial in Estonia. No official connection to the Russian government has been proven, but pro-Russian hackers, possibly from youth groups within the country, may have received unofficial government support. Russian businesses may have allowed the use of their networks for the attacks.

The Russian government has not limited its cyber attacks to Estonia. Russia was the first nation to combine large-scale cyber attacks on a nation while simultaneously launching a conventional invasion. This was done with their actions against Georgia in 2008. As Russian forces invaded and cut off the capital of Georgia, Tbilisi, from the coast, cyber vandalism and attacks were launched against Georgian government Web sites. A group of hackers from the breakaway area of Georgia, South Ossetia, vandalized government Web sites. Other attacks were organized that shut down major government, financial, and media outlets in Georgia. This appears to have been done by Russian citizens without official government support.

Patriotic hacking has been used to quell internal dissent, particularly in the PRC. The government attempted to crack down on Falun Gong, a Buddhist revival movement in China. The government began to fear the group as their membership grew larger than that of the Communist Party of China. They feared that a group that large could take power in China. The government began their crackdown of Falun Gong by disrupting servers in North America used by the group. Personal e-mail accounts provided by Google were hacked by Chinese government agents, possibly with help from Google employees. This was done to track human rights activists and Chinese journalists who were exposing the harsh treatment of Falun Gong members. These hacking activities were supported by patriotic hackers in China from groups known as the Green Army and the Red Hacker Alliance. This example shows that patriotic hacking has been used for more than state conflict and moved into internal repression.

Brad St. Croix

See also: Cyber Defence Management Authority (CDMA); Cyber War; Estonian Cyber Attack (2007); Georgian Cyber Attack (2008); Hacktivist; People's Republic of China Cyber Capabilities

Further Reading

Gutmann, Ethan. "Hacker Nation: China's Cyber Assault." *World Affairs* 173(1), 2010: 70–79.

Kerschischnig, Georg. *Cyberthreats and International Law.* The Hague, Netherlands: Eleven International Publishing, 2012.

Russell, Alison Lawlor, *Cyber Blockades.* Washington, D.C.: Georgetown University Press, 2014.

PEOPLE'S LIBERATION ARMY UNIT 61398

The highly secretive People's Liberation Army (PLA) Unit 61398 has become infamous for its ability to steal a variety of secrets from nations and companies around the globe, particularly the economic secrets of English-speaking nations. The unit is also known as the Third Office of the PLA General Staff Department Third Department Second Bureau. It is located in a 12-story building in Shanghai, People's Republic of China (PRC), and staffed by hundreds, perhaps thousands, of employees.

Much of what is known about the unit is due to a report released in 2013 by Mandiant Corporation. The American cyber-security company, established by former U.S. Air Force officer Kevin Mandia, rose to prominence with the report's release. The company had already been investigating Unit 61398 in light of Chinese cyber attacks against the *New York Times* after the newspaper reported on the vast familial wealth of an outgoing Chinese prime minister.

Mandiant Corporation has labeled the organization behind these attacks Advanced Persistent Threat 1 (APT1). An advanced persistent threat (APT) is a cyber attack by which an unauthorized user acquires access to a network and maintains access for a significant period of time in order to steal information.

Despite the many pieces of evidence pointing to Unit 61398, the question of attribution—or definitely determining the real source behind cyber attacks—persists. While it cannot be established absolutely that Mandiant is correct, the evidence provided in the report is overwhelming. Mandiant considers but ultimately dismisses the possibility that this could be a secret unit located nearby Unit 61398. That would not necessarily explain, for example, the impressive array of fiber-communication networks in the building that such a unit would require. The complex is also supported by a range of facilities, such as a kindergarten, usually only found at highly prestigious units. Scholars also point to the existence of a strong and large constituency of patriotic hackers in China as well as criminal operators who could also be behind the attacks. However, most of the attacks coming from this area occur during normal weekday working hours.

The primary goal of the unit is purported to be the theft of intellectual property. The unit, which has functioned since at least 2006, has targeted more than 141 companies and organizations, running many of these operations concurrently. While it has stolen information from obvious cyber-espionage industries such as telecommunications and advanced electronics, it has also targeted less obvious types of industries, including agriculture and health. This emphasis supports China's strategic goal of not only acquiring military secrets but economic information that can help China improve its global position, as presented in China's 12th Five-year Plan.

Unit 61398 uses social engineering, or the practice of tricking people into providing access to confidential information, and malware to gain access to networks. Using its English proficiency, the attackers entice people into clicking on links within e-mails, which is known as *spear phishing*. For example, they create e-mails using names that are recognizable to the recipient. Next, they establish a foothold that enables the unit to control systems remotely. Once the malware has become established, it is extremely difficult to locate and identify the intruder's actions. In the next step, the intruder focuses on privilege escalation, in which it seeks to obtain usernames and passwords to reach more secure information. Finally, the attack concludes with small transfers of information back to the unit. This process can average about one year, as antivirus software has difficulty identifying this malware.

Since the release of Mandiant's report, the United States has become more vocal about Chinese cyber attacks. In May 2013, the Pentagon made its strongest objections yet to Chinese cyber activities in a report presented to the U.S. Congress. In 2014, the United States indicted five Chinese military officers, all members of Unit

61398, for spying against six U.S. companies. The case constituted the first time a state actor had been charged for a cyber attack. The case is consistent with the report's findings that a military unit is being used to target economic information.

U.S. complaints against China have been undermined by Edward J. Snowden's release of documents claiming to show how the National Security Agency (NSA) has attempted to hack Chinese networks since 2009. From China's perspective, it is just as much a victim of cyber attacks as U.S. companies are. The U.S. government, however, avows that it only engages in hacking to protect its interests, not to steal intellectual secrets.

In light of the discussion about how a massive cyber attack could result in a reaction akin to the U.S. response to Pearl Harbor, it should be noted that war could be counter to China's long-term strategy. Scholars have pointed out that China is more interested in economic and regional power than in direct war with the United States. This strategy is highly influenced by the renowned military strategist Sun Tzu, who believed that the best way to win a war was to outsmart the enemy and avoid fighting altogether. As such, China seeks to do anything to strengthen its military and economic position while avoiding pushing so far that it would draw the United States into war. It also reflects China's belief that national security is not just limited to military matters, but runs the gamut of anything that can bolster China's position in the world, even if not traditionally thought of as "military."

Heather Pace Venable

See also: Attribution; Cyber Attack; Cyber Espionage; GhostNet; Malware; Operation Shady RAT; People's Republic of China Cyber Capabilities; Social Engineering; Spyware; Trojan Horse; *Unrestricted Warfare*

Further Reading

Ghafir, Ibrahim, and Václav Přenosil. "Advanced Persistent Threat Attack Detection: An Overview." *International Journal of Advances in Computer Networks and Its Security*, 2014: 154–158. http://www.seekdl.org/nm.php?id=3901.

Heckman, Kristin E., Frank J. Stech, Roshan K. Thomas, Ben Schmoker, and Alexander W. Tsow. "Countering Denial and Deception." In *Cyber Denial, Deception and Counter Deception*, 109–126. Edited by Kristin E. Heckman and Frank J. Stech. New York: Springer International Publishing, 2015.

Lindsay, Jon R. *China and Cybersecurity: Espionage, Strategy, and Politics in the Digital Domain.* New York: Oxford University Press, 2015.

Mandiant Corporation. *APT1: Exposing One of China's Cyber Espionage Units.* Alexandria, VA: Mandiant Corporation, 2013.

PEOPLE'S REPUBLIC OF CHINA CYBER CAPABILITIES

Cyber capabilities in the People's Republic of China (PRC) facilitate the country's economic growth, and its cyber capabilities also constitute an important part of the wider realm of information-dominance issues valued by leaders of the PRC and its People's Liberation Army (PLA). PRC's philosophy about information, the PLA's robust support of growing cyber assets that can operate within the context of PLA strategy, and contrasting definitions between Chinese and foreign voices in interpreting the requirements and implications of cyber capabilities play crucial roles in influencing China's cyber capabilities. The country's capabilities in the cyber realm continue to expand, and their impact carries complex implications.

Within the country, the idea of information dominance leads PRC to establish tools such as the Great Firewall to restrict domestic access to sites deemed subversive or otherwise dangerous to the regime. PRC officials have, furthermore, pointed to efforts made to skirt its restrictions and proclaimed these to constitute cyber attacks. Although misuse of such terms is common outside PRC, the country is essentially unique in condemning efforts to evade firewalls to constitute attacks. The definition rests on a conception of sovereignty that cedes control over information to the state and the party. A PRC white paper in 2010 declared that the state had the right to protect its own networks to eliminate criminal activity, threats to the state, and disruptions to the social order. Control of information figures importantly for the leadership's own maintenance, and this translates into efforts to dominate electronic information environments. Examples of censorship are presented as actions to ensure stability.

An ironic complement to the expansive definition of sovereignty has been a burgeoning interest in applying cyber capabilities to espionage. Defining security and national interests in military and economic terms, considerable espionage activity is traceable to the PRC, and targets for espionage often blur the boundaries between military and industrial espionage. A paramount example is the hack of contractors engaged in the design of the U.S. F-35 Joint Strike Fighter. The project is the most expensive technological development program in military history, and a significant portion of the mounting development costs may be related to the potential compromise of development data, as systems that may be compromised require redesign to reestablish their integrity in a finished airplane. The hackers who exfiltrated F-35 development data did so using methods that encrypted the stolen information as it was copied and removed. As a result, the task of determining what information had been accessed and taken became more complicated. Defense experts have pointed to similarities between PRC's new J-31 stealth fighter plane and the F-35. An array of defense-industry corporations, such as BAE Systems, have been targeted in these espionage efforts, and in the case of BAE Systems, hackers are believed to have been active on the network for a year and a half before their presence was detected.

Espionage has not been confined to government or corporate entities with obvious connections to national defense. In 2007, German chancellor Angela Merkel complained to PRC officials of Chinese hacks into the computer systems of that country's government ministries, and in 2008, the United Kingdom's internal security and counterintelligence office warned British companies doing business in the PRC that they were being targeted by Chinese hacking activity. In 2009, Canadian researchers took a lead role in uncovering a massive and coordinated action labeled GhostNet. It gained real-time control of computers, covertly accessing files and operating computer microphones and Web cameras. Nearly 1,300 computers were infected during the project's two-year span, and infected machines belonged to an array of government, media, and NGO entities in over 100 countries. The vectors for the action included both e-mails with remote-access Trojan horse payload attachments and lures to Web sites where infected files were downloaded. The ploy of attracting victims with files and e-mail addresses of purported Tibetan independence sympathizers represents one element of information suggesting that GhostNet originated with PRC, which sees Tibetan movements as destabilizing to its regime.

The following year, Google announced that it had been targeted by a highly sophisticated attack that struck the corporate infrastructure, in which intellectual property had been stolen. The actions against Google, known as Operation Aurora, made use of vulnerabilities identified in Microsoft Internet Explorer and utilized another Trojan horse method. The data breach in 2015, in which the personal identifying information of more than 20 million U.S. government employees and others was stolen from the Office of Personnel Management (OPM), is believed to have been the work of PRC hackers. Experts also believe that the PRC consciously permits the existence of a lucrative underworld of cyber-criminal elements.

PLA strategists nest cyber operations within the larger framework of information warfare. Following the U.S.-led coalition victory over Iraq in 1991, PLA analysts pointed to the role of U.S. communications technologies and networks in supporting operations and thereby dominating the physical battlefield. They contended that the best counter to this potent approach used by the United States involved the development of capabilities that could neutralize U.S. communications, through the destruction of communication satellites and targeting of U.S. cyber networks. As such, acts of war could be conducted not only by the uniformed military but also by ordinary citizens able to act as "fighters" because of their expertise with relevant technologies. Reflecting the influence of analysis during the 1990s about integrating cyber operations into People's War, PLA doctrinal publications have expressly identified information warfare as a key element in opposing a more formidable adversary.

It's likely that PRC cyber activities reflect the government's expansive definition of security and national interest. This includes espionage into the defense technologies of other states and efforts to maintain control over domestic access to information, but it also involves various efforts to surveil activities by nonmilitary entities overseas and to use information gained through industrial espionage to provide the PRC's own industries with advantageous positions in the global marketplace. Official denials of such activities in the cyber realm have habitually launched counteraccusations that any suggestion of PRC involvement in cyber espionage is an irresponsible claim.

Statistics can be selected to prove various assertions, and PRC officials often use them when arguing that the PRC is the world's leading victim of hostile cyber activity. However, many activities that PRC identifies as "attacks" include efforts to evade the Great Firewall or to use the cyber domain to voice ideas inimical or offensive to the regime. Measurements in 2012 did confirm that 23 percent of the global Internet population was in China, giving PRC an Internet presence (in terms of population) nearly equal to the United States and the European Union combined. Given that PRC's population of 1.38 billion is two-thirds larger than the combined U.S. and EU population, this implies PRC's online participation (in gross terms) as 60 percent that of the United States and the European Union.

With the world's largest total population and the world's largest online population, the PRC possesses important opportunities to mobilize its population in cyber. Even actions by botnets of controlled computers conducting actions such as a distributed denial-of-service (DDoS) attack require a degree of human coordination, and mobilization is an important factor affecting Chinese cyber capabilities. The phenomenon of patriotic hackers exemplifies both the potential power and the unbridled character of voluntary mobilization. Following a virtual collision of a U.S. surveillance plane and a PLA Air Force jet near China's Hainan Island in 2001, the Communist Party encouraged nationals to use the Internet to embarrass the United States.

The leveraging of patriotic hackers or hacker-activists (hacktivists) in the short run offers the tempting prospect of adding force multipliers to a competition in the cyber realm. Additionally, such actors are difficult to associate with a government, providing a degree of plausible deniability that can complicate the alternatives open to a targeted country. For example, researchers traced the origins of a hacking project labeled Byzantine Hades back to the PRC, but they were unable to definitively link the geographic location of the hackers to the PRC government itself.

Conversely, although the leveraging of nongovernment hackers can serve as a force multiplier in specific circumstances, the separation between the government and the hackers can complicate the government's ability to direct or curtail hacking efforts as effectively as might be possible when using official resources. The PLA indicated its interest in identifying and nurturing cyber talent through a series of regional hacker competitions in China in 2005. This resulted in the recruitment of a leader within the PRC's hacker community as a consultant for the Shanghai Public Security Bureau. However, significant complicating factors concern mobilization, particularly with respect to a people's war notion of hostile cyber activities. The raising of a cyber militia as a viable instrument of national policy requires more than the amassing of large numbers of people, an array of computers, and appropriate training.

The PLA itself is believed to have conducted military exercises exploring the organized use of computer viruses, starting in 1997, and to have expanded its studies in subsequent years. From about 2002 to 2005, in an action labeled Operation Titan Rain, hackers believed to be linked to the PLA infiltrated the computer systems of several entities within the U.S. Department of Defense (DoD) as well as the aerospace company Lockheed Martin, the National Aeronautics and Space Administration (NASA), and Britain's Foreign Office. To date, as is the case with other hackers, the operations that can be effectively linked to the PLA have engaged in nonlethal forms of cyber exploitation. Some entities within the PLA are known to be involved in some of the industrial espionage emanating from China.

The exact organizational structure for PLA cyber entities is not entirely known. However, analysts believe that the PLA General Staff Department's Third Department, with a signals intelligence and decoding role similar to the U.S. National Security Agency (NSA), is a hub of PLA cyber activity. The Beijing North Computer Center, Unit 61539, may serve as a PLA analog to the U.S. Cyber Command (USCYBERCOM). A dozen or more major cyber-training facilities are thought to be distributed throughout the PRC. The most infamous of the PLA organizations engaged in cyber actions is the Shanghai-based Unit 61398, to which the interception of voluminous amounts of militarily, economically, and politically significant U.S. intelligence information has been attributed.

The PRC possesses extensive cyber capabilities and regularly uses these to pursue an array of goals that it considers to be within the scope of its national interests. Control over domestically available information is one important area. It also includes considerable espionage and surveillance activities directed against foreign governments, businesses, activists, and citizens as well as the toleration of cyber crime and the nurturing of cyber talent for use in militias and sometime recruitment in the formal organs of the PLA.

Nicholas Michael Sambaluk

See also: Baidu; Cyber Crime; Cyber Espionage; Cyber Security; Cyber Weapon; Distributed Denial-of-Service (DDoS) Attack; Firewall; Google; Hacker; Identity Theft; Office of Personnel Management Data Breach; Operation Aurora; Operation Shady RAT; Operation Titan Rain; Patriotic Hacking; People's Liberation Army Unit 61398; Spyware

Further Reading

Chansoria, Monika. "Defying Borders in Future Conflict in East Asia: Chinese Capabilities in the Realm of Information Warfare and Cyber Space." *The Journal of East Asian Affairs* 26(1), Spring/Summer 2012: 105–127.

Deibert, Ronald. *Black Code: Surveillance, Piracy, and the Dark Side of the Internet.* Toronto: McClelland & Stewart, 2013.

Lindsay, Jon Ar., Tai Ming Cheung, and Derek S. Reveron, eds. *China and Cybersecurity: Espionage, Strategy, and Politics in the Digital Domain.* New York: Oxford University Press, 2015.

Mazanec, Brian M. *The Evolution of Cyber War: International Norms for Emerging-technology Weapons.* Lincoln, NE: Potomac, 2015.

Rid, Thomas. *Cyber War Will Not Take Place.* New York: Oxford University Press, 2013.

Singer, P. W., and Allan Friedman. *Cybersecurity and Cyberwar: What Everyone Needs to Know.* New York: Oxford University Press, 2014.

Springer, Paul J. *Cyber Warfare: A Reference Handbook.* Santa Barbara, CA: ABC-CLIO, 2015.

PHISHING

The term *phishing* refers to an attempt by a hacker or other illegal entity to obtain personal information for nefarious purposes. Phishing is a homophone for the commonly accepted term *fishing*, which refers to the act of casting bait in the hopes of hooking prey. In the cyber world, phishers use "bait" to obtain personal and sensitive material from their targets, such as usernames, passwords, and other identity information, that can be used for financial gain or to obtain access to protected computer systems.

To hook their prey, phishers use e-mail that appears to be from legitimate social media sites, banks, or online payment companies to trick people into entering their personal information into fake Web sites. These social-engineering techniques are able to deceive people because they believe the e-mail's substance to be factual. As the technique has evolved, new terms have come into being as well. *Spear phishing* refers to a specific attack against an individual. For example, an individual gets an e-mail from the bank or online payment service they commonly use. Because of the specificity involved, spear phishing has become the most successful form of attack. When hackers go after high-level executives or very important personalities, the term *whaling* describes this type of phishing attack.

To prevent phishing attacks, e-mail users can employ spam filters to isolate or highlight suspected phishing attempts. Increased e-mail defenses have caused hackers to employ other types of attacks, including instant messaging phishing as well as voice phishing.

Melvin G. Deaile

See also: Cyber Crime; Hacker; Identity Theft; Social Engineering; Spear Phishing

Further Reading

Hadnagy, Christopher. *Social Engineering: The Art of Human Hacking.* Indianapolis, IN: Wiley, 2011.

Verma, Nina. *Social Engineering: A Means to Violate a Computer System.* New Delhi, India: Global Vision Pub. House, 2011.

PRESIDENTIAL DECISION DIRECTIVE 63 (1998)

Presidential Decision Directive 63 (PDD-63) was a directive approved by President Bill Clinton on May 22, 1998, to create a framework and definitive policies to protect the United States' critical infrastructure, which includes both physical and cyber-based systems. PDD-63 set two goals: (1) by the end of 2000, the United States must have achieved the operating capability to protect the nation's critical infrastructure from deliberate and destructive acts; and (2) by 2003, the United States must have created protection mechanisms and the ability to maintain the protection of the infrastructure.

While these infrastructures used to act as independent systems, the advancement of information technology caused them to become automated and interlinked. With greater interdependence, nonconventional attacks on the cyber-supported and physical systems have the potential to cause greater disruption and destruction to the U.S. military and economy. PDD-63 came as a result of the findings from the President's Commission on Critical Infrastructure Protection (PCCIP). The commission focused upon aspects of the national infrastructure essential to the basic operations of the economy and government to include telecommunications, energy, banking and finance, transportation, water systems, public health services, and emergency services. PDD-63 became the founding document for the creation of multiple agencies, including the National Infrastructure Protection Center (NIPC), the United States Computer Emergency Readiness Team (US-CERT), and Critical Infrastructure Assurance Office (CIAO).

Under PDD-63, the U.S. federal government designated lead agencies to oversee various sectors of the economy considered vulnerable to attack. For example, the Department of Commerce received the task of securing the information and communications sector. Within each designated agency, a senior liaison official was selected to work with private sector organizations. The private sector then chose a sector coordinator as a counterpart to the liaison official. Together, these officials and private corporations worked to create a sector-security plan that was integrated into a National Infrastructure Assurance Plan. In addition, the sector liaisons worked with the national coordinator for security, infrastructure protection, and counterterrorism who chaired the Critical Infrastructure Coordination Group, which worked to develop and implement policy for the federal government's internal security.

On December 17, 2003, President George W. Bush signed the Homeland Security Presidential Directive-7 (HSPD), titled "Critical Infrastructure Identification, Prioritization, and Protection." This directive superseded PDD-63 and expanded the policies and development of critical infrastructure to protect the United States from terrorist attacks.

Heather M. Salazar

See also: Computer Emergency Response Team (CERT); Cyber Security; Department of Homeland Security (DHS); Infrastructure; National Infrastructure Protection Plan (NIPP); President's Commission on Critical Infrastructure Protection (PCCIP)

Further Reading

Clarke, Richard A., and Robert K. Knake. *Cyber War: The Next Threat to National Security and What to Do about It.* New York: HarperCollins, 2010.

National Telecommunications and Information Administration. Notice. "Presidential Decision Directive 63 on Critical Infrastructure Protection: Sector Coordinators." *Federal Register* 63(214), August 5, 1998: 41804–41806.

PRESIDENT'S COMMISSION ON CRITICAL INFRASTRUCTURE PROTECTION (PCCIP)

The President's Commission on Critical Infrastructure Protection (PCCIP) was a commission established in July 1996 to examine the scope and nature of the vulnerabilities and threats to the United States' critical infrastructure; to recommend a comprehensive national policy and implementation plan to protect these infrastructures; to determine legal and policy issues raised; and to propose statutory and regulatory changes required to implement recommendations. The PCCIP spent 15 months working on these tasks and submitted their report to President Bill Clinton in October 1997.

On July 15, 1996, President Clinton issued Executive Order 13010, creating the PCCIP and outlining the members, committees, and its mission. Robert T. Marsh, a U.S. Military Academy graduate, chaired the commission. Marsh holds master's degrees from the University of Michigan in instrumentation engineering and aeronautical engineering. PCCIP's membership included two individuals from each of the following departments: Treasury, Justice, Defense, Commerce, Transportation, and Energy. It also included representatives from the Central Intelligence Agency (CIS); the Federal Emergency Management Agency (FEMA); the Federal Bureau of Investigation (FBI); and the National Security Agency (NSA). The order created two committees within the PCCIP. The Principals Committee reported to the president following their review of all reports and recommendations submitted by the PCCIP. The Steering Committee had four members, all appointed by the president, and they approved the submission of reports to the Principals Committee.

The PCCIP concluded that no immediate threat existed but that the government needed to think differently about infrastructure protection due to the nation's heavy reliance on it. They identified eight critical infrastructures requiring protection: telecommunications; generation, transmission, and distribution of electric power; storage and distribution of gas and oil; water supplies; transportation; banking and finance; emergency services; and government services.

The commission recommended several measures to achieve greater protection from both physical and cyber threats and attacks. An increased level of cooperation and information sharing is needed between governmental agencies and private infrastructure. Protecting the infrastructure must be ingrained in society and should be done through education and awareness programs in the academic and professional environments. The PCCIP called on the federal government to lead by example in facing this new information age by increasing protection of its own infrastructures from attacks. In addition, it should streamline the legal structure that is behind technology's pace and move forward with the research and development of new technologies to counter these possible threats.

In October 1997, President Clinton received the commission's report and sent out for an extensive interagency review. That review resulted in the issuance of Presidential Decision Directive 63 in May 1998.

Heather M. Salazar

See also: Cyber Sabotage; Infrastructure; National Infrastructure Protection Plan (NIPP); Presidential Decision Directive 63 (1998)

Further Reading

President's Commission on Critical Infrastructure Protection. *Critical Foundations: Protecting America's Infrastructures.* Washington, D.C.: U.S. Government Printing Office, 1997.

U.S. Congress. Senate. Committee on the Judiciary. "The Nation at Risk—Report of the President's Commission on Critical Infrastructure Protection: Hearing before the

Subcommittee on Technology, Terrorism, and Government Information." 105th Cong., 1st sess., November 5, 1997.

U.S. President. Executive Order. "Executive Order 13010: Critical Infrastructure Protection." *Federal Register* 61(138), July 17, 1996: 37347–37350.

PREY

Prey is a 2002 novel by Michael Crichton. The plot, as in many of Crichton's works, employs speculation on emerging trends in science and technology as the foundation for a thriller involving a protagonist struggling against both technology and nature. Among the major scientific and technical themes explored are nanotechnology, biotechnology, and computer-based artificial intelligence (AI). Regarding AI, the plot discusses concepts related to artificial life, the creation and utility of genetic algorithms, and aspects of agent-based computing.

The novel revolves around out-of-work computer programmer Jack Forman, a homemaker taking care of three children while his wife, Julia, is an executive at a nanotechnology firm with a fabrication plant in the Nevada desert. Employing algorithms Jack developed at his former company, Julia's company devises organically based swarming nanobots to conduct real-time battlefield surveillance to fulfill a Department of Defense (DoD) contract. The company has lost control of some of the nanoswarms, which are rapidly evolving in unintended directions outside of the laboratory. In an ironic twist, Jack is rehired by his former company in a last-ditch effort to eradicate the now predatory and wild nanoswarms. Ultimately, Jack and members of his software team employ their unique knowledge of the software and other training they have acquired to save the world from the man-made threat looming from this technology convergence run amok.

The book elevated interest in nanotechnology and highlighted the role that advanced computing was playing in that field as well as in a number of other sciences.

John G. Terino

See also: Matrix, The; Terminator, The

Further Reading

Crichton, Michael. *Prey*. New York: Harper, 2002.

PRISM PROGRAM

The PRISM program is purported to be a collaboration between the U.S. National Security Agency (NSA), the U.K.'s Government Communications Headquarters (GCHQ), and major U.S.-based Internet service providers (ISPs), whereby the U.S. and U.K. government agencies can access data on company servers to extract audio and video files, photographs, e-mails, documents, and connection logs to facilitate intelligence gathering. The U.S. companies are alleged to include Microsoft, Google, Yahoo, Facebook, AOL, Skype, Apple, and YouTube, but each company has issued rebuttals to the effect that they have only complied with lawful requests for access. PRISM is not a departure from established practice in the United States; the NSA has collaborated with U.S. companies for decades in Special Source Operations and, more recently, on other NSA programs, such as BLARNEY, working in parallel with PRISM to collect metadata to conduct network traffic analyses.

PRISM was instigated following adverse media disclosures and lawsuits concerning a secret program of warrantless U.S. domestic surveillance; between 2004 and 2007, Foreign Intelligence Surveillance Act (FISA) judges issued surveillance orders that were alleged to have been secured in the absence of probable cause that an intelligence target or facility were connected to terrorism. Following a review, the FISA Court forced the U.S. government to develop lawful authority to undertake surveillance of foreign communications traffic transiting through U.S. servers; this led to the Protect America Act (2007) as well as the FISA Amendments Act (2008), which effectively rendered private companies immune to prosecution provided that they cooperated voluntarily with intelligence gathering.

The controversy that surrounds PRISM arises from the NSA's lawful mission of foreign intelligence gathering being achieved by sifting through servers on U.S. soil that facilitate the transit of international network traffic as well as hold the personal data of tens of millions of U.S. citizens. To ensure immunity from lawsuits, when the companies are issued a directive from the U.S. attorney general and the U.S. director of national intelligence to provide access to their servers by the FBI's Data Intercept Technology Unit (DITU), they must comply. If they do not comply, they can be compelled to do so by the U.S. Department of Justice (DOJ) under the authority of the U.S. Congress. Section 702 of the FISA Amendments Act authorizes the collection of communications content under PRISM and other programs, and Section 215 of the USA PATRIOT Act authorizes the collection of metadata from telephone companies. The FISA Court only approves the NSA's collection procedures; individual warrants are not required. PRISM purportedly does not directly access company servers; it is instead facilitated by collection managers who forward content tasking instructions directly to equipment installed at company-controlled locations.

Checks and balances do exist to ensure that only noncitizens outside the United States are targeted and that the acquisition, retention, and dissemination of information about U.S. citizens is minimized. In practice, analyses are undertaken by NSA staff inputting search terms (selectors) which are then used to examine collected data via signals intelligence activity designators (SIGADs) tasked for different types of data, such as the content of phone conversations or Internet metadata.

Analysts cannot specifically target someone reasonably believed to be a U.S. citizen communicating on U.S. soil; there must be at least 51 percent certainty their target is a foreign national. An analyst collects records on a target's contacts and their contacts' contacts (termed *contact chaining*); in the eventuality that a U.S. citizen is identified, the analyst must take steps to remove the data. Nevertheless, inadvertently acquired communications from U.S. citizens may be analyzed for up to five years. Moreover, communications that are reasonably believed to contain evidence of a crime that has been, is being, or is about to be committed can be forwarded to a U.S. domestic agency for action. Significantly, if communications are encrypted, they can be kept indefinitely. The PRISM program exemplifies a wider shift toward mass-collection techniques for intelligence gathering.

Graem Corfield

See also: Cyber Espionage; Encryption; National Security Agency (NSA); Snowden, Edward J.; The Onion Router (TOR)

Further Reading

Harding, Luke. *The Snowden Files: The Inside Story of the World's Most Wanted Man.* New York: Vintage Books, 2014.
Hayden, Michael. *Playing to the Edge: American Intelligence in the Age of Terror.* New York: Penguin, 2016.
Libicki, Martin. *Cyberspace in Peace and War.* Annapolis, MD: U.S. Naval Institute Press, 2016.

PROGRAMMABLE LOGIC CONTROLLER (PLC)

A programmable logic controller (PLC) consists of three components: an input module, a processing unit, and an output module. In operation, the processing unit scans the input signals, processes the data based on its programming, transmits an output signal, and then performs internal checks or programming updates. The significant feature of this device is its ability to reprogram the processing unit. This represents a versatility not found in the old hardwired relay systems, and for this reason, manufacturers have largely switched over to PLC units in production lines, starting in the early 1970s.

The processing unit's nonvolatile memory provides another attractive feature to manufacturers, as it retains programming through power shutdowns or outages. Standards commissions have defined the syntax and semantics for four of the controller programming languages: function block diagram, ladder diagram, structured text, and instruction list. The languages have evolved from simple relays functionality to a full range of functions, including counters, shift registers, and math operations. Using these languages, developers write new programs and update the PLC units remotely through built-in communications ports. These ports are often networked within a larger system, such as a supervisory control and data acquisition (SCADA) system. This networking represents a vulnerability not considered in most original designs, until Stuxnet was discovered in 2010.

Paul Clemans

See also: Cyber Sabotage; Supervisory Control and Data Acquisition (SCADA); Stuxnet

Further Reading

Bolton, William. *Programmable Logic Controllers.* 6th ed. Waltham, MA: Newnes, 2015.
Kandray, Daniel. *Programmable Automation Technologies.* New York: Industrial Press, 2010.

PUTIN, VLADIMIR

Vladimir Putin (1952–) is the president of the Russian Federation. Putin served as the prime minister (1999–2000), president (2000–2008), and prime minister again (2008–2012), and he returned to the presidency in 2012. Prior to entering politics, Putin spent 16 years in the Soviet State Security Committee (KGB) during the Cold War, an experience that left him skeptical about the intentions of the North Atlantic Treaty Organization (NATO) states toward Russia and framed his worldview. It also pressed upon him the importance of espionage and high-technology surveillance for states like Russia to obtain advantages in world affairs.

Few countries have been involved in as much conflict as Russia during Putin's reign. He has expanded Russia's cyber-warfare capability, which has been used aggressively as an instrument of foreign policy. Russia first demonstrated its cyber-warfare capacity in a 2007 incident involving Estonia. Roughly a year later, Russia used distributed denial-of-service (DDoS) attacks coupled with a kinetic offensive in a territorial conflict with Georgia. Cyber offensives were also part of Russia's conflict with Ukraine, beginning in 2014. Russia's military operations in support of the Assad regime in Syria have involved cyber attacks on Syrian opposition groups.

Joseph Hammond

See also: Bush, George W.; Cyber Espionage; Estonian Cyber Attack (2007); Georgian Cyber Attack (2008); Obama, Barack; Patriotic Hacking; Russia Cyber Capabilities

Further Reading

Givens, Austin. "Putin's Cyber Strategy in Syria: Are Electronic Attacks Next?" *Cyber Defense Review*, November 17, 2015. www.cyberdefensereview.org/2015/11/17/putins-cyber-strategy-in-syria-are-electronic-attacks-next.

Thomas, Timothy L. "Nation-state Cyber Strategies: Examples from China and Russia." In *Cyberpower and National Security*. Edited by Franklin D. Kramer, Stuart H. Starr, and Larry K. Wentz. Dulles, VA: Potomac Books, 2009.

Q

QUADRENNIAL DEFENSE REVIEW

The U.S. Congress established the Quadrennial Defense Review (QDR) in 1996 to review areas where the U.S. military can be reformed to better protect the nation. The QDR took on more importance after the 9/11 attacks and the War on Terror began in Afghanistan. The report is released every four years, and it is intended to ensure that the Department of Defense (DoD) conducts long-term planning in regard to defense policy for the next 20 years. It is presented to the Armed Services Committees of both the Senate and House of Representatives. The report must look at defense concerns on land, sea, air, space, and cyber space, it focuses on defense concerns on a worldwide scale. The inclusion of cyber space in the QDR shows how seriously the DoD is taking cyber threats not only to the U.S. military but the United States as a nation as well.

Several issues have been raised about the QDR and implementing the recommendations made within it. One concern is timing. Trying to plan so far ahead in terms of both physical and cyber security is extremely difficult. Technology changes so rapidly, especially information technology, that planning for 20 years into the future is difficult, if not impossible. There may be cyber threats that do not even exist at the time of the report and become real concerns in the near future. Certain events cannot be planned for, such as natural disasters, major cyber attacks, or man-made events, such as nuclear or biological attacks.

Preparedness is an important part of the QDR, as it is the only way to plan for the future. As conventional and cyber attacks can cause destruction on a national scale, they must be prevented before any damage can be caused. Economic concerns are a focus of the DoD, particularly relating to cyber warfare. Flexibility in response to threats and attacks has been highly recommended in every QDR. The reliance of communications on the Internet also receives attention from the DoD. As economic situations and national communication networks are open to cyber threats, the QDR allows for future planning to protect vital areas of the U.S. economy and national security.

The DoD works on the assumption that the U.S. military has the advantage in cyber war and defense. Research and development and funding of technology projects are an important part of the recommendations made in the QDR to maintain their superiority. The threats of an enemy, both state and nonstate, with advanced warfighting capabilities is a major concern of the DoD. To maintain this advantage, constant research is needed, as information technology (IT) advances at a very quick rate. The DoD plans to support projects that have the best potential for game-changing breakthroughs, particularly in cyber warfare.

The QDR highlights the importance of maintaining offensive options as well. The DoD will work under the laws of war, along with permission from the president, to eliminate any cyber threats in the United States and aboard. Cooperation between the different branches of the military is stressed in the QDR to respond to all manner of dangers. The QDR suggests setting up standing joint task forces to respond to all threats, whether they come from land, sea, air, space, or cyber space.

Cooperation with other U.S. government departments is an important part of the QDR's recommendations for protecting against cyber threats. Working with the Department of Homeland Security (DHS) and the Federal Bureau of Investigation (FBI) is critical, as these departments need to protect the communication and economic infrastructure of the United States. The DoD can provide important information and experience with law enforcements agencies in the areas of cyber threats.

The QDR also focuses on cooperation with private industry to conduct research and to protect vital infrastructures. Alliances are an important part of protecting the United States, especially in cyber defense. Resources and information can be shared with allies, which will allow better responses to threats to prevent attacks from occurring.

Brad St. Croix

See also: Cyber Defense; Cyber Security; Department of Defense (DoD); Department of Homeland Security (DHS); Federal Bureau of Investigation (FBI)

Further Reading

Hagel, Charles. *Quadrennial Defense Review.* Washington, D.C.: U.S. Department of Defense, February 2014.

Noonan, Michael P. "The *Quadrennial Defense Review* and U.S. Defense Policy." *Orbis* 50(3), 2006: 584–591.

Simon, Christopher A. *Public Policy: Preferences and Outcomes.* New York: Pearson Longman, 2007.

R

RAND CORPORATION

The RAND (Research and Development) Corporation is a think tank that provides strategic guidance, in-depth analysis, and policy examinations to the U.S. government, the U.S. military, and associated organizations. It was founded in 1948 as a collaborative partnership between the newly independent U.S. Air Force and the Douglas Aircraft Company, but it has grown far beyond its initial size and mission. RAND still receives funds from the U.S. government, but it has diversified to included finances from private donors, universities, and the health care industry, all of whom have benefited from previous RAND analyses. RAND now operates as a nonprofit organization with more than $250 million in annual revenues.

When General of the Air Force Henry H. Arnold envisioned the creation of RAND, he expected it to serve as a means of developing long-range technological projects. In this regard, Arnold thought that an independent agency would be best able to create major weapons improvements, including some projects on the order of the Manhattan Project that might revolutionize the nature of warfare. When the Douglas Aircraft Company became concerned that RAND's theoretical research would hinder the company's ability to bid on major defense procurement projects, RAND was spun off into a separate organization. Since that time, RAND has served in more of an advisory and analysis capacity with government and private agencies, rather than in direct pursuit of hard research objectives. RAND's current mission statement is "to help improve policy and decision making through research and analysis."

RAND's early contributions included major projects of systems analysis for the space program, computer science, and in developing artificial intelligence (AI). RAND's researchers were instrumental in developing both the theoretical concept and the actual structure of the Internet, and they have helped in the long-range planning for its improvement and governance. Most of RAND's research directly involves national security in some fashion, although it has also done major long-term studies for other aspects of the U.S. government. RAND has served as a magnet for top talent, with more than 30 Nobel Prize winners working with the organization in some fashion. Much of RAND's national security research is highly classified, but every piece of unclassified research is posted on the RAND Web site for free public access.

Paul J. Springer

See also: Arquilla, John; Libicki, Martin

Further Reading

Abella, Alex. 2009. *Soldiers of Reason: The RAND Corporation and the Rise of the American Empire.* Boston: Mariner Books, 2009.

Ware, Willis H., ed. *RAND and the Information Evolution: A History in Essays and Vignettes.* Santa Monica, CA: RAND Corporation, 2008.

RED TEAM

A *red team* can be defined as a group that engages in alternative analysis to challenge the assumptions and procedures of an organization or entity that it is beneficially testing. Red teams have many variations and include analytic, physical, and cyber-focused groups that may take on the persona of an opposing force (OPFOR). A cyber red team (CRT) exists within a subset of red teaming activity, typically performing penetration testing (pentesting) of computers and their networks. Both business (private sector) and governmental (public sector) cyber red teams exist as well as some independent collectives that view themselves as white hat, or positive, hacking groups. Examples of well-known cyber red teams include the cyber component of Sandia Lab's Information Design Assurance Red Team (IDART); the National Security Agency's Tailored Access Operations (TAO) group; and the iSec Partners, a white hat company.

Cyber red teams can operate in one of two types of environments. The first type is the actual computer operational environment, or, from a system administrator's perspective, the production environment. The strength of operating in this environment is that it provides the same picture that outside attackers would achieve, while the dangers of using it are that it can cause programs to crash, data to be lost, and sensitive information to be revealed. The production environment, in turn, can be further subdivided into black-box tests in which no prior knowledge of or access to it exists, white-box tests in which full knowledge and access of it exists, and gray-box tests that include some level of knowledge and access.

The second type of operational environment, called a *cyber range*, is a simulated one used specifically for red teaming purposes. The benefits of using this environment are that concepts, technologies, and policies can be tested as well as new cyber-defense professionals trained. The detriments of such ranges are that they can be costly to maintain and, ultimately, they represent simulated non-real-world environments that do not operate the same as way as a production environment.

When engaging in a cyber attack, a red team must overcome individual computer and broader network defenses, reminiscent of an onion-peeling approach. At the most basic noniterated level, it does this by means of a defined process or cycle, such as that derived from the four stages of preparation planning, reconnaissance and information gathering, the execution phase, and after-action analysis. A more advanced and iterated technical model engages in such attacks via a kill chain approach derived from reconnaissance and weaponizing and then the cyber-engagement zone phases of deliver, exploit, install, and command and control—actions that then repeat themselves over and over again.

Great variability exists in cyber red team certification. In the case of the U.S. Department of Defense (DoD), a well-defined cyber red team certification and accreditation process exists. From the commercial side, however, certified ethical hacking (CEH) training and confirmation is generally viewed as both outdated and fairly meaningless.

Robert J. Bunker

See also: Cyber Security; Defense Information Systems Agency (DISA); Mitnick, Kevin; White Hat

Further Reading

Brangetto, Pascal, Emin Çalişkan, and Henry Rõigas. *Cyber Red Teaming: Organisational, technical and legal implications in a military context.* Tallinn, Estonia: NATO Cooperative Cyber Defence Centre of Excellence (CCDCOE), 2015.

Chairman of the Joint Chiefs of Staff. *Department of Defense Cyber Red Team Certification and Accreditation.* CJCSM 6510.03, February 28, 2013.

Sandia National Laboratories. *The Information Design Assurance Red Team (IDART).* Sandia, NM: Sandia Corporation, 2009. http://www.idart.sandia.gov.

Zenko, Micah. *Red Team: How to Succeed by Thinking Like the Enemy.* New York: Basic Books, 2015.

REMOTE ADMINISTRATION TOOL (RAT)

A remote administration tool (RAT) is a piece of software that allows a remote computer user to control a computer or network as if physically located at the terminal in question. It typically includes full administrator privileges, which places the affected system under the total control of the remote user. While this concept is often used as a means to allow information technology professionals to troubleshoot computers via the Internet, it is also a common form of attack carried out through malware. Trojan horse programs, in particular, are often used to transmit a RAT into an infected system.

Once the remote user has gained administrative control of the target computer, he or she may be capable of browsing files, downloading or deleting data, or even activating the hardware associated with the computer. This might include turning on an attached camera or microphone for espionage purposes. Many of the most devastating cyber attacks, particularly those involving an advanced persistent threat (APT), have included the incorporation of RAT software to facilitate the attacker's ability to steal or destroy targeted information.

Paul J. Springer

See also: Advanced Persistent Threat (APT); Cyber Crime; Cyber Espionage; Ghost-Net; Malware; Operation Night Dragon; Operation Shady RAT; Operation Titan Rain; Trojan Horse

Further Reading

Lucas, Edward. *Cyberphobia: Identity, Trust, Security and the Internet.* New York: Bloomsbury, 2015.

Ventre, Daniel E. *Chinese Cybersecurity and Defense.* Hoboken, NJ: Wiley, 2014.

RIGA SUMMIT

Senior leaders from 26 North Atlantic Treaty Organization (NATO) nations held a summit in Riga, Latvia, to discuss the organization's mission and transformation in 2006. Member nations formed NATO in the late 1940s in response to Russian aggression and the formation of the Eastern Bloc. When the Soviet Union dissolved in 1989 and the Eastern bloc democratized, NATO searched for a new purpose to give meaning to its existence. Terrorism emerged as the new raison d'être, leading the member nations to redefine the threat and their required military capabilities in the NATO Defense Capabilities Initiative at the Washington, D.C., Summit in 1999. After the 9/11 tragedy, the fight against terrorism expanded to engage terrorist-sponsoring states and failed states, such as Afghanistan. The wars in Iraq and Afghanistan required not only significant military resources and political resolve but also nongovernmental organizations to conduct relief and construction efforts.

By 2006, many member nations questioned whether NATO had lost its focus and was now overstretched in its worldwide commitments. Member nations had begun to specialize their military capabilities as their defense budgets fell far below their commitment to 2 percent of their gross domestic products. Five years of operations in Afghanistan highlighted gaps in military capabilities between the nations and the operational readiness of the coalition force. At the same time, Vladimir Putin had come to power in Russia and was rebuilding its military power based on a new, aggressive nationalism. The Riga Summit brought member nations together to move national commitments to concrete actions for the purpose of transforming the NATO military into a capable, relevant force.

NATO's secretary general proposed six transformation objectives for the conference. Although the spotlight focused on Afghanistan, other discussions tackled such significant issues as equitable sharing of burdens and risks in combat zones; inclusion of nonstate actors in relief and construction efforts; and alignment of NATO and EU efforts. Military transformation requirements fell into one of five areas: joint maneuver and engagement; improved civilian-military relations; information superiority and NATO network-enabled capabilities; expeditionary operations; and sustainable, integrated logistics. Of those, the development and interoperability of member nations' information systems and the protection of those systems remained constant concerns.

After consideration of the progress to date and the projected threats, the member nations included statements of the need for information superiority and the ability to defend against cyber attacks in the summit's Comprehensive Political Guidance statement. The statement led NATO to prepare an assessment of its cyber-defense approach and to deliver it to Allied defense ministers in October 2007. The report highlighted the need to share information across NATO military partners while maintaining secure communications. Not surprisingly, the report points to the political aspects of this effort as the most relevant to developing common technical standards and protecting mechanisms both for information networks and unmanned aerial systems.

Paul Clemans

See also: Estonian Cyber Attack (2007); NATO Cooperative Cyber Defence Centre of Excellence (CCDCOE); North Atlantic Treaty Organization (NATO)

Further Reading

Libicki, Martin. *Crisis and Escalation in Cyberspace.* Santa Monica, CA: RAND Corporation, 2012.

Schmitt, Michael N. *Tallinn Manual on the International Law Applicable to Cyber Warfare.* New York: Cambridge University Press, 2013.

ROGERS, MICHAEL S.

Michael S. Rogers (1959–) is a U.S. Navy admiral who serves as commander of the U.S. Cyber Command (USCYBERCOM), director of the National Security Agency (NSA), and as chief of the Central Security Service (CSS).

Rogers is a native of Chicago. He attended Auburn University and graduated in 1981. He received his commission through the Naval Reserve Officers Training Corps, and he graduated with distinction from the National War College. He is also a Massachusetts Institute of Technology Seminar XXI fellow and Harvard Senior Executive in National Security alumnus, and he holds a master of science in national security strategy. He started his naval career as a surface warfare officer (SWO) aboard the USS *Caron*, working in naval gunfire support operations off Grenada and Beirut and maritime surveillance operations off El Salvador. He also served at the strike group level as the senior cryptologist on the staff of the commander for Carrier Group 2/John F. Kennedy Carrier Strike Group. In 1986, he was transferred from Unrestricted Line (URL) Officer to Restricted Line (RL) Officer and redesignated as a cryptology (now known as *information warfare*) officer aboard the USS *La Salle*. He has also led cryptologic direct support missions aboard U.S. submarines and surface units in the Arabian Gulf and Mediterranean.

Between 1998 and 2000, Rogers commanded Naval Security Group Activity in Winter Harbor, Maine. He also served at the Naval Security Group Department; at the Naval Communications Station in Rota, Spain; at Naval Military Personnel Command; as commander in chief, U.S. Atlantic Fleet; at the Bureau of Personnel as the cryptologic junior officer detailer; and at Commander, Naval Security Group Command, as the aide and executive assistant to the commander.

During the 2003 U.S. invasion of Iraq, Rogers joined the military's Joint Staff, where he specialized in computer network attacks. After becoming a flag officer in 2007, he served as director of intelligence for the military's Pacific Command. In 2009, he became director of intelligence for the Joint Chiefs of Staff, and he was subsequently named commander of U.S. Fleet Cyber Command (FCC) and commander of the U.S. Tenth Fleet, which is responsible for all U.S. Navy cyber-warfare efforts. As such, Rogers was the first RL officer to serve as a numbered fleet commander and the first Information Dominance Warfare officer to achieve the rank of vice admiral.

In January 2014, President Barack Obama announced Rogers's nomination as director of the NSA and the commander of the U.S. offensive cyber-space operations unit in the Department of Defense (DoD). Rogers succeeded General Keith B. Alexander, who served as director for nine years. The Senate unanimously approved Rogers's appointment as head of USCYBERCOM. Since assuming the directorship, Rogers has increased the command's capabilities and has made progress in building its 133-team cyber mission force, to be accomplished by 2018. As director, Rogers focuses on cyber defense, but as of January 2016, he plans to extend USCYBERCOM's focus to systems and platforms.

Angela M. Riotto

See also: Cryptography; Cyber Defense; Department of Defense (DoD); Encryption; National Security Agency (NSA)

Further Reading

Lovelace, Douglas C., Jr. *Terrorism: Commentary on Security Documents: Hybrid Warfare and the Gray Zone Threat.* Vol. 141. New York: Oxford University Press, 2016.

McGhee, James E. "Hack, Attack or Whack: The Politics of Imprecision in Cyber Law." *Journal of Law and Cyber Warfare* 4(1), Winter 2014: 13–41.

RUMSFELD, DONALD H.

Donald H. Rumsfeld is best known for serving two terms as secretary of defense, under presidents Gerald R. Ford (1975–1977) and George W. Bush (2001–2006). Rumsfeld was born in Chicago on July 9, 1932, and in 1954, he graduated from Princeton University in the Naval Reserve Officers Training Corps. Rumsfeld served as a pilot in the U.S. Navy from 1954 to 1957, after which he joined the Naval Reserve. In 1989, Rumsfeld retired as a captain.

At the age of 30, Rumsfeld was elected to the U.S. House of Representatives for the Illinois 13th Congressional District (1963–1969). In 1969, Rumsfeld joined the administration of President Richard Nixon, and in 1973, he was appointed the U.S. ambassador to the North Atlantic Treaty Organization (NATO). As the secretary of defense under President Ford, Rumsfeld guided the transition of the U.S. military to an all-volunteer force. In 1977, he was awarded the Presidential Medal of Freedom. After time in the private sector, Rumsfeld was reappointed as the secretary of defense in 2001, where he oversaw the invasions of Afghanistan in 2001 and Iraq in 2003.

President Bush also tasked Rumsfeld with modernizing the U.S. military. The resulting doctrine, termed the "Rumsfeld Doctrine" by journalists, emphasized a smaller but more flexible, deployable, and precise military force that employed network-centric warfare (NCW). In 2002, Rumsfeld warned of the threat of cyber war to national security and formed the Joint Task Force–Computer Network Operations.

Mary Elizabeth Walters

See also: Bush, George W.; Department of Defense (DoD); Net-centric Warfare (NCW)

Further Reading

Graham, Bradley. *By His Own Rules: The Ambitions, Successes, and Ultimate Failures of Donald Rumsfeld*. New York: Public Affairs, 2009.
Rumsfeld, Donald. *Known and Unknown: A Memoir.* New York: Sentinel, 2011.

RUSSIA CYBER CAPABILITIES

As the inheritor of much of the military and technological infrastructure of the former Soviet Union, the Russian Federation is one of the most technologically advanced nations on earth, particularly regarding cyber capabilities. The collapse of the Soviet Union allowed the rise of enormous Russian criminal networks, many of which have focused on the burgeoning field of cyber crime. The Russian economy, which has been in turmoil for decades, causes many individuals with advanced computer programming skills to turn to criminal activities when they have failed to find legitimate employment. The Russian intelligence services, which have always been regarded as some of the most capable in the world, have also turned toward cyber activities as a major means of conducting espionage activities.

The Russian government, realizing that it does not possess the resources necessary to directly challenge the military forces of the People's Republic of China or the United States, has embraced a form of hybrid warfare, relying on irregular forces backed by conventional units to bolster an aggressive foreign policy. In the cyber domain, this has led to the development of patriotic hackers, individuals willing to use their computer skills on behalf of the government's objectives, even if they may not be directly connected to the Russian government. These individuals have played an outsized role in resolving Russian conflicts with several neighbors and, in the process, have demonstrated how even relatively unsophisticated cyber attacks can have a significant effect if they are conducted on a grand scale.

The nations of Russia and Estonia have a long history of conflict, albeit in a very lopsided fashion. After centuries of Russian domination, the republic of Estonia proclaimed its independence in 1918 and achieved international recognition as a separate nation in 1920. In 1940, the Soviet Union invaded Estonia, but it only occupied the country for a few months before being driven out by Germany, who held the territory until 1944, when the Soviets again conquered the region. In the aftermath of World War II, Estonia was forcibly incorporated into the Soviet Union as a Soviet Socialist Republic, and it remained a part of the USSR until its collapse in 1991, when Estonia once again proclaimed independence.

In 2004, the small Baltic republic joined both the European Union and the North Atlantic Treaty Organization (NATO), two moves that irritated the Russian government, which saw its previous hegemony in the region in continual decline. In 2007, the Estonian legislature passed the Forbidden Structures Law, which required any public vestiges of the Soviet occupation of Estonia to be removed from public lands. This included a massive bronze statue of a Soviet soldier that had been erected in the capital city, Tallinn, at the end of World War II. The statue symbolized the Russian determination to defeat Nazi Germany and was surrounded by the graves of Red Army soldiers. Any attempt to remove it might upset the significant Russian minority in Estonia as well as the Russian government in Moscow. Nevertheless, the Estonian government chose to move the statue to a new and less prominent location in the national military cemetery, a move that absolutely infuriated citizens of Russian heritage and Russian nationalists throughout the much larger neighbor.

The statue's removal did not provoke a full-scale invasion by Russian forces, a move that might trigger a much larger conflict with NATO forces. Instead, the entire nation of Estonia was hit by a series of massive distributed denial-of-service (DDoS) attacks, primarily originating from Russia. Tens of thousands of botnet computers began to flood the Estonian computer servers with requests for information and Web site access. The result was essentially a massive cyber traffic jam, one that knocked hundreds of Estonian government and financial servers off-line.

Unlike a typical DDoS attack, which might be considered a nuisance and last only a few days, the DDoS attacks on the Estonian cyber system continued to increase in intensity and soon began to have a significant effect on the Estonian economy. Estonia is one of the most Internet-dependent societies on earth, with an enormous percentage of the population relying on the Internet for information, banking, and employment. The massive attacks against Estonian servers essentially brought the entire Internet to a nationwide halt. Every attempt to reset the servers brought a renewed flood of DDoS attacks, and soon over a million computers were included in the attacks, most of them probably being used without their owners' knowledge or consent.

The Estonian government reached out to its new economic and military partners for assistance, including a complaint to the North Atlantic Council, the governing body of NATO. Cyber experts rushed to Tallinn to offer assistance, but they could do little to halt the unprecedented flood of DDoS attacks. Attempts to trace the attackers demonstrated that the botnets were being reprogrammed to counter any efforts to stop the attacks. Unfortunately, the cyber-security technicians could not definitively prove the original source of the attacks, even though some evidence showed that much of the coding for the attack programs had been produced on Cyrillic-alphabet keyboards.

Entreaties for help from the Russian government fell on deaf ears. Not only did the Russians adamantly deny any responsibility for the attacks, they also refused to participate in any investigative attempts or to allow any cyber investigators access to Russian systems. Even when evidence demonstrated that the botnet controllers were in Russia, the government suggested that Russian patriots might have attacked on their own volition, for which they would not be punished by the Russian government.

Eventually, the diplomatic crisis faded and so did the attacks on the Estonian infrastructure. The bronze statue remained in its new location, although the Estonians did deign to engage in some beautification projects in the area to give it more prominence. NATO also created a cyber-defense center in Estonia, which opened in 2008. Of course, in the cyber domain, the location of such a center is largely irrelevant, but its presence on Estonian soil served as a symbol of NATO's resolve to defend the nation, whether against physical or cyber attacks.

In the year after the Estonian cyber attacks, the Russian government turned its attention to a different former Soviet vassal, the tiny Republic of Georgia on the Black Sea. Like Estonia, Georgia had attempted to take advantage of the chaos caused by World War I and the Bolshevik Revolution to declare independence from Russia. Its attempt proved far less successful, and once the Russian Civil War concluded in 1921, Soviet troops crushed the breakaway republic and brought it firmly back into the Soviet fold. When the Soviet Union collapsed, Georgia was one of the first republics to proclaim its independence, and, like Estonia, it sought to join NATO in the aftermath of the Cold War, although its application was rejected due to issues of autocratic governance and corruption. In 2008, Georgia became embroiled in a conflict with two of its semiautonomous provinces, South Ossetia and Abkhazia, each of which had a Russian-majority population. A Georgian invasion of South Ossetia provoked an immediate Russian military response, which quickly drove the Georgian armed forces out and threatened to overwhelm the entire Georgian nation.

Russian cyber forces acted decisively in support of the Russian invasion of Georgia. Massive DDoS attacks sought to isolate the Georgian population both from the Georgian government and from the rest of the world. Not only did the attacks seek to disable Georgian government servers and media outlets, they also sought to spread pro-Russian propaganda. Targeted attacks went after the Georgian banking system, and when Georgian banks cut their Internet connections with the hope of protecting their clients' information, Russian botnets began sending false messages simulating cyber attacks from the Georgian banks, aimed at the European banking system. This, in turn, triggered a host of defense mechanisms that only served to further isolate the Georgian banking system and to shut down any ability to process credit card payments in Georgia. Shortly afterward, the entire Georgian mobile phone network was taken off-line by DDoS attacks, effectively cutting off the small nation from most of the outside world.

Faced with overwhelming military and cyber force, the Georgian government was forced to sign a humiliating peace accord with the Russian government, dropping all claims to South Ossetia and Abkhazia, both of which soon voted to be annexed into Russia, and allowing Russian forces to retain control over a buffer zone until relieved by UN peacekeeping forces that never arrived.

As in the Estonian case from the year before, the Russian government denied that it had ordered any form of cyber offensive against Georgia and suggested that any such attacks must have been conducted by patriotic Russians on their own volition. In both cases, the cyber methodology was relatively crude, in that it involved a brute-force DDoS approach that required enormous botnets to continually evolve and continue their attacks. Despite the primitive approach, though, both attacks were remarkably effective and demonstrated the willingness and capabilities of the Russian government and its compatriots to use cyber attacks as a major force enabler to complement physical violence.

In February 2014, Ukrainian president Victor Yanukovych was ousted from office and fled to Russia for protection. Armed forces quickly began seizing positions in Eastern Ukraine and the Crimean Peninsula, both of which have a majority population of ethnic Russian heritage. On March 18, 2014, Russia formally annexed Crimea, over the protest of Ukraine and neutral observer nations. Pro-Russian militants in the easternmost provinces also demanded independence from the Ukrainian government and subsequent annexation by Russia. They may have received both covert funding and overt military assistance from the Russian government, although Russian president Vladimir Putin has repeatedly denied any such intervention into the affairs of Ukraine. Certainly, by the summer of 2014, Russian military units had entered portions of Eastern Ukraine and seized territory. Unsurprisingly, Russian cyber forces have been intimately involved in the conflict from its very beginning.

As was the case in Estonia in 2007 and Georgia in 2008, hackers in Russia began targeting Ukrainian government Web sites and major corporations, vandalizing Web sites and shutting down servers through DDoS attacks. These patriotic hackers also sought to control the flow of information from the disputed region to the rest of the world, in part by attempting to shut down media transmissions of conditions in the area and in part by overwhelming social media discussions of the crisis with coordinated messages defending the Russian position and actions.

Paul J. Springer

See also: Botnet; Cyber Crime; Dark Web; Estonian Cyber Attack (2007); Georbot; Georgian Cyber Attack (2008); Kaspersky Lab; Kaspersky, Yevgeniy "Eugene" Valentinovich; Patriotic Hacking; People's Republic of China Cyber Capabilities; Putin, Vladimir; Russian Business Network (RBN); Rustock Botnet; Snowden, Edward J.; United States Cyber Capabilities

Further Reading

Brenner, Joel. *America the Vulnerable: Inside the New Threat Matrix of Digital Espionage, Crime, and Warfare.* New York: Penguin, 2011.

Carr, Jeffrey. *Inside Cyber Warfare: Mapping the Cyber Underworld.* Sebastopol, CA: O'Reilly Media, 2009.

Clarke, Richard A., and Robert K. Knake. *Cyber War: The Next Threat to National Security and What to Do about It.* New York: HarperCollins, 2010.

Libicki, Martin. *Cyberspace in Peace and War.* Annapolis, MD: U.S. Naval Institute Press, 2016.

Singer, P. W., and Allan Friedman. *Cybersecurity and Cyber War: What Everyone Should Know.* New York: Oxford University Press, 2014.

Stiennon, Richard. *Surviving Cyber War.* Lanham, MD: Government Institutes, 2010.

Thomas, Timothy L. "Nation-state Cyber Strategies: Examples from China and Russia," 465–488. In *Cyberpower and National Security.* Edited by Franklin D. Kramer, Stuart H. Starr, and Larry K. Wentz. Dulles, VA: Potomac Books, 2009.

RUSSIAN BUSINESS NETWORK (RBN)

The Russian Business Network (RBN) is one of the largest cyber-crime organizations in the world. It offers hosting services for a wide variety of illegal Web sites, including ones that specialize in identity theft, credit card fraud, and child pornography. It also collaborates with the largest spam operators and malware distributers in cyber space. The RBN was registered in St. Petersburg, Russia, in 2006, and it quickly grew into an international criminal network. Many of its activities have proven impossible to trace by global authorities, in part because the Russian government turns a blind eye to the RBN's activities as long as it does not target Russian interests or institutions.

In addition to providing hosting services for illicit networks, the RBN also serves as a clearinghouse for cyber mercenaries, offering up enormous botnet resources for rental that can then be used in DDoS attacks. Businesses that have criticized the RBN for its practices have encountered an almost endless stream of attacks originating from the RBN's servers, which are housed on hundreds of networks in dozens of countries. The massive DDoS attacks on Estonia in 2007 and Georgia in 2008 may have been initiated by the RBN, possibly with some degree of government collusion. There is some evidence that the RBN's founder, who is known only by his online nickname "Flyman," may be related to a powerful Russian politician, which would account for some of the protections that the RBN has been able to claim from the Russian government.

Paul J. Springer

See also: Botnet; Cyber Crime; Cyber Espionage; Dark Web; Estonian Cyber Attack (2007); Georbot; Georgian Cyber Attack (2008); Malware; Patriotic Hacking; Putin, Vladimir; Russia Cyber Capabilities

Further Reading

Krebs, Brian. "Shadowy Russian Firm Seen as Conduit for Cybercrime." *Washington Post*, October 13, 2007.

"A Walk on the Dark Side." *The Economist*, August 30, 2007. http://www.economist.com/node/9723768.

Warren, Peter. "Hunt for Russia's Web Criminals." *The Guardian*, November 15, 2007.

RUSTOCK BOTNET

Rustock botnet is a spamming network that operated from around early 2006 until March 2011. This botnet operated over five years, making it one of the most persistent in history. The botnet affects Microsoft Windows computer users. At

Rustock's peak performance, the botnet was able to generate over 30 billion spam e-mails per day. Most of the spam e-mails sent were mostly junk pharmaceutical advertisements, such as counterfeit Viagra offers.

As a botnet, Rustock first had to infect computers using rootkit technology, which allows malware to stay under the radar from the user's presence and anti-virus software scans. This infection can be accomplished either through accessing an infected Web page or through a Trojan horse program embedded in an infected attachment. Once the computer is infected, the computer then tries to link up to a command and control server. The server transmits instructions to the infected computer, which then tries to distribute the malware and recruit other computers into the collective for further spam distributions or distributed denial-of-service attacks (DDoS). In Rustock's case, the goal was primarily distributing spam. Rustock's infection reached between 850,000 and 2.4 million machines.

During the early stages of Rustock's virus release on the Internet, the emergence was subtle as to not raise suspension. The botnet first experienced a setback in 2008 after its Internet service provider (ISP) that hosted control servers at McColo were shut down by Global Crossing and Hurricane Electric. McColo, a rogue network provider based in San Jose, was a known malware and botnet trafficking site. Half the world's spam came from this location. McColo's servers regained connection to the Internet for several hours, which allowed the botnet to transfer control to other servers somewhere in Russia, according to Trend Micro.

The botnet was finally taken down on March 16, 2011, by a consolidated effort from a consortium of company experts during Operation b107. The consortium consisted of Microsoft, Pfizer, FireEye, the University of Washington, the Netherland Police Agency, and CNCERT/CC, a Chinese security response organization. These coordinated efforts allowed the U.S. Marshal's Service to seize over 26 core servers in seven U.S. cities (Chicago, Columbus, Dallas, Denver, Kansas City, Scranton, and Seattle) along with two overseas locations. Internet providers were then able to block access to the ISP ranges used to control this spamming barrage. Because most of Rustock's servers were located within the United States, it evaded most detection efforts, which typically focused on intercepting overseas traffic.

Steven A. Quillman

See also: Botnet; Cyber Crime; Malware; Russian Business Network (RBN)

Further Reading

Bright, Peter. "How Operation b107 Decapitated the Rustock Botnet." *ARS Technica*, March 22, 2011.

Goodin, Dan. "Dead Network Provider Arms Rustock Botnet from the Hereafter: McColo Dials Russia as World Sleeps." *The Register*, November 18, 2008.

Krebs, Brian. "Host of Internet Spam Groups Is Cut Off." *Washington Post*, November 12, 2008.

Lanstein, Alex. "An Overview of Rustock." FireEye, March 19, 2011. https://www.fireeye.com/blog/threat-research/2011/03/an-overview-of-rustock.html.

SECOND ARMY/ARMY CYBER COMMAND

The U.S. Army Cyber Command (ARCYBER) was established in 2010 to centralize cyber warfare and information operations activities in an "operational level of war" command. ARCYBER functions as an operational army force reporting directly to the chief of staff of the army (CSA) at Headquarters, Department of the Army (HQDA). At the direction of the secretary of defense, the secretary of the army assigned ARCYBER to U.S. Strategic Command (USSTRATCOM) to function as the Army Force Component Headquarters of U.S. Army Cyber Command (ARCYBER). ARCYBER directs and conducts integrated electronic warfare, information, and cyber-space operations as authorized or directed. The mission of ARCYBER is to ensure freedom of action in and through cyber space and to deny freedom of action in and through cyber space to adversaries of the United States and its allies.

In 2014, the Second Army was reactivated, and its assigned elements comprise an army force retained by and assigned to the secretary of the army in accordance with Title 10, U.S. Code (USC), to carry out the "man, train and equip" functions assigned to the secretary of the army. Second Army is a direct reporting unit of the HQDA chief information officer in the execution of administrative, policy, management, architecture, and compliance responsibilities as delineated in applicable USC.

The commanding general, ARCYBER, and Second Army have headquarters elements at Fort Belvoir, VA; Fort Meade, MD; and Fort Gordon, GA. Subordinate units reporting directly to the commanding general are the Joint Force Headquarters–Cyber (JFHQ-C), Fort Gordon, GA; Network Enterprise Technology Command (NETCOM), Fort Huachuca, AZ; 780th Military Intelligence Brigade (MI BDE), Fort Meade, MD; First Information Operations (IO) Command (Land), Fort Belvoir, VA; and U.S. Army Cyber Protection Brigade (BDE), Fort Gordon, GA. NETCOM's mission is to install, engineer, operate, and defend army network capabilities; 780th MI BDE's mission is to conduct signals intelligence (SIGINT), execute computer network operations (CNO), enable dynamic computer network defense (CND), and achieve operational effects in support of army, combatant command and Department of Defense (DoD) operations; the mission of First IO Command (Land) is to provide deployable support teams, opposing forces support, reach-back planning and analysis, and specialized training, and the Cyber Protection BDE's mission is to evaluate and respond to unexpected and dynamic cyber situations; defend the nation in response to hostile action and imminent cyber threats; conduct global cyber-space operations to deter, disrupt, and defeat adversary's cyber-space efforts; and defend the United States through specialized cyber support missions. In 2014, the U.S. Army Cyber School was unveiled at Fort Gordon, with a mission to provide specialized training to build a highly skilled cyber effects and electronic warfare workforce. Soon after the opening of the cyber school, the U.S. Army Cyber Branch was established as a basic branch of the army, the first new army branch to be created since Special Forces in 1987.

Jeffrey R. Cares

See also: Department of Defense (DoD); U.S. Coast Guard Cyber Command (CGCYBER); U.S. Cyber Command (USCYBERCOM); U.S. Tenth Fleet

Further Reading

Brenner, Joel. *America the Vulnerable: Inside the New Threat Matrix of Digital Espionage, Crime, and Warfare.* New York: Penguin Press, 2011.

SECOND LIFE

Second Life is an online virtual community launched in 2003 by Linden Laboratories of San Francisco, California. Within a decade of its launch, Second Life had approximately 1 million regular users, *regular users* being defined as someone who logs into the system almost daily. Second Life is not classified as a game, as there is no scoring system, enforced competition, or objectives provided for users. Rather, Second Life users define how they will choose to interact with their online world.

Linden Laboratories and third-party providers have created a free set of programs to allow access to Second Life. Members of the Second Life community, who call themselves *residents*, build virtual representations of themselves (avatars) and then proceed to interact with other users, locations, and objects within the Second Life world. They can purchase access to virtual objects and property, which can be traded within the Second Life world, and avatars can also be used to build new content. Within the Second Life community, there is a virtual currency, Linden Dollars, that can be exchanged with a variety of real-world currencies.

One of the revolutionary aspects of this network is the ability to use an included three-dimensional modeling utility to allow the construction of virtual objects by residents of Second Life. Those objects can be programmed to interact with avatars through the incorporation of Linden Scripting Language commands. Users are allowed to copyright their creations within Second Life, a fact that has allowed some residents to develop lucrative businesses within the Second Life community.

Second Life has become an increasingly popular form of social media for real-world institutions. For example, many colleges, universities, and libraries have used Second Life as an outreach platform. Those organizations have often recreated their real-world physical structures in the Second Life world and then encouraged residents to visit and interact with their unique resources and collections. Similarly, artistic communities in Second Life have created virtual adaptions of art exhibits, music performances, and live theater. Sporting leagues within the Second Life platform offer a wide variety of competitive opportunities for residents so inclined.

One unique location within Second Life is Diplomacy Island. The Maldives was the first country to formally open an embassy within Second Life, and they were soon joined by a Swedish embassy. Other nations have begun to follow suit. These locations allow users to interact with computer-based "ambassadors" to discuss visas, trade inquiries, and other international issues. The embassies also offer an opportunity for host nations to promote their tourism industries and educate others about their culture.

Not surprisingly, religious organizations quickly grasped the outreach potential offered by a Second Life presence. An Egyptian Web site, Islam Online, purchased territory in Second Life to recreate the sacred Hajj in virtual form, allowing would-be pilgrims to inquire about specific challenges faced on the trip to Mecca. Several major Christian churches have established campuses in Second Life, and they encourage members from around the world to attend virtual services.

Military forces from around the world have also begun to use Second Life as a recruitment and outreach tool. In particular, countries that heavily recruit outside of their own borders have found Second Life to be a useful tool for contacting potential servicemembers. Intelligence agencies have also begun to use Second Life as a potential means to harvest information from global users, often through the practice of social engineering. Scientific communities have experimented with Second Life as a potential collaborative platform, bringing together interested researchers to coordinate efforts on specific projects and holding virtual conferences to exchange new concepts.

Jeffrey R. Cares

See also: Internet; Social Engineering

Further Reading

Boellstorff, Tom. *Coming of Age in Second Life: An Anthropologist Explores the Virtually Human.* Princeton, NJ: Princeton University Press, 2008.

Malaby, Thomas M. *Making Virtual Worlds: Linden Lab and Second Life.* Ithaca, NY: Cornell University Press, 2009.

SERVER

A server is a network computer that stores information and executes tasks for clients. Tasks may include access to Web sites, file retrieval, and e-mail services. One particularly important example of server technology is the Domain Name System (DNS), which searches various name servers for Internet Protocol (IP) addresses. Shopping cart technology, which enables secure electronic commerce (e-commerce), is another example of server software. Servers are also used to control functions on a local area network (LAN), such as printing.

The terms *host* and *server* are often used synonymously, but not all hosts are servers. Servers are often distinguished by their specialized functions (such as a name server or commerce server) and their ability to share workloads with clients. This distribution of tasks reduces network traffic and requires less processing power. The client-server relationship is considered a technological advance from the terminal-host relationship, in which a host computer performs all the work as directed by the user through a terminal.

Client-server technology developed in the 1980s, as the expanded use of personal computers (PCs) and LANs increased user capabilities and created a need for more efficient networking processes. Novell's Netware 2.0 operating system, released in 1985, helped standardize this new concept.

Christopher G. Marquis

See also: Authentication; Domain Name System (DNS); E-commerce; Encryption; Software; Tier 1 Internet Service Provider

Further Reading

Jansen, Erin. *NetLingo: The Internet Dictionary.* Ojai, CA: NetLingo, Inc. 2002.
Moschovitis, Christos J. P., Hilary Poole, Tami Schuyler, Theresa M. Senft. *History of the Internet: A Chronology, 1843 to the Present.* Santa Barbara, CA: ABC-CLIO, 1999.

SHAMOON VIRUS

The Shamoon virus is a self-replicating modular computer virus that was discovered in August 2012 by Seculert, Kaspersky Lab, and Symantec Corporation. Shamoon appears to be a program designed primarily for cyber sabotage. The virus affects both Microsoft Windows client and server-based machines and is spread from one infected computer to another within the network. According to Symantec, the virus contains three components: a dropper, a wiper, and a reporter. The dropper is the primary component that initiates the copying and execution of itself as well as embedding the other components into the system. The wiper is the destructive component that deletes files and overwrites files with corrupted JPEG images. The reporter transmits the virus information back to the attacker. The virus basically renders the infected computer systems unusable.

The virus appears to only attack energy companies. The most notable attacks were on Saudi Aramco, the Saudi Arabian national oil company, and RasGas, a natural gas company in Qatar. The Saudi Aramco attack occurred on August 15, 2012, and infected approximately 30,000 computers, while the RasGas attack occurred on August 27, 2012. Both companies spent over a week restoring their services. A group calling itself Cutting Sword of Justice claimed responsibility for the attack on Saudi Armaco, although it appears that a disgruntled Aramco employee initiated the attack.

Steven A. Quillman

See also: Aramco Attack; Cyber Sabotage; Malware

Further Reading

Springer, Paul J. *Cyber Warfare: A Reference Handbook.* Santa Barbara, CA: ABC-CLIO, 2015.
Zetter, Kim. "Qatari Gas Company Hit with Virus in Wave of Attacks on Energy Companies." *Wired,* August 30, 2012.

SILK ROAD

Silk Road is the name of the online black market Web site launched in 2011 by creator Ross William Ulbricht, known by the pseudonym "Dread Pirate Roberts." Silk Road was notorious for allowing individuals to purchase illicit or illegal substances and items without fear of being discovered by law enforcement. The name is derived from the ancient Silk Road, which connected the Asian continent to the Middle East, Africa, and Europe.

The cyber Silk Road was hidden from investigators on what is known as the *dark web*. Silk Road used the Onion Router (TOR) to protect the identity of those visiting the site by using techniques that stop investigators' ability to trace Internet traffic back to users. TOR is able to hide the identity of individuals by weaving their connection over the Internet through multiple servers; thereby making any attempt to trace back useless, as there is no clear point of origin.

Additionally, users paid using Bitcoin, an electronic currency. Bitcoin is a decentralized and virtual currency that is unable to be traced back to the buyer. Shoppers on the Silk Road exchanged their individual currency online for Bitcoins. Therefore, when consumers made a purchase, the only record of exchange showed a transaction of cyber monies.

In October 2013, the Federal Bureau of Investigation (FBI) discovered, and gained control over, the administrative server for Silk Road. Afterward, they were able to seize control of the marketplace and forced the site out of business, although similar sites have emerged to fill the vacuum left by its closure.

Jason R. Kluk

See also: Bitcoin; Cyber Crime; Dark Web; Federal Bureau of Investigation (FBI); The Onion Router (TOR)

Further Reading

Chander, Anupam. *The Electronic Silk Road: How the Web Binds the World Together in Commerce.* New Haven, CT: Yale University Press, 2013.
Libicki, Martin. *Cyberspace in Peace and War.* Annapolis, MD: U.S. Naval Institute Press, 2016.

SIPRNET

The Secret Internet Protocol Router Network (SIPRNet) is a computer network maintained and used by the Department of Defense (DoD) and other government agencies to transmit information classified at the "Secret" level. In addition to secure communications via e-mail, SIPRNet is capable of hypertext document access and video teleconferencing. Because SIPRNet is designed for the transmission of classified materials, access to the network is strictly controlled. Users must hold an appropriate security clearance and can only work on certain computer terminals capable of accessing the network. The hardware required for SIPRNet access is provided by the users' organizations and is unique to the network.

Like the unclassified NIPRNet and the "Top Secret" JWICS network, SIPRNet allows for the centralized control of cyber-security issues and enterprise-level responses to cyber threats. Transfer of materials onto and off of the SIPRNet requires adherence to a set of formal security protocols designed to prevent the loss of classified data. Materials from the SIPRNet were included in Bradley Manning's massive 2010 leak of classified materials to WikiLeaks. SIPRNet has been exposed to malware on at least one occasion, an event that demonstrated that the network possessed insufficient internal security measures, meaning that once the network had been penetrated, the malware spread very rapidly throughout SIPRNet.

SIPRNet operates at a lower transmission speed than NIPRNet, largely due to the requirements of security considerations. The centralized security system allows for rapid responses to cyber threats. Nevertheless, SIPRNet is the key mechanism for operational planning and other day-to-day DoD communications activities. SIPRNet supports the Global Command and Control System (GCCS) and the Defense Message System (DMS), each of which are vital to daily military operations.

Jeffrey R. Cares

See also: ARPANET; Cyber Defense; Department of Defense (DoD); Domain Name Server; JWICS Network; NIPRNet

Further Reading

Brenner, Joel. *America the Vulnerable: Inside the New Threat Matrix of Digital Espionage, Crime, and Warfare.* New York: Penguin Press, 2011.

SNOWDEN, EDWARD J.

Edward J. Snowden (1983–) is a former Central Intelligence Agency (CIA) employee and U.S. government contractor. His revelation of classified and other information that he obtained as part of his interactions with the U.S. intelligence community generated a great deal of attention around the world. This information involved areas of intrusion on the privacy of individuals and organizations in the United States and digital and computer security and led to a vigorous debate across the globe on these issues. This debate continues today. Snowden fled the country in anticipation that he would face prosecution for his unauthorized actions and traveled to Russia, where he was first granted a year of temporary asylum and then, in August 2014, three years of formal residency in Russia. Documents collected under questionable circumstances continue to be released by Snowden and his contacts among journalists around the world. These documents describe a variety of secret and largely unaccountable practices across the domestic and international intelligence community.

Born on June 21, 1983, in Elizabeth City, North Carolina, Snowden was raised in an upper-middle-class family. His father, Lonnie Snowden, was an officer in the U.S. Coast Guard, and his mother, Elizabeth B. Snowden, was a court official and, as of this writing, serves as the chief deputy at the U.S. District Court for the

Judicial District of Maryland. When Snowden was in high school, he contracted mononucleosis and was unable to attend school for more than eight months. He did not return to high school, but instead completed the General Equivalency Diploma (GED) examination and then attended but did not graduate from Anne Arundel Community College in Maryland. He has also completed work toward a master's degree through an online program at the University of Liverpool in the United Kingdom.

Snowden enlisted in the U.S. Army Reserve, but he was discharged from the program after breaking both legs in a training accident. Later, he worked for less than a year as a security guard at the University of Maryland's Center for Advanced Study of Language at the university's College Park, Maryland, campus. After attending a job fair, where he described himself as a "computer wizard," Snowden was hired by the CIA in the global communications division at CIA headquarters in Langley, Virginia. His responsibilities included monitoring the security status of agency computers and participating in the creation of programs to protect the security of data collected and generated across the CIA's areas of responsibility.

During his work first with the CIA and then with various contractor organizations, Snowden discovered that the CIA and other arms of the U.S. intelligence community were operating in ways that he found morally and ethically questionable. As early as 2009, Snowden began collecting "Top Secret" documents to support his beliefs while working as a contractor for the Dell Computer Corporation. This document collection continued as Snowden proceeded through a variety of assignments, where he was exposed to more detailed information regarding these practices, which he found objectionable. The documents eventually became part of a series of files that Snowden produced on practices that he found invasive and disturbing.

Snowden was able to collect this information as a result of his various assignments in the CIA and later when he was transferred to the National Security Agency (NSA). It was at the NSA that he collected the bulk of the material that would later be released as part of his unauthorized disclosures on the practices of these agencies. In May of 2013, Snowden told his NSA employers that he needed a leave of absence for treatment of epilepsy and flew to Hong Kong, China, where he had arranged a meeting with journalists from *The Guardian*, a prominent newspaper in the United Kingdom, and a filmmaker, Laura Poitras, to begin the process of releasing the documents he had collected. Poitras's documentary on his story, called *Citizen Four*, won the Academy Award for Best Documentary for 2015, and did much to publicize Snowden's justification for his actions. When *The Guardian* published the first of his documents, he sought and eventually received temporary asylum in Russia rather than return to the United States, where he would almost certainly have faced charges for the unauthorized release of classified information.

The documents supplied to the press by Snowden show that the U.S. intelligence community and its partners around the world, including agencies of the United Kingdom, Israel, and Germany, among others, indicate that these agencies are involved in mass surveillance of U.S. citizens domestically and around the world. This surveillance is conducted without the required warrants and in the absence of probable cause; much of the data appeared to be the sort of routine records that are produced when people use computers, fixed and mobile phones, and other devices to communicate with each other. The surveillance goes well beyond that which might be performed for legitimate law enforcement or counterterrorism purposes and includes collection of data from civilian organizations, such as cell phone service providers, in situations that are removed from any demonstrable intelligence value or purpose. These disclosures have caused U.S. officials to admit a need for investigation and greater transparency in the intelligence-gathering activities of the U.S. government. They have also been deeply embarrassing to U.S. officials, who, while appearing to support the requirements of the U.S. Constitution with regard to permissible searches and seizures, have permitted the warrantless gathering of private data to continue.

Snowden's accounts of policy abuses in the NSA and other arms of the U.S. intelligence community are not without confirmation. In 2016, *The Guardian* published an account of a former assistant inspector general at the Pentagon, John Crane, who, like Snowden, had concerns about certain practices of the intelligence agencies he was associated with. Crane attempted to bring his concerns about what he felt were wasteful, illegal, and unconstitutional actions by the NSA, but he found that the system in place to address such concerns was not productive. He then forwarded his concerns to members of the U.S. Congress and initiated a whistle-blower complaint to the Pentagon's Inspector General's office under the understanding that his identity would not be revealed. The Inspector General's office subsequently revealed Crane's identity to the Justice Department, and a criminal prosecution against him was started. Crane was charged with 10 felony counts of espionage. The charges were eventually dropped, but Crane was professionally ruined. He resigned from the NSA in January 2013.

According to Snowden, Crane's experience demonstrated inadequacies in the checks and balances in the NSA and support his claim that these checks and balances were likewise inadequate to protect him had he pursued his grievances through existing channels. Snowden has stated that these problems illustrate the insincerity of the claims of a variety of U.S. officials, including President Barack Obama and Secretary of State Hillary Clinton, that Snowden's grievances would have been heard and protections against recriminations provided had he made use of the avenues available to employees of the intelligence agencies of the United States. Snowden has subsequently called for a complete overhaul in the whistle-blower protections available to those in the U.S. intelligence community to protect those who seek to expose wrongdoing.

After a year of temporary asylum in Russia, Snowden was granted three years' formal residency there, starting in August 2014, and documents from his collection continue to be published. These documents reveal a variety of secret and unaccountable practices across the domestic and international intelligence community. Attempts to extradite Snowden from his asylum in Russia have so far been unsuccessful. Vladimir Putin, a former intelligence agent himself, has stated unequivocally that Russia will take no part in Snowden's return to the United States, but he also made it clear that he did not wish for Snowden's presence in Russia to further damage relations with the United States. According to Putin, if Snowden wishes to remain in Russia, he must refrain from causing additional harm to the United States. What actions would constitute harm, however, were not specified, and this statement has not stopped the continued release of Snowden's documents. The controversy continues as of this writing. Meanwhile, at least 19 proposals for legislative reform of the intelligence community's practices are pending in the U.S. Congress.

A subject of debate that continues, Snowden has variously been called a hero, a whistle-blower, a dissident, and a traitor. His disclosures continue to fuel intense public interest and serious concerns about mass surveillance, government secrecy, and the balance that should exist between information privacy and national security in a free society. In the summer of 2013, the U.S. Department of Justice unsealed charges against Snowden under the Espionage Act of 1917 that are pending.

Mary Lynn Bartlett

See also: Central Intelligence Agency (CIA); Cyber Espionage; National Security Agency (NSA); PRISM Program; United States Cyber Capabilities

Further Reading

Fidler, David P., ed. *The Snowden Reader.* Bloomington, IN: Indiana University Press, 2015.

Gellman, Barton. *Dark Mirror: Edward Snowden and the Surveillance State.* London: Penguin, 2016.

Greenwald, Glenn. *No Place to Hide: Edward Snowden, the NSA, and the U.S. Surveillance State.* New York: Metropolitan Books, 2014.

Harding, Luke. *The Snowden Files: The Inside Story of the World's Most Wanted Man.* New York: Vintage Books, 2014.

SOCIAL ENGINEERING

Social engineering is the deliberate study, manipulation, and use of a target's social context, values, and interests to elicit desired behavior. The use of cognitive biases—the expectations people have about the social contract, markers of authority, trust, and personal vanity—to provoke actions far predates the social science that labeled them and is a key component of salesmanship, politics, police work, and religion, although in its most exploitative form it is the basis of confidence games, psychic cold readings and financial scams. Traditional social engineering most often takes place in person, with a premium placed on the ability of the practitioner to read the visual and social clues of a situation and use them, and requires significant social skills and the ability to operate in a complex interpersonal situation without being caught or exposed.

In a 21st-century world of information security, social engineering is a much broader practice of exploitation to gain access to private information or secured networks for the purpose of illicit or illegal use. Some plans still require personal contact and may be schemes to walk past security in a building by wearing the uniform of an expected package delivery service or convincing a receptionist that the intruder needs access to a phone or a restroom. Organizations that do not dispose of confidential materials properly can be exploited by a determined dumpster diver. Other plans that take advantage of physical proximity may include leaving flash drives in employee spaces, labeled in ways that make it hard for people to resist plugging them into their work computers and thus exposing the network to viruses and hacking. A skilled social engineer can also often get targets to reveal key information about themselves in person by signing them up for prizes, surveys, or petitions, all of which is just a continuation of the traditional skill set of con men.

Internet access opened new vistas for social engineering. The relative newness of the technology and the open availability of massive amounts of personal information have been a boon for scammers, hackers, and thieves. People who take steps to protect their person and property face-to-face are often not attuned to the dangers posed by downloading online games, answering "fun" quizzes that ask for the personal data most likely to be answers to security challenges (childhood address, grandparents' names, high school mascots, etc.), or friending strangers in chat rooms and on social media. Phishing attacks play on the assumed authority of banks and organizations like eBay to threaten people that their accounts are under suspension, panicking recipients, who then lose their account numbers and logins to scammers. The relatively low cost of sending thousands of e-mails promising love with exotic partners or fortunes lost in the Nigerian civil war makes the handful of responses worthwhile to online social engineers who will work the mark over an extended period of time for money and access. Additionally, an experienced social engineer can quickly find background on targets' political and religious beliefs, family, location, and hobbies with ease, thanks to the ubiquity of apps like Foursquare, Facebook, Twitter, and Yelp. A target can then be lured into downloading a coupon for a favorite restaurant, going to a chat room for a niche hobby, or even approached in person once faux commonalities are established with this information.

Because skillful social engineering exploits intimate vulnerabilities, it is very difficult to prevent. Information-security training may mean little to the receptionist who lets in the interloper who makes friendly small talk and asks to leave a package on a "friend's" desk or to the person so excited about free tickets to a favorite event that he clicks on a suspect link and is then too embarrassed to report it to IT. Security firms can conduct tests of an organization's security, but the myriad opportunities for socially engineered attacks are endlessly adaptable and require an enormous investment in training, empowering employees to refuse to obey people they don't know and creating a desire to protect company data. Individual people, even those who consider themselves technology savvy or wise to scams, probably have some bias or blind spot that can be exploited by a clever and determined opponent. In a world of technological warfare and security, social engineering assures that human error and habits remain a vulnerability and opportunity.

Margaret D. Sankey

See also: Authentication; Hacker; Phishing; Spear Phishing

Further Reading

Hadnagy, Christopher. *Social Engineering: The Art of Human Hacking.* Indianapolis, IN: Wiley, 2011.

Russell, Ryan. *Hack Proofing Your Network: Internet Tradecraft.* Rockland, MD: Syngress, 2000.

Verma, Nina. *Social Engineering: A Means to Violate a Computer System.* New Delhi, India: Global Vision Pub. House, 2011.

SOFTWARE

Computer software is composed of encoded information in programmed form. It can be used to supply a computer with commands, or it can supply information or functions to the computer user. Software, in contrast to computer hardware, has no physical form and, as such, requires computer hardware to function. In the same fashion, computer hardware that is not equipped with software has no utility to a user. Computer software comes in many forms, including computer programs, informational libraries, documentation systems, and digital media. Sophisticated computer programs have been written that are capable of devising less-complex programs without the intervention of a human programmer.

The most basic form of software is executable code that provides machine language instructions for a computer processor. Most machine languages consist of binary value groups that can change a computer's status from a preceding state. These instructions can be used to change the information stored on a central processing unit, which would not be directly observable by the user, or it might change the value of anything provided on the computer display for the user. Typically, a processor carries out the instructions provided in the order received, although it is possible to program the processor to jump from one point in the program to another.

The vast majority of software is created in high-level programming languages that are far more efficient for programmers and then translated via compilers or interpreters into a form more easily used by a machine. It is possible, although time-consuming, to produce software directly in a low-level programming language, which then allows a faster translation to machine language using an assembler, but such approaches are relatively rare.

Jeffrey R. Cares

See also: Hardware; Malware

Further Reading

Clarke, Richard A., and Robert K. Knake. *Cyber War: The Next Threat to National Security and What to Do about It.* New York: HarperCollins, 2010.

SOLAR SUNRISE

Solar Sunrise is the code name for a series of cyber attacks on networks of the U.S. Department of Defense (DoD) by three individuals exploiting a well-known operating system vulnerability from February 1 to February 26, 1998. The name came from the operating system being used by the DoD, Sun Microsystem's Solaris.

This system's vulnerabilities allowed the hackers to gain access to government networks. The hackers, two California teenagers and their teenage Israeli mentor, used moderately sophisticated tools to probe the system for its vulnerabilities. Once the weaknesses were determined, they implanted a program to gather data from unclassified network computers. They later returned to retrieve the collected data. Targeting key parts of the defense network, the attacks compromised over 500 computer systems and acquired hundreds of network passwords. Fortunately, the government reported that no classified data was removed.

The investigation into the Solar Sunrise attacks showed the difficulty of quickly identifying the originators of cyber attacks. The U.S. Air Force's Information Warfare Center in San Antonio, Texas, picked up several unauthorized intrusions. The newly established National Infrastructure Protection Center (NIPC) headed a multiagency investigation to identify those responsible. Some initially believed that Russia perpetrated the DoD attacks. Initial intrusions were first tracked to Abu Dhabi in the United Arab Emirates. As the attack occurred during a period of international instability over weapons inspections, some U.S. government officials believed that the intrusions into the networks were the work of Iraq or its sympathizers. Misidentifying the real perpetrator or acting on unproved suspicions is a real danger in responding to cyber attacks.

The attacks raised the question that if they had been perpetrated by another nation-state, how could the United States have responded? What would have been an appropriate response? Could attacks like Solar Sunrise directed by a nation-state or nonstate organizations be defined as acts of war? Identifying the perpetrators and their possible sponsors remains a major difficulty.

The DoD had not determined the implications of these attacks before larger attacks occurred. At least 11 additional attacks had the same profile. Attacks were widespread and appeared to come from sites in Israel, the United Arab Emirates, France, Taiwan, and Germany. The Moonlight Maze attack was more extensive and was not uncovered for approximately two years, after it had compromised over 2 million computers, including systems in the Pentagon, U.S. Department of Energy (DOE), and the Command Center of Space and Naval War Systems (SPAWAR). Investigations led to accusations of involvement by Russia and the Moscow Science Academy.

The success of these attacks and additional similar attacks against the air force, navy, and Marine Corps computers worldwide that contained a similar signature demonstrated the danger associated with the government and the military using commercial off-the-shelf software systems (COTS). While the use of COTS lowers procurement costs, the products are developed by multinational corporations with programmers who may have anti-American allegiances. COTS allow the government to keep up with continuing developments, and the systems come with training and documentation to educate users. In addition, new hires can come in with some experience with the operating system if it is used in other areas and industries.

Lori Ann Henning

See also: Advanced Persistent Threat (APT); Hacker; Moonlight Maze; Tenenbaum, Ehud "Udi"

Further Reading

Anderson, Robert H, and Richard O. Hundley. "The Implication of COTS Vulnerabilities for the DoD and Critical U.S. Infrastructure: What Can/Should the DoD Do?" Santa Monica, CA: RAND, 1998.

Binnendijk, Hans, ed. *Transforming America's Military*. Washington, D.C.: National Defense University Press, 2002.

Springer, Paul J. *Cyber Warfare: A Reference Handbook*. Santa Barbara, CA: ABC-CLIO, 2015.

SOLID-STATE DRIVE (SSD)

Solid state refers to electronic circuitry that is constructed completely out of semiconductors. Solid-state drives (SSD) store data on interconnected flash memory chips. Unlike hard disk drives (HDD) that are magnetic, SSDs do not have any moving parts. Data is stored in erasable and rewriteable circuitry. They are not the same as the flash memory used in USB thumb drives. Both the type of memory and speed are different. SSDs use less power than HDDs, allowing for faster data access, cooler running temperatures, and more reliability. Computers with SSD can boot in seconds, do not have a problem with fragmentation, and are quieter than computers with HDD. SSDs also can be built smaller, making them lighter than more traditional hard drives. SSDs are more durable because they are nonmechanical, and they are less likely to be damaged by being dropped. The disadvantages of SSDs are that they have a limited life span and they are more expensive per GB than HDDs. The increased usage of SSD started in the late 2000s, during the rise of netbooks, but they still remain an expensive choice.

SSDs may also have a security issue. Erasing data from SSDs can be difficult, if not impossible. Researchers at the University of California, San Diego, Non-Volatile Systems Laboratory (NVSL) have questioned the ability to erase data on SSDs. With HDD, overwriting memory locations is not a problem. SSDs with flash memory must have each location erased before reusing. HDD protocols may not work, and magnets are ineffective. Computers' built-in sanitizing commands are not reliable, overwriting the entire visible address space has poor results, and degaussing has no effect. While encrypted SSDs' data can be made useless if the encryption key is deleted, the same problem remains with successfully and confidentially deleting the locations where the encryption key was stored. It may not be possible at this time to successfully destroy the data on a SSD without physically destroying the circuitry.

Lori Ann Henning

See also: Encryption; Hardware

Further Reading

Parsons, June Jamrich, and Dan Oja. *New Perspectives on Computer Concepts: Brief.* Boston, MA: Course Technology, 2014.

Wei, Michael, Laura M. Grupp, Frederick E. Spada, and Steven Swanson. "Reliably Erasing Data from Flash-based Solid State Drives." *Proceedings of the 9th USENIX Conference on File and Storage Technologies*, 2011.

SONY HACK

The Sony Hack was a November 2014 incident whereby hackers from the Democratic People's Republic of Korea (North Korea) launched an attack against the servers of Sony Pictures Entertainment in Los Angeles, California. The hackers sought to prevent the release of the comedy film *The Interview*, which depicted the assassination of North Korean leader Kim Jong-un.

Prior to the attack, Sony poorly protected its networks from intrusion. It is believed that the hackers first accessed Sony's network in September 2014. Over the next two months, the hackers eventually granted themselves administrator privileges that provided unlimited access to the company's network. Subsequently, the hackers then downloaded significant amounts of critical information from the servers without attracting notice because Sony encrypted almost none of its data. In addition, the hackers slowly copied the data from Sony servers to their own to hide the file transfers among Sony's legitimate data traffic.

The company learned of the breach on November 24, 2014, when a short video from a group calling itself the Guardians of Peace played on Sony's networked computers. Soon after, the hacker's malware erased data on approximately half of Sony's computers and servers and also caused Sony's network to crash. For many weeks afterward, Sony conducted business with very little network connectivity as technicians scrubbed the infected machines. This led company employees to conduct business through in-person meetings, hard copy communications, and even by reactivating obsolete computers and Blackberry smartphones held in storage. Eventually, Sony built an entirely new network with much tougher security protocols. It is estimated that the direct effects of the attack cost Sony $41 million in the months that followed, not including any potential lawsuits stemming from the release of personal information.

On November 29, journalists received e-mails from the Guardians of Peace that linked to more than 100 terabytes of information. Seven more leaks of data occurred in the days and weeks that followed. The hackers released significant amounts of sensitive company data, including employee records and e-mails between producers and high-ranking studio executives. The e-mails proved especially embarrassing to the company's leadership, as they revealed personal and creative disagreements as well as pay disparities among top actors and actresses. WikiLeaks eventually made much of this data available for download. The hackers also released digital copies of unreleased Sony films to the Web for illegal distribution by torrent sites, potentially costing the studio millions of dollars in revenue. The fallout from the attack also cost shareholders, as the company's stock price fell more than 10 percent in late 2014. In addition, the hack also contributed to Sony Motion Pictures Group cochairperson Amy Pascal's decision to step down from her position in early 2015.

On December 16, the Guardians of Peace sent a cryptic e-mail implying that theaters showing *The Interview* would suffer attacks like those of September 11, 2001. As a result, many theater chains soon announced that they had dropped the film from their release schedules. Sony CEO Michael Lynton sought to cancel *The

Interview because of the threats, but a public backlash, including critical remarks from President Barack Obama, caused Sony to reverse course. Many independent theaters went forward with plans to release the film as scheduled on Christmas Day. Sony also released *The Interview* for digital download on Christmas Eve. *The Interview* grossed $40 million from the limited release and digital downloads, but the film's lack of a wide release to theater chains meant that it failed to recoup the company's investment.

Initially, many speculated that a disgruntled employee had caused the Sony Hack. On December 19, 2014, the Federal Bureau of Investigation (FBI) publicly attributed the attack to North Korea.

Ryan Wadle

See also: Cyber Crime; Cyber Espionage; Dark Web; Malware; North Korea Cyber Capabilities; Patriotic Hacking; The Onion Router (TOR); Torrent; WikiLeaks

Further Reading

Elkind, Peter. "Inside the Hack of the Century." *Fortune*, July 1, 2015. http://fortune.com /sony-hack-part-1.

Hess, Amanda. "Inside the Sony Hack." *Slate*, November 22, 2015. http://www.slate.com /articles/technology/users/2015/11/sony_employees_on_the_hack_one_year_later .single.html.

Libicki, Martin. *Cyberspace in Peace and War.* Annapolis, MD: U.S. Naval Institute Press, 2016.

Seal, Mark. "An Exclusive Look at Sony's Hacking Saga." *Vanity Fair*, March 2015. http:// www.vanityfair.com/hollywood/2015/02/sony-hacking-seth-rogen-evan-goldberg.

SPEAR PHISHING

Spear phishing is a form of social-engineering attack, whereby targeted communications, typically over the Internet, seek to influence the recipient into undertaking an action that is to the attacker's benefit (and usually to the recipient's detriment). Although such attacks most commonly take place over e-mail, almost any other form of online communications may be (and usually has been) used, including social-networking sites, Web forums, chat, voice/phone calls, and even removal media such as compact flash USB drives. In contrast to e-mail spam, spear phishing attacks are personalized to the recipient, using information that may be gleaned from a variety of sources, such as social networks, and may impersonate a personal or professional acquaintance or family member. Typical goals for spear phishing attacks include convincing the target to reveal financial or other personal information (such as credit card numbers) or access credentials (such as passwords), installing malicious software posing as legitimate or required; or undertaking an action that will subvert the security of the target's system (e.g., set a password to a known value, or open a document that contains an exploit for a vulnerability in the corresponding document reader).

Spear phishing attacks have been prevalent in the past few years. This is primarily because of their relative ease and flexibility, compared to alternatives such as server-side software exploitation. A second advantage to using such attacks is that they target a part of an organization's IT infrastructure (user devices such as desktop computers) that is more challenging to secure and offers more opportunities for attackers to hide and persist because of less uniformity and higher unpredictability stemming from their direct interaction with users.

Angelos D. Keromytis

See also: Hacker; Phishing; Social Engineering

Further Reading

Hadnagy, Christopher. *Social Engineering: The Art of Human Hacking.* Indianapolis, IN: Wiley, 2011.

Verma, Nina. *Social Engineering: A Means to Violate a Computer System.* New Delhi, India: Global Vision Pub. House, 2011.

SPOOFING

Spoofing is a category of cyber attack in which the attackers disguise themselves to convince the targets to give them access to their systems or data. Spoofing attacks vary widely in their methods and levels of technological sophistication.

The most common type of spoofing attack is Internet Protocol (IP) spoofing. IP spoofing alters the packets that a computer sends so that those packets appear to have been sent from a different machine. IP spoofing can be used to attack systems in several ways. The most common attack is the distributed denial-of-service (DDoS) attack. A DDoS attack floods the target with an overwhelming amount of information, slowing or shutting down the system. IP spoofing allows the attacker to both hide the source of the attack by making it appear to come from one or more different machines and to hinder efforts to defend the system by blocking information from particular IP addresses. Another common use of IP spoofing is to use it to defeat network-security measures that rely on authenticating IP addresses. By spoofing their IP addresses, the attacker can fool the security system into believing that the attacker has legitimate access to the network.

IP spoofing fools machines, but several types of spoofing target users. Phishing uses spoofed e-mail or social media accounts and messages to encourage recipients to disclose valuable personal or professional information. As anyone can set up an e-mail or social media account with any name, or pretend to be anyone within the contents of an e-mail or social media message, this type of spoofing is both easy and versatile. More technically sophisticated variants may use IP spoofing or other means to make it appear that phishing e-mails have come directly from the legitimate accounts or organizations they purport to be from.

Web spoofing is when an attacker creates a fraudulent Web site designed to get users to voluntarily enter the desired data. This may take the form of a phony log-in page for a real site, such as a bank or an e-mail account, where the user's information can then be used by the attacker. These spoofing techniques are often used in tandem for greater effectiveness.

While most spoofing efforts are targeted at personal computers, networks, or servers, similar principles can be used to attack other systems. Telephones and caller ID systems can be spoofed as well as GPS systems. As spoofing is a style of attack rather than a specific technique, it is almost endlessly variable and easily adapted to new systems or technologies.

Benjamin M. Schneider

See also: Distributed Denial-of-Service (DDoS) Attack; Phishing; Social Engineering; Spear Phishing; Trojan Horse

Further Reading

Lobo, Lancy, and Umesh Lakshman. *CCIE Security v4.0 Quick Reference.* Indianapolis, IN: Cisco Press, 2014.
Shostack, Adam. *Threat Modeling: Designing for Security.* Hoboken, NJ: John Wiley & Sons, 2014.
van der Linden, Maura A. *Testing Code Security.* Boca Raton, FL: CRC Press, 2007.

SPYWARE

Spyware is malicious computer software (malware) that is designed to surreptitiously collect information from a computer without the knowledge of the owner. It is also designed to collect information about the users of an infected computer and transmit the data to another computer user without consent. There are four primary types of spyware in common use: system monitors; Trojan horses; adware; and tracking cookies. The utilization of spyware can range from minor cyber criminals and vandals to state-sponsored espionage programs.

System monitors are programs that are created to collect information accessed on a host computer or input into the computer. The most common form of system monitors are keystroke loggers, which track every input into the system, copy it, and forward it to a third party. More sophisticated system monitors have proven capable of activating a target computer's camera or microphone as a means of eavesdropping on an unsuspecting user. Trojan horses are software programs that appear on the surface to be useful, or at least benign, but which contain hidden sections of malicious code. The most common form of Trojan horses attempts to establish vulnerabilities for later exploitation and, in some instances, may allow a malicious user to seize complete control over a victim's computer. Adware is spyware that observes a host computer's Internet activity and scans computer files to target advertisements more effectively. It can also be used as a means to display fraudulent advertisements. Tracking cookies are small programs that log and report a computer user's Internet behavior without the consent of the user being tracked.

Spyware has occasionally been inserted into genuine software. One example came from the Sony Corporation, which inserted spyware into music CDs that tracked the behavior of owners who loaded the music files onto their computers. Upon its discovery, Sony claimed that it had only used the software to combat digital piracy and illegal peer-to-peer sharing of content, but the spyware was demonstrated to have tracked all of the victims' activities online, not just their behavior regarding music files.

Spyware is not usually classified as a computer virus, as it is rarely designed to spread itself throughout a network. However, a small industry of antispyware software creators has emerged to combat the massive expansion of spyware. Because spyware is generally installed without the user's knowledge, it is considered malware and, as such, has been explicitly banned in some countries, but it continues to proliferate. In particular, spyware is common on illicit Web sites, where merely visiting a Web site can trigger an automatic download of the software.

Jeffrey R. Cares

See also: Cyber Attack; Hacker; Malware

Further Reading

Brenner, Joel. *America the Vulnerable: Inside the New Threat Matrix of Digital Espionage, Crime, and Warfare.* New York: Penguin Press, 2011.

SQL INJECTION

Structured Query Language (SQL) injection attacks append an SQL command to the end of a legitimate response within a form field. The programming accepts the command along with a user's response and executes the malicious code. Most interactive software applications use form fields to collect information from users. For example, form fields may be found at the Google homepage search, an Amazon product search, or vendors' credit card purchase information Web sites. In each case, an Internet user enters data for a search (i.e., a query), and the data is used to query a database and to return the requested information. This is only an Internet example; however, many commercial and residential software applications perform the same operations. The SQL injection adds a delimiter and a SQL command to the user's response. A delimiter such as a semicolon (;) indicates the beginning of a command. SQL procedures are unable to discriminate between user's response data, and these commands are executed as long as they contain a syntactically valid query. There is a misconception that SQL injections only affect the Microsoft SQL Servers, when, in fact, any database allowing multiple statements to run in the same connection is susceptible. Examples of other susceptible databases include Access, Oracle, and MySQL.

These attacks continue to be successful because of the ease of implementation and the dynamic, interactive access users have to databases. The functionality was first published in 1998, when a user with the screen name "Rain Forest Puppy" documented how easy they were to implement. Since then, user interaction with databases via Web site or user interfaces exponentially increased, and SQL injections have matured along with the countermeasures. For example, an

SQL injection successfully penetrated one of the world's leading software-security firms, Kaspersky Lab, in 2009. Many other successful attacks have occurred to compromise usernames and passwords, utilities' user accounts, and credit card information. While any information stored in a database can be compromised, most of these attacks are thwarted by software developers and information technology administrators.

The malicious code's success depends on the ability to get to the back-end database, so there are straightforward methods to defending against the attacks. Generally, there are four safeguards that may be put in place to significantly reduce the risk. First, type-safe SQL Parameters, an SQL Server tool, may be used to validate the type and length of data being received. This tool treats input as a literal value vice an executable code so that it is impervious to embedded SQL commands. Second, filters protect against SQL injections by removing escape and delimiter characters, such as the semicolon (;), from inputs. Third, multiple transaction SQL statements can be compiled into one execution plan, called a *stored procedure*. These stored procedures are less susceptible to manipulation when used along with filters or parameters. Finally, administrators should review their code for execution statements and error reporting to detect and mitigate successful attacks.

Paul Clemans

See also: Cyber Attack; Hacker; Malware; SQL Slammer Worm

Further Reading

Cherry, Denny. *Securing SQL Server: Protecting Your Database from Attackers.* New York: Syngress Publishing, 2015.

Clarke, Justin. *SQL Injection Attacks and Defense.* New York: Syngress Publishing, 2012.

SQL SLAMMER WORM

A worm is a computer virus that is designed to spread itself as quickly as possible to, in theory, move through entire networks. The power of destructive worms has only continued to grow. In 2003, the SQL Slammer worm was first detected as it rapidly spread through the World Wide Web. The virus required only 374 bytes, making it far too small to do anything truly damaging to an individual computer, other than using its memory and communications systems. However, it spread so quickly that it managed to shut down the entire global Internet for more than 12 hours. Essentially, each infected computer began sending copies of the virus as fast as possible, which in turn caused Internet routers to become overwhelmed by the traffic and crash. As each router crashed, it shifted the burden of transmissions onto other routers, putting an exponential number of routers at risk.

Further compounding the problem, the individual routers sent updates to all other routers, informing them of the loss of neighboring systems, which increased the strain on the network. As routers were restarted, they sent a similar message to all neighboring routers, with similar effects. The result was a cascade of router crashes, essentially bringing the entire Internet to a standstill until router software could be updated with a patch that Microsoft had actually released six months earlier.

After more than a decade, Slammer is still one of the most commonly detected viruses in the world, in part because billions of computer users in the world use pirated copies of operating system software, such as Microsoft Windows, that are not eligible for security patches. That same year, the MS Blaster worm followed shortly after Slammer and had nearly the same level of success, a fact that not only exposed yet another software vulnerability but also showed that fixing one problem will do nothing to protect against the next exploit discovered by malicious programmers.

Paul J. Springer

See also: Malware; MS Blaster Worm; MyDoom Virus; SQL Injection; Worm

Further Reading

Carr, Jeffrey. *Inside Cyber Warfare: Mapping the Cyber Underworld.* Sebastopol, CA: O'Reilly Media, 2009.

Singer, P. W., and Allan Friedman. *Cybersecurity and Cyberwar.* New York: Oxford University Press, 2014.

STUXNET

Stuxnet, originally known as Rootkit.Tmphider, is considered the first malicious malware designed to target a specific type of industrial control system (ICS). An ICS includes any software that controls industry production and distribution, like oil or natural gas. Stuxnet manipulated Microsoft Windows operating systems and exploited its vulnerabilities to infect its intended target. The most notable attack was against Iran's nuclear facilities, specifically their uranium-enrichment centrifuges. It is believed that Stuxnet's intent was to shut down Iran's nuclear capabilities or at the very least impede any progress.

In June 2010, Virusblokada, an antivirus company in Minsk, Belarus, was hired by an Iranian client to investigate an anomaly in a computer. The anomaly was believed to be a glitch, as the computer was continually rebooting itself. Sergey Ulasen, an analyst at Virusblokada, eventually discovered Stuxnet, and the firm immediately notified the international community and began working to discover its origins. Thus far, Symantec Corporation, an American technology company, has the most detailed account of Stuxnet available to the public. Reports indicated that not only did Stuxnet destroy 1,000 of the 5,000 centrifuges at Iran's nuclear facility in Natanz, but that there were also up to 9,000 new infections daily at the Bushehr nuclear power plant, which would make the centrifuges spin out of control and ultimately self-destruct.

Stuxnet was a 500-kilobyte computer worm that was installed onto a computer with a flash drive or USB, transferring from one computer system to the next within a local area network (LAN). Because Stuxnet is a computer worm, it was able to duplicate itself to spread throughout a network without attaching itself to any specific file and reprogrammed integral systems. Therefore, Stuxnet was difficult to detect once uploaded because it bypassed any antivirus program by simulating legitimate software.

Allegedly, Stuxnet was devised to destroy or impair centrifuges used in Iran's nuclear program through supervisory control and data acquisitions (SCADA) systems. SCADA systems are computer-based devices that monitor and control the operations of a program. These can be electrical power grids, railway transportation, or, in this case, nuclear facilities. It allows human operators to remotely access data and perform automated or manual commands. SCADA systems include a master terminal unit (MTU), a remote terminal unit (RTU), a communication apparatus, and the system software. The MTU is essentially the core of the SCADA system, while the RTU circulates information it has gathered and stored. The communication apparatus then transfers the information that goes in and out between the MTU and RTU while the system software commands the control boundaries and can respond to irregularities. The intended target within the SCADA system was the programmable logic controllers (PLC), which would allow the authors of Stuxnet to spy on the systems. PLCs are small computers that are responsible for the operational functions of the system, such as timers, switches, and relays. As with SCADA systems, PLCs are not connected to the Internet.

Stuxnet, therefore, used the SCADA system to distribute the worm and specifically targeted the PLC that controlled the centrifuges used in uranium enrichment. Stuxnet was tailored in such a way to spread to other personal computers (PCs) that were operating on the same shared network with the originally infected PC. The SCADA system was likely vulnerable to this type of attack due to the lack of personnel training or proper network security. Moreover, the Stuxnet code is available to view online as are its vulnerabilities. Most importantly, Web addresses of SCADA systems are also available online, which worries security analysts because nonstate groups or terrorist organizations can figure out how to use it.

Iran was likely the intended target given the number of setbacks its uranium enrichment facility had suffered. Stuxnet's design intentionally disrupted Iran's nuclear-enrichment networks by targeting ICSs. The Iranian Atomic Energy Organization stated that the malware was likely transferred to their facility's computer with a USB drive by someone working in the facility. Stuxnet targeted the ICS that controlled the centrifuge operations in the Natanz nuclear facility, which employed software from German electronics company Siemens called SIMATIC STEP 7. A human operator is required to monitor and control the exterior devices that operate such equipment as the centrifuge rotors, or propellers. Therefore, Stuxnet targeted Siemens SIMATIC STEP 7 PLCs, which run on Microsoft Windows operating systems, because it could easily penetrate this particular system. The Stuxnet code directed the centrifuge controller to speed up for a given time, return to normal operating standards, slow down, and then return to normal once again. This variation in speed caused irreparable damage to the centrifuge.

According to Symantec, there have been three versions of Stuxnet, although only the first version caused any damage. Stuxnet operators employed the worm in three waves: June and July 2009, March 2010, and April and May 2010. Stuxnet used two authorized digital certificates from Taiwanese firms, Realtek and JMicron, to install a rootkit, which is a program that can gain complete control over a computer and can boot and reboot repeatedly. With the certificates and rootkit installation, Stuxnet essentially blended in with authentic software. The rootkit identifies SIMATIC files and then exploits a Siemens vulnerability, which is a password embedded into the SIMATIC software to gain access to the network to infect the control systems. It can then communicate with network servers on the Internet by uploading reports of what has been found and subsequently infected. The worm managed to get as far as it did because it was designed to also bypass any firewalls and other networks or computers that did not have direct Internet connections.

Ultimately, the Symantec report explained that once the worm replicated itself, it spread through local area networks (LAN) and server message blocks (SMB), repeatedly duplicating the process and injecting itself into remote computers and STEP 7 programs. It would update itself within a LAN, evading security products by replicating a precise ICS and altering and concealing any Siemens PLCs. Stuxnet manipulated three vulnerabilities to penetrate Iran's uranium enrichment program. First, it exploited the default passwords embedded in the SCADA systems. Second, it penetrated the Microsoft Windows rootkit and used it to spread across linked computer networks. Finally, it harnessed four previously unknown zero-day vulnerabilities within all Windows operating systems, which is typically used to damage computer programs, other computers, or an entire network. It is known as zero-day because the software's creator has zero days to plan and direct any modifications against the operation.

While investigating Stuxnet, analysts at the Russian-based international software security group, the Kaspersky Lab, discovered traces of the file Flame, a 20-megabyte file considered Stuxnet's predecessor that also penetrated networks undetected. While Stuxnet was designed to destroy a system, Flame was intended for spying. It had the ability to search for keywords and report a synopsis of what it was looking for. Flame penetrated systems immediately after a Windows 7 update in which a user would assume that they were downloading a Microsoft update, but they were downloading Flame instead. Flame was primarily used in Iran but also across other countries in the Middle East.

After Stuxnet, Siemens and Microsoft worked to provide solutions for the PLCs and zero-day flaws. Additionally, VeriSign invalidated the stolen Realtek and JMicron certificates. Countries affected by Stuxnet include Iran, Indonesia, India, Pakistan, Germany, China, and the United States. In November 2012, Chevron was the first U.S. corporation to have been infected by the Stuxnet worm. No group or country has claimed responsibility for creating Stuxnet or the attacks against Iran's nuclear facilities. Security analysts believe that given the malware's sophistication and complexity, it must have been developed by a state rather than an individual or group. Countries believed to have the monetary assets and expert capability to develop Stuxnet are the United States, Israel, the United Kingdom, Russia, China, and France. Iran accused NATO, the United States, and Israel's elite

Unit 8200 security agency for the Stuxnet attack, which all have denied. Stuxnet proved to the international community that cyber terrorism is the next credible threat the world is facing. As a result of Stuxnet's devastating capabilities, countries are spending hundreds of millions of dollars on cyber-defense programs. Stuxnet established a new class of malware, thereby setting a high standard for cyber-security infrastructure.

Alma Keshavarz

See also: Certificates; Flame Worm; Iran Cyber Capabilities; Israel Cyber Capabilities; Kaspersky Lab; Malware; Programmable Logic Controller (PLC); Russia Cyber Capabilities; Supervisory Control and Data Acquisition (SCADA); Symantec Corporation; United States Cyber Capabilities; Zero-Day Vulnerability

Further Reading

Chen, Thomas M. *Cyberterrorism after Stuxnet.* Carlisle, PA: U.S. Army War College Strategic Studies Institute, 2014.

Collins, Sean, and Stephen McCombie. "Stuxnet: The Emergence of a New Cyber Weapon and Its Implications." *Journal of Policing, Intelligence and Counter Terrorism,* 7(1), 2012: 80–91.

Kerr, Paul K., John Rollins, and Catherine A. Theohary. *The Stuxnet Computer Worm: Harbinger of an Emerging Warfare Capability.* Washington, DC: 2010.

Lindsay, Jon R. "Stuxnet and the Limits of Cyber Warfare." *Security Studies,* 22(3), 2013: 365–404.

Poroshyn, Roman. *Stuxnet: The True Story of Hunt and Evolution.* Denver, CO: Outskirts Press, 2013.

Zetter, Kim. *Countdown to Zero Day: Stuxnet and the Launch of the World's First Digital Weapon.* New York: Crown Publishers, 2014.

SUN MICROSYSTEMS

Sun Microsystems is a defunct technology company that was responsible for creating much of the modern computer, server, and networking architecture between 1980 and 2010, including UNIX, RISC/SPARC, NFS, Java, and MySQL. Unlike many competitors, Sun encouraged open-source collaboration and development, particularly within its Java environment.

Sun Microsystems was founded by Andy Bechtolsheim, Bill Joy, Scott McNealy, and Vinod Khosla in the early 1980s at Stanford University. Bechtolsheim began the company by designing the Sun-1, a UNIX workstation. Over the next several years, the company incorporated and continued to develop workstations based on the Berkeley reduced instruction set computing (RISC) strategy. Sun also developed an in-house operating system called SUN OS, later renamed Solaris. This marked it as a competitor in the "workstation wars" of the decade. Sun developed a reputation for building reliable, high-end, innovative systems, including the powerful SPARC architecture in 1987 that largely replaced the Berkeley and other similar RISC-based processors. The company also created the Network File

System (NFS) in 1984, allowing clients to access network files in a manner similar to locally stored files.

During the 1990s, Sun transitioned from creating dedicated workstations to network-based products, becoming one of the dominant companies manufacturing networking solutions, storage systems, and supercomputers. The company developed the Java platform in the middle of the decade, marking a shift to virtual computing. Its main component, the Java Virtual Machine, was designed to work across multiple platforms and operating systems, providing a space for development of applications, including the JavaScript programming language run on the JVM compiler. In 1999, the company purchased StarDivision, giving it ownership of OpenOffice, the leading competitor to Microsoft Office. After the dot-com bubble, Sun shifted priorities again, concentrating on high-performance computing, including high-end multiprocessors for its servers. This allowed it to develop UltraSPARC, several supercomputers, and grid computing solutions, including in partnership with Microsoft. It also continued to develop software for its platforms, such as the purchase of MySQL AB in 2008. Most significantly, Sun began to release much of its software under GNU licenses, including the OpenSolaris OS and Java, including the JVM and its compiler. In 2010, Sun was purchased by Oracle and folded into the company.

During its existence, Sun played a prominent role in cyber warfare. One of the first worms, the Morris worm, spread into the wild on Sun computers in 1988. The Sadmind worm also infected Sun Solaris systems in 2000 and 2001, which ran a significant portion of the world's network infrastructure at the time. The latter infected Sun servers with anti-American messages originating from China, marking one of China's first forays into cyber warfare.

Most prominently, Sun systems were involved in the Solar Sunrise incident in early 1998. Three hackers, including Ehud "Udi" Tenenbaum, exploited a UNIX vulnerability in Solaris versions 2.4 and 2.6 to enter U.S. military computers, first at Andrews Air Force Base. Sun had previously warned about the vulnerability, but the systems affected were not repaired in time. The attack was initially feared to be the work of a foreign government, perhaps Iraq, particularly given the Eligible Receiver scenarios that presaged just such a cyber attack. However, the culprits were simply hobbyists, and all three were arrested within a month of the attack.

Jonathan Abel

See also: Cyber Attack; Hacker; Infrastructure; Microsoft Corporation; Server; Solar Sunrise; Tenenbaum, Ehud "Udi"; Worm

Further Reading

Hall, Mark. *Sunburst: The Ascent of Sun Microsystems.* Chicago: Contemporary Books, 1990.

Kaplan, Fred. *Dark Territory: The Secret History of Cyber War.* New York: Simon & Schuster, 2016.

Southwick, Karen. *High Noon: The Inside Story of Scott McNealy and the Rise of Sun Microsystems.* New York: John Wiley, 1999.

SUPERVISORY CONTROL AND DATA ACQUISITION (SCADA)

Supervisory control and data acquisition (SCADA) systems are a technology that enables data to be collected from remote industrial facilities and instructions sent to control them. SCADA systems are used to control pipelines, water and transportation systems, industrial plants, and critical infrastructure. SCADA systems operate by collecting real-time data and implementing standardized control programs that reduce human error and the cost of operating industrial plants. The use of SCADA systems has become more pervasive as low-cost PC-based systems have become available at the same time as advances in programmable logic controllers (PLC) and the Internet.

By using standard software, communication, and network protocols, and because of the need to operate in real time, SCADA systems are vulnerable to malicious code, distributed denial-of-service (DDOS) attacks, and modification of data. As a consequence, attacks on SCADA systems in critical national infrastructure, such as power generation, distribution, or transportation networks, have the potential to wreak havoc across industrial societies and present a risk of harm to humans. In the United States, the Department of Homeland Security (DHS) has responsibility for working with industry and across government to coordinate the identification, targeting, and addressing of vulnerabilities in critical national infrastructure arising from SCADA systems.

Graem Corfield

See also: Cyber Attack; Infrastructure; Programmable Logic Controller (PLC); Stuxnet

Further Reading

Krutz, Ronald. *Securing SCADA Systems.* Hoboken, NJ: Wiley, 2006.
Libicki, Martin C. *Cyberdeterrence and Cyber War.* Santa Monica, CA: RAND Corporation, 2009.

SYMANTEC CORPORATION

Symantec Corporation is a computer software company that specializes in computer-security products. It was founded on March 1, 1982, in Mountain View, California, by Gary Hendrix. Symantec is the creator of the Norton antivirus security software, which is one of the most widely used antivirus programs in the consumer market. It helps to protect individuals from cyber threats and ensure hackers cannot access computers or networks. This is very important, as cyber threats are increasing each day and individuals are now open to threats not just from individual hackers but by state-sponsored individuals and teams designed to steal personal information.

Symantec formed a joint venture with Huawei in 2008, which combined Huawei's telecommunications network infrastructure and Symantec's security and storage software. Huawei is a Chinese-owned company, which has raised concerns over computer security in the United States and throughout the world. It is feared that the Chinese government may use this relationship for developing more sophisticated computer network attacks and defense for their own network. These strategies could be abused by both nonstate and state actors in China. This new venture demonstrates that global reach provides new business opportunities, but it could negatively affect American cyber security.

Brad St. Croix

See also: Antivirus Software; Malware

Further Reading

Carr, Jeffery. *Inside Cyber Warfare.* 2nd ed. Sebastopol, CA: O'Reilly Media, 2012.
Jager, Rama D., and Rafael Ortiz. *In the Company of Giants: Candid Conversations with the Visionaries of the Digital World.* New York: McGraw-Hill, 1997.

SYRIAN ELECTRONIC ARMY (SEA)

The Syrian Electronic Army (SEA) was formed on March 15, 2011, by a group of hackers supporting Syrian president Bashar al-Assad. Syria is the first Arab country with a public Internet army that has launched open cyber attacks on its enemies, through spamming, Web site defacement, malware, phishing, and distributed denial-of-service (DDoS) attacks. SEA has targeted government Web sites in the Middle East, Europe, and the United States. News organizations, Syrian opposition groups, and human rights groups have also been compromised. The attack style varies from serious political statements to pointed humor.

The foundation of SEA can be traced back to the Syrian Computer Society of the 1990s. A Syrian malware team was discovered on January 1, 2011. The following month, Syria lifted a ban on Facebook and YouTube. Antiregime protests soon emerged on Facebook. The Syrian Computer Society registered SEA's Web site on May 5, 2011, which signified the backing of the Syrian government. SEA initially claimed that it was not officially sanctioned but more like a group of patriotic hackers, but they removed all text that denied official sanction on May 27, 2011. By 2014, their activity showed links with Syrian, Iranian, Lebanese, and Hezbollah officials.

The Syrian Electronic Army's activities concentrate on four styles of attack. Their primary goal was attacks against Syrian rebels, using surveillance to discover their identities and locations. This was later expanded to include foreign aid workers. Secondary intrusions were made against Western news Web sites that were hostile to the Syrian government. Their third actions were spamming Facebook pages with proregime comments. The fourth concentration was global cyber espionage, targeting technology and media companies, allied military procurement officers, U.S. defense contractors, and foreign attachés and embassies. Their tools of attack included malware, phishing, and distributed denial-of-service (DDoS) attacks. They have used the Blackworm virus and spamming to achieve their goals.

Two members of the SEA were added to the FBI's "Cyber's Most Wanted" list on March 22, 2016: Ahmed al Agha and Firas Dardar ("The Shadow"). Both are believed to be in Syria, and there is a $100,000 reward for the capture of each. In 2013, they hacked into computers and threatened to damage, delete, or sell data unless paid a ransom. They compromised Twitter accounts of prominent U.S. media organizations and gained control of a U.S. Marine Corps recruiting Web site, urging marines to refuse orders. The FBI reported, "While some of the activity sought to harm the economic and national security of the Unites States in the name of Syria, these detailed allegations reveal that the members also used extortion to try to line their pockets at the expense of law-abiding people all over the world." The FBI agents and analysts continue to work with both domestic and international partners to curtail SEA operations.

Raymond D. Limbach

See also: Cyber Espionage; Hacker; Operation Orchard

Further Reading

Kaplan, Fred. *Dark Territory: The Secret History of Cyber War.* New York: Simon & Schuster, 2016.

Libicki, Martin. *Cyberspace in Peace and War.* Annapolis, MD: U.S. Naval Institute Press, 2016.

TALLINN MANUAL

Published in 2013, the *Tallinn Manual* resulted from a three-year-long study sponsored by the North Atlantic Treaty Organization's Cooperative Cyber Defence Centre of Excellence (NATO CCDCOE). The CCDCOE brought more than a dozen experts in cyber warfare and international law together to consider the extent to which current international law could be used to govern cyber warfare. Three individuals also attended in their official capacities, including representatives from U.S. Cyber Command (USCYBERCOM), NATO, and the International Committee of the Red Cross, because of its ties to upholding the Geneva Convention. It was chaired by Dr. Michael Schmitt, who is a professor and the chairman of the International Law Department at the U.S. Naval War College.

The committee arrived at 95 "black letter rules" that apply to what they consider generally accepted, customary international laws relevant to cyber warfare. Every committee member had to agree on each of these rules. They then provided commentary that included noting any disagreements among committee members as to the application or interpretation of these 95 laws. Because the manual was designed to be a practical work that could guide advisers rather than an academic one, the purpose of this commentary was to provide various options and considerations as opposed to definitive guidelines.

The manual gets its name from Tallinn, the capital city of Estonia, where CCDCOE is located. The impetus for the center's placement was the cyber attack Estonia suffered in 2007, when Russia launched an extensive number of distributed denial-of-service (DDoS) attacks over a dispute between the two nations. In 2008, Russia then launched a cyber attack against Georgia. These two events brought cyber warfare to prominence, resulting in the establishment of the CCDCOE in 2008.

The project sought to wrestle with three major issues: (1) Do current international laws apply to cyber warfare? The committee concluded that they do, just as already-extant international law applied to other technological developments, such as nuclear weapons. (2) The particularly challenging area is the determination of *jus ad bellum*, which is Latin for the "right to war," where states must consider whether it is legal to use force. The committee concluded that a cyber attack need not have kinetic consequences, or physical results, to be considered a use of force and thus a violation of international law. They pointed to the prominent case of *Nicaragua v. United States*, where the International Court of Justice determined that arming and training guerrillas constituted an act of war. Economic and political warfare, however, do not merit the same consideration. Thus, the committee concluded that cyber espionage and cyber intelligence are not acts of war. Still, economic attacks that cause massive societal upheaval could be considered justifiable in responding with force. As such, they merit future consideration as cyber war continues to evolve. In helping legal advisers to determine how the international community would view a forceful response to a cyber attack, the committee developed eight different criteria, ranging from severity, the most important one being the extent to which a nation's military was involved in an attack. (3) Finally, the committee considered *jus in bello*, the Latin term for "law in war." *Jus in bello* guides the conduct of states during conflict, particularly regarding the treatment of civilians. The committee concluded, among other determinations, that cyber attacks must not harm civilians in a physical sense or cause severe psychological harm. The majority of the committee agreed to a "functionality test." If a cyber attack against civilians necessitated some kind of repair to reestablish cyber functionality, the act should be considered illegal.

The first version of the manual, which is now being referred to as *Tallinn Manual 1.0*, focuses only on cyber war. A subsequent version, known as *Tallinn Manual 2.0*, was released in 2016. Its focus is on activities below the level of war, which include cyber terror, cyber espionage, and cyber crime.

The manual has received some critique for being exclusionary in its preference for American and Western European scholars. As Schmitt argues, though, he had two criteria: excellent international lawyers and those with experience advising on these matters. Others have argued that the manual is too concerned with self-defense rather than in providing nonmilitary solutions. Countermeasures receive greater attention in *Tallinn Manual 2.0*, as they are the most practical solutions for states.

Heather Pace Venable

See also: Cyber Attack; Cyber War; Estonian Cyber Attack (2007); Georgian Cyber Attack (2008); Just War; North Atlantic Treaty Organization (NATO); U.S. Cyber Command (USCYBERCOM)

Further Reading

Fleck, Dieter. "Searching for International Rules Applicable to Cyber Warfare—A Critical First Assessment of the New *Tallinn Manual*." *Journal of Conflict and Security Law* 18, 2013: 331–351.

"International Law and Cyber Warfare." C-Span. Washington, D.C.: March 28, 2013. http://www.c-span.org/video/?311806-1/panelists-explain-new-cyber-warfare-manual.

Schmitt, Michael N. "International Law in Cyberspace: The Koh Speech and *Tallinn Manual* Juxtaposed." *Harvard International Law Journal Online* 54, 2012: 13–37.

Schmitt, Michael N. *Tallinn Manual on the International Law Applicable to Cyber Warfare.* Cambridge, UK: Cambridge University Press, 2013.

TARGET CORPORATION HACK

In 2013, the Target Corporation was victimized by a sophisticated computer hack that obtained 40 million credit card numbers and 70 million mailing and e-mail addresses, phone numbers, and other personal information from customers. It is the second-largest retail cyber attack after the 2006 hack of TJX Companies that affected nearly 94 million credit cards.

On December 19, 2013, Target announced it was investigating a major data breach involving millions of customer credit and debit card records that took place between November 27 and December 15, 2013. It warned that up to 40 million credit and debit cards were affected, including names, card numbers, expiration dates, and CCV security codes. On December 27, Target announced that debit card PIN numbers were also stolen, albeit in encrypted form. On January 10, 2014, Target disclosed that the names, mailing addresses, phone numbers, and e-mail addresses of up to 70 million additional customers had also been stolen, bringing the possible number of affected persons to 110 million.

In the days before Thanksgiving 2013, hackers began installing malware in Target's security and payments system that was designed to steal every credit card used at the company's 1,797 U.S. stores. The malware was in place on November 30, and data began moving out on December 2 and continued unmolested for nearly two weeks. Data was automatically sent to three U.S. staging points and later routed to a server in Moscow, Russia. Federal law enforcement officials contacted Target with evidence of a breach on December 12, and Target confirmed it three days later.

The cyber-security company McAfee described the breach as a low-tech hack using BlackPOS-based malware—a common exploit kit for sale that that can be easily modified and applied with little programming skill. Cyber experts believe the hack was the work of a stolen credit card vendor operating out of Odessa, Ukraine, but no arrests have been made.

Target was heavily criticized for not taking preventative action. Six months before the attack, Target had installed a $1.6 million malware-detection tool from the cyber-security company FireEye. Their system produced multiple malware alerts beginning November 30, and Target's Symantec antivirus system also identified suspicious behavior on the same server over several days around Thanksgiving. A FireEye system option to automatically delete detected malware was turned off. Target headquarters took no action on the alerts until it was contacted by federal authorities.

The hack prompted a congressional hearing into Target's lack of action and placed national pressure on retail stores to adopt a more secure technology by using cards with embedded chips, as they are harder to counterfeit than magnetic strips. On March 5, 2014, Target announced it was investing $100 million to implement this technology. In March 2015, Target reached a $10 million class-action settlement with affected customers.

Steven B. Davis

See also: FireEye; Malware; TJX Corporation Hack

Further Reading

Carr, Bob. "Target Breach Is a Wake-up Call." *CSP* 25, May 2014: 28–30.

Libicki, Martin. *Cyberspace in Peace and War.* Annapolis, MD: U.S. Naval Institute Press, 2016.

Riley, Michael, et al. "The Epic Hack." *Bloomberg Business Week*, March 17, 2014: 42–47.

TENENBAUM, EHUD "UDI"

Ehud Tenenbaum, an Israeli computer hacker, first came to prominence in 1998 when he managed to break into the Pentagon's security system. Tenenbaum was only 18 when he was unmasked by FBI investigators reacting to his incursion into Pentagon systems. The Israeli and U.S. agencies took the intrusion seriously, but both countries concluded that Tenenbaum acted without malice or ill intent.

Tenenbaum was a typical teenage overachiever from a middle-class family who excelled in math and science. He graduated from high school with top marks, despite having dyslexia. He had been a hacker since the age of 15 and operated from his bedroom computer. For three years, Tenenbaum, known only as "the Analyzer," targeted various U.S. Air Force and U.S. Navy computer systems and NASA, as well as American university and federal research sites, such as the Lawrence Livermore National Laboratories.

In 2002, Tenenbaum went to jail for eight months because of his involvement in the Pentagon incursion, code-named "Solar Sunrise." After his release, it was difficult for him to find work, so he left Israel and lived in France and then Montreal, Canada. In 2009, Tenenbaum was arrested for masterminding a global operation that hacked into financial institutions. In 2012, Tenenbaum accepted a plea bargain that required him to repay $503,000 and spend three years on probation.

Christopher Menking

See also: Cyber Crime; Department of Defense (DoD); Hacker; Solar Sunrise

Further Reading

Cuthbertson, Richard. "Naive or Evil?" *The Leader-Post* (Regina, Saskatchewan), February 21, 2009.

Zetter, Kim. "'The Analyzer' Gets Time Served for Million-dollar Bank Heist." *Wired*, May 7, 2012.

TERMINATOR, THE

The Terminator is a 1984 film directed by James Cameron that stars Arnold Schwarzenegger and Linda Hamilton. In the film, Schwarzenegger plays a cybernetic organism—a robot covered in living tissue that looks and acts human—known as a Terminator, that is sent back in time from 2029 to 1984 to assassinate Sarah Connor, the mother of the leader of the human resistance in a future war against the machines, which had taken over the world. Her future son, John Connor, sends a human soldier, Kyle Reese, back to 1984 to protect Sarah from the Terminator. The film's financial and creative success led to four film sequels, a short-lived television series, and numerous other media properties.

The Terminator fueled anxieties over the growth of computing power and became a point of discussion for many futurists, who debated the impact of future technologies on society. In particular, the film anticipated the rise of artificial intelligence (AI) and automated weapons systems and depicted a dystopian future overrun by automated aircraft, armored vehicles, and robotic foot soldiers mercilessly hunting the remaining human population. In the film's first sequel, *Terminator 2: Judgment Day* (1990), it is explained that the killing machines spawned from a runaway artificial intelligence program named Skynet that had been used to control the United States' nuclear arsenal.

Ryan Wadle

See also: Matrix, The

Further Reading

French, Sean. *The Terminator.* New York: British Film Institute, 2008.

THE ONION ROUTER (TOR)

Known as TOR, the Onion Router is open-source software that allows individuals to operate anonymously on the Internet. TOR was developed by the Center for High Assurance Computer Systems (CHACS) of the U.S. Naval Research Laboratory and was intended to prevent network traffic analysis of U.S. Department of Defense (DoD) communications. By providing private, untraceable connections through public networks, the DoD was able to support such activities as multilevel secure communications over a single network, anonymous open-source intelligence (OSINT) gathering, and communications using networks controlled by third parties, such as coalition partners and even adversaries. Since 2002, TOR has been available to the public as a free download through a nonprofit organization.

TOR consists of both software that can be downloaded and installed on a computer and an overlay network of computers that manages its connections. TOR works by using a volunteer network of computers that anonymously relays encrypted traffic through its network. Each relay node in the network knows which neighboring node that information packets are coming from and going to but not the entire path to the final Internet Protocol (IP) address. TOR effectively creates a number of layers that conceal identities so that Internet-surveillance techniques are unable to trace the traffic back to its origin.

The TOR network consists of three types of relays: middle relays, bridge relays, and exit relays. Middle relays handle routed traffic and are constituted from volunteer TOR users who retain their anonymity. Bridge relays are alternative entry points into the TOR network, and like middle relays, these volunteer IPs are not publicly identifiable and retain their anonymity. However, when a user's data emerges at an exit relay to pass a request to the public Internet, it is possible to observe what is being sent and received because the traffic emerging from the exit relay retains the protocol and data that was issued at the origin. Critically, then, while TOR provides for end-user anonymity at the packet level (IP address), it does not provide for end-to-end data secrecy. Despite the exit relay constituting a weak link that can attract surveillance or IP blocking, TOR users continue to volunteer to act as an exit relay for reasons of social reciprocity that further engenders trust in the network.

One drawback to using TOR is performance-related; as Internet traffic is being routed through at least three relays, this will introduce latency in the TOR network that will appear as sluggishness to the user. While there is no expectation that users volunteer to act as relays, it is the case that the larger the network, the greater the anonymity of its users. Also, the greater the ratio of volunteers (relays) to users, the less latency will be encountered. TOR is the largest network of its kind.

Graem Corfield

See also: Cyber Security; Encryption; Internet; Internet Protocol (IP) Address

Further Reading

Dingledine, Roger, Nick Mathewson, and Paul Syverson. *Tor: The Second-generation Onion Router.* Naval Research Laboratory Release Number 03-1221.1-2602, 2003.

Singer, P. W., and Allan Friedman. *Cybersecurity and Cyberwar: What Everyone Needs to Know.* New York: Oxford University Press, 2014.

TIER 1 INTERNET SERVICE PROVIDER

The Internet consists of many networks around the globe that are owned or operated by various companies, called *Internet service providers (ISPs)*. ISPs provide Internet access to government, commercial, and residential customers to generate their profits. The largest bandwidth networks form the Internet backbone and are labeled as *Tier 1 networks*. The associated network owners are Tier 1 ISPs. Tier 1 ISPs directly connect with, or have access to, all other Tier 1 networks in their region without fees under a "settlement-free peering agreement." Communications between these networks are voluntarily exchanged under this agreement.

In 2015, Dyn Research estimated there to be about dozen Tier 1 ISPs in the world, such as Level 3, NTT, Telia Sonera, GTT, and Cogent. Some smaller networks, called Tier 2 networks, exist that practice peering with other networks but must purchase access to portions of the Internet. Finally, some networks exist that are almost completely dependent on other networks for their access and must purchase all their access to the Internet. These are classified as Tier 3 networks.

Paul Clemans

See also: Hardware; Internet; Internet Service Provider (ISP); Transmission Control Protocol/Internet Protocol (TCP/IP)

Further Reading

Clarke, Richard A., and Robert K. Knake. *Cyber War: The Next Threat to National Security and What to Do about It.* New York: HarperCollins, 2010.

Montgomery, Justin. "What's the Difference between Tier 1, 2 and 3 Carriers, and Who Are They in the US?" *Mobile Marketing Watch*, February 3, 2010. http://mobilemarketingwatch .com/whats-the-difference-between-tier-12-and-3-carriers-and-who-are-they-5182.

Zmijewski, Adam. "A Baker's Dozen, 2015 Edition." Dyn Research, 2016. http://research .dyn.com/2016/04/a-bakers-dozen-2015-edition.

TJX CORPORATION HACK

In 2007, TJX, the parent company of TJ Maxx, Office Max, and Marshalls, disclosed that hackers had compromised its network, stealing data for at least the previous 18 months. It was the largest breach of credit card data at that time, with an estimated 45 million compromised credit and debit cards. Later court filings raised that estimate to 94 million.

The hackers that compromised TJX found their target by simply driving around Miami looking for vulnerable wireless networks, a technique called *war-driving*. At the time of the breach, TJX used Wired Equivalent Privacy (WEP) encryption to secure its wireless networks. WEP, as an encryption protocol, had been broken in 2001. By 2003, it was possible to break the encryption in three seconds on a laptop, making it one of the weakest forms of security for wireless local area networks.

Once the hackers were able to crack the encryption for transmitting data from cash registers to computers inside the store, they were able to intercept wireless data and then collect information on system usernames and passwords as employees logged into the company's central systems in Massachusetts. Using this information, they were able to set up accounts on TJX's central system. Between mid-2005 and throughout 2006, the hackers were able to exfiltrate historic credit card and debit card information. The hackers were also able to intercept unencrypted transaction data sent to banks with a packet sniffer that they had installed on the network.

Cybercriminals led by Alberto Gonzalez perpetrated the hack. Gonzalez was no stranger to law enforcement. At the age of 14, the FBI had visited him at his high school after he compromised NASA systems. In 2003, a plainclothes detective followed him to an ATM and watched him use a series of debit cards to withdraw several hundred dollars at a time on each. After being interviewed by the U.S. Secret Service, Gonzalez agreed to become an informant for the Secret Service to avoid prosecution. As an informant, he provided evidence to prosecute over a dozen of his former colleagues from the Shadowcrew message boards. His work for the Secret Service eventually landed him a job as a paid informant, drawing a $75,000 annual salary until his arrest. In 2010, Gonzalez was sentenced to 20 years in prison for leading the TJX hack and an assortment of other cyber crimes.

In 2008, Nick Benson, a TJ Maxx employee, was terminated for disclosing confidential information after a firm TJX had hired to monitor the Internet for anything mentioning the company found an anonymous post on a computer-security Web site that highlighted deficiencies in the company's basic practices. Benson noted that when he was hired in 2005, his password and username were identical. After the breach, TJX sent out policies requiring employees to use more robust passwords. At his location, Benson noted that his store manager changed the log-in protocol to allow employees to log in to company servers using blank passwords. The manager went so far as to post usernames and passwords on a Post-it note next to one system. The store's local server was also running in administrator mode, allowing anyone who logged in to have elevated privileges across the network. Benson cited his management's unresponsiveness as his reason for going public.

In 2009, the PCI Security Standards Council released guidelines aimed at securing wireless networks, specifically those for payment-card transactions, in response to several high-profile hacks, including the TJX hack. The measures included regularly scanning networks for rogue access points, installing firewalls to isolate networks that process payment-card data from those that fail to do so, changing default passwords and settings on wireless devices, and using strong encryption.

Marcus Laird

See also: Cyber Crime; Cyber Security; Encryption; Hacker; JPMorgan Hack; Office of Personnel Management Data Breach; Sony Hack; Target Corporation Hack

Further Reading

Brenner, Joel. *America the Vulnerable: Inside the New Threat Matrix of Digital Espionage, Crime, and Warfare.* New York: Penguin, 2011.
Kaplan, Fred M. *Dark Territory: The Secret History of Cyber War.* New York: Simon & Schuster, 2016.
Verini, James. "The Great Cyberheist." *New York Times Magazine,* November 10, 2010.

TORRENT

A torrent is a computer file that contains metadata about files to be distributed and usually a list of network locations of trackers. Trackers assist users in the system to locate one another so they can form swarms, or efficient distribution systems. While there is a centralized directory of torrents on Web sites like BitTorrent, the data transmission is shared by the swarm members. Unlike a centralized system where individual computers download a large file from a single source, torrents allow for a decentralized system. A torrent file does not contain content, only information about files, including names, sizes, and folder structure. Using a peer-to-peer (P2P) system, one large desired program, document, or media file can be obtained by downloading and then combining small pieces of the desired file from multiple locations. Downloading is faster because computers are not all requesting the same file from a centralized source. The torrent system is designed for when many users all demand the same file at the same time, what is called *multicasting*. This system can prevent distributed denial-of-service (DDoS) attacks from succeeding.

The danger of these kinds of systems is that the providers do not offer their users security or anonymity. The IP addresses of the computers that make up each swarm are not hidden. This exposes users with insecure systems to possible attack. A high volume of traffic on the Internet is P2P; this could possibly make discovering malicious traffic more difficult, as so many systems are sharing information for perfectly legal purposes.

Lori Ann Henning

See also: Botnet; Internet

Further Reading

Bailey, Matthew. *Complete Guide to Anonymous Torrent Downloading and File Sharing: A Practical, Step-by-step Guide on How to Protect Your Internet Privacy and Anonymity Both Online and Offline while Torrenting.* United States: Nerel Publications, 2013.

Chiang, Mung. *Networked Life: 20 Questions and Answers.* New York: Cambridge University Press, 2012.

TRANSMISSION CONTROL PROTOCOL/INTERNET PROTOCOL (TCP/IP)

Transmission Control Protocol and Internet Protocol (TCP/IP) are two complementary sets of conventions established for the purpose of sending data across multiple computer networks, enabling the operation of the Internet. Transmission Control Protocol (TCP) establishes a uniform standard for data transfers between host computers, and Internet Protocol (IP) enables data to seamlessly travel from one network to another.

In 1974, American computer scientist Vinton G. Cerf of Stanford University and electrical engineer Robert E. Kahn of the Advanced Research Projects Agency (ARPA) published a paper describing their ideas for sharing data across networks. Their concept, then called "TCP," was successfully demonstrated in 1977, when a data file was sent through the Packet Radio Network (PRNET) to ARPA's network (ARPANET) to the Atlantic Packet Satellite Network (SATNET) and back through ARPANET to its destination. By 1980, IP was distinguished from TCP for the specific purpose of passing data through "gateway" computers between networks.

TCP/IP usage spread rapidly. ARPANET adopted it in 1983, and Sun Microsystems included it in their workstations as part of the UNIX operating system. The privatization of the Internet in the 1990s, and the establishment of the World Wide Web with TCP/IP as a foundation, solidified its status as the standard Internet protocol.

Christopher G. Marquis

See also: ARPANET; Defense Advanced Research Projects Agency (DARPA); Internet; Sun Microsystems

Further Reading

Abbate, Janet. *Inventing the Internet.* Cambridge, MA: The MIT Press, 2000.

Hafner, Katie, and Matthew Lyon. *Where Wizards Stay Up Late: The Origins of the Internet.* New York: Simon & Schuster 1996.

TROJAN HORSE

A Trojan horse is a malware program used to steal private informataion. It is used by hackers to infiltrate computer networks and implant unauthorized commands. Usually, the Trojan is sent by e-mail, with computer users enticed to open an attachment or follow a download link. Once the target has done this, a hidden file in the target executes a program that allows the hacker to gain access to the hacked computer. The Trojan allows the intruder to scan the activities of the computer. In general, the access to sensitive data allows the hacker to use this data for theft or espionage. As the Trojan horse is usually not affecting other programs, it is much harder to detect than most malware.

Kaspersky Lab, a leading cyber-security firm, defines 19 different types of Trojans, depending on their behavior. Antivirus programs have provided a high level of security against most known Trojans, but new variants are constantly being developed. With new technological possibilities, highly skilled hackers and secret agencies might try to find a new backdoor for their Trojans to gain access to secure networks and use them to place other forms of malware.

Frank Jacob

See also: Cyber Attack; Cyber Espionage; Hacker; Malware

Further Reading

Carr, Jeffrey. *Inside Cyber Warfare: Mapping the Cyber Underworld.* Sebastopol, CA: O'Reilly Media, 2009.
Singer, P. W., and Allan Friedman. *Cybersecurity and Cyber War: What Everyone Should Know.* New York: Oxford University Press, 2014.

24TH AIR FORCE

In October 2008, Secretary of the Air Force Michael B. Donley and Air Force Chief of Staff General Norton A. Schwartz announced the creation of a new Numbered Air Force (NAF) to oversee the U.S. Air Force's cyber-space operations. Established on August 18, 2009, at Joint Base San Antonio-Lackland, Texas, under the command of Major General Richard E. Webber, the 24th Air Force served as the U.S. Air Force's operational-level organization responsible for planning and executing cyber-space operations in support of air force and joint force commanders. The 24th Air Force originally consisted of a headquarters staff, the 624th Operations Center, and three wings: the 67th Network Warfare Wing, the 688th Information Operations Wing, and the 689th Combat Communications Wing. During the first 14 months after its activation, the new NAF focused on building its organizational structure, increasing manning, and maturing its relationships with Air Force Space Command and U.S. Cyber Command (USCYBERCOM). The 24th Air Force reached full operational capability on October 1, 2010.

Operating in a climate of reduced resources and policy constraints, the 24th Air Force carried out its operations at a time when many senior government officials and policy makers expressed significant interest in military cyber-space operations. This emphasis has shaped the environment in which the NAF executed its three primary roles. First, as a Numbered Air Force assigned to Air Force Space Command, 24th Air Force organized, trained, and equipped cyber-space forces and operated, maintained, and defended the air force's network. Second, in its role as Air Force Cyber Command (AFCYBER), the NAF served as the service cyber component to USCYBERCOM and presented forces to that subunified command charged with the operation and defense of DoD networks. Finally, with the establishment of the USCYBERCOM Cyber Mission Force in 2013, the 24th Air Force staff also functioned as the Joint Force Headquarters–Cyber (JFHQ-C), charged with directing assigned cyber mission force teams.

Since its establishment, the 24th Air Force has focused on instilling a culture of mission assurance rather than information assurance and has emphasized efforts to operationalize its cyber-space forces. This has been accomplished through the implementation of standard planning processes, conceptualizing cyber-space operations using warfighting terminology rather than complex technical terms, and the introduction of AFCYBER Force Packages, which were discrete elements designed to carry out specific missions. The 24th Air Force also conducted the full range of cyber-space operations, including offensive, defensive, and network operations, as directed by higher headquarters, using seven cyber-space weapon systems approved by the Chief of Staff of the Air Force in March 2013. Finally, the 24th Air Force, partnering with the 25th Air Force, has taken steps to develop multidomain concepts through the convergence of cyber-space intelligence, surveillance, and reconnaissance (ISR) and electronic warfare.

As of 2016, the 24th Air Force consisted of nearly 6,000 active-duty service-members, civilians, and contractors assigned to the headquarters staff, the 624th Operations Center, the 67th Cyberspace Wing, the 688th Cyberspace Wing, and the 5th Combat Communications Group. In addition, nearly 9,000 additional members of the Air National Guard and Air Force Reserve supported the NAF as well.

Gregory W. Ball

See also: Department of Defense (DoD); Second Army/Army Cyber Command; United States Cyber Capabilities; U.S. Coast Guard Cyber Command (CGCYBER); U.S. Cyber Command (USCYBERCOM); U.S. Tenth Fleet

Further Reading

Lord, William T. "Cyberspace Operations: Air Force Space Command Takes the Lead." *High Frontier* 5(3), 2009: 3–6.

Vautrinot, Suzanne M. "Sharing the Cyber Journey." *Strategic Studies Quarterly* 6(3), 2012: 71–87.

Wilson, Major General Burke E. Wilson. "Embedding Airmenship in the Cyberspace Domain: The First Few Steps of a Long Walk." *Cyber Defense Review* 1(1), 2016: 21–26.

U

UNITED STATES CYBER CAPABILITIES

When all the organizations within the United States that are involved in cyber operations are taken into account, the United States is by far the most powerful nation currently active in the cyber domain. These organizations include government agencies and private corporations, and they are augmented by an enormous number of private actors with extensive cyber experience. However, the American economy and society are extremely dependent on the Internet, perhaps more so than any major power on earth, and as such, the United States is also subject to enormous threats originating from the cyber domain. While the exact capabilities of the U.S. government are a closely held secret, numerous authorities have implicated U.S. agencies in the most sophisticated cyber attacks publicly known and suggested that these examples are merely a small part of the total American strength in the cyber domain.

The United States was by far the earliest nation involved in cyber activities, in large part because most of the early computer advances were made in the United States. Likewise, the first effort to network computers occurred in the United States, when the Advanced Research Projects Agency debuted ARPANET as a means to connect defense-related researchers at multiple sites. When the first computer networks were envisioned, there was little effort given to the notion of security, as they were anticipated to be a tool used by only a handful of researchers and government agencies, rather than the primary means of communication for the human population around the globe. The architecture of the early unsecured networks continues to have an influence on the structure of the modern Internet, despite decades of malware demonstrating the need to undertake a greater effort at cyber security.

The American portion of the global Internet is by far the largest segment held by a single nation. Being the earliest adopter of cyberspace provided a significant advantage, as did American economic resources, a technologically savvy population, and a large citizen base. The United States has the world's largest economy and biggest university system, both of which have also driven expansion into the cyber domain. In terms of raw computing power, the United States possesses the most processing and storage capacity of any nation. It is also the source of most of the driving innovations regarding computers, including being the largest producer of computer equipment and the creator of ubiquitous software commonly in use around the world. All of these factors contribute to the current American hegemony in cyber space.

The most prominent American presence on the Internet, from a cyber-warfare perspective, is that of the U.S. Department of Defense (DoD). All military services maintain a major presence in the cyber domain, plus the services have a number of joint initiatives combining the capabilities of all. DoD cyber activity operates under the umbrella of the U.S. Cyber Command (USCYBERCOM), headquartered in Fort Meade, Maryland. Established in 2009, this four-star command is colocated with the headquarters of the National Security Agency (NSA), a key actor within the intelligence collection realm. The commander of USCYBERCOM, Admiral Michael S. Rogers, is also the director of the NSA, making him a key actor in the U.S. cyber effort. This structure has led some critics to claim that the U.S. government is blurring the lines between military operations, which are governed by Title 10 of the U.S. Code, and intelligence agencies, which are governed by Title 50. Similar accusations have been made regarding the U.S. conduct of warfare in the physical realm, particularly during the ongoing struggle against Al Qaeda, the Islamic State in Iraq and Syria (ISIS), and other terror organizations.

Under USCYBERCOM, each of the services maintains its own cyber force. The U.S. Army Cyber Command (ARCYBER) is headquartered with Second Army and is responsible for defending army networks from external intrusions. Under certain circumstances, with presidential approval, Second Army, like other service commands, may undertake offensive cyber operations. The U.S. Fleet Cyber Command (FCC) is maintained with U.S. Tenth Fleet, which defends the navy's networks and can likewise potentially undertake cyber attacks. The U.S. Air Force, which prior to 2009 was the DoD's lead agency for the cyber domain, activated the 24th Air Force to serve as its key cyber command.

In addition to the individual services, there are also specific DoD agencies responsible for certain aspects of military operations, including the Defense Information Systems Agency (DISA), which takes the lead in providing network security for the DoD. The Defense Advanced Research Projects Agency (DARPA) is a DoD-funded organization that seeks to make technological leaps forward by uniting researchers toward a common goal. One of the most well-known examples, of course, is the Internet itself, but DARPA has been responsible for dozens of key innovations within the field of computer design and is currently examining the possibility of building organic computer systems and advanced artificial intelligence (AI) capabilities.

Defense communications occur on three different networks, depending on the level of classification of material being transmitted. At the highest level, the JWICS system is the most secure and is the only network upon which materials classified "Top Secret" are allowed to be stored or transferred. Documents that are classified "Secret" can be transmitted on the Secret Internet Protocol Router Network (SIPRNet), which is somewhat less secure than JWICS but is still not connected to the Internet per se. Daily communications that are not classified, including those that are still confidential, may be transmitted via the Non-classified Internet Protocol Router Network (NIPRNet), which has much greater connectivity to the World Wide Web.

U.S. intelligence agencies have found the Internet to be a tremendous means of conducting espionage activities. The primary intelligence actors in the cyber domain are the National Security Agency (NSA) and the Central Intelligence Agency (CIA). The NSA is one of the largest intelligence agencies in the world and was initially founded to concentrate on signals intelligence (SIGINT). By the 21st century, the NSA had established itself as one of the most sophisticated cyber operations in the world. It remains the lead agency for SIGINT, to include the interception of data traveling through the Internet. The NSA also has a key role in the encryption and decryption of data and is most likely the lead agency for strategic offensive operations in cyber space. It goes to great lengths to remain unnoticed by the public at large and rarely offers commentary on allegations of its possible involvement in cyber activities.

In 2013, former NSA contractor Edward J. Snowden leaked an enormous number of sensitive documents to global media agencies. These documents demonstrated that the NSA was involved in a massive intelligence-collection operation targeting the U.S. public, essentially creating electronic files on every citizen active on the Internet. Snowden's revelations also demonstrated that the NSA had targeted the personal communications of world leaders, including several key allies of the United States. The CIA traditionally focuses on human intelligence (HUMINT) collection methods, including the stereotypical methods of spying on foreign nations. While the NSA is more likely to absorb and analyze enormous volumes of data, the CIA has traditionally preferred targeted espionage activities, focusing in particular on foreign government activities.

The security of the United States and its citizenry is also entrusted to the Department of Homeland Security (DHS) and the Federal Bureau of Investigation (FBI). DHS is the lead agency for protecting key infrastructure, particularly critical elements of U.S. transportation, communications, and the electrical grid, all of which would be lucrative targets for an enemy nation-state in the event of a major cyber war. The FBI is the lead agency for investigating cyber crime, cyber terrorism, and engaging in cyber counterespionage operations. As such, the FBI's responsibilities heavily overlap with those of the DoD and DHS, in large part because many cyber attacks are not immediately classifiable as crime, espionage, terrorism, or acts of warfare.

One of the major military strengths of the United States for the past two centuries has been the ability of private industrial corporations and the U.S. government to cooperate in times of war. The same remains true in the cyber domain, as many of the largest and most sophisticated cyber companies are headquartered in the United States and were created by American citizens. For example, Apple, Google, Intel, and Microsoft, each of which is a titan within its own sector of the technology industry, are all American companies, and each has cooperated with the U.S. government on a variety of cyber initiatives. Many of the world's leading cyber-security companies are also based in the United States, including FireEye, McAfee, and Symantec Corporation (Norton). While these companies are by no means under the control of the U.S. government, they tend to share information relatively freely with the federal government.

The United States has an enormous number of private citizens who are very active on the Internet and who play almost every role imaginable in a cyber-warfare scenario. There are thousands of U.S. "white hat" hackers who seek means to penetrate cyber defenses as a hobby. Upon success, they notify the affected companies or software designers, sometimes receiving a bounty in return. Unfortunately, the United States also has an extremely high number of "black hat" hackers who seek to penetrate cyber networks for personal gain, often for criminal purposes. In some ways, these hackers are an irritant, as they tend to engage in cyber crime and their most common targets are fellow U.S. citizens. However, at times, they become incensed at an external actor and turn their capabilities against an enemy of the U.S. government. Many of the leading elements of the hacker collective Anonymous appear to be operating in the United States. That group had "declared war" on the Islamic State in Iraq and Syria (ISIS), Mexican drug cartels, and the government of North Korea, with interesting effects.

The United States faces a number of rising competitors within the cyber realm, most notably the People's Republic of China and the Russian Federation. Nonstate actors also represent a potential threat to American networks, as terror organizations, criminal networks, and military forces all seek means to upset U.S. advantages in the physical domain. To maintain its competitive advantage in the cyber domain, the United States will need to emphasize the formal education of cyber operators, recommit itself to upgrading the nation's cyber infrastructure, and improve cyber security throughout the public and private sectors. Failure to do so could lead to the rise of peer nations that can steal U.S. innovations almost as quickly as they are developed and might outproduce American industry in military-related hardware. Should the United States lose its comparative advantage in cyber space, it might also face a corresponding threat in the physical realm.

Paul J. Springer

See also: ARPANET; Department of Defense (DoD); Department of Homeland Security (DHS); EINSTEIN (Cyber System); Hacker; JWICS Network; Manning, Bradley; National Cyber Security Strategy; National Security Agency (NSA); NIPRNet; People's Republic of China Cyber Capabilities; PRISM Program; Russia Cyber Capabilities; Second Army/Army Cyber Command; SIPRNet; Snowden, Edward J.; 24th Air Force; U.S Coast Guard Cyber Command (CGCYBER); U.S. Cyber Command (USCYBERCOM); U.S. Tenth Fleet

Further Reading

Brenner, Joel. *America the Vulnerable: Inside the New Threat Matrix of Digital Espionage, Crime, and Warfare.* New York: Penguin, 2011.

Carr, Jeffrey. *Inside Cyber Warfare: Mapping the Cyber Underworld.* Sebastopol, CA: O'Reilly Media, 2009.

Clarke, Richard A., and Robert K. Knake. *Cyber War: The Next Threat to National Security and What to Do about It.* New York: HarperCollins, 2010.

Gellman, Barton. *Dark Mirror: Edward Snowden and the Surveillance State.* London: Penguin, 2016.

Greenwald, Glenn. *No Place to Hide: Edward Snowden, the NSA, and the U.S. Surveillance State.* New York: Metropolitan Books, 2014.

Harding, Luke. *The Snowden Files: The Inside Story of the World's Most Wanted Man.* New York: Vintage Books, 2014.

Kaplan, Fred M. *Dark Territory: The Secret History of Cyber War.* New York: Simon & Schuster, 2016.

Libicki, Martin. *Cyberspace in Peace and War.* Annapolis, MD: U.S. Naval Institute Press, 2016.

Singer, P. W., and Allan Friedman. *Cybersecurity and Cyber War: What Everyone Should Know.* New York: Oxford University Press, 2014.

Springer, Paul J. *Cyber War: A Reference Handbook.* Santa Barbara, CA: ABC-CLIO, 2015.

Stiennon, Richard. *Surviving Cyber War.* Lanham, MD: Government Institutes, 2010.

UNRESTRICTED WARFARE

In 1999, two political air force colonels of the People's Liberation Army (PLA), Qiao Liang and Wang Xiangsui, wrote a book, *Unrestricted Warfare*. It primarily focuses on how China can defeat technologically superior opponents. Instead of a direct military confrontation, it calls for victory by other means, to include using international law and economic pressure. The first English translation was produced by an obscure publisher in Panama and subtitled *China's Master Plan to Destroy America*.

The authors argue that the primary weakness of the United States in military matters is that it views a revolution in military concepts in terms of technology and new capabilities. They state that the United States does not consider the larger picture of legal and economic factors and thus is vulnerable to attack. The authors propose that new means, such as political and financial coercion, will prove more effective than traditional military action. Any state that does not acknowledge these warnings might be vulnerable. The best-known alternative attack is through data networks vital to financial, transportation, and communication institutions. The ability to shut down any power grid would be devastating to both civilian and defense areas. Within economic warfare, disastrous results on a global level can be inflicted without taking any military offensive. Political action could change policy through government and nongovernmental organizations. Their last tenet is the use of terrorism to shatter a nation's sense of security. They conclude that globalization has broken down the differences between warfare and nonwarfare and that a grand warfare method combines all dimensions.

Raymond D. Limbach

See also: Cyber War; GhostNet; Informatization; Operation Night Dragon; Operation Shady RAT; People's Liberation Army Unit 61398; People's Republic of China Cyber Capabilities

Further Reading

Liang, Qiao, and Wang Xiangsui. *Unrestricted Warfare.* Beijing: PLA Literature and Arts Publishing House, 1999.

Lindsay, Jon R., Tai Ming Cheung, and Derek S. Reveron, eds. *China and Cybersecurity: Espionage, Strategy, and Politics in the Digital Domain.* New York: Oxford University Press, 2015.

USA PATRIOT ACT

On October 26, 2001, President George W. Bush signed into law the Uniting and Strengthening America by Providing Appropriate Tools Required to Intercept and Obstruct Terrorism Act (USA PATRIOT Act). Leading up to its passage, there was resounding support for the increased measures found in the act within Congress and the general public to mitigate the potential for additional attacks and create a sense of security. Passage of the act significantly increased the executive branch's global reach and the executive authority to carry out preventative actions against terrorist threats directed against the United States.

September 11, 2001, served as the catalyst in codifying increased measures by the government that were preexisting and established in law as well as previously rejected due to their infringement on constitutional rights and individual freedoms. A mentality of acceptance, crisis management, and an increased tolerance for expanded law enforcement activities gave the administration and government a mandate from the American people.

Prior to September 11, 2001, the 1978 Foreign Intelligence Surveillance Act (FISA) and the 1996 Antiterrorism Act were two fundamental laws governing actions both internal and external to the United States. Following the 9/11 attacks against the American homeland, action was demanded by the public. If the government was to effectively assess, deter, prevent, and react to the evolving situation and recent attacks, it needed to act swiftly. The first proposal arrived at the Senate floor on September 13 and was approved after 30 minutes of debate. Patrick Leahy (D-VT) was the only senator to oppose the bill on the basis of speed, lack of information presented, and concern for the degradation of civil liberties. The next attempt to pass comprehensive security measures was presented by the U.S. attorney general as the Mobilization Against Terrorism Act (MATA), which become the Antiterrorism Act (ATA) of 2001 after limited negotiation.

In retrospect, there was limited debate on what some would consider the most important legislation of the current century, yet minority voices of opposition did generate enough leverage to eventually have the MATA-ATA tabled for a more bipartisan proposal. Following this rejection, the administration immediately began drafting the Uniting and Strengthening America Act (USA Act), which was eventually signed into law as the USA PATRIOT Act.

The final bill passed in the House by a majority of 356–66 and in the Senate with a margin of 98–1. On October 26, 2001, President George W. Bush signed the USA PATRIOT Act into law and ushered in broad and sweeping changes to the application and interpretation of U.S. government responsibility and authority in regard to terrorism. The USA PATRIOT Act has served as the security initiative for the protection, safety, and survival of the American way of life, according to the U.S. government. What is not fully addressed are the incurred costs on civil liberties and the implications of these expanded powers.

The act allows for expanded traditional wiretaps, the application of pen registers, tracking and tracing of electronic communications, and multijurisdictional orders, and it lowers the standard for attaining a search warrant. Senator Russell Feingold (D-WI) addressed significant concerns about giving law enforcement agencies the power to investigate crimes outside the realm of terrorism, to include monitoring computer systems without consent and the power to conduct search and seizures without meeting the threshold of previously existing probable cause. Ultimately, the utilization of cyber space and the application of intelligence processes within the domain changed the U.S. approach to terrorism and redefined authorities across executive agencies.

Jose Alberto Rivas Jr.

See also: Bush, George W.; Cyber Security; Cyber Terrorism; Foreign Intelligence Surveillance Act (FISA)

Further Reading

Atkin, Michelle Louise. *Balancing Liberty and Security: An Ethical Study of U.S. Foreign Intelligence Surveillance, 2001–2009.* Lanham, MD: Rowman & Littlefield, 2013.

Ball, Howard. *The USA Patriot Act of 2001: Balancing Civil Liberties and National Security: A Reference Handbook.* Santa Barbara, CA: ABC-CLIO, 2004.

Wong, Kam C. *The Impact of the Patriot Act on American Society: An Evidence Based Assessment.* New York: Nova Science, 2007.

U.S. COAST GUARD CYBER COMMAND (CGCYBER)

The U.S. Coast Guard Cyber Command (CGCYBER) was established on June 23, 2009, under the command of Rear Admiral Robert E. Day Jr., USCG. Located at the headquarters of the U.S. Coast Guard (USCG) headquarters in Washington, D.C., CGCYBER consists of 63 military personnel and 17 civilians. CGCYBER maintains a liaison detachment at the headquarters of the U.S. Cyber Command (USCYBERCOM) at Fort Meade, Maryland.

The mission of CGCYBER is to identify and protect against threats to the USCG's portion of the Department of Defense Information Network (DODIN). CGCYBER provides cyber capabilities that foster excellence in the execution of Coast Guard operations, support Department of Homeland Security (DHS) cyber missions, and serve as the Service Component Command to USCYBERCOM. CGCYBER is a designated Computer Network Defense Security Provider, and it reports to USCYBERCOM on matters related to DODIN.

CGCYBER is headed by a USCG admiral with collateral duties as the Coast Guard's chief information officer (CIO) and the assistant commandant for command, control, communications, computers, and information technology. CGCYBER is divided into five departments: Certification and Accreditation, Information Assessments, Network Operations Security, Compliance and Reporting, and Plans and Policy.

Coast Guard Commandant Admiral Paul Zukunft unveiled the USCG's cyber strategy on June 15, 2015, at the Center for Strategic and International Studies in Washington, D.C. This strategy identified three distinct strategic priorities crucial to the Coast Guard's mission: defending cyber space, enabling operations, and protecting infrastructure.

Jim Dolbow

See also: Department of Defense (DoD); Department of Homeland Security (DHS); United States Cyber Capabilities; U.S. Cyber Command (USCYBERCOM)

Further Reading

U.S. Coast Guard. *United States Coast Guard Cyber Strategy.* Washington, D.C., 2015. https://www.uscg.mil/seniorleadership/DOCS/cyber.pdf.

U.S. CYBER COMMAND (USCYBERCOM)

The U.S. Cyber Command (USCYBERCOM) is a subunified command under U.S. Strategic Command (USSTRATCOM). USCYBERCOM was formed in 2010 by consolidating two USSTRATCOM subordinate organizations: the Joint Functional Component Command–Network Warfare and Joint Task Force–Global Network Operations. USCYBERCOM plans and executes operations in support of DoD's primary cyber missions: defend DoD networks, systems, and information; defend the U.S. homeland and U.S. national interests against cyber attacks of significant consequence; and provide cyber support to military operational and contingency plans. USCYBERCOM plans, coordinates, integrates, synchronizes, and conducts activities to direct the operations and defense of the Department of Defense Information Network (DODIN). It also prepares, when directed, to conduct full-spectrum military cyber-space operations to enable actions in all domains, ensure U.S. and allied freedom of action in cyber space, and deny the same to adversaries.

USCYBERCOM is located at Fort Meade, Maryland, colocated with the National Security Agency/Central Security Service (NSA/CSS). U.S. Army General Keith B. Alexander was the first commander; he was replaced by U.S. Navy Admiral Michael S. Rogers in April 2014. General Alexander had been the G2 for the U.S. Army prior to commanding USCYBERCOM, while Admiral Rogers had commanded U.S. Fleet Cyber Command/U.S. Tenth Fleet. The commander of U.S. Cyber Command is also the director of the NSA, a position known as the DIRNSA. This dual-hatting structure has both advantages and disadvantages and is under constant review to determine whether or not to continue that structure.

USCYBERCOM's main operational instrument of cyber power is the Cyber National Mission Force, which conducts cyber-space operations to disrupt and deny adversarial attacks against national critical infrastructure. It is the U.S. military's first joint tactical command with a dedicated mission focused on cyber-space operations. It plans to create 133 cyber mission teams by the end of fiscal year 2018. The plan is for these 133 teams to consist of 13 national mission teams to defend the United States and its interests against cyber attacks of significant consequence by performing full-spectrum cyber operations; 68 cyber protection teams to defend priority DoD networks and systems against priority threats; 27 combat mission teams to provide support to combatant commands by generating integrated cyber-space effects in support of operational plans and contingency operations; and 25 support teams to provide analytic and planning support to the national mission and combat mission teams. The combat mission teams are similar to the national mission teams, but rather than serving at the national level, they conduct cyber-space operations to achieve combatant commanders' objectives and are geographically and functionally aligned under one of four Joint Force Headquarters–Cyber (JFHQ-C) in direct support of geographic and functional combatant commands:

- JFHQ-C Washington supports U.S. Special Operations Command, U.S. Pacific Command, and U.S. Southern Command.
- JFHQ-C Georgia supports U.S. Central Command, U.S. Africa Command, and U.S. Northern Command.
- JFHQ-C Texas supports U.S. European Command, USSTRATCOM, and U.S. Transportation Command.
- JFHQ-DODIN defends the DODIN.

The DoD has cyber strategy and doctrine. These are nested in the overall U.S. cyber strategy as produced by the National Security Council (NSC) and coordinated across the U.S. government. The service chiefs also develop their own strategy and doctrine and will provide cyber operations capabilities for deployment and support to combatant commands as directed by the secretary of defense and remain responsible for compliance with USSTRATCOM's direction for operation and defense of DODIN.

The DoD, the Joint Staff, and the services have published a variety of important cyber publications:

- The White House published the *International Strategy for Cyberspace* in 2011.
- DoD published *The DoD Cyber Strategy* in 2015.
- The Joint Staff published Joint Publication 3-12 (R), *Cyberspace Operations*, in 2013.
- The army published Field Manual 3-38, *Cyber Electromagnetic Activities*, and is currently developing a new cyber branch and military occupational specialty to facilitate the development of its cyber workforce.
- The navy has a set of approaches, including the *Department of the Navy Cybersecurity/Information Assurance Workforce Management, Oversight and Compliance*; the *Navy Information Dominance Corps Human Capital Strategy 2012–2017*; *Navy Cyber Power 2020*; the *U.S. Navy Information Dominance Roadmap 2013–2028*; and the *Navy Strategy for Achieving Information Dominance 2013–2017*. The service also created the Information Dominance Corps, a unified body that produces precise, timely warfighting decisions by bringing together the intelligence, information professional, information warfare, meteorology and oceanography communities and members of the space cadre.

- The Marine Corps has Marine Corps Doctrinal Publication 1-0, *Marine Corps Operations*. The service recognizes five types of cyber operations: network operations, defensive and offensive cyber operations, computer network exploitation, and information assurance.
- The Air Force codified its cyber doctrine in Air Force Doctrine Document 3-12, *Cyberspace Operations*, published in 2010 and updated in 2011. It has also created its own cyber branch by carving out part of the air force communications community.

Each of the services also has its own cyber organizations. Under their Title 10 U.S. Code role as force providers to the combatant commanders, the services recruit, train, educate, and retain the military cyber force. These are U.S. Army Cyber Command/Second Army, U.S. Fleet Cyber Command/U.S. Tenth Fleet, 24th Air Force, and U.S. Marine Corps Forces Cyber Command.

The U.S. Army Cyber Command (ARCYBER), or Second Army, is the single information technology provider for all network communications and is responsible for the army section of DODIN. The U.S. Intelligence and Security Command conducts intelligence, security, and information operations for military commanders and national decision makers. The command is also responsible for the Joint Forces Headquarters–Cyber in Georgia.

U.S. Fleet Cyber Command (FCC) and U.S. Tenth Fleet compose combined headquarters at Fort Meade, Maryland. FCC is the staff organization to organize forces, and Tenth Fleet is the operational staff that provides command and control. FCC has a mission set similar to the other services: direct cyber-space operations globally to deter and defeat aggression and to ensure freedom of action to achieve military objectives in and through cyber space; organize and direct cryptologic operations worldwide and support information operations and space planning and operations, as directed; execute cyber missions as directed; direct, operate, maintain, secure, and defend the navy's portion of DODIN; deliver integrated cyber, information operations, cryptologic, and space capabilities; deliver global cyber network operational requirements; assess cyber readiness; and manage, man, train, and equip functions associated with Navy Component Commander and Service Cryptologic Commander responsibilities The mission of Tenth Fleet is to serve as the Numbered Fleet for Fleet Cyber Command, to exercise operational control of assigned forces, and to coordinate with other naval, coalition, and joint task forces to execute the full spectrum of cyber, electronic warfare, information operations, and signal intelligence capabilities and missions across the cyber, electromagnetic, and space domains.

Marine Corps Forces Cyber Command has two subordinate elements: the Marine Corps Network Operations and Security Center and L Company of the Marine Corps Support Battalion. It has also been innovative in its deployment of cyber forces, with the Marine Air-Ground Task Force Cyberspace and Electronic Warfare Coordination Cell being embedded into the Marine Expeditionary Unit onboard ships where it provides support directly to deployed forces.

Air Forces Cyber, or the 24th Air Force, is self-described as an "Operational warfighting organization that executes full spectrum cyberspace operations to ensure friendly forces maintain a warfighting advantage." It has several subordinate elements:

- The 624th Operations Center serves as the cyber operations center for the air force.
- The 67th Cyberspace Wing operates the Air Force Information Network, which is the Air Force section of DODIN.
- The 688th Cyberspace Wing delivers proven information operations engineering and infrastructure capabilities.
- The 5th Combat Communications Group delivers expeditionary communications, information systems, engineering and installation, air traffic control, and weather services to the president, secretary of defense, and combatant commanders.

The U.S. DoD identifies four types of cyber actions: cyber-space defense; cyber-space intelligence, surveillance, and reconnaissance (ISR); cyber-space operational preparation of the environment (OPE); and cyber-space attack. According to DoD, cyber-space defense is intended to defend DoD or other friendly cyber space. Specifically, they are passive and active cyber-space defense operations to preserve the ability to utilize friendly cyber-space capabilities and protect data, networks, net-centric capabilities, and other designated systems. Cyber-space ISR is an intelligence action that includes ISR activities in cyber space conducted to gather intelligence that may be required to support future operations, including offensive or defensive cyber operations. These activities synchronize and integrate the planning and operation of cyber-space systems in direct support of current and future operations. Cyber-space ISR focuses on tactical and operational intelligence and on mapping adversarial cyber space to support military planning. Cyber-space ISR requires appropriate deconfliction and cyber-space forces that are trained and certified to a common standard with the intelligence community. Cyber-space OPE consists of the nonintelligence-enabling activities conducted to plan and prepare for potential follow-on military operations. OPE requires cyber-space forces trained to a standard that prevents compromise of related intelligence operations. ISR and OPE operations conducted by DoD in cyber space are conducted pursuant to military authorities and must be coordinated and deconflicted with other departments and agencies in the U.S. government.

Cyber-space attacks are actions that create various direct-denial effects in cyber space and manipulation that leads to denial that is hidden or that manifests in the physical domains. These specific actions are

- *Deny*—to degrade, disrupt, or destroy access to, operation of, or availability of a target by a specified level for a specified time. Denial prevents adversary use of resources.
- *Degrade*—to deny access (a function of amount) to, or operation of, a target to a level represented as a percentage of capacity. Level of degradation must be specified. If a specific time is required, it can be specified.

- *Disrupt*—to completely but temporarily deny (a function of time) access to, or operation of, a target for a period of time. A desired start and stop time are normally specified. Disruption can be considered a special case of degradation where the degradation level selected is 100 percent.
- *Destroy*—to permanently, completely, and irreparably deny (time and amount are both maximized) access to, or operation of, a target.
- *Manipulate*—to control or change the adversary's information, information systems, or networks in a manner that supports the commander's objectives.

Cyber attack is a popular phrase, but not one that is defined to any degree of precision. Under international law, there are "armed attacks" and there is the "use of force" as mentioned in the UN Charter. Although there is a high level of congruence between the opinions of the United States and those of international organizations and other states on other norms for cyber space, the United States has articulated a different definition of what an armed attack is than what the rest of the world considers to be an armed attack. However, most international actors agree that existing international law is in effect in cyber space and that certain existing norms developed for use in other areas are applicable in cyber space, including specific law of war rules, "even though those rules were developed before cyber operations were possible," as well as norms under international law, such as upholding fundamental freedoms, respect for property, valuing privacy, protection from crime, and the right of self-defense. There are several Web pages that allow one to watch in real time as a variety of cyber attacks occur.

According to Admiral Michael S. Rogers, the release authority for cyber-space attacks is the president of the United States. If the president authorizes these operations, they are conducted by the Cyber National Mission Force or one of the combatant commands.

G. Alexander Crowther

See also: Alexander, Keith B.; Department of Defense (DoD); National Security Agency (NSA); Rogers, Michael S.; Second Army/Army Cyber Command; 24th Air Force; United States Cyber Capabilities; U.S. Coast Guard Cyber Command (CGCYBER); U.S. Tenth Fleet

Further Reading

Kaplan, Fred M. *Dark Territory: The Secret History of Cyber War.* New York: Simon & Schuster, 2016.

Libicki, Martin. *Cyberspace in Peace and War.* Annapolis, MD: U.S. Naval Institute Press, 2016.

Rid, Thomas. *Cyber War Will Not Take Place.* New York: Oxford University Press, 2013.

Singer, P. W., and Allan Friedman. *Cybersecurity and Cyber War: What Everyone Should Know.* New York: Oxford University Press, 2014.

Springer, Paul J. *Cyber Warfare: A Reference Handbook.* Santa Barbara, CA: ABC-CLIO, 2015.

U.S. TENTH FLEET

The U.S. Tenth Fleet of the U.S. Navy, based at Fort Meade, Maryland, is the operational unit of the service's U.S. Fleet Cyber Command (FCC). These forces constitute the naval element of the larger U.S. Cyber Command (USCYBERCOM), which is also based at Fort Meade. As of 2016, Vice Admiral Jan E. Tighe commanded both the FCC and the Tenth Fleet.

Following the establishment of the USCYBERCOM on June 23, 2009, the navy required its own command to manage the fleet's cyber units. The navy created the Fleet Cyber Command and reestablished the Tenth Fleet on January 29, 2010. The Tenth Fleet took its name from the U.S. Navy's antisubmarine warfare command, originally led by Admiral Ernest J. King in the Battle of the Atlantic during World War II. Much as the original Tenth Fleet ensured the defeat of German submarines to allow the flow of supplies across the Atlantic, the new Tenth Fleet aims to ensure the navy's access to cyber space by coordinating the navy's efforts against cyber threats. The new cyber fleet includes larger task forces and smaller task groups organized to work on four key areas: network operations and defense, information operations, fleet and theater operations, and cryptological operations. These units are deployed at key navy installations in both the United States and overseas. As of 2014, the Tenth Fleet totaled approximately 15,000 officers, enlisted persons, and civilians with a budget allotment of $904 million.

The navy conceptualizes the cyber realm much like the service does the sea, as a global commons of information flowing through cyber space. To best exert its influence in cyber space, the navy seeks to control the domain through commanding critical nodes and lines of communication. The Tenth Fleet enables naval operations in both the real world and in cyber space through the direct attack of cyber threats by securing navy information networks, especially in high-threat environments, and providing navy units with an information advantage over its adversaries. To ensure proper execution of these operational goals, the Tenth Fleet seeks to develop a force of skilled cyber experts to support the continued development of critical information technologies in both government and private industry and to reform the navy's acquisition process so that the service can rapidly integrate new capabilities into the fleet.

Ryan Wadle

See also: Net-centric Warfare (NCW); Second Army/Army Cyber Command; 24th Air Force; U.S. Coast Guard Cyber Command (CGCYBER); U.S. Cyber Command (USCYBERCOM)

Further Reading

U.S. Navy. *The Navy Strategy for Achieving Information Dominance.* http://www.public.navy .mil/fccc10f/Strategies/Navy_Strategy_for_Achieving_Information_Dominance.pdf.

U.S. Navy. *U.S. Fleet Cyber Command/Tenth Fleet Strategic Plan 2015–2020.* http://www.navy .mil/strategic/FCC-C10F Strategic Plan 2015-2020.pdf.

W

WARGAMES

The 1983 movie *WarGames*, starring Matthew Broderick and Ally Sheedy, represented a significant turning point in U.S. cyber-security policy. Allegedly, President Ronald Reagan was so concerned about the plausibility of the movie that he ordered a study to determine the risk that hacking posed to national security. In the movie, Broderick's character randomly calls telephone numbers looking for computers with modems to play games. He discovers a computer filled with games that denies him access. He researches his target and discovers the lead programmer's backdoor. Unbeknown to the protagonist, the computer is actually a mainframe at the North American Aerospace Defense Command (NORAD) that is responsible for nuclear weapons command and control. The computer then initiates a sequence that almost causes a nuclear exchange with the Soviet Union.

WarGames was the first movie that fairly accurately portrayed hacking methodology of the time period. Many people in the government were relatively unfamiliar with hacking, as computer networking was at a very early state and dependent on telephone infrastructure. The idea that advanced national-security computers could be breached by unsophisticated hackers seemed implausible to many computer-security experts at the time, but the government study found otherwise.

The Reagan administration reacted by signing the first detailed national policy on cyber security, called the National Policy on Telecommunications and Automated Information Systems Security (NSDD-145). Although there were certainly groups within the federal government that were significantly concerned about cyber security, *WarGames* was the catalyst the government needed for action. Even today, this is still, perhaps, the most significant hacking movie, and it certainly had the greatest influence of any film on cyber-security policy.

Zachary M. Smith

See also: Matrix, The; Terminator, The

Further Reading

Brown, Scott. "*WarGames*: A Look Back at the Film That Turned Geeks and Phreaks into Stars." *Wired*, July 21, 2008.

Kaplan, Fred. "Cybersecurity's Debt to a Hollywood Hack." *New York Times*, February 21, 2016.

WEAPONS OF MASS DISRUPTION

From the end of World War II to the present, weapons of mass destruction (WMD) have been a persistent concerning topic. WMDs are generally broken into the categories of biological, chemical, and nuclear/radiological. They are noteworthy because they have the potential to cause enormous casualties and major disruptions in the social order. In the period since the end of the Cold War, the definition of WMD has come under debate, as cyber weapons have gained prominence in possessing great disruptive and destructive potential—weapons of mass disruption.

Perhaps the most iconic WMD is the nuclear weapon, powered by either fission or fusion. The only entities that possess these weapons are national governments, though certain terrorist groups have expressed interest in acquiring nuclear weapons. Throughout the Cold War, nuclear weapons formed the military basis of the conflict and the enforcement mechanism for deterrence. To this day, the threatened use of thousands of nuclear weapons provides the basis for international security and the prevention of large-scale conflict between major powers. Despite past and current security regimes being based on the threatened use of such weapons, several treaties and organizations have been fashioned to reduce the number and ultimate use of nuclear weapons.

Chemical weapons are those that use toxic or caustic chemicals to inflict harm. As with nuclear weapons, chemical weapons have the ability to inflict broad human damage and deny the use of large areas. They include nerve agents, blistering agents, and respiratory agents. Chemical weapons have been used in war and continue to be used as a method of crowd control. By and large, however, the Chemical Weapons Convention (CWC) of the 1990s has outlawed the use and possession of most chemical weapons.

Biological weapons are organic compounds that present dangers to humans when they are weaponized. Typical biological weapons include naturally occurring toxic substances and dangerous communicable pathogens. The Biological Weapons Convention generally outlawed the possession and employment of biological weapons. Given the potential for the mass destruction, death, and chaos that can be caused by WMDs, the proscription of the use of such instruments has grown in an increasingly globalized world. In large part, the ban is derived from the difficulty in using WMDs in a discriminating manner.

Cyber weapons' key resemblance to WMDs is their ability to create widespread effects in a short period of time. While they do not have the physical destructive potential of classical WMDs, they are often called *weapons of mass disruption* because of the enormous variety of ways in which a major campaign of cyber attacks could potentially interrupt even the most basic aspects of modern life by shutting down electrical grids, communications networks, and financial institutions.

Trevor Albertson

See also: Cyber War; Cyber Weapon; Infrastructure; *Unrestricted Warfare*

Further Reading

Kaplan, Fred M. *Dark Territory: The Secret History of Cyber War.* New York: Simon & Schuster, 2016.

Libicki, Martin. *Cyberspace in Peace and War.* Annapolis, MD: U.S. Naval Institute Press, 2016.
Singer, P. W., and Allan Friedman. *Cybersecurity and Cyber War: What Everyone Should Know.* New York: Oxford University Press, 2014.

WHITE HAT

The term *white hat* is usually used to refer to ethical hackers who are not using their skills to destroy or attack a computer system but to prevent such damage by testing it via simulated penetrations. The term harkens to Western films, where the good character usually wore a white hat while the bad one had a black hat. The ethically acting hacker is consequently a *white hat*, while the one who uses malware to gain unallowed access to personal data or is illegally intruding into a secured system is a *black hat* hacker.

A security test for the U.S. Air Force Multics system was one of the first instances of white hat hacking. As a consequence of this test, security issues could be discovered and improved before launch. The U.S. military uses white hat hackers to test new devices or programs to make sure these new technologies are capable of resisting any known form of cyber attack. Such tests do not solely include pentrating attacks against software and computer systems; they usually also try to simulate other forms of intrusion into private data, such as through corrupt e-mail messages. White hats are usually recruited by security agencies, the military, or private corporations to secure their hacking potential for the greater good, though some white hats engage in their activities as a hobby. Especially with regard to the future scenarios of a cyber war, these hackers will play a tremendously important role for national security.

Frank Jacob

See also: Black Hat; Cyber Security; Hacker; Patriotic Hacking

Further Reading

Haerens, Margaret, and Lynn M. Zott, eds. *Hacking and Hackers.* Detroit, MI: Greenhaven Press, 2014.
Holt, Thomas J., and Bernadette H. Schell. *Hackers and Hacking: A Reference Handbook.* Santa Barbara, CA: ABC-CLIO, 2013.
Levy, Steven. *Hackers: Heroes of the Computer Revolution.* Beijing: O'Reilly, 2010.

WHITELIST

A whitelist is a grouping of identifiers representing authorized or confirmed benign entities or content. Such identifiers may include Internet Protocol (IP) addresses, domain names, file hashes, or e-mail addresses. Whitelists may be used for two purposes:

1. To precisely define the entities with which a host or network may communicate with or the content that may be allowed to enter or reside in a system or network.
2. To indicate authorized exceptions for a security mechanism that would otherwise block or restrict such communications or contents.

The primary uses of whitelisting fall in the second category, as a way of addressing limitations in security mechanisms (e.g., ensuring that a critical mail server will never be accidentally blocked). However, the high volumes of malware in recent years has inspired the creation of systems and the use of security policies that explicitly define complete sets of allowed software (e.g., as identified by a hash of the code). In such environments, all other software will be prevented from executing (or, with less strict settings, an alert will be raised). This may be contrasted with a blacklist approach, where the system may prevent execution of malicious software that is included in the blacklist. The choice between blacklisting and whitelisting primarily depends on the relative prevalence of malicious versus benign entities, the ability or difficulty to precisely define one or the other class of entities, and the degree of dynamism in the system (e.g., the rate at which new benign or malicious software may be encountered).

Angelos D. Keromytis

See also: Blacklist; Cyber Defense; Internet

Further Reading

Brenner, Joel. *America the Vulnerable: Inside the New Threat Matrix of Digital Espionage, Crime, and Warfare.* New York: Penguin Press, 2011.

WI-FI

Wi-Fi is a means for electronic devices to connect to a wireless local area network (WLAN) without requiring a hardwired connection. Most Wi-Fi networks utilize ultra high frequency (UHF) and super high frequency (SHF) radio bands, although it is possible to operate on other sections of the electromagnetic spectrum. WLAN allows any wireless-capable device to access and utilize the WLAN network, assuming the device meets the necessary password or encryption requirements that are created to protect the network.

The most common means to access Wi-Fi networks are personal computers, smartphones, and tablet computers, although an increasing array of devices are now Wi-Fi enabled. Home appliances, video-game consoles, digital computers, and network printers are now commonly connected to WLAN through wireless access points. These access points, also called *hotspots*, have ranges of approximately 20 meters indoors and 100 meters outdoors, although obstructions and electromagnetic interference can reduce the effective range. Wireless access points (WAP) can be used to connect wireless devices to a wired network. Often, the same router that is used to connect a local network to the Internet will also have a built-in wireless hotspot.

Because Wi-Fi does not require a physical connection, it is by definition less secure than wired networks. Any wireless-enabled device can theoretically detect all WLAN hotspots within range, even if it does not have the password to connect to the network. Further, many open WLAN systems (such as those commonly provided at airports, hotels, and other public locations) have little or no security, making users who connect to them without an encryption protocol subject to detection and interception. Unfortunately, many computer users falsely assume that they possess anonymity when using Wi-Fi networks and thus expose themselves to significant cyber threats.

Cyber criminals have taken advantage of the open nature of many public Wi-Fi nodes to engage in identity theft, financial crimes, and cyber vandalism. In particular, intercepting signals for credit card transactions has proven extremely lucrative. State-sponsored cyber actors, especially intelligence-collection agencies, have established open Wi-Fi networks in public locations as a means to trawl for potentially useful intelligence through the interception of unsecured communications. One favored tactic has been to offer free Wi-Fi access in social gathering spaces near major work centers of the targeted population. For these reasons, savvy computer users utilize encryption algorithms to protect their data and establish virtual private networks as a means to conceal their vital computer information.

Jeffrey R. Cares

See also: Cloud Computing; Cyber Defense; Hardware; Internet; Internet Service Provider (ISP); Malware

Further Reading

Brenner, Joel. *America the Vulnerable: Inside the New Threat Matrix of Digital Espionage, Crime, and Warfare.* New York: Penguin Press, 2011.

WIKILEAKS

WikiLeaks considers itself a nonprofit media organization, though it is most noted for publishing leaked documents, videos, or other media documenting government or corporate wrongdoing on its Web site. The Web site was launched in 2007 by noted hacktivist Julian Assange. Assange also serves as the editor-in-chief and director of the Web site. WikiLeaks is owned by the organization the Sunshine Press.

Assange first thought of the idea of WikiLeaks in 2005 while at his home in Melbourne, Australia. He wanted to create a Web site where anyone could anonymously post documents. In 2006, he reached out to fellow hacktivist John Young, founder of the Web site Cryptome, to register the domain WikiLeaks.org on behalf of Assange. WikiLeaks works by allowing whistle-blowers to upload content to a secure, anonymous drop box. Assange also gathered together a group of Chinese dissidents and techies from the United States, Australia, South Africa, and Europe to serve as WikiLeaks' advisers. Assange wanted to create a system where the identity of whistle-blowers was hidden, even from the organization itself. Secure communications and the protection of whistle-blowers' identities were of utmost importance to Assange from WikiLeaks' founding.

One of WikiLeaks' first stories revolved around a leaked document accusing Somali leader Sheik Hassan Dahir Aweys of planning to assassinate the leaders of the Somali government. Assange himself wrote an analysis of the piece and posted it directly to the WikiLeaks Web site. WikiLeaks also became the source of a 2007 story alleging corruption by the Kenyan president Daniel arap Moi. WikiLeaks also published other documentation concerning the treatment of prisoners in Guantanamo and the costs of the war in Afghanistan. WikiLeaks was also the site where Anonymous-affiliated hacktivist David Kernell uploaded the contents of Sarah Palin's hacked e-mail account.

In early 2010, it is alleged that a soldier named Bradley Manning had contacted Assange about a number of documents that WikiLeaks might desire. Later that year, WikiLeaks released a U.S. State Department cable related to the 2008 Icelandic banking scandal. WikiLeaks then released a video titled "Collateral Murder." The video provides footage of two American Apache helicopters opening fire on what appeared to be unarmed Iraqi civilians. Among those killed in the attack were two *Reuters* journalists covering the war. This video was followed by two more releases of material documenting U.S. actions in Iraq and Afghanistan known as the "Iraqi War Logs" and the "Afghan War Diary," respectively. In 2010, WikiLeaks partnered with news outlets the *New York Times*, *The Guardian*, and *Der Spiegel* to release a huge archive of redacted U.S. Department of State cables. Disagreements over the handling and release of the material led to a split between Assange and longtime collaborators at *The Guardian*. Relations between Assange and the *New York Times* became equally acrimonious when the *New York Times* released a very unflattering portrayal of Assange.

As a result of the release of the diplomatic cables, it was revealed that former secretary of state Hilary Clinton had directed employees to spy on UN secretary Ban Ki Moon as well as other UN employees and U.S. allies. It also revealed the names of Arab countries pressing the United States to bomb Iranian nuclear facilities. State Department cables also acknowledged ongoing high-level corruption in African countries such as Egypt, Kenya, and the Sudan. It also documented U.S. knowledge of corporate wrongdoing in various countries. Later documents released in 2015 uncovered that the United States was spying on French presidents Nicholas Sarkozy, Jacques Chirac, and Francois Hollande; German chancellor Angela Merkel; and several Brazilian government officials.

Since the release of documents outlining the treatment of prisoners in Guantanamo Bay, WikiLeaks and Julian Assange have drawn the attention of the U.S. government. In 2010, Department of Justice (DOJ) officials began to explore the possibility of charging Assange under the 1917 Espionage Act. A few weeks after the release of the "Afghan War Logs," the Department of Defense (DoD) organized a 150-person WikiLeaks Task Force meant to investigate Assange's and WikiLeaks' activities. The task force was made up of high-level military intelligence officials working around the clock to stop Assange and WikiLeaks.

After Manning's arrest, the Pentagon began to explore the possibility that he was manipulated by Assange to collect material for publication by WikiLeaks. U.S. government officials spoke broadly about the threat WikiLeaks and Assange posed to U.S. national security, and the Obama administration pressed European and Australian governments to detain Assange and prevent him from crossing international borders. In August 2010, Swedish authorities issued an arrest warrant for Assange under allegations of rape and sexual misconduct stemming from incidents with two Swedish women earlier that year. Assange was arrested in London, but supporters soon posted bail.

Assange petitioned the U.K. courts to not extradite him to Sweden to face charges. His attorneys argued that Swedish extradition was tantamount to a death sentence, as he feared Sweden would then send him to the United States to face the death penalty on espionage charges. The U.K. courts denied the request, causing Assange to seek asylum at the London office of the Ecuadorian embassy. In 2016, the United Nations convened a Working Group on Arbitrary Detention. The group found Assange's arbitrary detention by Sweden and the United Kingdom was a violation of his human rights. Regardless, U.K. authorities are still looking to extradite him to face rape charges in Sweden. As of this writing, Assange still resides at the Ecuadorian embassy in London. His Swedish rape charges are set to expire in 2020.

Prior to his arrest, Assange was seeking residency in Sweden to make WikiLeaks a Swedish-based organization. He chose Sweden because free speech laws make it illegal for journalists to reveal sources. Additionally, WikiLeaks' servers are based in Sweden, making it nearly impossible for the United States to shut them down, as they previously had when Amazon hosted the Web site. The Swedish Pirate Party also agreed to pay for hosting as well as technical upkeep on the Web site, and they also agreed to keep hidden and not record the Internet Protocol (IP) addresses of any WikiLeaks users. This is to ensure anonymity for whistle-blowers and users alike.

WikiLeaks has few employees and is mostly administered by volunteers. It is financed through private donations. In December 2009, due to a shortage of funds, WikiLeaks disabled all but the drop box functions of the Web site until funds could be raised to pay for operating costs. In 2010, Paypal suspended WikiLeaks' accounts and froze all their assets. In response, Anonymous launched Operation Payback to get Paypal to reverse its actions against WikiLeaks. Valitor (an Icelandic company related to Visa and MasterCard) also prevented donations from being made using its credit cards; however, this action was deemed illegal by Icelandic courts. Donations to WikiLeaks are technically made to the Wau Holland Foundation, which then disperses the funds to pay employee salaries and other daily operation costs.

WikiLeaks has undergone drastic restructuring since 2010. Prior to 2010, it had functioned similar to other "wiki" Web sites, where all users could upload and discuss posts. However, now all posts are vetted by an internal editorial board, with Assange having final approval for all material posted to the Web site. The editorial board consists of subject matter experts and computer programmers who work to verify the authenticity of documents. Users are no longer permitted to edit, alter, or comment on any posts. The organization has also had an employee restructuring, with many former supporters no longer working with WikiLeaks, the most famous being longtime WikiLeaks supporter Daniel Domscheit-Berg, who was suspended by Assange. Other collaborators and supporters have equally been dismissed, left, or become Federal Bureau of Investigation (FBI) informants.

Supporters of WikiLeaks argue that the Web site and others like it represent the rise of a digital "fifth estate," or a sociopolitical organization powerful enough to influence public opinion and policy making. The fifth estate is able to speak truth to power, even when the fourth estate, that is, the mainstream media, cannot or will not. Supporters have also argued that the rise of WikiLeaks has ushered in a new era of accountability, where governments and other powerful organizations can be held to higher standards of transparency, thereby enhancing global governance, democracy, and freedom of speech. However, because WikiLeaks releases classified information, often unedited, critics argue the organization poses a threat to national security, undermines diplomatic efforts, and puts lives at risk.

Human rights organizations have urged WikiLeaks to redact the names of civilians on the documents it releases. Assange himself has publicly stated that if WikiLeaks continues to release unedited documents, it could one day have "blood on its hands." WikiLeaks has also spawned a variety of similar whistle-blower Web sites, many focused on particular organizations (e.g., the European Union) or a specific industry (e.g., the coal mining industry).

Barbara Salera

See also: Anonymous; Assange, Julian; Hacktivist; Manning, Bradley; Snowden, Edward J.

Further Reading

Fowler, Andrew. *The Most Dangerous Man in the World: The Explosive True Story of Julian Assange and the Lies, Cover-ups and Conspiracies He Exposed.* New York: Skyhorse, 2011.

Greenberg, Andy. *This Machine Kills Secrets: Julian Assange, the Cypherpunks, and Their Fight to Empower Whistleblowers.* New York: Plume, 2013.

Madar, Chase. *The Passion of Bradley Manning.* London: Verso, 2013.

Nicks, Denver. *Private Bradley Manning, WikiLeaks, and the Biggest Exposure of Official Secrets in American History.* Chicago: Review Press, 2013.

WORM

Computer worms are programs that self-propagate across systems. The distinction from a computer virus is that such propagation occurs without the need for user involvement (e.g., to copy files to/from removable media, such as a flash drive, or to execute an infected program). In most cases, this means that the worm is capable of identifying and exploiting one or more vulnerabilities in target systems, which allows a new instance of its code to start execution there. As a result, worms are generally capable of propagating across a network much faster than a virus, whose propagation speed is limited to that of the human activity that helps spread it. Fast-spreading worms, such as the SQL Slammer worm, whose code fit within a single UDP packet, are able to infect almost all possible targets within 10 minutes.

Such fast-spreading worms have sometimes caused network-stability problems as secondary effects of their aggressive scanning and propagation activity.

The three primary components of a worm are target identification, propagation, and payload. Target identification involves finding new systems to infect and partly depends on the communication medium. For worms that rely on removable media, targeting consists of infecting each new such medium (e.g., a USB stick) and determining whether any new systems on which that medium is inserted are already infected. For Internet worms (or, more generally, worms in networked environments), target identification has historically been done as a mix of an explicit hit list of targets that is compiled ahead of time by the worm creator and scanning the network to identify vulnerable hosts.

Worms seen in the wild have mostly used a pure-scanning approach, with each instance of the worm randomly probing and infecting remote systems. However, most such worms have been launched against an initial set of known vulnerable systems that had been identified a priori. Academic work has shown that it is possible to create even faster-spreading worms by making heavier use of such precompiled hit lists, at the risk of exposure due to the scanning activity. In general, the logistic function provides a good model of the propagation speed of worms; the same behavior is seen for infectious diseases in the biological domain.

Propagation is the method for how a worm replicates itself and spreads. Although the majority of worms in the early years of the 21st century exploited software bugs that allowed for remote code injection and control flow hijacking, primarily using buffer overflow bugs, other worms have exploited features, such as removable media auto-execution; configuration weaknesses, such as open services or disabled authentication; and stolen or predictable credentials. Several worms also demonstrated the use of multimode propagation (i.e., using a variety of attack vectors), including the first widely publicized Internet worm, the 1989 Morris worm.

The payload component refers to code that is not relevant for target identification and propagation and which may be invoked to achieve an effect on all or a subset of infected systems. Many of the worms seen in the wild have not carried an explicit payload; rather, their sole purpose appears to have been propagation. A notable exception is the Stuxnet worm, which appears to have targeted specific supervisory control and data acquisition (SCADA) systems for destruction. Other payloads seen in the wild include deletion of files, installation of backdoors, and even patching of systems to prevent other worms from propagating.

Angelos D. Keromytis

See also: Antivirus Software; Conficker Worm; Malware; MS Blaster Worm; SQL Slammer Worm; Stuxnet

Further Reading

Bowden, Mark. *Worm: The First Digital World War.* New York: Grove Press, 2011.
Springer, Paul J. *Cyber Warfare: A Reference Handbook.* Santa Barbara, CA: ABC-CLIO, 2015.

Z

ZERO-DAY VULNERABILITY

A zero-day vulnerability is an error in the code of a program that exposes it, and potentially the system or network that runs it, to a hacker who becomes aware of the exploitable mistake. It is called a *zero-day vulnerability* because the first warning that the hole exists usually comes in the form of a cyber attack that exploits it, one leaving a cyber defender zero days to patch the hole before damage commences. Zero-day vulnerabilities are a serious threat precisely because they are revealed through an attack. A zero-day attack can come through almost any piece of malware, including Trojan horses, worms, and viruses.

Hackers prize the discovery of zero-day vulnerabilities, in part because knowledge of their existence and how to exploit them can be sold to unscrupulous users. The larger the vulnerability, and the more systems running unpatched software that might be exploited, the larger the payday for discovering it. Some software companies now offer bounties to hackers that discover these vulnerabilities and point them out to the company rather than selling them on the underground market. The companies then create patches and push them out to users, effectively blocking the vulnerability before it becomes publicly known.

Cyber attacks that exploit zero-day vulnerabilities have a high probability of success, particularly if they use more than one such opportunity. However, the discovery and hoarding of zero-day vulnerabilities is expensive and somewhat risky. Software companies constantly test their own software for errors and might discover a problem before a hacker has the opportunity to take advantage of a discovery. Other hackers might find the vulnerability and exploit it, making it visible to the companies and subject to repairs. Thus, there is always a certain degree of pressure to take advantage of a zero-day vulnerability as soon as possible, lest the opportunity evaporate.

Nation-states with advanced cyber programs spend an inordinate amount of time and resources on the discovery of zero-day vulnerabilities. These exploitable errors create remarkable opportunities for cyber espionage and might even facilitate large-scale attacks in a future cyber war. Some analysts pointed out that Stuxnet, the malware program that significantly damaged the Iranian nuclear program, utilized four zero-day vulnerabilities, making it an enormous investment for whomever created it. They argue that the use of such a large number of zero-day exploits demonstrates that the program must have been the work of a nation-state, although there is no definitive proof as to the identify of Stuxnet's creators.

Paul J. Springer

See also: Antivirus Software; Cyber Espionage; Dark Web; Hacker; Malware; Stuxnet

Further Reading

Poroshyn, Roman. *Stuxnet: The True Story of Hunt and Evolution.* Denver, CO: Outskirts Press, 2013.

Rosenzweig, Paul. *Cyber Warfare: How Conflicts in Cyberspace Are Challenging America and Changing the World.* Santa Barbara, CA: Praeger, 2013.

Primary Documents

1. Remarks of President Barack Obama on Securing the Nation's Cyber Infrastructure, Washington, D.C., May 29, 2009

Barack Obama's first presidential election campaign harnessed the power of cyber space in ways that no candidate had ever done before, including using the Internet for unprecedented amounts of fund-raising and directly communicating with supporters. In this major policy speech, President Obama outlines his plan to improve the cyber security of the United States through several major steps to protect U.S. cyber networks. Although critics argued that the president's plan did not do nearly enough to protect the nation's cyber infrastructure, it still represented a major shift in the federal approach to cyber security and defensive preparations for cyber war.

It's long been said that the revolutions in communications and information technology have given birth to a virtual world. But make no mistake: This world—cyberspace—is a world that we depend on every single day. It's our hardware and our software, our desktops and laptops and cell phones and Blackberries that have become woven into every aspect of our lives.

It's the broadband networks beneath us and the wireless signals around us, the local networks in our schools and hospitals and businesses, and the massive grids that power our nation. It's the classified military and intelligence networks that keep us safe, and the World Wide Web that has made us more interconnected than at any time in human history.

So cyberspace is real. And so are the risks that come with it.

It's the great irony of our Information Age—the very technologies that empower us to create and to build also empower those who would disrupt and destroy. And this paradox—seen and unseen—is something that we experience every day.

It's about the privacy and the economic security of American families. We rely on the Internet to pay our bills, to bank, to shop, to file our taxes. But we've had to learn a whole new vocabulary just to stay ahead of the cyber criminals who would do us harm—spyware and malware and spoofing and phishing and botnets. Millions of Americans have been victimized, their privacy violated, their identities stolen, their lives upended, and their wallets emptied. According to one survey, in the past two years alone cyber crime has cost Americans more than $8 billion.

I know how it feels to have privacy violated because it has happened to me and the people around me. It's no secret that my presidential campaign harnessed the Internet and technology to transform our politics. What isn't widely known is that during the general election hackers managed to penetrate our computer systems. To all of you who donated to our campaign, I want you to all rest assured, our fund-raising Web site was untouched. (Laughter.) So your confidential personal and financial information was protected.

But between August and October, hackers gained access to e-mails and a range of campaign files, from policy position papers to travel plans. And we worked closely with the CIA—with the FBI and the Secret Service and hired security consultants to restore the security of our systems. It was a powerful reminder: In this Information Age, one of your greatest strengths—in our case, our ability to communicate to a wide range of supporters through the Internet—could also be one of your greatest vulnerabilities.

This is a matter, as well, of America's economic competitiveness. The small businesswoman in St. Louis, the bond trader in the New York Stock Exchange, the workers at a global shipping company in Memphis, the young entrepreneur in Silicon Valley—they all need the networks to make the next payroll, the next trade, the next delivery, the next great breakthrough. E-commerce alone last year accounted for some $132 billion in retail sales.

But every day we see waves of cyber thieves trolling for sensitive information—the disgruntled employee on the inside, the lone hacker a thousand miles away, organized crime, the industrial spy and, increasingly, foreign intelligence services. In one brazen act last year, thieves used stolen credit card information to steal millions of dollars from 130 ATM machines in 49 cities around the world—and they did it in just 30 minutes. A single employee of an American company was convicted of stealing intellectual property reportedly worth $400 million. It's been estimated that last year alone cyber criminals stole intellectual property from businesses worldwide worth up to $1 trillion.

In short, America's economic prosperity in the 21st century will depend on cybersecurity.

And this is also a matter of public safety and national security. We count on computer networks to deliver our oil and gas, our power and our water. We rely on them for public transportation and air traffic control. Yet we know that cyber intruders have probed our electrical grid and that in other countries cyber attacks have plunged entire cities into darkness.

Our technological advantage is a key to America's military dominance. But our defense and military networks are under constant attack. Al Qaeda and other terrorist groups have spoken of their desire to unleash a cyber attack on our country—attacks that are harder to detect and harder to defend against. Indeed, in today's world, acts of terror could come not only from a few extremists in suicide vests but from a few keystrokes on the computer—a weapon of mass disruption.

In one of the most serious cyber incidents to date against our military networks, several thousand computers were infected last year by malicious software—malware. And while no sensitive information was compromised, our troops and defense personnel had to give up those external memory devices—thumb drives—changing the way they used their computers every day.

And last year we had a glimpse of the future face of war. As Russian tanks rolled into Georgia, cyber attacks crippled Georgian government Web sites. The terrorists that sowed so much death and destruction in Mumbai relied not only on guns and grenades but also on GPS and phones using voice-over-the-Internet.

For all these reasons, it's now clear this cyber threat is one of the most serious economic and national security challenges we face as a nation.

It's also clear that we're not as prepared as we should be, as a government or as a country. In recent years, some progress has been made at the federal level. But just as we failed in the past to invest in our physical infrastructure—our roads, our bridges and rails—we've failed to invest in the security of our digital infrastructure.

No single official oversees cybersecurity policy across the federal government, and no single agency has the responsibility or authority to match the scope and scale of the challenge. Indeed, when it comes to cybersecurity, federal agencies have overlapping missions and don't coordinate and communicate nearly as well as they should—with each other or with the private sector. We saw this in the disorganized response to Conficker, the Internet "worm" that in recent months has infected millions of computers around the world.

. . . From now on, our digital infrastructure—the networks and computers we depend on every day—will be treated as they should be: as a strategic national asset. Protecting this infrastructure will be a national security priority. We will ensure that these networks are secure, trustworthy and resilient. We will deter, prevent, detect, and defend against attacks and recover quickly from any disruptions or damage.

. . . First, working in partnership with the communities represented here today, we will develop a new comprehensive strategy to secure America's information and communications networks. To ensure a coordinated approach across government, my cybersecurity coordinator will work closely with my chief technology officer, Aneesh Chopra, and my chief information officer, Vivek Kundra. To ensure accountability in federal agencies, cybersecurity will be designated as one of my key management priorities. Clear milestones and performances metrics will measure progress. And as we develop our strategy, we will be open and transparent, which is why you'll find today's report and a wealth of related information on our Web site, www.whitehouse.gov.

Second, we will work with all the key players—including state and local governments and the private sector—to ensure an organized and unified response to future cyber incidents. Given the enormous damage that can be caused by even a single cyber attack, ad hoc responses will not do. Nor is it sufficient to simply strengthen our defenses after incidents or attacks occur. Just as we do for natural disasters, we have to have plans and resources in place beforehand—sharing information, issuing warnings and ensuring a coordinated response.

Third, we will strengthen the public/private partnerships that are critical to this endeavor. The vast majority of our critical information infrastructure in the United States is owned and operated by the private sector. So let me be very clear: My administration will not dictate security standards for private companies. On the contrary, we will collaborate with industry to find technology solutions that ensure our security and promote prosperity.

Fourth, we will continue to invest in the cutting-edge research and development necessary for the innovation and discovery we need to meet the digital challenges of our time. And that's why my administration is making major investments in our information infrastructure: laying broadband lines to every corner of America; building a smart electric grid to deliver energy more efficiently; pursuing a next generation of air traffic control systems; and moving to electronic health records, with privacy protections, to reduce costs and save lives.

And finally, we will begin a national campaign to promote cybersecurity awareness and digital literacy from our boardrooms to our classrooms, and to build a digital workforce for the 21st century. And that's why we're making a new commitment to education in math and science, and historic investments in science and research and development. Because it's not enough for our children and students to master today's technologies—social networking and e-mailing and texting and blogging—we need them to pioneer the technologies that will allow us to work effectively through these new media and allow us to prosper in the future. So these are the things we will do.

Let me also be clear about what we will not do. Our pursuit of cybersecurity will not—I repeat, will not—include monitoring private sector networks or Internet traffic. We will preserve and protect the personal privacy and civil liberties that we cherish as Americans. Indeed, I remain firmly committed to net neutrality so we can keep the Internet as it should be—open and free.

Source: Obama, Barack. "Remarks by the President on Securing Our Nation's Cyber Infrastructure." The White House, May 29, 2009. https://www.whitehouse .gov/the-press-office/remarks-president-securing-our-nations-cyber-infrastructure.

2. Excerpts of Secretary of State Hillary Clinton on Internet Freedom, Washington, D.C., January 21, 2010

Secretary of State Hillary Clinton delivered these remarks before a gathering of Internet freedom activists, U.S. political leaders, and international visitors. Her remarks demonstrate both the U.S. resolve to protect its own cyber space and a belligerent approach to any nations that have a different view of the importance of Internet freedom. Her remarks were interpreted by some authoritarian governments as a deliberate effort by the United States to undermine their control of the Internet in their nations and as a call to arms for insurgents in China, Iran, and North Korea to use the Internet as a means to communicate with fellow rebels and increase their resistance to the government forces.

The spread of information networks is forming a new nervous system for our planet. When something happens in Haiti or Hunan, the rest of us learn about it in real time—from real people. And we can respond in real time as well. Americans eager to help in the aftermath of a disaster and the girl trapped in the supermarket are connected in ways that were not even imagined a year ago, even a generation ago. That same principle applies to almost all of humanity today. As we sit here, any of you—or maybe more likely, any of our children—can take out the tools that many carry every day and transmit this discussion to billions across the world.

Now, in many respects, information has never been so free. There are more ways to spread more ideas to more people than at any moment in history. And even in authoritarian countries, information networks are helping people discover new facts and making governments more accountable.

During his visit to China in November, for example, President Obama held a town hall meeting with an online component to highlight the importance of the Internet. In response to a question that was sent in over the Internet, he defended the right of people to freely access information, and said that the more freely information flows, the stronger societies become. He spoke about how access to information helps citizens hold their own governments accountable, generates new ideas, encourages creativity and entrepreneurship. The United States' belief in that ground truth is what brings me here today.

Because amid this unprecedented surge in connectivity, we must also recognize that these technologies are not an unmitigated blessing. These tools are also being exploited to undermine human progress and political rights. Just as steel can be used to build hospitals or machine guns, or nuclear power can either energize a city or destroy it, modern information networks and the technologies they support can be harnessed for good or for ill. The same networks that help organize movements for freedom also enable al-Qaida to spew hatred and incite violence against the innocent. And technologies with the potential to open up access to government and promote transparency can also be hijacked by governments to crush dissent and deny human rights.

In the last year, we've seen a spike in threats to the free flow of information. China, Tunisia, and Uzbekistan have stepped up their censorship of the Internet. In Vietnam, access to popular social networking sites has suddenly disappeared. And last Friday in Egypt, 30 bloggers and activists were detained. One member of this group, Bassem Samir, who is thankfully no longer in prison, is with us today. So while it is clear that the spread of these technologies is transforming our world, it is still unclear how that transformation will affect the human rights welfare of the world's population.

On their own, new technologies do not take sides in the struggle for freedom and progress, but the United States does. We stand for a single Internet where all of humanity has equal access to knowledge and ideas. And we recognize that the world's information infrastructure will become what we and others make of it. Now this challenge may be new, but our responsibility to help ensure the free exchange of ideas goes back to the birth of our republic.

There are many other networks in the world. Some aid in the movement of people or resources, and some facilitate exchanges between individuals with the same work or interests. But the Internet is a network that magnifies the power and potential of all others. And that's why we believe it's critical that its users are assured certain basic freedoms. Freedom of expression is first among them. This freedom is no longer defined solely by whether citizens can go into the town square and criticize their government without fear of retribution. Blogs, e-mails, social networks, and text messages have opened up new forums for exchanging ideas, and created new targets for censorship. As I speak to you today, government censors somewhere are working furiously to erase my words from the records of history. But history has already condemned these tactics.

Some countries have erected electronic barriers that prevent their people from accessing portions of the world's networks. They've expunged words, names, and phrases from search engine results. They have violated the privacy of citizens who engage in nonviolent political speech. These actions contravene the Universal Declaration of Human Rights, which tells us that all people have the right "to seek, receive and impart information and ideas through any media and regardless of frontiers." With the spread of these restrictive practices, a new information curtain is descending across much of the world. And beyond this partition, viral videos and blog posts are becoming the samizdat of our day.

As in the dictatorships of the past, governments are targeting independent thinkers who use these tools. In the demonstrations that followed Iran's presidential elections, grainy cell phone footage of a young woman's bloody murder provided a digital indictment of the government's brutality. We've seen reports that when Iranians living overseas posted online criticism of their nation's leaders, their family members in Iran were singled out for retribution. And despite an intense campaign of government intimidation, brave citizen journalists in Iran continue using technology to show the world and their fellow citizens what is happening inside their country. In speaking out on behalf of their own human rights, the Iranian people have inspired the world. And their courage is redefining how technology is used to spread truth and expose injustice.

Some nations, however, have co-opted the Internet as a tool to target and silence people of faith. Last year, for example, in Saudi Arabia, a man spent months in prison for blogging about Christianity. And a Harvard study found that the Saudi government blocked many Web pages about Hinduism, Judaism, Christianity, and even Islam. Countries including Vietnam and China employed similar tactics to restrict access to religious information.

Now, just as these technologies must not be used to punish peaceful political speech, they also must not be used to persecute or silence religious minorities. Now, prayers will always travel on higher networks. But connection technologies like the Internet and social networking sites should enhance individuals' ability to worship as they see fit, come together with people of their own faith, and learn more about the beliefs of others. We must work to advance the freedom of worship online just as we do in other areas of life.

A connection to global information networks is like an on-ramp to modernity. In the early years of these technologies, many believed they would divide the world between haves and have-nots. But that hasn't happened. There are 4 billion cell phones in use today. Many of them are in the hands of market vendors, rickshaw drivers, and others who've historically lacked access to education and opportunity. Information networks have become a great leveler, and we should use them together to help lift people out of poverty and give them freedom from want.

Now, we have every reason to be hopeful about what people can accomplish when they leverage communication networks and connection technologies to achieve progress. But make no mistake—some are and will continue to use global information networks for darker purposes. Violent extremists, criminal cartels, sexual predators, and authoritarian governments all seek to exploit these global networks. Just as terrorists have taken advantage of the openness of our societies to carry out their plots, violent extremists use the Internet to radicalize and intimidate. As we work to advance freedoms, we must also work against those who use communication networks as tools of disruption and fear.

Governments and citizens must have confidence that the networks at the core of their national security and economic prosperity are safe and resilient. Now this is about more than petty hackers who deface Web sites. Our ability to bank online, use electronic commerce, and safeguard billions of dollars in intellectual property are all at stake if we cannot rely on the security of our information networks.

States, terrorists, and those who would act as their proxies must know that the United States will protect our networks. Those who disrupt the free flow of information in our society or any other pose a threat to our economy, our government, and our civil society. Countries or individuals that engage in cyber attacks should face consequences and international condemnation. In an Internet-connected world, an attack on one nation's networks can be an attack on all. And by reinforcing that message, we can create norms of behavior among states and encourage respect for the global networked commons.

Source: Clinton, Hillary. "Remarks on Internet Freedom." U.S. State Department, January 21, 2010. http://www.state.gov/secretary/20092013clinton/rm/2010/01/135519.htm.

3. Excerpts from the *Tallinn Manual on the International Law Applicable to Cyber Warfare*, NATO Cooperative Cyber Defence Centre of Excellence, 2010

In 2010, NATO's Cooperative Cyber Defence Centre of Excellence, headquartered at Tallinn, Estonia, invited experts in international law, cyber security, and information technology to draft a manual of rules for cyber warfare. The manual is not binding on even the member states of NATO, but it does offer a means to open discussion on the creation of international law governing cyber conflict. In this regard, it follows the long history of international laws of armed conflict that began through similar international conferences. This manual seeks to apply the laws of physical warfare to the cyber domain and also recognizes that some aspects of cyber war, including the means of attack and the individuals involved, differ markedly from the physical world.

Rule 5. A State shall not knowingly allow the cyber infrastructure located in its territory or under its exclusive governmental control to be used for acts that adversely and unlawfully affect other States.

Rule 6. A State bears international legal responsibility for a cyber operation attributable to it and which constitutes a breach of international obligation.

Rule 7. The mere fact that a cyber operation has been launched or otherwise originates from governmental cyber infrastructure is not sufficient evidence for attributing the operation to that State but is an indication that the State in question is associated with the operation.

Rule 8. The fact that a cyber operation has been routed via cyber infrastructure located in a State is not sufficient evidence for attributing the operation to that State.

Rule 9. A State injured by an internationally wrongful act may resort to proportionate countermeasures, including cyber countermeasures, against the responsible State.

Rule 10. A cyber operation that constitutes a threat or use of force against the territorial integrity or political independence of any State, or that is in any other manner inconsistent with the purposes of the United Nations, is unlawful.

Rule 11. A cyber operation constitutes a use of force when its scale and effects are comparable to noncyber operations rising to the level of a use of force.

. . .

Rule 16. The right of self-defence may be exercised collectively. Collective self-defence against a cyber operation amounting to an armed attack may only be exercised at the request of the victim-State and within the scope of the request.

. . .

Rule 20. Cyber operations executed in the context of an armed conflict are subject to the law of armed conflict.

. . .

Rule 28. Mercenaries involved in cyber operations do not enjoy combatant immunity or prisoner of war status.

Rule 29. Civilians are not prohibited from directly participating in cyber operations amounting to hostilities but forfeit their protection from attacks for such time as they so participate.

Rule 30. A cyber attack is a cyber operation, whether offensive or defensive, that is reasonably expected to cause injury or death to persons or damage or destruction to objects.

Rule 31. The principle of distinction applies to cyber attacks.

Rule 32. The civilian population as such, as well as individual civilians, shall not be the object of cyber attack.

. . .

Rule 36. Cyber attacks, or the threat thereof, the primary purpose of which is to spread terror among the civilian population, are prohibited.

. . .

Rule 51. A cyber attack that may be expected to cause incidental loss of civilian life, injury to civilians, damage to civilian objects, or a combination thereof, which would be excessive in relation to the concrete and direct military advantage anticipated is prohibited.

. . .

Rule 61. Cyber operations that qualify as ruses of war are permitted.

. . .

Rule 66. (a) Cyber espionage and other forms of information gathering directed at an adversary during an armed conflict do not violate the law of armed conflict. (b) A member of the armed forces who has engaged in cyber espionage in enemy-controlled territory loses the right to be a prisoner of war and may be treated as a spy if captured before re-joining the armed forces to which he or she belongs.

. . .

Rule 77. Prisoners of war and interned protected persons shall not be compelled to participate in or support cyber operations directed against their own country.

. . .

Rule 84. Diplomatic archives and communications are protected from cyber operations at all times.

Rule 85. Collective punishment by cyber means is prohibited.

. . .

Rule 93. A neutral State may not knowingly allow the exercise of belligerent rights by the parties to the conflict from cyber infrastructure located in its territory or under its exclusive control.

Source: Schmitt, Michael N. *Tallinn Manual on the International Law Applicable to Cyber Warfare.* Cambridge: Cambridge University Press, 2013. Copyright © Cambridge University Press. Reprinted with permission of Cambridge University Press.

4. Excerpts of "International Strategy for Cyberspace," May 2011

Many Western nations, the United States included, make their national security strategies available to the public. Of course, these strategy documents offer more of a general guide to the nation's priorities and goals than a practical examination of how those goals will be reached. Nevertheless, the U.S. cyber-space strategy is an important example that clarifies not only how the American government envisions the needs of the international cyber-space community but what underpins its understanding of the interaction of nations. Take note that while much of the document is extremely optimistic regarding the future of the Internet, there is a lightly veiled threat that any form of cyber attack may provoke a kinetic retaliation from the United States. Further, the American conception that all the people of the world should have free, open access to the Internet and should be granted liberty and privacy in its use is anathema to the totalitarian regimes of the world that abhor the idea of open information-sharing among their subject populations. As the United States tries to push such a vision on a global scale, it is essentially sowing the seeds of revolt among those populations.

The Future We Seek

The cyberspace environment that we seek rewards innovation and empowers individuals; it connects individuals and strengthens communities; it builds better governments and expands accountability; it safeguards fundamental freedoms and enhances personal privacy; it builds understanding, clarifies norms of behavior, and enhances national and international security. To sustain this environment, international collaboration is more than a best practice, it is a first principle.

Our Goal

The United States will work internationally to promote an open, interoperable, secure, and reliable information and communications infrastructure that supports international trade and commerce, strengthens international security, and fosters free expression and innovation. To achieve that goal, we will build and sustain an environment in which norms of responsible behavior guide states' actions, sustain partnerships, and support the rule of law in cyberspace.

Stability through Norms

The United States will work with like-minded states to establish an environment of expectations, or norms of behavior, that ground foreign and defense policies and guide international partnerships. The last two decades have seen the swift and unprecedented growth of the Internet as a social medium; the growing reliance of societies on networked information systems to control critical infrastructures and communications systems essential to modern life; and increasing evidence that governments are seeking to exercise traditional national power through cyberspace. These events have not been matched by clearly agreed-upon norms for acceptable state behavior in cyberspace. To bridge that gap, we will work to build a consensus on what constitutes acceptable behavior, and a partnership among those who view the functioning of these systems as essential to the national and collective interest.

The Role of Norms

In other spheres of international relations, shared understandings about acceptable behavior have enhanced stability and provided a basis for international action when corrective measures are required. Adherence to such norms brings predictability to state conduct, helping prevent the misunderstandings that could lead to conflict.

The development of norms for state conduct in cyberspace does not require a reinvention of customary international law, nor does it render existing international norms obsolete. Long-standing international norms guiding state behavior—in times of peace and conflict—also apply in cyberspace. Nonetheless, unique attributes of networked technology require additional work to clarify how these terms apply and what additional understandings might be necessary to supplement them. We will continue to work internationally to forge consensus regarding how norms of behavior apply to cyberspace, with the understanding that an important first step in such efforts is applying the broad expectations of peaceful and just interstate conduct to cyberspace.

The Basis for Norms

Rules that promote order and peace, advance basic human dignity, and promote freedom in economic competition are essential to any international environment. These principles provide a basic roadmap for how states can meet their traditional international obligations in cyberspace and, in many cases, reflect duties of states that apply regardless of context. The existing principles that should support cyberspace norms include:

- Upholding Fundamental Freedoms: States must respect fundamental freedoms of expression and association, online as well as off.
- Respect for Property: States should in their undertakings and through domestic laws respect intellectual property rights, including patents, trade secrets, trademarks, and copyrights.
- Valuing Privacy: Individuals should be protected from arbitrary or unlawful state interference with their privacy when they use the Internet.
- Protection from Crime: States must identify and prosecute cybercriminals, to ensure laws and practices deny criminals safe havens, and cooperate with international criminal investigations in a timely manner.
- Right of Self-Defense: Consistent with the United Nations Charter, states have an inherent right to self-defense that may be triggered by certain aggressive acts in cyberspace.

Deriving from these traditional principles of interstate conduct are responsibilities more specific to cyberspace, focused in particular on preserving global network functionality and improving cybersecurity. Many of these responsibilities are rooted in the technical realities of the Internet. Because the Internet's core functionality relies on systems of trust (such as the Border Gateway Protocol), states need to recognize the international implications of their technical decisions, and act with respect for one another's networks and the broader Internet. Likewise, in designing the next generation of these systems, we must advance the common interest by supporting the soundest technical standards and governance structures, rather than those that will simply enhance national prestige or political control. Emerging norms, also essential to this space, include:

- Global Interoperability: States should act within their authorities to help ensure the end-to-end interoperability of an Internet accessible to all.
- Network Stability: States should respect the free flow of information in national network configurations, ensuring they do not arbitrarily interfere with internationally interconnected infrastructure.
- Reliable Access: States should not arbitrarily deprive or disrupt individuals' access to the Internet or other networked technologies.
- Multi-stakeholder Governance: Internet governance efforts must not be limited to governments, but should include all appropriate stakeholders.
- Cybersecurity Due Diligence: States should recognize and act on their responsibility to protect information infrastructures and secure national systems from damage or misuse.

While cyberspace is a dynamic environment, international behavior in it must be grounded in the principles of responsible domestic governance, peaceful interstate conduct, and reliable network management. As these ideas develop, the United States will foster and participate fully in discussions, advancing a principled approach to Internet policy-making and developing shared understandings appropriate to each issue.

Defense: Dissuading and Deterring

The United States will defend its networks, whether the threat comes from terrorists, cybercriminals, or states and their proxies. Just as importantly, we will seek to encourage good actors and dissuade and deter those who threaten peace and stability through actions in cyberspace. We will do so with overlapping policies that combine national and international network resilience with vigilance and a range of credible response options. In all our defense endeavors, we will protect civil liberties and privacy in accordance with our laws and principles.

Defense Objective

The United States will, along with other nations, encourage responsible behavior and oppose those who would seek to disrupt networks and systems, dissuading and deterring malicious actors, and reserving the right to defend these vital national assets as necessary and appropriate.

Dissuasion

Protecting networks of such great value requires robust defensive capabilities. The United States will continue to strengthen our network defenses and our ability to withstand and recover from disruptions and other attacks. For those more sophisticated attacks that do create damage, we will act on well-developed response plans to isolate and mitigate disruption to our machines, limiting effects on our networks, and potential cascade effects beyond them.

Strength at Home

Ensuring the resilience of our networks and information systems requires collective and concerted national action that spans the whole of government, in collaboration with the private sector and individual citizens. For a decade, the United States has been fostering a culture of cybersecurity and an effective apparatus for risk mitigation and incident response. We continue to emphasize that systematically adopting sound information technology practices—across the public and private sectors—will reduce our Nation's vulnerabilities and strengthen networks and systems. We are also making steady progress towards shared situational awareness of network vulnerabilities and risks among public and private sector networks. We have built new initiatives through our national computer security incident response team to share information among government, key industries, our critical infrastructure sectors, and other stakeholders. And we continually seek new ways to strengthen our partnership with the private sector to enhance the security of the systems on which we both rely.

Strength Abroad

This model of defense has been successfully shared internationally through education, training and ongoing operational and policy relationships. Today, through existing and developing collaborations in the technical and military defense arenas, national share an unprecedented ability to recognize and respond to incidents— a crucial step in denying would-be attackers the ability to do lasting damage to our national and international networks. However, a globally distributed network requires globally distributed early warning capabilities. We must continue to produce new computer security incident response capabilities globally, and to facilitate their interconnection and enhanced computer network defense. The United States has a shared interest in assisting less developed nations to build capacity for defense, and in collaboration with our partners, will intensify our focus on this area. Building relationships with friends and allies will increase collective security across the international community.

Deterrence

The United States will ensure that the risks associated with attacking or exploiting our networks vastly outweigh the potential benefits. We fully recognize that cyberspace activities can have effects extending beyond networks; such events may require responses in self-defense. Likewise, interconnected networks link nations more closely, so an attack on one nation's networks may have impact far beyond its borders.

In the case of criminals and other non-state actors who would threaten our national and economic security, domestic deterrence requires all states have processes that permit them to investigate, apprehend, and prosecute those who intrude or disrupt networks at home and abroad. Internationally, law enforcement organizations must work in concert with one another whenever possible to freeze perishable data vital to ongoing investigations, to work with legislatures and justice ministries to harmonize their approaches, and to promote due process and the rule of law—all key tenets of the Budapest Convention on Cybercrime.

When warranted, the United States will respond to hostile acts in cyberspace as we would to any other threat to our country. All states possess an inherent right to self-defense, and we recognize that certain hostile acts conducted through cyberspace could compel actions under the commitments we have with our military treaty partners. We reserve the right to use all necessary means—diplomatic, informational, military, and economic—as appropriate and consistent with applicable international law, in order to defend our Nation, our allies, our partners, and our interests. In so doing, we will exhaust all options before military force whenever we can; will carefully weigh the costs and risks of action against the costs of inaction; and will act in a way that reflects our values and strengthens our legitimacy, seeking broad international support whenever possible.

Military: Preparing for 21st Century Security Challenges

Since our commitment to defend our citizens, allies, and interests extends to wherever they might be threatened, we will:

- **Recognize and adapt to the military's increasing need for reliable and secure networks.** We recognize that our armed forces increasingly depend on the networks that support them, and we will work to ensure that our military remains full equipped to operate even in an environment where others might seek to disrupt its systems, or other infrastructure vital to national defense.

Like all nations, the United States has a compelling interest in defending its vital national assets, as well as our core principles and values, and we are committed to defending against those who would attempt to impede our ability to do so.

- **Build and enhance existing military alliances to confront potential threats in cyberspace.** Cybersecurity cannot be achieved by any one nation alone, and greater levels of international cooperating are needed to confront those actors who would seek to disrupt or exploit our networks. This effort begins by acknowledging that the interconnected nature of networked systems of our closest allies, such as those of NATO and its member states, creates opportunities and new risks. Moving forward, the United States will continue to work with the militaries and civilian counterparts of our allies and partners to expand situational awareness and shared warning systems, enhance our ability to work together in times of peace and crisis, and develop the means and method of collective self-defense in cyberspace. Such military alliances and partnerships will bolster our collective deterrence capabilities and strengthen our ability to defend the United States against state and non-state actors.

- **Expand cyberspace cooperation with allies and partners to increase collective security.** The challenges of cyberspace also create opportunities to work in new ways with allied and partner militaries. By developing a shared understanding of standard operating procedures, our armed forces can enhance security through coordination and greater information exchange; these engagements will diminish misperceptions about military activities and the potential for escalatory behavior. Dialogues and best practice exchanges to enhance partner capabilities, such as digital forensics, work force development, and network penetration and resiliency testing will be important to this effort. The United States will work in close partnership with like-minded states to leverage capabilities, reduce collective risk, and foster multistakeholder initiatives to deter malicious activities in cyberspace.

Moving Forward

The benefits of networked technology should not be reserved to a privileged few nations, or a privileged few within them. But connectivity is no end unto itself; it must be supported by a cyberspace that is open to innovation, interoperable the world over, secure enough to earn people's trust, and reliable enough to support their work.

Thirty years ago, few understood that something called the Internet would lead to a revolution [in] how we work and live. In that short time, millions now owe their livelihoods—and even their lives—to advances in networked technology. A billion more rely on it for everyday forms of social interaction. This technology propels society forward, accomplishing things previous generations scarcely thought possible. For our part, the United States will continue to spark the creativity and imagination of our people, and those around the world. We cannot know what the next great innovation will be, but are committed to realizing a world in which it can take shape and flourish.

This strategy is a roadmap allowing the United States Government's departments and agencies to better define and coordinate their role in our international cyberspace policy, to execute a specific way forward, and to plan for future implementation. It is a call to the private sector, civil society, and end-users to reinforce these efforts through partnership, awareness, and action. Most importantly, it is an invitation to other states and peoples to join us in realizing this vision of prosperity, security, and openness in our networked world. These ideals are central to preserving the cyberspace we know, and to creating, together, the future we seek.

Source: "International Strategy for Cyberspace: Prosperity, Security, and Openness in a Networked World." The White House, May 2011. https://www.whitehouse.gov/sites/default/files/rss_viewer/international_strategy_for_cyberspace.pdf.

5. Excerpts of Secretary of Defense Leon Panetta on Cyber Security, October 11, 2012

Secretary of Defense Leon Panetta, speaking to the Business Executives for National Security, laid out both the current capabilities of the U.S. Department of Defense and its short-term priorities for the cyber-space domain. In his speech, he suggested that the United States had largely solved the fundamental attribution problem for cyber attacks, while also noting the incredible vulnerabilities of American infrastructure and the failure of private companies to undertake even the most basic cyber-security precautions. Unlike many leaders in comparable positions, Panetta seems optimistic that cyber defense and deterrence are both technically feasible and fiscally possible.

Cyberspace has fundamentally transformed the global economy. It's transformed our way of life, providing 2 billion people across the world with instant access to information, to communication, to business opportunities. Cyberspace is the new frontier, full of possibilities to advance security and prosperity in the 21st century. And yet, with these possibilities also come new perils and new dangers. The Internet is open. It's highly accessible, as it should be. But that also presents a new terrain for warfare. It is a battlefield of the future where adversaries can seek to do harm to our country, to our economy, and to our citizens. I know that when people think of cybersecurity today, they worry about hackers and criminals who prowl the Internet, steal people's identities, steal sensitive business information, steal even national security secrets. Those threats are real, and they exist today. But the even greater danger—the danger facing us in cyberspace goes beyond crime and it goes beyond harassment. A cyber attack perpetrated by nation-states or violent extremist groups could be as destructive as the terrorist attack on 9/11. Such a destructive cyber-terrorist attack could virtually paralyze the nation.

Let me give you some examples of the kinds of attacks that we have already experienced. In recent weeks, as many of you know, some large U.S. financial institutions were hit by so-called distributed denial-of-service attacks. These attacks delayed or disrupted services on customer Web sites. While this kind of tactic isn't new, the scale and speed with which it happened was unprecedented. But even more alarming is an attack that happened two months ago when a very sophisticated virus called Shamoon infected computers in the Saudi Arabian state oil company Aramco. Shamoon included a routine called a "wiper," coded to self-execute. This routine replaced crucial systems files with an image of a burning U.S. flag. But it also put additional garbage data that overwrote all the real data on the machine. More than 30,000 computers that it infected were rendered useless and had to be replaced. It virtually destroyed 30,000 computers. Then just days after this incident, there was a similar attack on RasGas of Qatar, a major energy company in the region. All told, the Shamoon virus was probably the most destructive attack that the private sector has seen to date.

These attacks mark a significant escalation of the cyber threat, and they have renewed concerns about still more destructive scenarios that could unfold. For example, we know that foreign cyber actors are probing America's critical infrastructure networks. They are targeting the computer control systems that operate chemical, electricity, and water plants and those that guide transportation throughout this country. We know of specific instances where intruders have successfully gained access to these control systems. We also know that they are seeking to create advanced tools to attack these systems and cause panic and destruction and even loss of life.

An aggressor nation or extremist group could use these kinds of cyber tools to gain control of critical switches. They could, for example, derail passenger trains or even more dangerous, derail trains loaded with lethal chemicals. They could contaminate the water supply in major cities or shut down the power grid across large parts of the country. The most destructive scenarios involve cyber actors launching several attacks on our critical infrastructure at one time, in combination with a physical attack on our country. Attackers could also seek to disable or degrade critical military systems and communication networks. The collective result of these kinds of attacks could be a cyber Pearl Harbor, an attack that would cause physical destruction and the loss of life. In fact, it would paralyze and shock the nation and create a new, profound sense of vulnerability.

The Department of Defense, in large part through the capabilities of the National Security Agency, NSA, has developed the world's most sophisticated system to detect cyber intruders and attackers. We are acting aggressively to get ahead of this problem, putting in place measures to stop cyber attacks dead in their tracks. We are doing this as part of a broad whole of government effort to confront cyber threats.

The Department of Defense also has a role. It is a supporting role, but it is an essential role. And tonight, I want to explain what that means. But first let me make clear what it does not mean. It does not mean that the Department of Defense will monitor citizens' personal computers. We're not interested in personal communications or in e-mails or in providing the day to day security of private and commercial networks. That is not our goal. That is not our job. That is not our mission. Our mission is to defend the nation. We defend. We deter, and if called upon, we take decisive action to protect our citizens. In the past, we have done so through operations on land and at sea, in the skies and in space. In this century, the United States military must help defend the nation in cyberspace as well. If a foreign adversary attacked U.S. soil, the American people have every right to expect their national defense forces to respond. If a crippling cyber attack were launched against our nation, the American people must be protected. And if the commander in chief orders a response, the Defense Department must be ready to obey that order and to act.

To ensure that we fulfill our role to defend the nation in cyberspace, the department is focusing upon three main tracks. One, developing new capabilities. Two, putting in place the policies and organizations we need to execute our mission. And three, building much more effective cooperation with industry and our international partners.

First, developing new capabilities. DoD is investing more than $3 billion annually in cybersecurity because we have to retain that cutting-edge capability in the field. Following our new defense strategy, the department is continuing to increase key investments in cybersecurity even in an era of fiscal restraint. Our most important investment is in skilled cyber warriors needed to conduct operations in cyberspace. Just as DoD developed the world's finest counterterrorism force over the past decade, we need to build and maintain the finest cyber force and operations. We're recruiting, we're training, the best and the brightest in order to stay ahead of other nations. It's no secret that Russia and China have advanced cyber capabilities. Iran has also undertaken a concerted effort to use cyberspace to its advantage. Moreover, DoD is already in an intense daily struggle against thousands of cyber actors who probe the Defense Department's networks, millions of times a day.

Throughout the innovative efforts of our cyber operators, we've been trying to enhance the department's cyber defense programs. These systems rely on sensors, they rely on software to hunt down the malicious codes before it harms our systems. We actively share our own experience defending our systems with those running the nation's critical private sector networks. In addition to defending the department's networks, we also help deter attacks. Our cyber adversaries will be far less likely to hit us if they know that we will be able to link to the attack or that their effort will fail against our strong defenses. The department has made significant advances in solving a problem that makes deterring cyber adversaries more complex, the difficulty of identifying the origins of that attack. Over the last two years, DoD has made significant investments in forensics to address this problem of attribution, and we're seeing the returns on that investment. Potential aggressors should be aware that the United States has the capacity to locate them and to hold them accountable for their actions that may try to harm America.

But we won't succeed in preventing a cyber attack through improved defenses alone. If we detect an imminent threat that will cause significant, physical destruction in the United States or kill American citizens, we need to have the option to take action against those who would attack us to defend this nation when directed by the president. For these kinds of scenarios, the department has developed the capability to conduct effective operations to counter threats to our national interests in cyberspace. Let me be clear that we will only do so to defend our nation, to defend our interests, to defend our allies, and we will only do so in a manner that is consistent with the policy principles and legal frameworks that the department follows for other domains including the law of armed conflict.

Which brings me to the second area of focus, policies and organization. Responding to the cyber threat requires the right policies and organizations across the federal government. For the past year, the Department of Defense has been working very closely with other agencies to understand where are the lines of responsibility when it comes to cyber defense. Where do we draw those lines? And how do those responsibilities get executed? As part of that effort, the department is now finalizing the most comprehensive change to our rules of engagement in cyberspace in seven years. The new rules will make clear that the department has a responsibility, not only to defend DoD's networks, but also to be prepared to defend the nation and our national interests against an attack in or through cyberspace. These new rules make the department more agile and provide us with the ability to confront major threats quickly.

Three years ago, the department took a major step forward by establishing the United States Cyber Command, under the leadership of General Keith Alexander, a four-star officer who also serves as the director of the National Security Agency. Cyber Command has matured into what I believe is a world-class organization. It has the capacity to conduct a full range of missions inside cyberspace. The threat picture could be quickly shared with DoD's geographic and functional combatant commanders, with DHS, with FBI and with other agencies in government. After all, we need to see an attack coming in order to defend against that attack. And we're looking at ways to strengthen Cyber Command as well. We must ensure that it has the resources, that it has the authorities, that it has the capabilities required to perform this growing mission. And it must also be able to react quickly to events unfolding in cyberspace and help fully integrate cyber into all of the department's plans and activities.

And finally, the third area is to build stronger partnerships. As I've made clear, securing cyberspace is not the sole responsibility of the United States military or even the sole responsibility of the United States government. The private sector, government, military, our allies—all share the same global infrastructure, and we all share the responsibility to protect it. Therefore, we are deepening cooperation with our closest allies with the goal of sharing threat information, maximizing shared capabilities and determining malicious activities. The president, the vice president, secretary of state and I have made cyber a major topic of discussion in nearly all of our bilateral meetings with foreign counterparts. I recently met with our Chinese military counterparts just a few weeks ago. As I mentioned earlier, China is rapidly growing its cyber capabilities. In my visit to Beijing, I underscored the need to increase communication and transparency with each other so that we could avoid a misunderstanding or a miscalculation in cyberspace. This is in the interest of the United States, but it's also in the interest of China.

Ultimately, no one has a greater interest in cybersecurity than the businesses that depend on a safe, secure and resilient global, digital infrastructure. Particularly those who operate the critical networks that we must help defend. To defend those networks more effectively, we must share information between the government and the private sector about threats in cyberspace. We've made real progress in sharing information with the private sector. But very frankly, we need Congress to act to ensure that this sharing is timely and comprehensive.

Companies should be able to share specific threat information with the government, without the prospect of lawsuits hanging over their head. And a key principle must be to protect the fundamental liberties and privacy in cyberspace that we are all duty bound to uphold. Information sharing alone is not sufficient. We've got to work with the business community to develop baseline standards for our most critical private-sector infrastructure, our power plants, our water treatment facilities, our gas pipelines. This would help ensure that companies take proactive measures to secure themselves against sophisticated threats, but also take common sense steps against basic threats. Although awareness is growing, the reality is that too few companies have invested in even basic cybersecurity. The fact is that to fully provide the necessary protection in our democracy, cybersecurity legislation must be passed by the Congress. Without it, we are and we will be vulnerable.

Source: Panetta, Leon. "Remarks by Secretary Panetta on Cybersecurity to the Business Executives for National Security." U.S. Department of Defense, October 11, 2012. http://archive.defense.gov/transcripts/transcript.aspx?transcriptid=5136.

6. Excerpts from U.S. Department of Defense, Defense Science Board, Task Force Report: "Resilient Military Systems and the Advanced Cyber Threat," January 2013

In June 2011, the Defense Science Board (DSB) was tasked with examining the current state of cyber security in the Department of Defense (DoD) and offering recommendations for how the DoD could improve its cyber posture. The extensive report, of which excerpts are below, paints a grim picture of the cyber conditions confronting the DoD and concedes that there will be extensive penetrations of the U.S. cyber network, even if all the recommendations are carried out. Further, it is telling that the DSB considers it an important aspiration for the United States to rise to the level of worthy competitor in the cyber domain. The DSB views the potential of cyber warfare, which it believes will be a part of every future conflict, to present an existential threat to the nation matched only by the danger of nuclear weapons.

The United States cannot be confident that our critical Information Technology (IT) systems will work under attack from a sophisticated and well-resourced opponent utilizing cyber capabilities in combination with all of their military and intelligence capabilities (a "full spectrum" adversary). While this is also true for others (e.g., Allies, rivals, and public/private networks), this Task Force strongly believes the DoD needs to take the lead and build an effective response to measurably increase confidence in the IT systems we depend on (public and private) and at the same time decrease a would-be attacker's confidence in the effectiveness of their capabilities to compromise DoD systems. We have recommended an approach to do so, and we need to start now!

While DoD takes great care to secure the use and operation of the "hardware" of its weapon systems, these security practices have not kept up with the cyber adversary tactics and capabilities. Further, the same level of resource and attention is not spent on the complex network of information technology (IT) systems that are used to support and operate those weapons or critical cyber capabilities embedded within them. This Task Force was asked to review and make recommendations to improve the resilience of DoD systems to cyber attacks and to develop a set of metrics that the Department could use to track progress and shape investment priorities.

Over the past 18 months, the Task Force received more than 50 briefings from practitioners and senior officials throughout the DoD, Intelligence Community (IC), commercial practitioners, academia, national laboratories, and policymakers. As a result of its deliberations, the Task Force concludes that:

- The cyber threat is serious, with potential consequences similar in some ways to the nuclear threat of the Cold War.
- The cyber threat is also insidious, enabling adversaries to access vast new channels of intelligence about critical U.S. enablers (operational and technical; military and industrial) that can threaten our national and economic security.
- Current DoD actions, though numerous, are fragmented. Thus, DoD is not prepared to defend against this threat.
- DoD red teams, using cyber attack tools which can be downloaded from the Internet, are very successful at defeating our systems.
- U.S. networks are built on inherently insecure architectures with increasing use of foreign-built components.
- U.S. intelligence against peer threats targeting DoD systems is inadequate.
- With present capabilities and technology it is not possible to defend with confidence against the most sophisticated cyber attacks.
- It will take years for the Department to build an effective response to the cyber threat to include elements of deterrence, mission assurance and offensive cyber capabilities.

The DoD, and its contractor base are high priority targets that have sustained staggering losses of system design information incorporating years of combat knowledge and experience. Employing reverse engineering techniques, adversaries can exploit weapon system technical plans for their benefit. Perhaps even more significant, they gained insight to operational concepts and system use (e.g., which processes are automated and which are person controlled) developed from decades of U.S. operational and developmental experience—the type of information that cannot simply be recreated in a laboratory or factory environment. Such information provides tremendous benefit to an adversary, shortening time for development of countermeasures by years.

In addition, there is evidence of attacks that exploit known vulnerabilities in the domestic power grid and critical infrastructure systems. DoD, and the United States, is extremely reliant on the availability of its critical infrastructure.

Recent DoD and U.S. interest in counterfeit parts has resulted in the identification of widespread introduction of counterfeit parts into DoD systems through commercial supply chains. Since many systems use the same processors and those processors are typically built overseas in untrustworthy environments, the challenge to supply chain management in a cyber-contested environment is significant.

DoD is in the process of institutionalizing a Supply Chain Risk Management (SCRM) strategy that prioritizes scarce security resources on critical mission systems and components, provides intelligence analysis to acquisition programs and incorporates vulnerability risk mitigation requirements into system designs.

The success of DoD red teams against its operational systems should also give pause to DoD leadership. During exercises and testing, DoD red teams, using only small teams and a short amount of time, are able to significantly disrupt the "blue team's" ability to carry out military missions. Typically, the disruption is so great, that the exercise must be essentially reset without the cyber intrusion to allow enough operational capability to proceed. These stark demonstrations contribute to the Task Force's assertion that the functioning of DoD's systems is not assured in the presence of even a modestly aggressive cyber attack.

The benefits to an attacker using cyber exploits are potentially spectacular. Should the United States find itself in a full-scale conflict with a peer adversary, attacks would be expected to include denial of service, data corruption, supply chain corruption, traitorous insiders, kinetic and related non-kinetic attacks at all altitudes from underwater to space. U.S. guns, missiles, and bombs may not fire, or may be directed against our own troops. Resupply, including food, water, ammunition, and fuel, may not arrive when or where needed. Military Commanders may rapidly lose trust in the information and ability to control U.S. systems and forces. Once lost, that trust is very difficult to regain.

The impact of a destructive cyber attack on the civilian population would be even greater with no electricity, money, communications, TV, radio, or fuel (electrically pumped). In a short time, food and medicine distribution systems would be ineffective, transportation would fail or become so chaotic as to be useless. Law enforcement, medical staff, and emergency personnel capabilities could be expected to be barely functional in the short term and dysfunctional over sustained periods. If the attackers' effects were reversible, damage could be limited to an impact equivalent to a power outage lasting a few days. If an attack's effects cause physical damage to control systems, pumps, engines, generators, controllers, etc., the unavailability of parts and manufacturing capacity could mean months to years are required to rebuild and reestablish basic infrastructure operation.

The DoD should expect cyber attacks to be part of all conflicts in the future, and should not expect competitors to play by our version of the rules, but instead apply their own rules (e.g., using surrogates for exploitation and offense operations, sharing IP with local industries for economic gain, etc.).

Recommendations:

1. Protect the Nuclear Strike as a Deterrent (for existing nuclear armed states and existential cyber attack).

2. Determine the Mix of Cyber, Protected-Conventional, and Nuclear Capabilities Necessary for Assured Operation in the Face of a Full-Spectrum Adversary.
3. Refocus Intelligence Collection and Analysis to Understand Adversarial Cyber Capabilities, Plans and Intentions, and to Enable Counterstrategies.
4. Build and Maintain World-Class Cyber Offensive Capabilities (with appropriate authorities).
5. Enhance Defenses to Protect Against Low and Mid-Tier Threats.
6. Change DoD's Culture Regarding Cyber and Cyber Security.
7. Build a Cyber Resilient Force.

The network connectivity that the United States has used to tremendous advantage, economically and militarily, over the past 20 years has made the country far more vulnerable than ever to cyber attacks. At the same time, our adversaries are far more capable of conducting such attacks. The DoD should expect cyber to be part of all future conflicts, especially against near-peer and peer adversaries. This Task Force believes that full manifestation of the cyber threat could even produce existential consequences to the United States, particularly with respect to critical infrastructure. To maintain global stability in the emerging area of cyber warfare, the United States must be, and be seen as, a worthy competitor in this domain.

This Task Force developed a set of recommendations that, when taken in whole, creates a strategy for DoD to address this broad and pervasive threat. Cyber is a complicated domain and must be managed from a systems perspective. There is no silver bullet that will reduce DoD cyber risk to zero. While the problem cannot be eliminated, it can and must be determinedly managed through the combination of deterrence and improved cyber defense. Deterrence is achieved with offensive cyber, some protected-conventional capabilities, and anchored with U.S. nuclear weapons. This strategy removes the requirements to protect all of our military systems from the most advanced cyber threats, which the Task Force believes is neither feasible nor affordable. It will take time to build the capabilities necessary to prepare and protect our country from the cyber threat. We must start now!

Source: U.S. Department of Defense, Defense Science Board. "Task Force Report: Resilient Military Systems and the Advanced Cyber Threat." January 2013. http://www.acq.osd.mil/dsb/reports/ResilientMilitarySystems.CyberThreat.pdf.

7. Statement of General Keith B. Alexander, Commander, United States Cyber Command, before the Senate Committee on Armed Services, March 12, 2013

General Keith B. Alexander, the director of the National Security Agency and the commander of U.S. Cyber Command, gave a prepared statement to the U.S. Senate Committee on Armed Services. In that statement, he laid out the basic tenets of U.S. cyber policy and the current state of affairs in the cyber domain. This excerpt, titled "The Strategic Landscape," clarifies the role of U.S. Cyber Command in the American national defense structure. It pays particular attention to the threats that currently confront the United States in the cyber domain.

U.S. Cyber Command operates in a dynamic and contested environment that literally changes its characteristics each time someone powers on a networked device. Geographic boundaries are perhaps less evident in cyberspace, but every server, fiber-optic line, cell tower, thumb drive, router, and laptop is owned by someone and resides in some physical locale. In this way cyberspace resembles the land domain—it is all owned, and it can be reshaped. Most networked devices, for example, are in private hands, and their owners can deny or facilitate others' cyber operations by how they manage and maintain their networks and devices. Cyberspace as an operating environment also has aspects unique to it. Events in cyberspace can seem to happen instantaneously. Data can appear to reside in multiple locations. There is a great deal of anonymity, and strongly encrypted data are virtually unreadable. In cyberspace, moreover, sweeping effects can be precipitated by states, enterprises, and individuals, with the added nuance that such cyber actors can be very difficult to identify. The cyber landscape also changes rapidly with the connection of new devices and bandwidth, and with the spread of strong encryption and mobile devices. Despite the unique characteristics of cyberspace, states still matter because they can affect much of the physical infrastructure within their borders. Convergence is our watchword; our communications, computers, and networks are merging into one digital environment as our political, economic, and social realms are being re-shaped by the rush of innovation.

In this environment that is both orderly and chaotic, beneficial and perilous, we at USCYBERCOM have to focus on actors who possess the capability—and possibly the intent—to harm our nation's interests in cyberspace or to use cyber means to inflict harm on us in other ways. Unfortunately, the roster of actors of concern to us is growing longer and growing also in terms of the variety and sophistication of the ways they can affect our operations and security.

State actors continue to top our list of concerns. We feel confident that foreign leaders believe that a devastating attack on the critical infrastructure and population of the United States by cyber means would be correctly traced back to its source and elicit a prompt and proportionate response. Nonetheless, it is possible that some future regime or cyber actor could misjudge the impact and the certainty of our resolve.

We have some confidence in our ability to deter major state-on-state attacks in cyberspace but we are not deterring the seemingly low-level harassment of private and public sites, property, and data. As former Secretary of Defense Panetta explained to an audience in New York last October, states and extremist groups are behaving recklessly and aggressively in the cyber environment. Such attacks have been destructive to both data and property. The Secretary mentioned, for example, the remote assaults last summer on Saudi Aramco and RasGas, which together rendered inoperable—and effectively destroyed the data on—more than 30,000 computers. We have also seen repressive regimes, desperate to hold on to power in the face of popular resistance, resort to all manner of cyber harassment on both their opponents and their own citizens caught in the crossfire. Offensive cyber programs and capabilities are growing, evolving, and spreading before our eyes; we believe it is only a matter of time before the sort of sophisticated tools developed by well-funded state actors find their way to non-state groups or even individuals. The United States has already become a target. Networks and websites owned by Americans and located here have endured intentional, state-sponsored attacks, and some have incurred damage and disruption because they happened to be along the route to another state's overseas targets.

Let me draw your attention to another very serious threat to U.S. interests. The systematic cyber exploitation of American companies, enterprises, and their intellectual property continued unabated over the last year. Many incidents were perpetrated by organized cybercriminals. Identity and data theft are now big business, netting their practitioners large profits and giving rise to an on-line sub-culture of markets for stolen data and cyber tools for stealing more. Much cyber exploitation activity, however, is state-sponsored. Foreign government-directed cyber collection personnel, tools, and organizations are targeting the data of American and western businesses, institutions, and citizens. They are particularly targeting our telecommunications, information technology, financial, security, and energy sectors. They are exploiting these targets on a scale amounting to the greatest unwilling transfer of wealth in history. States and cybercriminals do not leave empty bank vaults and file drawers behind after they break-in—they usually copy what they find and leave the original data intact—but the damage they are doing to America's economic competitiveness and innovation edge is profound, translating into missed opportunities for U.S. companies and the potential for lost American jobs. Cyber-enabled theft jeopardizes our economic growth. We at USCYBERCOM work closely with our interagency partners to address these threats.

We must also watch potential threats from terrorists and hacktivists in cyberspace. The Intelligence Community and others have long warned that worldwide terrorist organizations like al Qaeda and its affiliates have the intent to harm the United States via cyber means. We agree with this judgment, while noting that, so far, their capability to do so has not matched their intent. This is not to downplay the problem of terrorist use of the Internet. Al Qaeda and other violent extremist groups are on the Web proselytizing, fund-raising, and inspiring imitators. We should not ignore the effectiveness with which groups like al Qaeda and its affiliates radicalize ever larger numbers of people each year—on more continents. The Federal Bureau of Investigation and other agencies cite instances in which would-be terrorists found motivation and moral support for suicide attacks at jihadist websites and chat rooms. This is an especially serious and growing problem in areas of hostilities where our troops and personnel are deployed. Another threat that is not growing as fast as we might have feared, on the other hand, is that of hacktivists with a cause or a grievance that leads them to target U.S. government and military networks. Our vulnerabilities to this sort of disruption remain, but 2012 saw fewer such incidents than 2011.

Source: Statement of Gen. Keith B. Alexander, USA, Commander, U.S. Cyber Command. *Department of Defense Authorization for Appropriations for Fiscal Year 2014 and the Future Years Defense Program.* Statement to the U.S. Senate, Committee on Armed Services, March 12, 2013. http://www.armed-services.senate.gov /imo/media/doc/stratcom_cybercom_fullcomm_hearing_031213.pdf.

8. Excerpts from U.S. Department of Defense, *The Department of Defense Cyber Strategy*, April 2015

The U.S. Department of Defense (DoD) periodically releases strategic documents that reflect its missions, roles, and efforts to defend the United States. In 2015, the DoD released its formal cyber strategy, an overview of the primary means by which the Department of Defense operates in cyber space. The document does not contain specifics regarding cyber attacks or defensive limits, but it does offer a broad perspective of the DoD's approach to cyber security and how it perceives its role in a mission that includes many other agencies, both public and private.

Three Primary Missions in Cyberspace

The President has established principles and processes for governing cyber operations. The purpose of these principles and processes is to plan, develop, and use U.S. capabilities effectively, and to ensure that cyber operations occur in a manner consistent with the values that the United States promotes domestically and internationally.

The Defense Department has three primary cyber missions. **First, DoD must defend its own networks, systems, and information.** The U.S. military's dependence on cyberspace for its operations led the Secretary of Defense in 2011 to declare cyberspace as an operational domain for purposes of organizing, training, and equipping U.S. military forces. The Defense Department must be able to secure its own networks against attack and recover quickly if security measures fail. To this end, DoD conducts network defense operations on an ongoing basis to securely operate the Department of Defense Information Network (DoDIN). If and when DoD detects indications of hostile activity within its networks, DoD has quick-response capabilities to close or mitigate vulnerabilities and secure its networks and systems. Network defense operations on DoD networks constitute the vast majority of DoD's operations in cyberspace.

In addition to defense investments, DoD must prepare and be ready to operate in an environment where access to cyberspace is contested. During the Cold War, forces prepared to operate in an environment where access to communications could be interrupted by the adversary's advanced capabilities, to include the potential use of an electromagnetic pulse that could disrupt satellite and other global communications capabilities. Commanders conducted periodic exercises that required their teams to operate without access to communications systems. Through years of practice and exercise, a culture of resilience took root in the military and units were ready and prepared to operate in contested environments.

Since the end of the Cold War, however, a younger generation has grown increasingly more accustomed to an environment of connectivity. The generation of military men and women that grew up since the end of the Cold War have had near constant access to information and communications, and the information revolution has led to a more agile and globally adaptive force. In the face of an escalating cyber threat, the lessons of the previous generations must now be passed down. The Defense Department must be able to carry out its missions to defend the country. Organizations must exercise and learn to operate without the tools that have become such a vital part of their daily lives and operations.

For its second mission, DoD must be prepared to defend the United States and its interests against cyberattacks of significant consequence.

While cyberattacks are assessed on a case-by-case and fact-specific basis by the President and the U.S. national security team, significant consequences may include loss of life, significant damage to property, serious adverse U.S. foreign policy consequences, or serious economic impact on the United States.

If directed by the President or the Secretary of Defense, the U.S. military may conduct cyber operations to counter an imminent or on-going attack against the U.S. homeland or U.S. interests in cyberspace. The purpose of such a defensive measure is to blunt an attack and prevent the destruction of property or the loss of life. DoD seeks to synchronize its capabilities with other government agencies to develop a range of options and methods for disrupting cyberattacks of significant consequence before they can have an impact, to include law enforcement, intelligence, and diplomatic tools. As a matter of principle, the United States will seek to exhaust all network defense and law enforcement options to mitigate any potential cyber risk to the U.S. homeland or U.S. interests before conducting a cyberspace operation.

The United States government has a limited and specific role to play in defending the nation against cyberattacks of significant consequence. The private sector owns and operates over ninety percent of all of the networks and infrastructure of cyberspace and is thus the first line of defense. One of the most important steps for improving the United States' overall cybersecurity posture is for companies to prioritize the networks and data that they must protect and to invest in improving their own cybersecurity. While the U.S. government must prepare to defend the country against the most dangerous attacks, the majority of intrusions can be stopped through relatively basic cybersecurity investments that companies can and must make themselves.

Third, if directed by the President or the Secretary of Defense, DoD must be able to provide integrated cyber capabilities to support military operations and contingency plans.

There may be times when the President or the Secretary of Defense may determine that it would be appropriate for the U.S. military to conduct cyber operations to disrupt an adversary's military-related networks or infrastructure so that the U.S. military can protect U.S. interests in an area of operations. For example, the United States military might use cyber operations to terminate an ongoing conflict on U.S. terms, or to disrupt an adversary's military systems to prevent the use of force against U.S. interests. United States Cyber Command (USCYBERCOM) may also be directed to conduct cyber operations, in coordination with other U.S. government agencies as appropriate, to deter or defeat strategic threats in other domains.

To ensure that the Internet remains open, secure, and prosperous, the United States will always conduct cyber operations under a doctrine of restraint, as required to protect human lives and to prevent the destruction of property. As in other domains of operations, in cyberspace the Defense Department will always act in a way that reflects enduring U.S. values, including support for the rule of law, as well as respect and protection of the freedom of expression and privacy, the free flow of information, commerce, and ideas. Any decision to conduct cyber operations outside of DoD networks is made with the utmost care and deliberation and under strict policy and operational oversight, and in accordance with the law of armed conflict. As it makes its investments and builds cyber capabilities to defend U.S. national interests, the Defense Department will always be attentive to the potential impact of defense policies on state and non-state actors' behavior.

Source: U.S. Department of Defense. "The Department of Defense Cyber Strategy." April 2015. http://www.defense.gov/Portals/1/features/2015/0415_cyber-strategy /Final_2015_DoD_CYBER_STRATEGY_for_web.pdf.

Chronology

1948	The RAND (Research and Development) Corporation is formed, creating a direct partnership between the U.S. Air Force and the Douglas Aircraft Company.
1952	The National Security Agency (NSA) is established to oversee all U.S. government signal intelligence collection efforts as well as signal counterintelligence activities.
1958	The U.S. government creates the Advanced Research Projects Agency (ARPA), later renamed the Defense Advanced Research Projects Agency (DARPA), an organization dedicated to preventing strategic surprise through technological development.
	Jack St. Clair Kilby invents the integrated circuit while working for Texas Instruments. It is the first great leap forward in miniaturization since the completion of the transistor.
	Seymour Cray, an engineer for the Control Data Corporation, finishes the first supercomputer, a machine that pushes the limits of processing speed for any given technology. Cray's first model relies upon transistors and will soon be surpassed by integrated circuit machines.
1968	Intel Corporation is founded in Santa Clara, California, and quickly becomes the world's leading producer of microprocessors.
1969	ARPANET is introduced, linking a handful of government and academic computer networks.
1972	The Transmission Control Protocol/Internet Protocol (TCP/IP) system is created, providing a specific model for how data should be formatted, addressed, transmitted, routed, and received by computers on a network.
1976	Steve Jobs and Steve Wozniak start Apple Computer Corporation and begin to build home computers designed for ease of use.
1978	The Foreign Intelligence Surveillance Act is passed, limiting the ability of federal intelligence agencies to engage in domestic surveillance without court approval.
1979	The first computer worm is developed, but it is not released on a network.

1983	The movie *WarGames* is released, in which a young hacker nearly starts a nuclear war by accessing a Department of Defense computer system.
	The Domain Name System (DNS), a hierarchical naming system for computers connected to networks, is created.
	MILNET, the dedicated U.S. military network, is split from ARPANET.
1984	William Gibson publishes the science fiction novel *Neuromancer*, in which the term "cyberspace" is coined.
	The term "Internet" is created, and the TCP/IP system is selected for communication on it.
1988	The Morris Worm is released from a Massachusetts Institute of Technology laboratory, where it was developed by student Robert Morris. It infects thousands of machines on the nascent Internet and reveals the lack of protections against such programs.
	Donald Gene Burleson is the first American convicted for the malicious use of software after writing code to destroy the payroll data of his former employer, creating one of the first logic bombs in history.
	The first computer emergency response team (CERT) is formed by DARPA at Carnegie Mellon University in response to the effects of the Morris Worm.
1993	The Mosaic Web browser is released by the National Center for Supercomputing Applications (NCSA) at the University of Illinois at Urbana-Champaign. This Web browser makes the Internet accessible for nonexpert home users.
1995	The U.S. Congress requires a national policy to protect information infrastructure from strategic effect as part of the fiscal year 1996 Department of Defense budget authorization bill.
	Admiral Arthur K. Cebrowski publicly describes the U.S. military's new concept of network-centric warfare, an attempt to incorporate sensors, commanders, and operators into a single system, making for a reflexive, adaptive military organization.
1997	The U.S. Department of Defense conducts Eligible Receiver, its first information warfare exercise. The 35-person red team easily demonstrates an ability to hack into power grids, government Web sites, and industry networks using off-the-shelf technology.
1998	Moonlight Maze hacking attacks against government, academic, and corporate networks begins. It is not discovered until 2000, and the culprits have never been identified, although the attacks have been traced to a server in Russia.

In the Solar Sunrise incident, two California high school students and their teenage Israeli mentor compromised more than 500 computer networks, but because they did not remove any classified data, the Department of Justice declined to press charges.

The U.S. federal budget includes $1.14 billion for critical infrastructure cyber security.

Larry Page and Sergey Brin incorporate Google while PhD students at Stanford University.

The Internet Corporation for Assigned Names and Numbers (ICANN) is founded in Los Angeles, California. It coordinates multiple databases to assign unique namespaces on the Internet, ensuring its smooth function.

The President's Commission on Critical Infrastructure Protection (PCCIP) is created.

Three thousand Chinese hackers attack Indonesian government Web sites to protest anti-Chinese riots in Indonesia.

1999   The science fiction blockbuster *The Matrix* is released, in which the protagonist discovers that the entire human population on earth is living in a virtual reality world.

Chinese colonels Qiao Liang and Wang Xiangsui release *Unrestricted Warfare*, a book advocating unconventional strategies to defeat the United States or other technologically advanced nations, including massive cyber-attack campaigns.

2000   The ILOVEYOU virus spreads so quickly that it causes $10 billion in damages.

2001   The USA PATRIOT (Uniting and Strengthening America by Providing Appropriate Tools Required to Intercept and Obstruct Terrorism) Act is passed, creating massive new opportunities for signal intelligence collection in both domestic and international locations.

The Code Red worm exploits a vulnerability in Microsoft's Internet Information Server software, allowing defacement of infected Web sites and possible theft or destruction of data.

The Nimda worm uses a five-method approach to spread, including through backdoors created by the Code Red worm.

The U.S. federal budget includes over $2 billion for critical infrastructure cyber security.

The U.S. Department of Homeland Security is established.

2002   NATO begins its Network-Enabled Capabilities transformation, adopting the network-centric warfare concept for the military alliance.

2003	The U.S. government releases its first National Cyber Security Strategy.
	Titan Rain cyber attacks target U.S. government and corporate networks, eventually exfiltrating more than 20 terabytes of data before being discovered. The attacks are eventually traced to China, which denies all culpability.
	The SQL Slammer worm is released. It spreads so quickly that it completely shuts down the entire Internet for 12 hours. Ten years later, it remains one of the most commonly detected pieces of malware.
	The MS Blaster worm replicates much of SQL Slammer's success, demonstrating the transitory nature of most security fixes.
	John McAfee, creator of McAfee antivirus software, announces the identification of nearly 60,000 computer virus threats, with an additional 10 to 15 discovered daily.
	The Department of Homeland Security announces the creation of the U.S. Computer Emergency Response Team at Carnegie Mellon University.
2004	The Mydoom worm spreads throughout computers operating any recent version of Windows, causing $2 billion in damages worldwide.
2005	General Keith B. Alexander is named director of the National Security Agency, and the organization begins attempts to collect the full electronic communication stream of entire global regions.
2006	General Michael Hayden is named director of the Central Intelligence Agency (CIA), returning from retirement to assume the position as a four-star U.S. Air Force general.
	Google begins censoring Chinese search results, as required by the Chinese government, in exchange for doing business in the People's Republic of China.
2007	Israel bombs a suspected Syrian nuclear facility, using a cyber attack to blind the Syrian air defense network in the process.
	Estonia decides to move a bronze statue depicting a Soviet soldier, provoking a massive cyber attack by Russian hackers against the Baltic nation's cyber infrastructure.
	The NSA commences PRISM, a massive data-collection program that targets foreign communications that pass along the backbone of the Internet.
	Distributed denial-of-service (DDoS) attacks are launched against the Internet's core domain name servers, essentially stopping almost all Internet traffic.

2008	Russian hackers contribute to an attack on the republic of Georgia, cutting off Georgia's access to news outlets and attacking Georgian government Web sites.
	WikiLeaks publishes a State Department cable alleging that foreign hackers stole 50 megabytes of e-mail messages as well as usernames and passwords.
	TJX Corporation reports a breach of its credit card information, a cyber attack that eventually costs the company more than $250 million.
	Israel launches Operation Cast Lead against Palestinian militants in the Gaza Strip. A massive cyber war erupts between Israeli and Arabic hackers. Both state and nonstate hackers are involved on both sides.
	The U.S. military bans the use of all flash drives due to the high incidence rate of worms and viruses on the devices.
2009	A North Korean cyber attack uses a botnet to bring down U.S. and South Korean government Web sites in response to a planned joint military exercise near the Korean peninsula.
	Five million machines participate in a coordinated attack against Israeli Internet infrastructure during Israeli attacks in the Gaza Strip.
	French naval databases are infected by the Conficker worm, forcing the grounding of naval aircraft.
	Google, the Internet's largest search engine, announces that it will no longer filter results in the People's Republic of China, largely because Chinese hackers have penetrated Google's software and used it to persecute religious dissidents.
	Hamas hacktivists deface 800 American and Israeli Web sites.
	North Korean government hackers launch attacks in response to UN sanctions over nuclear weapons testing.
	Canadian researchers discover "GhostNet," a network of infected computers in 103 countries that are all connected to a single espionage effort against the Tibetan government-in-exile.
2010	U.S. Cyber Command (USCYBERCOM) is activated at Fort Meade, Maryland. It incorporates the separate cyber organizations of each of the military services as well as the National Security Agency.
	The Stuxnet virus is first discovered and publicly reported. Earlier versions of the worm had already significantly damaged the Iranian nuclear program at Natanz.

Google reveals it was attacked as a means to track and hit Chinese subversives.

The "Iranian Cyber Army" hacks the Chinese search engine Baidu and disrupts its service.

2011   Secretary of Defense Robert Gates announces that the United States may consider cyber attacks to be acts of war and retaliate in any fashion it deems appropriate.

The Georbot worm infects Georgian government systems, allowing both snooping and exfiltration of data. A Georgian CERT team reverses the attack, seizes control of the botmaster's computer, and manages to film him with his own Web camera.

2012   The Shamoon virus attack against Saudi Aramco renders 30,000 workstations unusable. A previously unknown group, Cutting Sword of Justice, claims responsibility.

The Flame worm is discovered and publicized. It is quickly regarded as the most complex malware ever developed.

The *New York Times* claims the U.S. government engineered the Stuxnet virus. The government refuses to verify the claims, but the Federal Bureau of Investigation (FBI) begins searching for the source of the leaks about Stuxnet.

The Gauss worm is discovered targeting Lebanese financial institutions used by Hezbollah.

The director of the National Security Agency declares that cyber attacks on U.S. infrastructure increased 1,600 percent between 2009 and 2011.

An Iranian hacker group, Izz ad-Din al-Qassam, launches Operation Ababil, a sustained DDoS attack against Western financial and corporate targets. The attacks continue throughout 2013.

Al Qaeda's recruitment and propaganda Web sites are attacked and knocked offline for two weeks.

2013   NSA contractor Edward J. Snowden engages in a massive whistle-blowing operation, exposing an enormous domestic surveillance program undertaken by the NSA.

Target Corporation reports a data breach in which more than 50 million consumers' credit card information was stolen. The company had failed to engage in even the most basic security measures.

Major media outlets, including the *New York Times*, *Washington Post*, and *Bloomberg News*, announce that they have been under continual Chinese cyber attack for years.

North Korean hackers release DarkSeoul, a malware program targeting South Korean media and financial corporations and specifically designed to evade South Korean antivirus software.

The Syrian Electronic Army hacks into U.S. and European media outlets that have urged intervention in the Syrian civil war.

Hackers encrypt elements of Al Qaeda's English-language Web site, making it unreadable.

Israeli cyber-security experts foil an attempt by the Syrian Electronic Army to disrupt water supplies to the city of Haifa.

Edward J. Snowden releases documents demonstrating that the United States had engaged in cyber espionage against China.

President Barack Obama issues an executive order instructing the United States to aid allies being attacked by North Korean and Iranian hackers.

Mandiant Corporation, a cyber-security firm, releases a massive report detailing sustained Chinese cyber attacks, probably launched by PLA Unit 61398, against hundreds of Western private corporations and government agencies.

FireEye purchases Mandiant for $1.05 billion.

2014   Admiral Michael S. Rogers is named commander of USCYBERCOM and director of the NSA, continuing the pattern of one military officer commanding both organizations.

A U.S. federal grand jury returns indictments for five members of the Chinese PLA Unit 61398, who are accused of cyber espionage, cyber sabotage, and other computer crimes against private American corporations.

A member of the Islamic State in Iraq and Syria (ISIS) beheads American journalist James Foley on a live video feed broadcast through the Internet.

JP Morgan Chase reveals it is the victim of a cyber attack that compromised 83 million accounts.

Sony Corporation is hacked, probably by North Korean state agencies.

2015   Al Qaeda Electronic emerges, the first cyber franchise of the global terror organization.

The FBI indicts four men, including two Israelis, for hacking JP Morgan Chase's servers.

Kaspersky Lab announces the discovery of Equation Group, an organization reportedly linked to the creation of Stuxnet and Flame.

Microsoft opens its Cyber Defense Operations Center and signs an information-sharing agreement with NATO.

According to the UN International Telecommunications Union, 3.2 billion people use the Internet.

The U.S. Office of Personnel Management detects a data breach affecting 22.1 million current, former, and prospective federal government employees' records.

The CIA launches the Directorate for Digital Innovation.

Hacker collective Anonymous declares war on ISIS.

Apple Inc. refuses an FBI demand that it break the security features on an Apple iPhone that had belonged to a terrorist in San Bernardino, California.

2016   The European Union announces new rules on net neutrality that require all citizens have Internet access.

Microsoft purchases LinkedIn, expanding its social media presence.

The European Union and NATO sign the Technical Arrangement on Cyber Defense.

Two members of the Syrian Electronic Army are added to the FBI's Cyber Most-Wanted list.

Tallinn Manual 2.0 is released, focusing on cyber terror, cyber espionage, and cyber crime.

Kevin Mandia is named CEO of FireEye.

WikiLeaks publishes 28,000 files from Democratic National Committee internal communications, exposing dissent within the party.

Russian hackers are accused of interfering in the U.S. presidential election on behalf of Republican nominee Donald Trump.

2017   President Barack Obama commutes the 35-year sentence of Bradley [Chelsea] Manning after 6 years.

WikiLeaks publishes more than 8,000 documents demonstrating the CIA's immense ability to break into encrypted devices and networks.

Bibliography

Abbate, Janet. *Inventing the Internet*. Cambridge, MA: The MIT Press, 2000.

Alfreda, Dudley, and James Braman. *Investigating Cyber Law and Cyber Ethics: Issues Impacts and Practices*. Hershey, PA: IGI Global, 2011.

Anderson, Ross. *Security Engineering*. Indianapolis, IN: Wiley, 2008.

Andress, Jason, and Steve Winterfield. *Cyber Warfare: Techniques, Tactics and Tools for Security Practitioners*. Waltham, MA: Syngress, 2011.

Arquilla, John, and David Ronfeldt. "Cyberwar Is Coming!" *Comparative Strategy*, 12(2), Spring 1993: 141–165.

Arquilla, John, and David Ronfeldt, eds. *In Athena's Camp*. Santa Monica, CA: RAND Corporation, 1997.

Awan, Imran, and Brian Blakemore. *Policing Cyber Hate, Cyber Threats, and Cyber Terrorism*. Burlington, VT: Ashgate, 2011.

Bartlett, Jamie. *The Dark Net: Inside the Digital Underworld*. New York: Melville House, 2015.

Bayuk, Jennifer L. *Cyber Security Policy Guidebook*. Hoboken, NJ: Wiley, 2012.

Blaker, James K. *Transforming Military Force: The Legacy of Arthur Cebrowski and Network Centric Warfare*. Westport, CT: Praeger Security International, 2007.

Blane, John V., ed. *Cyberwarfare: Terror at a Click*. New York: Novinka Books, 2002.

Bossler, Adam M., and Thomas J. Holt. *Cybercrime in Progress: Theory and Prevention of Technology-enabled Offenses*. Basingstoke: Routledge, 2016.

Bousquet, Antoine. *The Scientific Way of Warfare: Order and Chaos on the Battlefields of Modernity*. New York: Columbia University Press, 2009.

Bowden, Mark. *Worm: The First Digital World War*. New York: Atlantic Monthly Press, 2011.

Brenner, Joel. *America the Vulnerable: Inside the New Threat Matrix of Digital Espionage, Crime, and Warfare*. New York: Penguin Press, 2011.

Brenner, Joel F. *Glass Houses: Privacy, Secrecy, and Cyber Insecurity in a Transparent World*. New York: Penguin, 2013.

Brenner, Susan W. *Cyberthreats: The Emerging Fault Lines of the Nation State*. New York: Oxford University Press, 2009.

Bryen, Stephen D. *Technology Security and National Power: Winners and Losers*. New Brunswick, NJ: Transaction Publishers, 2016.

Bush, George W. *Decision Points*. New York: Crown Publishers, 2010.

Campbell-Kelly, Martin, William Aspray, Nathan Ensmenger, and Jeffrey R. Yost. *Computer: A History of the Information Machine*. Boulder, CO: Westview Press, 2013.

Carlin, John. "A Farewell to Arms," *Wired*, May 1997. https://www.wired.com/1997/05/netizen-2.

Carr, Jeffrey. *Inside Cyber Warfare: Mapping the Cyber Underworld*. Sebastopol, CA: O'Reilly Media, 2009.

Ceruzzi, Paul E. *Computing: A Concise History*. Cambridge, MA: The MIT Press, 2012.

Chander, Anupam. *The Electronic Silk Road: How the Web Binds the World Together in Commerce*. New Haven, CT: Yale University Press, 2013.

Chapple, Mike, and David Seidl. *Cyberwarfare: Information Operations in a Connected World.* Burlington, MA: Jones and Bartlett Learning, 2015.

Clarke, Richard A., and Robert K. Knake. *Cyber War: The Next Threat to National Security and What to Do about It.* New York: HarperCollins, 2010.

Coleman, Gabriella. *Hacker, Hoaxer, Whistleblower, Spy: The Many Faces of Anonymous.* London: Verso, 2014.

Deibert, Ronald. *Black Code: Surveillance, Piracy, and the Dark Side of the Internet.* Toronto: McClelland & Stewart, 2013.

Deibert, Ron, and Rafal Rohozinski. *Tracking Ghostnet: Investigating a Cyber Espionage Network.* Toronto: Centre for International Studies, University of Toronto, 2009.

Demchak, Chris. *Wars of Disruption and Resilience: Cybered Conflict, Power, and National Security.* Athens: University of Georgia Press, 2011.

DeNardis, Laura. *The Global War for Internet Governance.* New Haven, CT: Yale University Press, 2014.

Dunham, Ken, and Jim Melnick. *Malicious Bots: An Inside Look into the Cyber-criminal Underground of the Internet.* Boca Raton, FL: CRC Press, 2009.

Erickson, Jon. *Hacking: The Art of Exploitation.* 2nd ed. San Francisco: No Starch Press, 2008.

Fowler, Andrew. *The Most Dangerous Man in the World: The Explosive True Story of Julian Assange and the Lies, Cover-ups and Conspiracies He Exposed.* New York: Skyhorse, 2011.

Gellman, Barton. *Dark Mirror: Edward Snowden and the Surveillance State.* London: Penguin, 2016.

Graham, David. "Cyber Threats and the Law of War." *Journal of National Security Law & Policy.* Vol. 4:87, 2010.

Green, A. James, ed. *Cyber Warfare: A Multidisciplinary Analysis.* New York: Routledge, 2015.

Greenberg, Andy. *This Machine Kills Secrets: Julian Assange, the Cypherpunks, and Their Fight to Empower Whistleblowers.* New York: Plume, 2013.

Greenwald, Glenn. *No Place to Hide: Edward Snowden, the NSA, and the U.S. Surveillance State.* New York: Metropolitan Books, 2014.

Hadnagy, Christopher. *Social Engineering: The Art of Human Hacking.* Indianapolis, IN: Wiley, 2011.

Haerens, Margaret, and Lynn M. Zott, eds. *Hacking and Hackers.* Detroit: Greenhaven Press, 2014.

Hafner, Katie, and Matthew Lyon. *Where Wizards Stay Up Late: The Origins of the Internet.* New York: Simon & Schuster, 1996.

Halpin, Edward, Philippa Trevorrow, David Webb, and Steve Wright, eds. *Cyberwar, Netwar, and the Revolution in Military Affairs.* New York: Palgrave MacMillan, 2006.

Harding, Luke. *The Snowden Files: The Inside Story of the World's Most Wanted Man.* New York: Vintage Books, 2014.

Hardy, Marianna, ed. *The Target Store Data Breaches: Examination and Insight.* New York: Nova Science Publishers, 2014.

Harris, Shane. *The Watchers: The Rise of America's Surveillance State.* New York: Penguin Press, 2010.

Hayden, Michael V. *Playing to the Edge: American Intelligence in the Age of Terror.* New York: Penguin Press, 2016.

Healey, Jason, ed. *A Fierce Domain: Conflict in Cyberspace, 1986 to 2012.* Washington, D.C.: Atlantic Council, 2014.

Heickerö, Roland. *The Dark Sides of the Internet: On Cyber Threats and Informational Warfare.* Translated by Martin Peterson. New York: Peter Lang Publishing Group, 2013.

Holt, Thomas J., and Bernadette H. Schell. *Hackers and Hacking: A Reference Handbook.* Santa Barbara, CA: ABC-CLIO, 2013.

Isaacson, Walter. *The Innovators: How a Group of Hackers, Geniuses, and Geeks Created the Digital Revolution.* New York: Simon & Schuster, 2014.

Johnson, Thomas A., ed. *Cybersecurity: Protecting Critical Infrastructures from Cyber Attack and Cyber Warfare.* Boca Raton, FL: CRC Press, 2015.

Kaplan, Fred. *Dark Territory: The Secret History of Cyber-War.* New York: Simon and Schuster, 2016.

Kerschischnig, Georg. *Cyberthreats and International Law.* The Hague, Netherlands: Eleven International Publishing, 2012.

Kizza, Joseph Migga. *Guide to Computer Network Security.* London: Springer, 2015.

Knake, Robert K. *Internet Governance in an Age of Cyber Insecurity.* New York: Council on Foreign Relations, 2010.

Kramer, Franklin D., Stuart H. Starr, and Larry K. Wentz, eds. *Cyberpower and National Security.* Dulles, VA: Potomac Books, 2009.

Lee, Wenke, Cliff Wang, and David Dagon. *Botnet Detection: Countering the Largest Security Threat.* New York: Springer, 2008.

Levy, Steven. *Hackers: Heroes of the Computer Revolution.* Beijing: O'Reilly, 2010.

Leyden, John. "Hack on Saudi Aramco Hit 30,000 Workstations, Oil Firm Admits." *The Register*, August 29, 2012.

Li, Jennifer J., and Lindsay Daugherty. *Training Cyber Warriors: What Can Be Learned from Defense Language Training?* Santa Monica, CA: RAND, 2015.

Liang, Qiao, and Wang Xiangsui. *Unrestricted Warfare.* Beijing: PLA Literature and Arts Publishing House, 1999.

Libicki, Martin. *Brandishing Cyberattack Capability.* Santa Monica, CA: RAND Corporation, 2013.

Libicki, Martin. *Conquest in Cyberspace: National Security and Information Warfare.* New York: Cambridge University Press, 2007.

Libicki, Martin. *Cyberdeterrence and Cyberwar.* Santa Monica, CA: RAND Corporation, 2009.

Libicki, Martin. *Cyberspace in Peace and War.* Annapolis, MD: U.S. Naval Institute Press, 2016.

Lindsay, Jon R., Tai Ming Cheung, and Derek S. Reveron, eds. *China and Cybersecurity: Espionage, Strategy, and Politics in the Digital Domain.* New York: Oxford University Press, 2015.

Lucas, George. *Ethics and Cyber Warfare: The Quest for Responsible Security in the Age of Digital Warfare.* Oxford: Oxford University Press, 2016.

Mahmood, Zaigham, ed. *Continued Rise of the Cloud: Advances and Trends in Cloud Computing.* London: Springer, 2014.

Mandiant Corporation. *APT1: Exposing One of China's Cyber Espionage Units.* Alexandria, VA: Mandiant Corporation, 2013.

Marvel, Elisabette M., ed. *China's Cyberwarfare Capability.* New York: Nova Science Publishers, 2010.

Mitnick, Kevin. *Ghost in the Wires: My Adventures as the World's Most Wanted Hacker.* New York: Little, Brown and Company, 2011.

Moschovitis, Christos J. P., Hilary Poole, Tami Schuyler, and Theresa M. Senft. *History of the Internet: A Chronology, 1843 to the Present.* Santa Barbara, CA: ABC-CLIO, 1999.

Mueller, Milton. *Networks and States: The Global Politics of Internet Governance.* Cambridge, MA: MIT Press, 2010.

Murray, Charles J. *The Supermen: The Story of Seymour Cray and the Technical Wizards behind the Supercomputer.* New York: John Wiley & Sons, 1997.

Nagaraja, Shishir, and Ross Anderson. *The Snooping Dragon: Social-malware Surveillance of the Tibetan Movement*. Cambridge: Computer Laboratory, University of Cambridge, 2009.

Nicks, Denver. *Private Bradley Manning, WikiLeaks, and the Biggest Exposure of Official Secrets in American History*. Chicago: Review Press, 2013.

Olson, Parmy. *We Are Anonymous: Inside the Hacker World of LulzSec, Anonymous and the Global Cyber Insurgency*. New York: Back Bay Books, 2012.

Poindexter, Dennis F. *The Chinese Information War: Espionage, Cyberwar, Communications Control and Related Threats to United States Interests*. Jefferson, NC: McFarland, 2013.

Poroshyn, Roman. *Stuxnet: The True Story of Hunt and Evolution*. Denver, CO: Outskirts Press, 2013.

Reveron, Derek S., ed. *Cyberspace and National Security: Threats, Opportunities, and Power in a Virtual World*. Washington, D.C.: Georgetown University Press, 2012.

Richards, Julian. *Cyber-war: The Anatomy of the Global Security Threat*. London: Palgrave, 2014.

Rid, Thomas. *Cyber War Will Not Take Place*. New York: Oxford University Press, 2013.

Rosenzweig, Paul. *Cyber Warfare: How Conflicts in Cyberspace Are Challenging America and Changing the World*. Santa Barbara, CA: Praeger, 2013.

Schmitt, Michael N., ed. *Tallinn Manual on the International Law Applicable to Cyber Warfare*. New York: Cambridge University Press, 2013.

Schneier, Bruce. *Secrets and Lies: Digital Security in a Digital World*. New York: John Wiley & Sons, Inc., 2000.

Shakarian, Paulo, Jana Shakarian, and Andrew Ruef. *Introduction to Cyber-Warfare: A Multi-disciplinary Approach*. Waltham, MA: Syngress, 2013.

Singer, P. W., and Allan Friedman. *Cybersecurity and Cyberwar: What Everyone Needs to Know*. New York: Oxford University Press, 2014.

Spinello, Richard A. *Cyberethics: Morality and Law in Cyberspace*. Sudbury, MA: Jones & Bartlett, 2011.

Springer, Paul J. *Cyber Warfare: A Reference Handbook*. Santa Barbara, CA: ABC-CLIO, 2015.

Stiennon, Richard. *Surviving Cyber War*. Lanham, MD: Government Institutes, 2010.

Stocker, Gerfried, and Christine Schöpf. *Info War*. New York: Springer-Verlag, 1998.

Stryker, Cole. *Hacking the Future: Privacy, Identity, and Anonymity on the Web*. New York: Overlook Duckworth, 2012.

Taddeo, Mariarosaria. *The Ethics of Cyber Conflicts: An Introduction*. London: Taylor and Francis Group, 2016.

Tapscott, Don, and Alex Tapscott. *Blockchain Revolution: How the Technology behind Bitcoin Is Changing Money, Business, and the World*. New York: Penguin, 2016.

Thomas, Timothy L. 2009. "Nation-state Cyber Strategies: Examples from China and Russia." *Cyberwar and Information Warfare*, edited by Daniel Ventre. Hoboken, NJ: John Wiley & Sons, 2011.

Verma, Nina. *Social Engineering: A Means to Violate a Computer System*. New Delhi, India: Global Vision Pub. House, 2011.

Vigna, Paul, and Michael J. Casey. *The Age of Cryptocurrency: How Bitcoin and the Blockchain Are Challenging the Global Economic Order*. New York: St. Martin's Press, 2015.

Wang, Jie, and Zachary A. Kissel. *Introduction to Network Security: Theory and Practice*. Hoboken, NJ: Wiley, 2015.

Weiman, Gabriel. *Terror on the Internet: The New Arena, the New Challenges*. Washington, D.C.: USIP, 2006.

Zettner, Kim. *Countdown to Zero Day: Stuxnet and the Launch of the World's First Digital Weapon*. New York: Broadway Books, 2015.

Contributors

Editor

Dr. Paul J. Springer
Professor and Chair
Department of Research
Air Command and Staff College
Maxwell Air Force Base, Alabama

Contributors

Dr. Jonathan Abel
Assistant Professor
University of Texas at Arlington

Dr. Trevor Albertson
Assistant Professor
Department of Airpower
Air Command and Staff College
Maxwell Air Force Base, Alabama

Dr. Gregory W. Ball
Command Historian
24th Air Force
Lackland Air Force Base, Texas

Dr. Mary Lynn Bartlett
Profession of Arms Center of
Excellence
Department of Leadership
Air Command and Staff College
Maxwell Air Force Base, Alabama

Dr. Lisa Beckenbaugh
Assistant Professor
Department of Research
Air Command and Staff College
Maxwell Air Force Base, Alabama

Dr. Terry L. Beckenbaugh
Associate Professor
Department of International Security
Studies
Air Command and Staff College
Maxwell Air Force Base, Alabama

**Lieutenant Colonel Michael A.
Bonura, PhD**
U.S. Army

Dr. Robert J. Bunker
Division of Politics and Economics
Claremont Graduate University

Major Spencer Calder
U.S. Army

Jeffrey R. Cares
Captain
U.S. Navy, Retired
Founder and Chairman
Alidade, Inc.

**Lieutenant Colonel George L.
Chapman**
U.S. Air Force

Roger J. Chin
PhD Candidate
Department of Political Science
Claremont Graduate University

Lieutenant Colonel Paul Clemans
Chief of Academic Research and
Publications
Department of Research

Air Command and Staff College
Maxwell Air Force Base, Alabama

Lieutenant Colonel Jeremy Cole
Instructor
eSchool of Graduate Professional
Military Education
Maxwell Air Force Base, Alabama

Dr. Daniel Connelly
Assistant Professor
Department of International Security
Studies
Air Command and Staff College
Maxwell Air Force Base, Alabama

Wing Commander Graem Corfield
Royal Air Force, United Kingdom

Dr. G. Alexander Crowther
Senior Research Fellow, Cyber Policy
National Defense University

Dr. Ronald N. Dains
Associate Professor and Chair
Department of International Security
Studies
Air Command and Staff College
Maxwell Air Force Base, Alabama

Lukas K. Danner
PhD Candidate
Department of Politics & International
Relations
Florida International University

Steven B. Davis
PhD Candidate
Department of History
Texas A&M University

Dr. Melvin G. Deaile
Associate Professor
Department of Warfighting
Air Command and Staff College
Maxwell Air Force Base, Alabama

Jim Dolbow
Military Legislative Assistant
U.S. Senate

Dr. Manas Dutta
Assistant Professor
Department of History
Kazi Nazrul University, India

Joseph Hammond
Independent Scholar

Michael Hankins
PhD Candidate
Department of History
Kansas State University

Major Brandee J. Harral
Chief, Personnel Management
Air Command and Staff College
Maxwell Air Force Base,
Alabama

Dr. Jordan R. Hayworth
Assistant Professor
Department of Airpower
Air Command and Staff College
Maxwell Air Force Base,
Alabama

Dr. Lori Ann Henning
Instructor
History of Technology
Auburn University

Dr. Roy Franklin Houchin II
Associate Professor
Department of Strategy
Air War College
Maxwell Air Force Base,
Alabama

Jonathan Hoyland
PhD Candidate
Royal Holloway
University of London

Dr. Frank Jacob
Assistant Professor
Department of History
City University of New York

Dr. Angelos D. Keromytis
Program Manager
Information Innovation Office
Defense Advanced Research Projects
Agency

Alma Keshavarz
PhD Candidate
Department of Political Science
Claremont Graduate University

Jason R. Kluk
PhD Candidate
Department of History
East Stroudsburg University

Major Marcus Laird
U.S. Air Force

Raymond D. Limbach
Independent Scholar

**Major Christopher G.
Marquis**
Instructor
Department of Warfighting
Air Command and Staff College
Maxwell Air Force Base,
Alabama

Dr. Augustine Meaher IV
Associate Professor
eSchool of Graduate Professional
Military Education
Maxwell Air Force Base,
Alabama

Christopher Menking
PhD Candidate
Department of History
University of North Texas

**Lieutenant Colonel Robert Y.
Mihara**
U.S. Army

John J. Mortimer
PhD Candidate
Department of History
University of Southern Mississippi

Dr. Deonna D. Neal
Associate Professor
eSchool of Graduate Professional
Military Education
Maxwell Air Force Base, Alabama

**Lieutenant Colonel Steven A.
Quillman**
Director of Staff
Department of Research
Air Command and Staff College
Maxwell Air Force Base,
Alabama

Dusan Repel
PhD Candidate
Royal Holloway
University of London

Angela M. Riotto
PhD Candidate
Department of History
University of Akron

Major Jose Alberto Rivas Jr.
U.S. Air Force Reserve

Heather M. Salazar
PhD Candidate
Ohio University

Dr. Barbara Salera
Assistant Professor
Department of International Security
Studies
Air Command and Staff College
Maxwell Air Force Base, Alabama

Dr. Nicholas Michael Sambaluk
Associate Professor
eSchool of Graduate Professional Military Education
Maxwell Air Force Base, Alabama

Dr. Margaret D. Sankey
Director of Research and Electives
Air War College
Maxwell Air Force Base, Alabama

Benjamin M. Schneider
PhD Candidate
Department of History
George Mason University

Major Zachary M. Smith
U.S. Air Force

Brad St. Croix
PhD Candidate
Department of History
University of Ottawa

Dr. John G. Terino
Associate Professor and Chair
Department of Airpower
Air Command and Staff College
Maxwell Air Force Base, Alabama

Dr. Heather Pace Venable
Assistant Professor
Department of Airpower
Air Command and Staff College
Maxwell Air Force Base, Alabama

Dr. Ryan Wadle
Associate Professor
eSchool of Graduate Professional Military Education
Maxwell Air Force Base, Alabama

Mary Elizabeth Walters
PhD Candidate
Department of History
University of North Carolina

Dr. Anna Zuschlag
University Lecturer
Department of History
Western University, Canada

Index

Page numbers in **bold** indicate the location of main entries.